Russell Smith has combined the careers of singer and academic. He is one of Australia's foremost bass-buffos. He began his operatic career in England, Ireland and Wales before working for ten years in various German opera houses. In 1970 he returned to Australia with his young family to lecture in vocal studies and instigate an operatic program at the Tasmanian Conservatorium of Music. In 1971 he co-founded the Tasmanian Opera Company. He has performed with the Australian Opera and every regional company and has directed operas and opera workshops in Germany, United States, Canada, Korea and Australia.

He also maintained a career as a recitalist, covering the gamut of vocal music in concerts, oratorio, studio broadcasts and performance with the state orchestras. In 1993 he was awarded the Medal of the Order of Australia for services to the performing arts as a singer and teacher of opera. In 1997 he received a PhD. for his dissertation on the life and work of Peter Dawson.

Peter Burgis has an international reputation as a performing arts historian, discographer and sound archivist. He is a world authority on Australian composition and performers and in 1984 received the inaugural Jack Davey Pater Award for professional excellence in the broadcasting arts and sciences. He was founder and director of the National Library of Australia's sound archive, 1974–1984; and of the National Film and Sound Archive (now ScreenSound) 1984–1989; and was vice-president of the International Association of Sound Archives 1981–1987 and chairman of the Australian branch 1979–1984. Since 1988 he has been curator of the Australian Institute of Recorded Sound (AIRS) at Port Macquarie, New South Wales, the world's largest collection of Australian sound recordings. He has produced 200 record issues of historical Australian sounds on LP disc, cassette and compact disc; including the ten-disc Peter Dawson Centenary record set, *Ambassador of Song* in 1982. His current projects are a national discography of recordings by Australian entertainers at home and abroad (1890–1960) and a discography of Australian patriotic and national songs.

Peter Dawson as a rising young singer, 1902.

PETER DAWSON

The World's Most Popular Baritone

with complete song title discography

Russell Smith & Peter Burgis

Currency Press, Sydney

First published in 2001
by Currency Press Pty Ltd,
PO Box 2287, Strawberry Hills, NSW, 2012, Australia
enquiries@currency.com.au
www.currency.com.au

National Library of Australia CIP data
Smith, Russell Hugh.
    Peter Dawson : the world's most popular baritone : with complete song title discography.
    Bibliography.
    Includes index.
    ISBN 0 86819 603 7.
    1. Dawson, Peter, 1882-1961. 2. Dawson, Peter, 1882-1961 - Discography. 3. Baritones (Singers) - Australia - Biography. 4. Popular music - Australia - History and criticism. 5. Popular music - Australia - Discography. I. Burgis, Peter. II. Title.
    ISBN 0 86819 603 7.

 Publication of this title was assisted by the Commonwealth Government through the Australia Council, its arts funding and advisory body.

Cover design by Kate Florance, Currency Press
Set by Currency Press in 11 point Garamond
Printed by Hyde Park Press, Richmond, South Australia

Foreword

PETER BURGIS

Peter Dawson first came to my attention in the 1940s when I was a schoolboy in Newcastle (NSW) with a wind-up gramophone and a beat-up copy of 'On The Road To Mandalay'. In the 1950s I started gathering discs and cylinders by Australians, a field ignored by most collectors. The collection expanded in the 1960s with the addition of vast quantities of 78s discarded by radio stations. Many were by Peter Dawson.

In 1968, becoming concerned about the future of my collection I wrote to the major libraries to ask about their sound archives. It soon became apparent that most were oblivious of sound scholarship. The one exception was the National Library of Australia, in Canberra, whose chief, Harold (later Sir Harold) White came to our home in Sydney in 1969 to discuss my proposal for a national sound archive. I pointed out that records were audio documents essential to our education in an audio-visual world; and that nowhere in their homeland did institutional record collections exist of either Nellie Melba or Peter Dawson. Mr White, who was fond of Dawson, announced he would rectify this and he proved true to his word. I was enlisted as a consultant; and in 1973 was invited to join the staff of the National Library to establish a national sound archive.

One of my first priorities was to create an archive of Peter Dawson, whom I considered Australia's most acclaimed male vocalist. To achieve this we needed his personal papers, if they existed. We needed to find Mrs Dawson. However, this proved difficult as Constance Bedford Dawson, then aged 77, lived in retirement, shunning attention due to natural shyness and deteriorating health. Eventually, however, in 1976 she agreed to meet me on a fixed day at North Sydney railway station entrance, at 10am. She would wear a blue dress and a red rose.

Our meeting went very well. I learnt that Peter's personal papers did exist – a minor miracle in view of his nomadic ways. Appropriately, they were stored at John Bull Removalists, Newport, where we drove to inspect them. There we discovered dozens of cartons and tea chests, covered in dust and cobwebs. The storage account was overdue (by some years!) and the collection had been saved from dumping only because it was housed in a remote corner. The papers of the world's most popular baritone had lain untouched for 15 years.

Mrs Dawson was delighted (and relieved) to donate her husband's collection to the National Library. It proved a marvellous windfall of scrap books, sheet music, paintings, photographs, diaries, sketches, manuscripts, contracts, business reports, magazines, concert programs, cartoons, letters, and gramophone discs, which became the basis of a highly successful major public exhibition at the library in 1982 to celebrate Dawson's centenary. EMI (Australia) asked me to produce a ten-LP set entitled *Ambassador of Song*, which, with sound transfers by Chris Long, became a best-seller internationally.

For many years I kept in touch with Con, sharing lunches when in Sydney and reminiscing about Peter. Constance was a kind person, very proper, disciplined, with strong views; but witty and proud of her British heritage and firmly devoted to Peter's memory.

In November 1985 I was a member of *The Old Fashioned Show*, presented by Nancye Bridges & Her Company in the Concert Hall of the Sydney Opera House. My act was to play, from a pre-recorded tape, short excerpts by Australian entertainers and to link them with stories about their songs. The culmination was Peter Dawson's 'Waltzing Matilda' booming through the darkened auditorium. It brought a huge round of applause from the audience of 2,000, which on this occasion included Constance. Upon hearing that Mrs Dawson was present the audience gave her a special cheer. Nellie Melba's 'Home, Sweet Home' had preceded 'Waltzing Matilda' and it was a nice feeling to know that after all these years our two greatest singers had been heard in the Sydney Opera House.

In 1990, after Russell Smith had begun his doctoral thesis, we first discussed the possibility of writing this book together. In August he wrote: 'I too am fired with enthusiasm. The idea of a co-operative effort makes the task seem less mind-boggling.' From his experience of the vast range of Dawson's songs he believed that the popular stereotype belied the complexities of Dawson's life. His objective was to build up a profile of Peter Dawson from original sources. His first major task was to analyse and catalogue the Peter Dawson papers, which had transferred with me when I became the 'Sound' in the National Film and Sound Archive (now known as ScreenSound Australia). He then scoured Australia's major archives before setting off for England to search through the extensive EMI and BBC written archives.

We finally joined forces in 1996. After years of gathering information, sifting, analysing, investigating, interviewing, organising and writing, our minds may well be a trifle boggled but our enthusiasm has remained fully fired. I am particularly appreciative of the unique skills which Russell has brought to the project, including his expertise in voice production and acting; his understanding of the tribulations of stage life; his grasp of Dawson's repertoire; and his broad musicological knowledge and discipline.

Our biography demonstrates how the phenomenon of Dawson's achievement was inextricably linked to his social environment, the politics of the period, Australia's emotional ties to the British Empire, and the global influence of the burgeoning advertising and communications industry. We hope we have produced a fresh, independent and stimulating view of a national icon.

Our thanks to Dr Katharine Brisbane and Currency staff for support, guidance and an enthusiasm which matched our own.

> Bright is the ring of words
> When the right man rings them
> Fair the fall of songs
> When the singer sings them

Robert Louis Stevenson

Peter Dawson recording at the Gramophone Company, Hayes, Middlesex, 1920, in a studio 'so small it would hardly have held a full-size billiard table'. The conductor surveyed his kingdom from the raised dais, whilst the technician and his apparatus were housed in the recording cabinet.

Contents

Illustrations

This book is dedicated to our wives,
Anje and Carolyn,
in appreciation of their patience and support
during the long years of collection, research and
preparation of the manuscript.

Acknowledgements

All source material is held or has been sighted by the authors. The text is based on the doctoral dissertation: Russell Smith: *The Life and Repertoire of the Australian Baritone, Peter Dawson: 1882-1961: An Historical and Musicological Enquiry*, University of Tasmania, 1997, unpublished; with additional information in Russell Smith and Peter Burgis, *Preparatory Notes for a Biography of Peter Dawson 1882-1961*, forthcoming. An extensive bibliography may be found in the doctoral dissertation.

All illustrations, unless otherwise stated, are in the possession of the authors. Of particular value has been Peter and Nan's family album, in the possession of Nan Dawson's niece, Mrs Anne Jacquet, who lives in Sydney.

The spelling in quotations from archival material (letters, books, programmes, newspapers, etc.) has been retained. The spelling in these documents reflects the character of their authors and the period. In the general text spelling has been standardised; the deliberate incorporation of any misspelling indicated by [sic]. In general, composer, recording date, accompaniment and type of recording have been omitted from the main text. Accurate listings can be found in the Song Title Discography.

We gratefully acknowledge the support, encouragement and painstaking attention to detail given by so many individuals and archives in bringing this work to fruition: Australian Archives, Canberra, Sydney, Hobart; Australian Broadcasting Corporation, Sydney, Adelaide, Hobart; BBC Written Archives, Caversham, UK; Her Majesty's Theatre Archives, Perth; National Library of Australia's Performing Arts Collection; Adelaide Festival Centre; Performing Arts Museum of Victoria; Phonographic Society of South Australia; ScreenSound Australia (formerly National Film and Sound Archive) Canberra and Sydney; State Libraries of South Australia, Tasmania, Victoria; the *Advertiser,* Adelaide; the *Mercury,* Hobart; University libraries: Baillieu Library, University of Melbourne; Barr Smith Library, University of South Australia; Morris Miller Library, University of Tasmania.

Frank Andrews (UK); Kylie Antonio (WA), Barry Badham (NSW); Paul

Baker (UK); Barry Balmayne *(Call Boy,* UK); Tony Barker *(Music Hall,* UK); David Bayes (UK); Ernie Bayly (UK); Idelette Beute (SABC Sound Archives, South Africa); Lyall Beven (Tasmania); Ken Boness (Victoria); Colin J. Bray (Canada); the late Nancye Bridges (NSW); Dr Katharine Brisbane (Currency Press, NSW*); Dr* Jeff Brownrigg (Canberra); Sir Frank Callaway (WA); Bob Carlisle (UK); Peter Cliffe (UK); Mike Comber (UK); Peter Copeland (British Library National Sound Archive); Ronald T. Corbett (Victoria); Rod Cornelius (NZ); David Crisp (NSW); John S. Dales (UK); Anne Davenport (UK); Dr Jim Davidson (Victoria); Robert Dawe (SA); the late Constance Bedford Dawson (NSW); Smoky Dawson (NSW); Andrew Deas (UK); Colin Doman (UK); Harold Dooley (NSW); Peter Downes (NZ); Dr Ruth Edge (EMI Archives, Hayes, Middlesex); Dr Richard Ely (Tasmania); Alex Finch (SA); Dennis Foreman (UK); Elizabeth Frost (ACT); John Geale (NSW); John R. Gomer (UK); Richard Green (National Library of Canada); David E. Gyger *(Opera Australia,* NSW); Chris Hamilton *(Hillandale News,* UK); John Hanna *(Sound Record,* NSW); Terry Harrower (Victoria); Michael Hegarty (UK); Alan Heinecke (NSW); Sally Hine (BBC Broadcast Archives); Greg Hocking (Victoria); Lawrence F. Holdridge (USA), Charles A. Hooey (Canada); Ron Hughes (founder of the Peter Dawson Appreciation Society, UK); Ann Jacquet (NSW); Jamie Kelly (Victoria); Michael Kinnear (Victoria); Barbara Lewis (NSW); Chris Long (Victoria); Rachel Lord (Radio New Zealand Sound Archives); Larry Lustig *(Record Collecter,* UK); Timothy Massey (UK); Rex McLean, (Tasmania); Jack Mitchell (NSW); Tony Mobbs (EMI Archives, UK); William R. Moran (USA); Doug, Arthur and Barbara Mullins (SA); Valantyne Napier (Victoria); the late Ken Neate (Germany); Chris Neave (NSW); Walter Norris *(Phonographic Record,* NZ*);* Stanley Paine (UK); Allan Palmer (UK); Bob Pelham (WA); Rodney Poynter (NSW); Michael Quinn (Queensland); Professor John Rickards (Victoria); the late Doug Robertson (ACT); Bill Robertson (NSW); Emeritus Professor Michael Roe (Tasmania); Brian Rust, (UK); the late Hal Saunders (NSW); Anne-Maria Schwirtlich (Australian Archives, Canberra) the late Rex Shaw (NSW); Clive Simmonds (UK); John Simpson (Queensland); Bruce Skilton (ACT); the late Ken Snell (Victoria); John Spence (ABC Radio Archives, NSW); John Sutcliffe (NZ); Mike Sutcliffe (NSW); Don Taylor (Tasmania); Emeritus Professor Rod Thomson (Tasmania); Guy Tranter (ABC, Sydney); Sue Tronser (NSW); Bill Tully (ACT); Bill Turnbull (NSW); Wayne Turner (UK); Max Tyler (UK); Frank Van Straten (Victoria); John D. Vose (UK); John Watson (UK); the late Len Watts (UK); Ron Wills (NSW); Christian Zwarg (Germany).

Introduction

'The World's Most Popular Baritone?'
'That's what they say! They say he recorded 3,500 titles and sold more than 13 million records!'
'Peter Dawson?'
'Yes! Peter Dawson!'
'Never heard of him!'

Admirers of Peter Dawson may be surprised to learn that their icon is hardly known to post-World War II generations. In the four decades since he died our conception of Australia has changed dramatically: the post-war policies of immigration coupled with the accelerating change in international travel and communications have produced three times the population and a far more cosmopolitan community than he and his contemporaries could ever have imagined. During his lifetime Australia was part of the British Empire and everyone was a British Subject with automatic right of entry into Great Britain. Gradually the old Empire fragmented and transformed into a Commonwealth of Nations but when Peter Dawson climbed to fame and attained his dominant position as 'The World's Most Popular Baritone', the power of the British Empire was at its apex.

For generations Peter Dawson was a household name. His life read like a fairytale: in 1937 the Gramophone Company of London wrote: 'Once upon a time there was a young man called Peter Dawson. In the year 1905 he walked into a recording studio, and lived happily ever after!' His admirers certainly believed it, and the public relations departments of the dynamic recording industry, always masters of the superlative, ensured that they did. Newspaper reports, programmes, press releases, record covers, interviews, biographies told 'The Peter Dawson Story' the way his employers liked it, the way he liked it, the way the impresarios liked it, and the way the public liked it.

Dawson's rise to fame began in 1904 and lasted until his death in 1961. 'With the death of Peter Dawson tens of thousands of middle-aged and older admirers who never even saw, let alone met him in person, will feel that they have lost a friend', wrote British record authority W. A. Chislett in his obituary. For Peter Dawson's voice had become an intimate part of people's lives. 'Peter Dawson songs' became part of folklore. Whether it was 'Wandering the King's Highway', 'When the Sergeant Major's On Parade', 'The Floral Dance', 'I Travel the Road', 'Old Father Thames', 'The Cobbler's Song', 'On the Road to Mandalay' or 'Along the Road to Gundagai' – songs became famous because Peter Dawson had sung them. Even 'Waltzing Matilda' did not become famous until Peter Dawson sang it.

A 'Peter Dawson song' was a song anyone could sing – from Uncle Charlie, thumb-in-waistcoat beside the aspidistra in the drawing room, to old Fred around the pub 'pianer'. These were the pop songs of his era: ballads sung by a robust baritone who could give them character and meaning. The spirit of generations live on in those songs for they accompanied the great changes that have taken place in Australia. The generations who could remember Australia as a collection of colonies, remember Federation, remember World War I, the Depression, World War II and the good times between, knew the martial tunes, the sentimental songs, the ballads that Peter Dawson sang. His songs were first heard on the early talking machines, accompanied the advent of radio, the talkies, electrical recording and finally television. His songs were sung as the horse and buggy gave way to the automobile, as travel by ship gave way to the aeroplane, as the Coolgardie safe gave way to the refrigerator. For half a century Peter Dawson sang the songs the Empire loved and wanted to hear and he loved singing them.

It is hard to imagine today just how popular Peter Dawson was. His popularity compares favourably with modern day superstars – and lasted a lifetime. Today he would have been the darling of the chat shows for Peter Dawson was as approachable as his songs. He loved company and always retained a basic energy, a youthfulness, an infectious good humour, a love of pranks, an 'Australianness', which was contagious. Coming from a strict nonconformist household in an Australian colony before Federation, he became the embodiment of a young nation with an unquestioning acceptance of the infallibility of the British Empire and the Crown.

It is unfortunate that this popular picture of the legendary Peter Dawson leaves us with only the shell of the man. Despite his enormous recording output, this side of his career commanded less than a third of his time: the bulk of his working life was devoted to singing concerts. Exploiting the fame generated by the recording industry he could be heard in the most exalted concert halls, the most popular music-halls or with his own companies of 'international artists' touring South Africa, India, New Zealand or Australia. He sang the whole gamut of vocal music and is still admired for his excellent vocal technique. He was a brilliant advocate for the performance of English art songs; to this day some critics still regard him as the pre-eminent singer of Handel coloratura and, although he was never an opera singer, many consider that he made the definitive recordings of some popular baritone arias. It is axiomatic that a person who achieves fame must have the capacity to achieve fame. Fundamental to Dawson's success, apart from his voice and personality, was his superior musicianship. This is abundantly clear in his quality recordings but more particularly in some fifty songs he composed, like that rousing marching song, 'Boots', which became in effect his signature tune.

Yet, despite the rhetoric of the publicists, his popularity remained restricted to the British Empire; he was virtually unknown in the rest of Europe or the Americas and never toured there. But for his generation of Australians 'The World' and 'The British Empire' were synonymous.

Surprisingly, there is only one substantial book on the life of Peter Dawson: his own autobiography, *Fifty Years of Song*, published in London in 1951. Reference book authors, reporters and admirers regard it with almost biblical reverence. It is a sound starting point but, as in all autobiographies, the past gets blurry, some events overlap or get out of sync, and the protagonists present themselves in the best possible light. So it is high time that we turned to documents of the period to uncover a more accurate story of the life and career of Peter Dawson.

Thomas and Alison Dawson, c. 1900.

The formative years

Peter Smith Dawson was born in Adelaide in the colony of South
Australia on 31 January 1882. He was the eighth of nine children
born into a strict but generous Presbyterian family. The Adelaide he
knew was not the city we know today; it was a small principal town less
than fifty years old. Until attention was focussed on his vocal abilities, the
young, happy-go-lucky Peter Dawson believed he was destined to inherit a
partnership in his father's iron-working business and to remain in the city of
his birth. His strength of character, his professional dedication and stamina
were formed in the late Victorian era, in the years prior to Federation.

Queen Victoria had ascended the throne in June 1837 and ruled till her
death in 1901. She was monarch of a rich, powerful, far-flung empire that
covered 'almost one-quarter of the land's surface and more than one-quarter of the total population'.[1] In the latter years of her reign Peter Dawson's
Australia was still a collection of independent colonies – New South Wales,
Victoria, Tasmania, Queensland, South Australia, and Western Australia –
which all had ties to England but 'their origins were diverse, their capitals
were widely separated from one another, and the outlook of their people
… was parochial in the extreme'.[2]

South Australia and Western Australia differed in their origins from the
eastern colonies. These two colonies were not established as penal colonies
or by individual settlers; they were created artificially by developers in England:
South Australia was established by subscription in London after the *South
Australian Act* was declared in 1834. The first settlers sought to transport the
life they knew in Great Britain onto this foreign soil and in the struggle they
suffered many hardships. They were impossibly distant from Sydney, sea
routes were hazardous, overland transport was primitive and slow, and, as
the State was bounded to the north by desert, it became agricultural rather
than pastoral, running to small holdings in the main. It had a strong Protestant

doctrinaire foundation. South Australia was socially progressive but economically poor.

Peter Dawson's parents, to whom he was very attached, were Scottish immigrants.[3] His father, 'Thomas Dawson, Iron Worker' (1842-1919) was born in Kirkcaldy. He arrived in Adelaide aboard the *Alchemist*, in 1860. Peter described him as dour.[4] He must have been a strong-willed boy for he ran away to sea 'at about age 12 and remained an ordinary seaman for seven years'. Peter's mother, 'Alison Dawson, formerly Miller' (1841-1916) arrived in Adelaide on the *Morning Star* on 15 February 1863, aged twenty-one. When they married on 5 November 1867 at Mount Lofty – 'where farmers from Scotland had clustered'[5] – Thomas had already started a business close to the centre of the city which was to become 'T. Dawson & Sons, Plumber, Gasfitter, Tank and Cannister Maker'.

The eldest son, James, was born in 1868 followed by Violet, Agnes, Thomas, Alison, David, William, Peter and finally Jessie in 1883.[6] The parents may have had a strict Presbyterian code but Peter's generous, sunny nature, his ability to charm all those around him and his lack of financial responsibility in later life suggests that he was probably looked after and spoilt by his older brothers and sisters.

Growing up in a nonconformist immigrant family in a little city more like a country town was hardly the environment expected to produce an international singer. The innocent boy had to wait until after puberty to discover the quality of his adult voice and his destined career. Peter Dawson never mentions any musical training before his voice broke, yet certain abilities indicate that he acquired important musical skills by some kind of osmosis, for music played a major if incidental role in the lives of committed church families.

Peter Dawson's parents had arrived in Adelaide when the settlement was barely thirty years old: young Peter saw the light of day less than fifty years after land had been parcelled out in England. The total population of Australia before Federation was only about 3,000,000 of which South Australia represented twelve per cent. During Peter's youth and adolescence the total population of South Australia grew from 275,000 to 358,000. His City of Adelaide was the size of a small provincial town today; it had reached only 39,000 when he left in 1902.[7]

Adelaide was dubbed 'The City of Churches' as early as 1872 after a visit to Adelaide by the English writer Anthony Trollope, for churches had played a dominant role in the social fabric of Adelaide since its inception. First came the Anglicans, then the Methodists, who became 'the most potent religious movement in nineteenth century South Australia'. The Catholic Irish also sought religious freedom there, as did Lutheran Germans; and Presbyterian preachers followed the Scottish emigrants.

From the beginning Australia accepted religious pluralism. Officially there was no state religion; however, because of the strong ties to England, there were ingrained perceptions. The Anglicans believed they had a special relationship with the state; the other Protestant sects kept careful watch on them; and the Catholics, who held a grievance against England, regarded themselves as a persecuted minority and kept to themselves.[8]

Trollope's romantic idyll, however, is not supported by all sources; some advise that churches were in 'a very small proportion to the public-houses'. 'Adelaide! That town of parsons, pubs, and prostitutes!', jibed Nellie Melba when the 44-year-old international diva from Victoria met the 23-year-old Dawson at a recording session in London in 1905.[9] For in the last decades of the nineteenth century Adelaide was still more like a frontier town, with rough hostelries catering to itinerant labourers, seamen, cattlemen and immigrants with needs other than those of the settled families.

There has been much debate about Peter Dawson's actual date of birth. The 'birth was entered at the General Registry Office, this 19th day of March, 1882' and it is now generally accepted that he was born on 31 January 1882. But in an old passport a handwritten note dated 1 October 1954 reads: 'Peter Smith Dawson. Born Adelaide South Australia on 31.1.1881. Birth Certificate produced.'[10]

As the next-eldest brother, William, was born 1 April 1880, it is just possible that Peter could have been born on 31 January 1881. He certainly seems to have believed it because as late as 30 October 1960, a year before he died, his younger sister, Jessie, sent him a copy of his birth certificate to prove that he was born in 1882:

> Certified copy of Registration of Birth, Book 79, No 88, 1882, District of Adelaide, 321 … Correction of Entry: When Born Jan 31st, 1882. Correction entered this 5th day of December 1901.

Peter seemed equally confused about his place of birth. One interview claimed: 'He hates "swank" and calls the place where he was born East Adelaide and not St. Peters, which, according to him, is a title given it by snobs'; but he was actually born in Cassel Street in the City of Adelaide.[11] The family home in Cassel Street was within walking distance of the family business, T. Dawson & Sons, which was in Waymouth Street, the light industrial area near the saleyards, running from Light Square. Shortly after Peter's birth the family moved to 6 Fifth Avenue, East Adelaide, where he spent his childhood and went to primary school. Only Jessie, the youngest sister, was born at Fifth Avenue.[12] St Peters may have become a posh address later, but in his day it was East Adelaide, until a corner was cut off just before the Dawsons left the district.[13]

From 1887 to 1893 he attended the East Adelaide Primary School. Social, economic and cultural attitudes had changed dramatically since the days of the fledgling colony. In support of the argument that schooling would reduce crime and vice and make South Australian children more productive workers and politically responsible adults, compulsory, non-sectarian education had become law with the Education Act of 1875. 'Impressive public institutions were erected in the urban landscape'. The East Adelaide Primary School, which was opened in 1886, was 'one of the last public schools to be established in the inner suburban areas of Adelaide.'[14]

Originally the basic education in South Australia was 'the three Rs' plus a 'thorough training in the duties of responsible citizenship'. In 1885, when the East Adelaide Primary was still being built, the curriculum underwent reform to become 'instructions in the principles of morality, reading, spelling, writing, arithmetic, English grammar and composition, geography, history, poetry, elementary natural history or science, drill'. Until 1890 elementary schooling was compulsory but not free, which partially explains why 'schooling took second place to work in a society dominated by need for hard manual work'. Labour was at a premium. Although children between the ages of seven and thirteen were required to attend for 'a minimum of seventy days in each half-year' very few children attended every day. Some absenteeism was blamed on endemic children's diseases and epidemics but there was also an underlying acceptance of child labour in the maintenance of the family economy. Sons of day labourers missed more days than sons of skilled workers and shopkeepers; girls missed even more than boys, because their household duties included looking after younger children, doing the Monday wash and cooking. However, the curriculum was taught as if everyone attended fulltime, so it is not surprising that only about ten per cent made the annual promotion to the top class (Grade IV), before reaching the compulsory leaving age of 13.

Primary school attendance was divided into two years of Junior School, then Grades I-IV. Young Peter Dawson's school record indicates that he began on 3 April 1887 when the family was living at 'Fifth Avenue, East'. With the exception of absences in the second quarters of 1888 and 1893 – which suggests illnesses – Peter attended far more than the minimum and progressed each year. He was in Grade IV when he passed the 'Compulsory Standard' exam in early 1893, but stayed on for another three quarters of a year, finishing in September 1893. So, if we accept his date of birth as 1882, he completed his primary school education between the ages of five and eleven, instead of the compulsory seven to thirteen. Peter had an excellent school record for the times; he rarely missed school and passed all the grades with flying colours.

Although there was nothing remarkable in his early life to suggest he would make singing his career, music was integral to middle-class homes and the Church. Even before they left England the first emigrants had 'formed the South Australian Literary Society' with the express purpose of enriching the cultural life of their future colony; and when they 'came to South Australia they brought their musical instruments with them'.[15] The increasingly affluent Victorian middle class had created a demand for simple romantic compositions, which were inoffensive in polite society,[16] a market which accelerated dramatically once pianos could be produced cheaply. 'The advent of the upright piano at thirty guineas helped to make every home a concert room. A house without a piano was barely furnished'.[17]

As young Peter remembered it, 'there was no outstanding musical talent in the family but his mother had a sweet voice and with nine children in the house the piano got a thrashing.'[18] The family would have sung the Scottish folk songs Dawson loved and sang throughout his career. They probably also sang catchy imported songs like 'Come Back to Erin' or the nationalistic anthem, 'Song of Australia', composed as recently as 1859 by the German immigrant Carl Linger, which enjoyed immense popularity in South Australia. But most of all they would have sung hymns and Sunday school songs, the only music permitted on Sundays, for 'strict Presbyterianism sent them all to church twice every Sunday, and forbade piano-playing on the Sabbath'.[19]

The Dawsons attended St Andrew's Presbyterian Church in Wakefield Street, one of three 'solidly middle-class' city congregations. It is obvious from the career he chose and the music he favoured that Peter's musical abilities developed primarily in the church and through activities tangential to the church. 'Many churches had choirs of some musical quality' which supported the singing of their congregations through the performance of anthems and oratorios, so Peter, and some of his brothers and sisters too, would have sung in the choir from childhood.

While Peter was not training professionally as a musician at this time his latent ability was being nourished by this environment. The hymns he took for granted were published in the *Presbyterian Hymnal* codified in 1870 and again in 1895. Like other nonconformist hymnals, it was based on the reformed Church of England hymnal, *Hymns Ancient and Modern*, 1860.

No. 6 Fifth Avenue, East Adelaide, where the Dawson family moved shortly after Peter was born. It was here that he spent his childhood; and below, his parents at No. 6 South Terrace, Adelaide, where they moved in 1900.

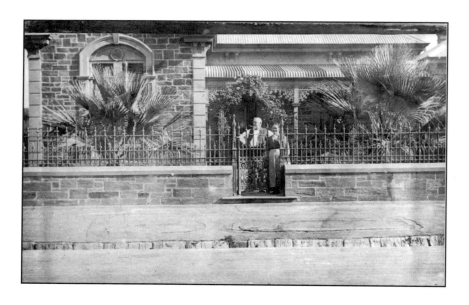

Sales of 150 million in the following century indicate the extraordinary influence of this hymnal throughout the English-speaking world.[20] The principle underlying its reform was 'the desire for hymn tunes in the romantic idiom which reflected the romantic movement in secular music.' Unwittingly, Peter was being educated for his future career by hymns like 'Rock of Ages, cleft for me', 'There is a green hill far away' or 'Eternal Father, strong to save'; and when he thundered Arthur Sullivan's 'Onward Christian Soldiers' or joined in the rousing bass line of the Wesleyan 'O, for a thou-ou-ou-sand tongues to sing my great Redeemer's praise'.

On Sunday the family was dressed in their Sunday best and the piano fell silent. But the lively children were permitted to play sacred music on Thomas Dawson's 'big American organ'.[21] Perhaps the songs they belted out were hymns, but more likely they were the easier, livelier, less romantic, less substantial music they had learned in Sunday school, which catered especially for the children. The church had evolved a 'cluster of organisations and societies' for 'all age-groups and leisure interests' to provide 'a wholesome counter-attraction to the moral dangers of the hotel bar and the billiard saloon'. There was a never-ending round of social activities and fund-raising functions, tennis and cricket matches, and particularly, the annual Sunday school picnic and the Sunday school concert.

Around 1900 the Sunday schools 'were approaching a peak of popularity and prestige' and with them the popularity of the simpler gospel music by the American evangelists, Moody and Sankey and the Scot Alexander Somerville. The theology was 'clear, straightforward, unambiguous and conservative'; if anything in Alexander's 'there was more pushing of sentiment towards sentimentality'. Some theologians regarded these as pernicious American songs with 'rum-tum-tiddity' tunes, 'trite and sterile, mere jingles devoid of spiritual nourishment', a threat to good solid reformed hymns, hymns 'with grit in them'. But the demand for 'Sankey's' and 'Alexander's' was prodigious.[22] Peter grew up with Sunday school songs like 'Jesus wants me for a sunbeam', 'Jesus loves me this I know, for the Bible tells me so', 'Shall we gather at the river, the beautiful, the beautiful, the river' and the hand-clapping 'Give me that old-time religion'.

'Methodists, Baptists, Congregationalists and Presbyterians shared a common hymnody, read the same devotional literature, instructed their children from the same International Sunday School lessons – their forms of worship were virtually identical.'[23] As nonconformist denominations in Adelaide were remarkably homogeneous this commonality in music led to fraternisation among congregations. One of Peter's earliest excursions onto the concert platform was a Grand Entertainment given by the College Park

Congregational Sunday School Children in St Peter's Town Hall on 1 October 1889. A Miss Foale won the First Prize in the Senior Division; Peter's sister, Elsie, six years his senior, the Second Prize, Middle Division; and the seven-year-old Peter was 'Prize Taker, Junior Division'.[24]

One of Peter Dawson's pronounced musical skills was his ability to read music at sight – an ability which gave him an enviable advantage over many of his contemporaries. Gerald Moore, the famous accompanist with whom he had a long association, wrote that 'with the possible exception of John McCormack he was one of the finest sight-readers of any singer I have met'; Peter could take up a new song 'and be ready and willing to perform or record it forthwith'.[25] Sight-reading is not a gift; it is a very studied form of musicianship, generally associated with those who have read music pro-lifically since childhood. But Dawson did not study an instrument as a child nor is there evidence of any formal musical training. His sister Jessie was his accompanist and it was she who taught him the notes of his first *Messiah* solos.[26] Later his wife or a professional accompanist played for him when he was rehearsing new programmes. His sight-reading skills must have de-veloped unconsciously from singing music in his church environment writ-ten in tonic-solfa:

> New trends in Christian hymnody emerged in the nineteenth century … surge of interest in the teaching of sight-singing … the 'movable do' method, or tonic sol-fa system developed by Curwen, resulted in the wide-spread popularity [of this method]. [27]

Sometimes only the words of the tonic-solfa – doh, re, mi, fa, sol, lah, ti, doh – were printed under the words of hymns. At others, as in Peter's oldest Bass Album, published in Glasgow around 1850, both musical nota-tion and tonic-solfa were written together.[28] Our study of his compositions has revealed that he called all keys 'major', which indicates that his brilliant sight-reading skills derived from singing tonic-solfa during his formative years in Adelaide.

While these environmental influences may be observed in retrospect, they would have meant little to young Peter at the time. During the 1880s he was just a kid at primary school on the edge of a big town. Land was cheap, there was a shortage of labour, wages were high and full employment gave security: 'The employee as well as the employer looked forward to owning his own house and garden.' Unfortunately, there came a point where 'practically everyone was living beyond his means and the public and private interest bill was rising'. In December 1889 a major building society went into liquidation: the boom ended; the great depression of the 1890s began.

Despite the depressed economy Peter was enrolled at a private second-ary school, the Pulteney Street School, from 1893–1898. This church school close to the city centre was originally 'intended for the children of the work-ing classes' but had become an all-boys school in 1884. 'Being a church school, it charged low fees in order to compete with the state schools'.[29] At the Pulteney School 'boys were encouraged to sit for the Preliminary Ex-amination conducted by the University of Adelaide', so, as post-primary school education was unusual for the times, the suspicion arises that old Thomas Dawson thought Peter might have prospects different from those of his brothers.

Although Peter stayed at the school until he was nearly seventeen, far beyond the compulsory leaving age, he never stressed the academic side of his education. He preferred to talk about his athletic or drawing prowess. 'As a boy he went in for most sports, doing particularly well as a swimmer and as time went on winning both junior and senior championships at school.'[30] 'When Peter Dawson was a boy he prided himself on his draw-ing, in which he had Hans Heysen as a school-fellow rival.'[31] Peter certainly received a certificate for his 'first examination in the art of Swimming' on 3 April 1895 and a prize for Drawing that year; but Hans Heysen (1877–1968) was five years older than Peter and they never went to school to-gether. By the time Dawson spoke at his old school (Sir) Hans Heysen had become one of Australia's foremost painters, so Dawson evidently made the connection to give colour to his story.

In 1896 Peter not only received another prize as Champion Swimmer but also for Work, Writing, Drawing and Shorthand and, to judge from a reunion photograph with an old Boer War sergeant, taken when Dawson toured Australia in 1931, Drill was also part of the curriculum. On that occasion he also told the boys at school that when he was a student they used to bombard departing wedding parties from peashooters and make darts out of pens and shoot them into the wooden ceilings.[32]

About 1895, while Peter was still at school, the family moved onto a farm at Windsor on the North-East Road. Peter speaks of riding a great deal with his elder brothers, David, who was an expert judge of horses, and Will, who was a 'class rider' and buckjump performer. 'Thomas drove a horse and trap to work each day and took the sons to school and work'. Today Windsor is relatively close to the city, but in 1895 the farm – 'only a few acres' – was a good hour's drive out into the country.[33]

No matter what dreams his parents might have had for the boy, in 1899, at the age of 17, Peter went to work. 'Working life began for all the Dawson

boys, Jim, Tom, Dave, Will and Peter, in their father's business.'[34] Although
Peter said he became an apprentice plumber, the term 'apprenticeship' was
a pretty loose word in those days: 'no one in authority knew whether any
new worker was an apprentice or not'.[35] His 1918 army record listed his
occupation as: 'Trade or Calling: Vocalist, Master Plumber', 'Apprentice:
No'; but Peter thought better of it, crossed out 'No' and replaced it with:
'Yes. Apprenticed to T. Dawson'. Later, reference to plumbing proved a
useful advertising ploy, for it implied that any simple artisan could make it to
the top. In March 1931 the London *News-Chronicle* wrote: 'A plumber, whose
voice has brought enjoyment to millions'; the *Daily Express* quoted Dawson:
'I was an ironworker in Australia until I was 20 years of age, and took a
master plumber's certificate at the School of Mines in Adelaide.' Both purported to come from interviews but actually came from the same EMI
press release.[36]

By the time Peter started work his father was nearing 60. Despite the
depression the business must have thrived for that year it moved a couple
of blocks to larger premises in Gilbert Street on the southern side of the
city. As the four sons were now employed there, the family moved back to
the city, to 6 South Terrace, where the parents remained until they died. On
11 October 1899 the Boer War began. Although it was not an Australian
war, men from some of the colonies chose to participate, among them
Peter's twenty-six-year-old brother, Thomas, who served for three years.[37]

Peter was now about to find the voice that would change the direction of
his life. Descriptions of his early study habits and his first performances
indicate that Peter Dawson was about eighteen years old when his voice
was 'discovered'. His own account was that the robust young voice caught
people's attention when he was singing as a chorister at St Andrew's Church,
Wakefield Street. 'As my mother and father thought that I should at least
aspire to becoming soloist in the choir I took up singing lessons for my own
amusement.'[38]

During puberty a boy's soprano voice breaks: sometimes it squeaks,
sometimes it rumbles, finally the last vestiges of the child's voice disappear
and it settles into the deeper adult male voice. Due to this state of flux a
man's voice cannot be trained until he is seventeen or eigheen years. Very
few become tenors, a few may become true basses: the generic male singing
voice is the baritone.

Initially Peter seemed to have a bass voice. He was encouraged to study
by his first teacher and mentor, the organist Charles Stevens. Most biographies
attribute Peter's success to his English teacher, Sir Charles Santley, but it was

Charles Stevens who recognised Peter's potential, gave him his first lessons, prepared the adolescent for competitions and gave him his first opportunities to sing publicly. He not only persuaded Peter's parents that their son had the talent to become a professional singer, but put his hand in his pocket to help send the boy to London to study.

It was a sign of the sophisticated cultural ambition of this burgeoning colonial city that a man like Stevens should have settled in Adelaide. This was Charles J. Stevens (c.1842–1911) 'who had been a member of the Chapel Royal Choir contemporaneously with Arthur Sullivan and who had worked with both Mendelssohn and Gounod in the preparation of their works'.[39] The immigrant society had been quick to set up musical activities to enrich its cultural life and in May 1880 the newly formed Adelaide Orchestral Society gave its first concert. In 1887, Stevens arrived to become organist at 'Christ Church, North Adelaide and Unitarian Church, Wakefield Street'. He quickly established the Adelaide Choral Society and also set up the Adelaide Orpheus Society.

Stevens was not only a product of reformed Victorian church music but of the great choral festivals that were centrepieces of English musical activity. Mendelssohn died soon after the production of his last oratorio, *Elijah*, which was written for the Birmingham Festival of 1846. It 'touched off the emotional spring of Victorian religious respectability as no other work had done [and] for a long time was considered inferior only to Handel's *Messiah*.' In 1882 Gounod's *Redemption*, also written for the Birmingham Festival, joined this pantheon of romantic oratorios that counterbalanced the fervour for Handel, which George Bernard Shaw claimed was sung by the English with 'the zest of the Chosen People in an age of mercantile expansion'. Unlike his contemporaries Shaw believed that Mendelssohn had created 'his richest musical spice to suit the compound of sanctimonious cruelty and base materialism which his patrons, the British Pharisees, called their religion'. However, the continued popularity of *Elijah* and *Messiah* to this day testifies to the impact of that Victorian theology, transplanted to Australia by church organists and choral conductors like Charles Stevens, caught in the euphoria of the reigning musical influences of their time.[40] Stevens produced his first *Messiah* in 1887, the year he arrived in Adelaide; Mendelssohn's *Elijah* and Gounod's *Redemption* soon followed.

The experienced Stevens was the first to recognise the potential of his young chorister but others later claimed the honour of introducing him to his teacher. One of these was John James Virgo, a preacher and amateur singer, who claims to have recognised Peter's vocal quality the year before he was given his first chance to sing *The Redemption*.[41] A report in the Adelaide

Advertiser on 5 October 1949 seems more apocryphal: 'One night while a game of skittles was in progress at the National Hotel, players heard a man at the piano singing in robust, rich notes. He was found to be Peter Dawson. They got in touch with Mr C J Stevens, conductor of the Orpheus Society, and I think he took Peter under his wing.'

Until attention was focussed on his vocal abilities, the happy-go-lucky young man believed he was destined to inherit a partnership in his father's iron-working business; but once he had embraced the intense discipline and dedication required to become a professional singer his life was transformed. From now on all his activities were subject to the priority of a daily regime of scales and vocal exercises; and in preparing Victorian concert material of increasing complexity. These were designed to gradually produce a consistent tone and extend the limited range of his natural voice to encompass the difficulties inherent in ballads, art songs, and arias from opera and oratorio. 'When I was 18 I used to get up at 6, practise scales for half an hour before breakfast and get to work at 7.30. Then after I had finished work at 5 I used to have tea and start lessons again. Hard work, eh? I don't suppose you would get many young chaps to do it now, but it didn't do me any harm.'[42]

Once Peter had accepted this essential professional baggage 'he would ride his horse out to Stevens' place at Wayville for lessons.' The Australian comedian Roy Rene (Mo) remembered those lessons too. He was about eight at the time. 'Peter Dawson ... lived round the corner from my home and went to his singing lessons in North Adelaide on a huge white horse – at any rate, it seemed a pretty big horse to me then. I double-banked with him on the way, and held the horse until the lesson was over.'[43]

As Stevens' protegé, it was a logical progression from solos with the church choir to competitions and solo performances with Stevens' secular choir. There are conflicting versions of his first appearances:

• he 'made his debut with the orchestra in July 1899'.
• in 1900 he sang the 'baritone part in Gounod's *Redemption* ... by Adelaide Choral Society. This was his first public appearance'.
• 'at the age of 17, he scored a success in a bass part in Gounod's *Redemption*, produced by the Adelaide Choral Society. Then he entered for a Ballarat singing contest, winning the first prize and a gold medal for a bass solo'.
• 'Dawson made his debut as a serious singer when, at seventeen, he sang in Gounod's *Redemption* in Adelaide; at eighteen he sang the bass solos in Handel's *Messiah* ... in the same year he won

first prize and gold medal against all comers at Ballarat. Can you wonder why plumbing palled!'[44]

There is a bit of romantic confusion here. When Peter Dawson turned eighteen in January 1900 his aspiration was not to become a singer but a prizefighter, 'an ambition further strengthened when at nineteen he won an amateur boxing championship'.[45] At eighteen Peter was still untrained or had just started singing lessons. *Redemption* might have been performed in 1899 but not with Peter; nor was he one of the soloists for the Adelaide Choral Society's performance of *Messiah* reported in the *Observer*, 30 December 1899; nor could we find proof of another performance of Gounod's *Redemption* in 1900.

Peter Dawson made his debut in the Adelaide Town Hall on 28 July 1900. He sang 'Blow, Blow Thou Winter Wind' (Serjeant) and the sizeable Gounod aria, 'She alone charmeth my sadness' with the Adelaide Grand Orchestra conducted by Charles Stevens.[46] This aria is a common, but unwise, choice for young basses because it lies fairly low and climaxes with a final low E; as a beginner young Dawson could not have sung the mellifluous line with the technical skill for which he later became known.

Addressing a luncheon from the stage of the Adelaide Town Hall in 1931, Dawson recalled that he had become 'Champion Soloist' on that very same platform at the Adelaide Exhibition of 1900: 'Well do I remember the first song I sang here. It was "O Ruddier than the cherry" and I stood there wearing what I thought was the shiniest pair of tan boots in the world. My old master, Mr. C. J. Stevens, saw them and said:

"My boy, you can't wear those."

"Why can't I? What's wrong with them?"

"Black, they must be black."

"Well, it's too late now and anyway they go well with my song, at any rate".[47]

That he continued to participate in church music is confirmed by a programme for 23 July 1900. Little Miss Moody sang 'Abide with me'; 'Miss M. Samson and Mr P. S. Dawson' were the soloists in 'Hosanna in the highest' (Stainer), 'Crossing the Bar' (Woodward) and 'I waited for the Lord' (Mendelssohn) with the Combined Choirs of St Andrews & St Giles at St Giles' Presbyterian Church in Norwood. Peter Dawson's first appearance as the bass soloist in *Messiah* was in December 1900; the much-touted success at Ballarat was in January 1901, two weeks before his nineteenth birthday.

The references to the Ballarat success imply that his outstanding gifts were immediately recognised at one of Australia's premier competitions;

but the Royal South Street Singing Competition did not earn its reputation as a mecca for young Australian singers until much later. Peter certainly won the prize – with the set piece, 'J. Christopher Mark's fine composition, "The Bandit Chief".' Seventeen competitors had entered but only nine came forward. In pronouncing 'P.S. Dawson an easy winner' the adjudicator, Professor Peterson, said that the standard was good but Dawson 'stood out head and shoulders above the other competitors'. However, the excitement of that 'Eighteenth Day, Evening Session, Thursday 17th January 1901' was not the Bass Solo but the choral event at the Albert Hall 'with its enormous seating capacity'. There, small specialist choral groups were being adjudicated in parallel with the competition for bass voices in the more intimate Her Majesty's.[48] As soon as the Bass Solo section had been decided, judge, competitors and audience rushed down the main street to the other hall for the Massed Choirs Competition, Professor Peterson to adjudicate, the singers to join their choirs. The real reason for Peter's presence was as one of the extra singers in the sixty-voice Augmented Kent Town Methodist Choir conducted by E. Harold Davies, Mus. Bac.

The Kent Town Methodist Church belonged to one of a handful of rich Protestant churches, 'sometimes referred to as fashionable, even aristo-cratic', whose choir members took part in choral competitions 'to stimulate their enthusiasm and competence'.[49] As it was quite common for Protestant singers to move 'freely from one church to another and from one denomi-nation to another', the choristers had taken the train to Ballarat, a small gold-mining town 56 miles from Melbourne. Travelling by train was a relatively new experience for the line had only been open since 1887.[50] The young Presbyterian bass was not in the Small Choir so he was free to compete against eight other amateur bass voices in the solo section before participat-ing in the centrepiece of the competition, the major choral event. The Aug-mented Kent Town Choir was not placed.

Young Dawson did not escape to Melbourne to spend his prize-money, as he was wont to relate later. The 'Grand Demonstration & Distribution of Prizes' took place in the large Albert Hall the following 23 October. After the chairman's address 'Mr Peter Dawson, Adelaide' sang 'She alone charmeth my sadness' and then hurried up to Her Majesty's Theatre to sing another deceptively simple bass aria, 'Item 8, Mozart's "Within these hal-lowed portals".' Each offering was accorded an [unnamed] encore.

During these initial two years of Dawson's formal vocal development the political situation in the colony changed dramatically. The land-boom col-lapse of the 1890s had revealed the financial vulnerability of the isolated

colonies and accelerated the arguments for some limited form of federa-
tion. By 1900, after much debate the states reached agreement. *An Act to
Constitute the Commonwealth of Australia* was proclaimed in London on 17
September 1900.

On 22 January 1901 Queen Victoria died after a reign of nearly sixty-
four years. Edward VII succeeded to the throne and the Royal House of
Saxe-Coburg-Gotha continued its reign. A few months later, on 9 May
1901, the Duke of York opened the first Commonwealth Parliament of
Australia in Melbourne's Exhibition Building. The Constitution limited the
new Parliament to four main areas of responsibility: a white Australia policy,
defence, tariffs and labour legislation. Like Canada, Australia became a le-
gally independent colony. 'The ties with the mother country were not broken; they now rested on sentiment rather than law; they were voluntary
instead of compulsory.'[51]

Photos of Peter Dawson in his twenties show a handsome man with
well-formed features, a straight nose, lively eyes and masses of dark wavy
hair. Listeners to his robust baritone might well picture a tall rugged individual but our hero was only five foot six and a half inches (1.7m.). From
his 1918 army record: 'Complexion: Dark; Eyes: Grey; Hair: Dark Brown;
Distinctive Marks: 7 vacs. L.; Dentally fit; Tattoos both Arms and Chest'.

By this time Dawson had also acquired those 'manly vices' learnt in the
schoolyard and in working life. One sign of 'trying to be a man before he
had grown out of being a boy' were the tattoos. Peter's father, who 'though
not a sailor, had one of the brands of the trade in the form of a large
crucifix tattooed on his forearm', was his role model. Peter's tattoos 'may
have proved the extent of his ardour for a few youthful sweethearts but in
later life proved a minor embarrassment.'[52]

Peter also aped his father by adopting 'the black rank twist favoured by
seamen' and 'developed a pair of lungs that could enjoy it.'[53] He smoked
heavily – not a habit singers should emulate. Today, when the dangers of
smoking have been widely canvassed, and a large portion of the population
has given up the addiction, we tend to forget how popular and how
sophisticated smoking was thought to be. It suggested manliness and
worldliness. In films a male character was defined by the way he smoked;
how the cigarette hung from his lips or from his fingers. Comedy kids were
always caught smoking in the shed or behind the back fence; smoking in a
woman implied 'modernity' if not immorality.

As a tough young tradesman Dawson also acquired the habits of swearing
and gambling, but not drinking. Although there are plenty of examples of
his enjoying a flutter, drinking is seldom reported. Although his last diaries

The young Peter, Adelaide 1900.

carry many entries of champagne celebrations and in later years he claimed that 'he enjoyed a drink whenever he felt like it, and did not think that fine Scotch whisky had done him anything but good', his nephews remember that 'Uncle Peter was not a big drinker; he could not drink'.[54] In his early recording days, at least, his producer said that 'Dawson in the matter of drink was a quasi-teetotaller'.[55] Perhaps the influence of his upbringing had had its effect, but Peter was definitely a social animal by nature; he loved a party and sat down to many a social meal, so it would hardly be surprising if on occasion he imbibed more than a thimbleful.

Dawson's written and spoken formal language remained relatively simple and showed limited style and vocabulary, even after long exposure to the public. In formal situations his language became platitudinous and pontificating, but when he was relaxed he loved to entertain those around him in a variety of accents, with the rough language and rough humour of male society and 'Smoke nights'. The larrikin element combined comfortably with an assiduous Presbyterian work ethic and morality.

By 1901 Peter's ambitious gift for singing was becoming apparent. Inspired by Charles Stevens' picture of more exciting possibilities in London, he was itching to try his luck overseas. But how good was he at this stage? Although he was tackling the perils of 'O Ruddier than the cherry', 'She alone charmeth my sadness' and 'Within these hallowed portals', he had received only elementary training. When he sang the difficult *Messiah* bass solos in the Adelaide Town Hall on Christmas Day 1901, just prior to his impending departure, the critic in the *Register* classified Miss Ethel Hantke and Messrs. F. G. H. Allen and P.S. Dawson as 'three young and inexperienced vocalists, who may be described as students and amateurs'.[56] Fortunately, 'viewed from the amateur's standpoint, they proved eminently pleasing, and in several instances gave rich promise of future excellence'. Handel's work had been severely cut, ending with the 'Hallelujah' chorus, so that the concert could finish by 10pm; therefore Peter did not have to sing the difficult 'The trumpet shall sound' with its high tessitura. Apart from one slip, Peter was much praised for the other three arias of which 'Why do the nations' 'evoked a furore of applause'.

Exciting as such a reception may have been, there was a quantum leap between singing as an amateur in Australia and deciding to join the singing profession overseas. Initially, Dawson's parents were not prepared to support such an idiotic idea. Their loyalty was to their chosen society and security for their children. Singing as a hobby was all right but going to London? 'Ye're ma richt haund mon, sae let me hear na muir o' that damned singing business!,'[57] said his father. But he had reckoned without the visionary Charles Stevens.[58] A paragraph appeared in the local paper: 'Mr. C.J. Stevens, Conductor A.G.O. and other musical authorities are so convinced of the wonderful future in store for this Vocalist that they are defraying the cost of sending him to Europe to undergo a complete course of training.'

Thomas Dawson and Charles Stevens struck a compromise. Thomas reckoned it was about time someone visited his brother in Glasgow so Peter and his eldest brother, James, could go there. They could get off the boat in London and Peter could audition for the famous teacher Stevens had recommended and they could then determine the next step.

The decision was made. On 25 March 1902, the night before they left, a send-off party was organised at the church. The hopes shared by Peter's church community and his mentor were eloquently expressed in a testimonial, written in elegant copperplate and signed by the minister and elders:[59]

> We the undersigned wish to convey to Mr Peter Dawson the very best wishes of the congregation of St Andrews Presbyterian Church before his departure to the Old country. Mr Dawson has been connected with the congregation for a number of years and during all that time has rendered most valuable services in the Church Choir taking a prominent part in the solo singing much to the delight of the congregation. His character as a young man has always been exemplary and while we deeply regret his departure from us yet we rejoice to know that this opportunity has come for the future culture of his voice and the development of his musical abilities.
> In assuming the musical profession he carries with him the very best wishes of the congregation and nothing will give them greater pleasure than to hear of his gaining high distinction in the musical world.
> We hope and pray that God will protect and bless him and should he return to South Australia we assure him of a hearty welcome from the Congregation at St Andrews Presbyterian Church.

In his biography Dawson wrote that he and James left Adelaide on 26 March 1902 on board the White Star liner, S.S. *Afric*.[60] The ship was indeed the S.S. *Afric* but the brothers did not sail from Adelaide; the ship left from Melbourne: 'The S.S. *Afric* ... will be dispatched from Railway Pier, Port Melbourne ... on Thursday, 27th Inst. Passengers should leave Adelaide by Express on Tuesday 25th.'[61] The advertisement was not completely accurate. They did leave Adelaide on 26 March, but, as the ship's manifest indicates, Mr J. H. Dawson and Mr P. Dawson were among the Third Class passengers, who sailed from Melbourne to London via Hobart and Capetown on 29 March, 1902.[62]

Such a long journey had its social occasions. An old photo shows Peter and James 'in fancy dress on deck of S.S. "Afric" 1902', and in 1951, on a *Morning-Tea Chat with Edith Pearn* at 7LA, Launceston, Peter filled in some other details.[63]

> We came down to Hobart and picked up 16,000 cases of apples then off we went round the Cape of Good Hope – the South African war was on at the time – martial law so we weren't allowed ashore – some wag got ashore anyway and brought back a bag of dirt – he put it on the deck and told us to walk over it and we could say we'd been on African soil – we were like kids – I did it – then our first place ashore was Madeira.'[64]

According to his book the *Afric* berthed at Tilbury at the end of May, on Derby Day at the end of the Boer War. As he put it: 'the South African War had just come to its long-drawn out end; peace had been declared the very day on which I arrived in London. The huge crowds returning from Epsom! Everyone singing, everyone happy, all carefree.' Because of the cost, the length and discomforts of such a journey, not to mention the dislocation from home and family, few Australians were prepared to undertake the 12,000 mile journey at that time. But like the youngest son in folk tales, our 20 year-old hero left home to seek his fortune in 'the leisurely, gracious hub of the world that was London of the day'. [65]

Annie Mortimer Noble: 'To Pete with love from Nan, 2/7/1904'.

'To Miss Nan Noble, kindest regards Peter Dawson'. The young lover, c.1904. In the possession of Ann Jacquet.

Peter, cousin David Dawson, Jim and (standing) Captain Riddell. In the possession of Ann Jacquet. Below: Peter's first composition, 1903. In the possession of the Documentation Collection – ScreenSound Australia, National Screen and Sound Archive.

Settling in London

It was the beginning of the Edwardian era. Nothing seemed to have changed since the Queen had died, yet the Boer War had begun the subtle process of undermining the inter-relationship between class structures in England. Returning soldiers among the working classes had tasted independence. A growing dissatisfaction with rule by a bourgeoisie grown rich on the spoils of Empire would gradually become visible.

The boys left the *Afric*. They gazed around them in excitement and amazement at the crowds returning from Epsom and celebrating the end of the Boer War. They were soon swept into the mêlée. Peter lost track of James and lost his posh new bowler. There were a few of the first motor cars but Dawson most vividly recalled the great charabancs pulled by four or five horses, the coachman in front, his assistant riding on the backplate. Rough kids ran beside them shouting, 'Throw down your mouldy coppers, throw down your mouldy coppers', and the well-heeled racegoers showered their coppers all over these kids. 'I remember someone from one of these charabancs made a face at them and all together, as one kid they made a face back and cried: "Throw down your mouldy coppers, Ugly!"'.[1]

This is the way Dawson told the story. However, in recollecting, he had mingled some indelible impressions from those first few weeks in England. The Boer War had ended on 31 May; Derby Day was 4 June; but the boys had already arrived in London by mid-May. By 1902 there were ships capable of making the run in six weeks. Although the S.S. *Afric*, 'half steam, half sail', was one of the slower boats it could still make it in eight. On this trip the ship had stopped in Hobart on 1 April, left Table Bay on 25 April, left Tenerife (not Madeira) on 11 May and arrived in London on 18 May.[2]

Before setting off for Glasgow to visit his uncle, the young colonial called on the eminent voice teacher, Charles Santley. Dawson never tired of telling the story of his first meeting with that august practitioner. It was retold in many variants; sometimes James was with him, sometimes the audition piece varied. This was where the already-familiar joke about the Handel aria, 'O ruddier than the cherry' began.[3]

Every singer has made that first step of singing for a famous teacher. It is a pretty scary experience, no matter how much gumption they might have. For all his cheek, Peter Dawson was no different. In honour of the occasion he put on his best clothes. Clothes maketh the man! Clothes reflect class, taste, education, panache. So Peter was very careful to get it right: he wore a braided tail coat, striped trousers and waistcoat, a shining silk top hat and – tan shoes. Tan boots with formal dress must have looked singularly gauche – but they matched the audition aria. In the event, Santley liked the young South Australian's voice but was not prepared to teach him immediately, so when he heard that the Dawson boys were going to Glasgow he suggested that Peter take some preliminary lessons while he was there.

The Scottish Dawsons lived at Rutherglen, to the south east of Glasgow on the River Clyde. Dawson's uncle, Captain James Dawson, was the owner of the Rock Line of sailing vessels – each named after well-known Scottish rocks such as the Bass Rock in the Firth of Forth.[4] The family connection to the sea is reflected in many photos and one extant painting by Dawson himself titled 'Gathering storm over Holy Island, Lamlash Isle of Arran', an island which 'Jim, Dave, Peter, Uncle James' visited for recreation.[5] Family life in Rutherglen parallelled life in Adelaide: the boys became active members of the Presbyterian congregation. A photo of the sober staff of 'St Andrews Church Sunday School, Rutherglen' suggests they taught there and Dawson at least sang as soloist in the choir for he marked several songs in his presentation *Scottish Anthem Book*.[6]

Dawson returned to his routine of daily practice and took regular lessons with a certain Mr F. L. Bamford whom Santley is said to have recommended: 'Mr Bamford was a fine teacher. He took me through a labyrinth of vocal exercises, taught me arias, opera, oratorio and the classic songs.'[7] Peter-the-teetotaller Dawson also gained experience singing with the Glasgow Abstainers' Union, which held concerts in the Glasgow City Hall: 'We attempted our biggest musical salvation on Saturday nights,' he recalls. 'We went around raking the drunks from pubs and streets, persuading them to come to our concerts.'[8]

This idyll lasted for a year. After that we lose track of James, who presumably returned to Adelaide. Peter moved to London in the summer of 1903 and settled into digs at 25 Finchley Road, Kennington.[9] By late 1903 the moving finger of Fate was probably suffering exhaustion, for Peter Dawson had started lessons with Charles Santley, met his future wife, toured with Madame Albani, written his first composition and had his first encounters with the recording industry.

Santley, who started teaching Dawson around September, was not only the pre-eminent teacher but one of the most famous English baritones of his era.[10] Liverpool-born, Charles Santley (1834-1922) was nearing seventy in 1903. He had begun his career as an opera singer but now concentrated on oratorio and concerts. He had learned the vocal technique he passed on to his pupils from the legendary master of *bel canto*, Manuel Garcia. A recent biographer has written that though he was an especially dramatic actor and sang with great expression, he did not have a naturally beautiful voice. This does not seem to accord with George Bernard Shaw's opinion that Santley was a model for singing coloratura; nor the recollection of the Gramophone Company producer, Fred Gaisberg. Gaisberg had coaxed the dapper, elegant maestro into the studio in 1903 to record the popular aria, 'Now your days of philandering are over' from Mozart's *The Marriage of Figaro*. 'I remember the delight his still fresh voice gave me. I was particularly struck with his ease of production and freedom of tone emitted.'[11] On 16 December 1907 Santley became the first British singer to be knighted. In 1913 Columbia brought out a number of titles including 'The Rosary'; and the year he died – aged eighty-eight – he recorded 'The Rosary' for Columbia again.

This remarkable man became Peter Dawson's new teacher and mentor, and once lessons began there followed 'three years of hard work'.[12] Santley now clearly believed in the natural talent of his student for he immediately arranged Dawson's 'first real engagement, a tour of the West of England with Mme Albani', in which Santley also appeared – a momentous opportunity. At fifty-one the French-Canadian dramatic soprano, Emma Albani (1852-1930), famous for her triumphs at Covent Garden, was in her prime.[13]

These concerts were the usual smorgasbord of major attractions – Albani and Santley – supported by minor artists including the twenty-one-year-old Dawson. He recalled singing 'Hybrias the Cretan' (Elliott) and 'The Bedouin Love Song' (Pinsuti) in the first half, then 'Blow Blow Thou Winter Wind' and 'The Bandolero' (Stuart) in the second at the first concert at the Plymouth Guildhall on 22 October 1903. The *Western Daily Mercury* reported that 'the young Adelaide basso … appears to have scored a complete success'.[14]

Although Dawson had already sung at concerts during his stay in Glasgow, in his book he referred to this tour and also a concert at a church in Burnett Road, Stepney – not far from his digs – as his first engagements. He remembered the programme for the church concert as the well-known bass songs, 'I Fear No Foe', 'Rocked in the Cradle of the Deep', 'The Bandolero' and 'Long Ago in Alcala' Although these songs are typical repertoire for the period, and became some of his early hits, we cannot be sure that he actually sang them on this occasion.[15]

In late 1903, around the time he had to travel to the northern suburb of St John's Wood for his lessons with Santley, Dawson moved from the east side of London to the west. He settled into a bed-sitter at 1 Hanger Lane, Ealing, not far from Mill Hill Road, Acton, where a certain Miss Annie Mortimer Noble lived. Eighteen months later 'Nan' became his wife. Nan's family was to play an important role in Peter's life. Thomas John Noble and his wife, Annie, formerly Mortimer, lived at Golders Green for most of their married life. They had seven children: Fan, Nan (1881-1954), Harry, Tom, Eva, Bill and Con. The move from Kennington suggests that Dawson already knew Nan quite well. Later, he wrote that Nan's father 'ran the Ealing Theatre, where I met his daughter'. But as the youngest daughter, Constance Bedford Noble (1899-1987), remembers it, 'My father was manager of a very big musical hall in Camden Town called the Bedford and I was named after it.'[16] Dawson also described Thomas Noble as 'the box-office manager of the famous Alhambra Theatre in Leicester Square'. So it appears that Thomas Noble managed several music halls: the Bedford when Constance was born, the Ealing Theatre around 1903, and the Alhambra when Dawson performed there on 13 February 1905.[17]

Fan and Nan worked professionally. Fan generally hid behind the name Yolande Noble, but also employed her married name, Frances Groves, and the pseudonym Dora Whittaker. The American record critic Jim Walsh regarded her as 'a talented comedian; some of her Edison and Columbia records were sold in the States'.[18] Constance remembered that 'Fan would sit at the piano and sing and talk. Fan was a wonderful Principal Boy. She had a beautiful figure,' but of the two Nan, who usually sang under the name Annette George, was considered the singer: 'Nanny used to sing and Nanny used to be Principal Boy and Princess and all that sort of thing.'

As the couple's first meeting is not part of family folklore, we can only speculate about it. Harry Noble had become a close friend of Peter, and could have introduced him to the family; or he might have introduced himself to Nan after watching her perform. They might have been on the same music-hall programme. Although Dawson dates his own recording career from mid-1904, it is possible that he could have been used in backing groups in late 1903. As Nan's brother Tom was working on the cylinder side of the industry and it is likely she made some recordings around this time, there are enough threads to suggest that they might even have met in a recording studio.

Nan (left) and sister Fan, London stage starlets, c. 1902. Nan worked professionally as Annette George and Fan as Yolande Noble. In the possession of Ann Jacquet.

Rare photographs from the family album: Recording at the Gramophone &
Typewriter Company's City Road studio, late 1904, with twin acoustic horns, one
for the singer, one for the piano; and below composing in his bed-sitter at 1 Hangar
Lane, Ealing, 1904. In the possession of Ann Jacquet.

CH 640053865 X 12

D) Löschzunge herausbrechen, wenn die Aufzeichnung gesichert werden soll. Bei erneuter Aufnahme Löschsicherungsloch überkleben.

GB) To keep a recording permanently, remove the tab on the underside. To make a new recording, cover the space with a label.

F) Pour protéger vos enregistrements, brisez la languette de sécurité. Pour réenregistrer, collez une étiquette à cet endroit.

E) Si se desea asegurar la grabación, romper el seguro contra borrado. Para una nueva grabación basta tapar dicho seguro.

P) Para proteger a gravação, quebrar a patilha de segurança. Para gravar novamente basta tapar o furo com a etiqueta.

I) Per proteggere le vostre registrazioni eliminate il dispositivo di cancellazione. Per registrare di nuovo applicate un'etichetta.

NL) Wilt u uw opnames niet kwijt? Verwijder het wispalletje aan de achterzijde. Voor nieuwe opnames kunt u een plakbandje over het ontstane gaatje plakken.

RUS) В целях защиты записи от случайного стирания сломать предохранительный механизм. При появлении новой записи заклеить образовавшееся отверстие.

PL) Aby zabezpieczyć nagranie przed skasowaniem należy wsunąć blokadę do środka. Aby dokonać ponownego nagrania należy ja wysunąć tak aby zakryła cały otwór.

CZ) Chcete-li trvale uchovat svoji nahrávku, vylomte jazýček na hřbetu kazety. Pro novou nahrávku, přelepte otvor lepící páskou.

T) Yapmış olduğunuz kayıtları korumak için, kasetin arka kenarındaki güvenlik dilçiğini kırınız. Bu durumda tekrar kayıt yapmak istiyorsanız, aynı alana bir bant yapıştırınız.

1 2 3 4 5 6 7 8 9 0
1 2 3 4 5 6 7 8 9 0
1 2 3 4 5 6 7 8 9 0
1 2 3 4 5 6 7 8 9 0

He was also composing. In a series of early photographs Dawson can be seen in leggings and a large rakish hat composing and playing the banjo. Despite his lack of formal musicianship, writing music became a life-long occupation. He wrote at least 59 songs of which more than thirty were published and recorded. At the age of 75 he was photographed composing at the piano and at 77 was writing another song, 'Moonlight Fancy'.[19] His first extant composition, 'In Memorium [sic] of Daniel Dawson', is dated 'Ealing, Dec 31st 03'.[20]

From his compositions, his correspondence and the careful way he filed music, photographs and other documents, we know that Peter Dawson was an orderly person. With experience he became singularly adept at writing musical notation. However, in 1903 he was just beginning to explore this new medium: awkwardly written notation, some incorrect rhythm and unsuccessful harmonies indicate that he was in unfamiliar territory. The words were set syllabically and his 'serious' artistic language was still rooted in church jargon: 'In faith and peace and prayer, Till He whose home is ours unite us there, Sleep on dear heart and take thy peaceful sleep, God taketh …'.

The range of this song, a low G to a top E, and the general placement of the notes (*tessitura*) give a clue to Dawson's comfortable vocal range at the time.[21] As both the tessitura and the top E would be most uncomfortable for a natural bass, they indicate that Dawson was already an instinctive baritone. However, the concluding effect, a gentle descent to the low G, suggests that he still regarded himself as a bass. Where sopranos or tenors seek to impress with unusually high notes, the bass makes his mark with unexpectedly low notes – a technique Dawson had learned from 'She alone charmeth my sadness', 'Within these hallowed portals' and two popular Victorian bass songs, which he now added to his repertoire, 'Asleep in the Deep' (Petrie) and 'In Cellar Cool' (Fischer). The latter, a drinking song, uses wide leaps to suggest the effects of intoxication then finishes with an inebriated ad libitum D-R-I-N-K-I-N-G as a descending scale, G being the final low effect note.[22]

At twenty-two, Dawson's ambition was still to appear on the concert platform. At the turn of the century the prospective sources of livelihood for a serious young professional were classical concerts, church concerts, oratorio in churches or at festivals, opera and musical societies. However, through Nan's family Peter was introduced to lighter, popular songs, songs that suited his lively, gregarious nature and exposed a latent comic talent. They were also suitable for smoke nights, the music-hall, light summer seaside entertainment and pantomime. The question was: which engagements would determine his career?

ALHAMBRA

Manager - - Mr. GEORGE SCOTT

The National Theatre of Varieties

SPECIAL AND EXCLUSIVE PROGRAMME

COMMENCING

Monday, February 13th, 1905

1. **Overture**   8.0

A Scene from the Popular Ballet.

2. **ALL THE YEAR ROUND** 8.5

(Last Weeks.)

3. **SHADOW BROS.**   8.20

Hand Equilibrists.

4. **PETER DAWSON**   8.30

Bass.

5. **BOBBY PANDUR**   8.40

Le Roi de la Beauté Plastique.

6. **ORCHESTRAL SELECTION** 8.50

7. **THE FOUR HARVEYS** 9.0

In their Clever Wire Act.

8. **Miss KITTY TRANEY** 9.15

In her Novel Juggling and Sporting Act.

9. **TSCHIN-MAA TROUPE** 9.30

Of Chunchuses, Conjurers and Jugglers, from Liao-yang.

10. **The "URBAN" BIOSCOPE** ... 9.55

THE BEGGAR CHILD
A Story of Pathos and Humour.
THE JAPANESE ARMY BEFORE PORT ARTHUR
Photographed by Mr. Rosenthal, attached to the THIRD IMPERIAL JAPANESE ARMY since May last.
BLACK DIAMONDS.
Daily life of the Coal-Miner. Scenes round and about the Colliery District of the Black Country. (Photographs by Norden.)

11. **"ENTENTE CORDIALE"** 10.30

The Enormously Successful Grand Ballet Divertissement.

12. **PITROT**   11.10

Mobile Bar Performer. (Last Week.)

Mr. H. WOODFORD ... ... Business Manager and Secretary.
Mr. CHAS. WILSON ... ... Stage Director.
Mr. G. W. BYNG ... ... Musical Director.

BOX OFFICE Open from 10 to 10.   **Doors Open at 7.45.**

TELEPHONE Nos. 5060 & 5065 GERRARD.

MILES & CO. LTD., PRINTERS, 68-73, WARDOUR STREET, W.

The Alhambra Theatre, Leicester Square, programme for 13 February 1905. The musical director on the 1905 bill was G. W. Byng, who in the 1920s supervised many of Peter's HMV recordings.

A career begins: creating the myth

The owners of the Gramophone rejoice
To hear it likened to the human voice.
The owners of the Human Voice disown
Its least resemblance to the Gramophone.[1]

When Dawson stood at the crossroads in 1903 he had not reckoned with the fledgling recording industry. '"The gramophone was at first regarded as an instrument of torture," Mr Dawson said to me. "Only extremely loud noises could make any impression on the early recording machines."'[2] Hardly the right medium for an aspiring concert artist.

Despite advertisements praising the excitement of the new-fangled talking machines, recording techniques and recorded sound were fairly primitive in the infant pre-1900 days. Looking back, the Gramophone Company chief, Alfred Clark, reflected that

> the early days of the gramophone now begin to take on the atmosphere of a fairy story. I remember when only half a dozen male singers could record well and only three records could be made each time the artists sang. It was impossible to make a record of a female voice or a violin.[3]

In 1877 the American inventor, Thomas Edison first demonstrated his talking machine, a cylinder, which he called the 'phonograph'. By 1903 he had developed a very successful recording business which had spread to Great Britain and Europe. The only opposition to cylinders was to come from the 'gramophone' a new system of recording by etching a flat zinc disc that had been patented in Washington in 1888 by the German emigrant, Emile Berliner.[4] Originally the turntable on which the disc lay could only be turned by means of a hand-driven crankshaft; this device was first used commercially by a toy seller in Berlin.[5] The Berliner Gramophone was launched in late 1893, when the first disc catalogue appeared. Berliner's original discs were of vulcanised rubber. In 1897 he switched to a more reliable shellac composition but his disc was still unable to gain any serious foothold until the engineer, Eldridge Johnson, invented a spring motor for the turntable. This made the gramophone a real competitor to cylinders, even though the market still regarded it as 'an amusing toy with very squeaky results'.

In May 1898 the Gramophone Company of London, the company with which Peter Dawson's name became associated, was registered 'with a working capital of £3000 and the exclusive rights to sell gramophone merchandise throughout Europe'. The general manager, William Barry Owens, an ex-lawyer turned promoter who had worked for one of the American disc companies, set up his headquarters at 31 Maiden Lane, just off the Strand.[6] The company imported and assembled the parts for the 1898 Berliner/Johnson Improved Model talking machine, the one seen on *His Master's Voice* labels.

In July 1898 the Gaisberg brothers, Fred and Will, who had also worked with American companies, joined Owens' Gramophone Company as its sound engineers. Fred Gaisberg converted a small room in the basement of Maiden Lane into a recording studio to produce his one-sided masters, but, in anticipation of possible difficulties with British unions, these were pressed by Emile Berliner's brother, Joseph, in a factory erected for that purpose in Hannover.[7]

There were several reasons for the eventual success of the Gramophone Company of London: the most basic was the gradual recognition of the greater convenience of a flat disc over a bulky cylinder but more importantly, discs could be made in hundreds of copies, like printing. To this was added the dramatic effect of American salesmanship on the British market, which changed the concept of advertising so completely that repercussions are felt to this day. Owens was a promoter. Owens was a salesman. He introduced his products 'with a minimum of social punctilio' with full-page advertisements in London newspapers that had none of the customary British reserve in layout or copy.[8] A third positive attribute was the musical sensibility of Fred Gaisberg. This small, quiet man, who had originally been a pianist, was destined to remain the artistic power behind the commercial throne up to and beyond World War II.[9]

The first United Kingdom recordings were made in August 1898. Some contend they were of an Australian vocalist, Syria Lamonte, for she recorded 21 titles between 2 August and 3 October. Legend has it that she was a barmaid at Owens' hotel in the Strand, but the English discographer, Brian Rust, advised us that 'Syria Lamonte, the girl who made the first London disc session, was the owner of a sweet pure voice that betokens expert training, whoever she was.'[10] Little is known about her. She appeared in Melbourne music-halls between 1894 and 1896 and, like Peter Dawson later, her picture appeared on popular cigarette cards, so she must have been well known in London at this time.

Initially the masters were of zinc with record information etched into the centre of the shellac pressings; but in 1900 the Gramophone Company was able to buy the rights to paper labels and to a secret wax recording process which Eldridge Johnson had invented. This was the wax master method that remained in use until 1949 (even some long-playing records).

To boost the company profile Fred Gaisberg travelled regularly to European opera houses to seek out internationally-known singers like Adelina Patti, Nellie Melba, Lilli Lehmann, Emma Calvé, Victor Maurel, Mattia Battistini and Pol Plançon, who were objects of adoration in the most envied vocal profession. In Russia, the Gramophone Company representative had the bright idea of identifying his opera stars with a special red label and selling these as exclusive recordings – at a higher price. The first *Red Label* catalogue, which included the young Feodor Chaliapin, appeared in September 1902. 'Red Labels established the Company and its trademark, gave it status and pushed it well to the forefront of the talking machine industry'.[11] But it was Fred Gaisberg's 1902 recording of the young Italian tenor, Enrico Caruso, in a studio set up in a Milanese hotel room, which finally marked the coming-of-age for disc recording. Caruso's sales topped those of all other artists, giving rise to the remark that no one was sure whether Caruso had made the gramophone or the gramophone had made Caruso.[12]

In early 1903, Will Gaisberg went to Varese in Italy to add the *tenore robusto*, Francesco Tamagno (1850-1905), to his *Red Label* artists. But Tamagno, who had created Verdi's Otello, did not consider a *Red Label* exclusive enough and insisted on his own special label. This super-exclusive *Tamagno* label cost £1 when normal 7in. records cost 2/6, the 10in. 'concert' cost 5/–; the exclusive *Red Label* 10in. 10/–; and the 12in. 15/–. Affronted, our diva insisted on her own *Melba* label which had to sell for a guinea – one shilling more! These were all single-sided discs. Playing speeds could be adjusted between 70 and 82 rpm, which altered the pitch. No doubt many a soprano became a contralto – and vice versa.

Some early Peter Dawson records, known as 'G&Ts', carry the identification 'Manufactured by The Gramophone & Typewriter Ltd. and Sister Companies'. Salesman Owens, misreading the future of the recording industry, had joined the ranks of those who believed the primitive talking machine was a passing craze. He decided to diversify by becoming distributor of the Lambert typewriter and in 1900 '& Typewriter' was added to the company name. But the Lambert was so ungainly that sales were poor, causing the Company financial problems and forcing Owens' resignation in 1904. The company, however, did not drop '& Typewriter' until 1908.

By 1900 the Gramophone Company already had a catalogue of 5,000 records. By March 1904 the interested purchaser could choose from 12,000. Disc competition came principally from Zonophone, whose list of celebrity artists was similar, so in 1903 the Gramophone Company acquired Zonophone and retained that trademark until the 1930s for its low-priced records. The Gramophone Company was slowly making its mark in the market battle with cylinders, but cylinders were still much more prevalent. 'Viewed side by side, the gramophone seemed a poor relation, the phonograph a bejewelled *grande dame*'.[13] Headed by the old master, Thomas Edison, the dominant cylinder company was Edison – not to be confused with its next rival, Edison Bell.

Just as the disc had achieved a reasonable recording quality our young Australian bass arrived on the scene. According to the official story Dawson began an exclusive solo recording career with the Gramophone Company in 1904 and remained under contract until 1955. The titles recorded, numbers sold, length of his recording career, even his income appear to be of mythical proportions. It was reported that:

- 'his eventual total was more than 13 million sales of some 3,500 titles';
- 'he calculates that he has sold thirteen and a half million records of one sort or another, most of them at the comforting royalty of five per cent';
- 'his association with the H.M.V. organisation for over fifty years is unique in the annals of the recording industry. His recording of over three and a half thousand titles will probably never be surpassed by any artist. Calculated on a basis of proportion to total sales, there can be little doubt that his fourteen million records sold represented a higher percentage than any other recording artist.'[14]

Fifty years! 3,500 titles! 13-14 million sales! Royalties of 5%! These figures originate from record company publicity, interviews, programmes and Peter Dawson's autobiography. Yet as extraordinary as they may appear, the American record specialist, Jim Walsh, found these sales figures 'woefully under-estimated', because 'even in the fledgling days of the phonograph industry a 5,000 sale was considered the break-even point'.[15] Using this figure, Walsh argued that total sales would be at least 17.5 million. However, as Dawson himself had 'said that many of his records sold in the hundreds of thousands', Walsh raised his claim to 26 million. A similar figure can be found in the 1984 *Guinness Book of Records*: 'his sales exceeded 21 million by the start of World War II and possibly over 25 million before the LP era'.

Like so many aspects of the Peter Dawson fable, the number of titles and their sales figures remain tantalisingly unverifiable, too large to be questioned and so large that the reader might think Peter Dawson one of the immortals. Perhaps he was, for there is unanimous agreement on his popularity and rarely a critical remark about his work. Broadly, critics and biographers share Walsh's opinion that 'he has been the most important recording artist in the phonograph's 84-year history – not excluding Caruso or even Elvis Presley!'

But beware the Peter Dawson legend! It is the product of the intrusion of aggressive American advertising into England, of a new, hard sell to which both Dawson and the Gramophone Company remained loyal. Dawson's first recordings were cylinders, but he was soon making discs; we first hear of him as a soloist but he was soon singing in various ensembles and may have sung ensembles earlier. Exclusivity with the Gramophone Company began in 1907, but there are gaps in the continuity. There was a brilliant rise to a peak of popularity in the early 1930s, then an aggressive rear-guard action for the rest of his life.

When his Australian biographer, James Glennon, tried to trace all Dawson's records, EMI advised him that it would be quite impractical because 'Dawson recorded for many companies … under many different names'.[16] Fortunately, we have now been able to prepare the first complete song title discography. As far as we can tell there were only about 1,500 recordings for the Gramophone Company. Even after adding the cylinders he recorded and pirated material on cylinder and disc; Gramophone Company material pressed in Australia, New Zealand, India, Canada; the minor Australian companies; material originating from radio, film and television – and even allowing for new discoveries – the discography seems unlikely to extend to more than 2,000 titles.

When did Peter Dawson's recording career begin? The question has intrigued researchers for years. It is a truism that 'most performers are less than 100 per cent accurate when they try to recollect details of their recording careers';[17] so let us take a moment to compare the popular perceptions with the known facts.

The Gramophone Company claimed that Peter Dawson first auditioned, unsuccessfully, for the venerable J. E. Hough, the head of the Edison Bell cylinder company.[18] Hough's American sound engineer, Russell Hunting, however, recognised that this youngster had potential and gave the wink to his friend Fred Gaisberg. Fred invited Peter to audition:[19] 'I remember as though it were yesterday,' Peter recalled, 'I sang "Long ago in Alcala, Tra la la, Tra la la" and Fred Gaisberg played the piano for me, and his brother Will made the record.' This audition led to his first record, 'a popular hit called "Navajo", which appeared in the 1904 catalogue'.[20]

On another page of his memoirs we find Dawson excited over another first: 'It was the custom for the recording to be announced by Harry Bluff, who gave me my first thrill when he said: "The Bandolero", sung by Peter Dawson, Edison Bell record.'[21] Trouble is, Dawson never recorded 'The Bandolero' for that company. On yet another page, Dawson admits that one of his earliest recordings was 'Navaho' [sic] on an Edison Bell cylinder under the name of Leonard Dawson.[22] So the audition for Mr Hough must have been successful after all.

Confused? Here are some facts. The first Peter Dawson cylinders listed in the Edison Bell catalogue were EB 6383, 'Thy Beaming Eyes' and EB 6384, 'To My First Love'. EB 6382, which cannot be traced, could also be a Dawson title. The 1903 Indian-Negro pop song, 'Navajo', recorded with orchestra in July/August 1904, was EB 6398. So at first glance, one of the numbers prior to 'Navajo' would seem to be Dawson's first recording – but we cannot be positive because Edison Bell did not always release cylinders in sequence.

To further complicate matters, Edison Bell shared premises in Euston Road with the Lambert Company and *Lambert* cylinders were recorded in the same studio as Edison Bell, so an artist might sing the same song for both companies on the same day. As a result many songs by the same performer appeared in both the Edison Bell and Lambert catalogues, so 'Leonard' Dawson singing 'Navajo' on *Lambert* issue No. 5100 could have come from the same session as EB 6398, the following session or the previous session. However, the *Lambert* catalogue shows that nine other Dawson numbers, 5087–5094 and 5099, precede 5100. As the earliest number, 5087, 'Drink to Me Only With Thine Eyes', was part of Dawson's 'natural' repertoire, it could well be a nominee for his first recording. About this time, however, he also recorded 'Navahoe' for *Nicole* discs under the name of Mr C. Adams.

There is another wild-card possibility that goes back to his meeting with Nan. In 1904 a popular hit like 'Navajo' was still uncharacteristic repertoire for the young Australian, but not for Nan's music-hall family. Her younger brother, Tom, was the 'Mr. T. J. Noble, who also worked for Edison, later under Russell Hunting, and was assistant Pathé recording supervisor throughout Europe. He had been one of the experts of National Company Ltd. at its British and some of its Continental laboratories.'[23] Peter was now family. He made recordings with Fan under the name 'Will Danby' and we have recently received a report that Edison cylinder 20076, 'Smile, Smile, Smile', was recorded by Will Danby and Anne Mortimer – that is, Nan. As several of the Noble family were involved with the talking machine industry we cannot ignore the possibility that Dawson could have sung in backing groups from the time he knew them – late 1903 to mid-1904.

While the jury is still out on the question of the actual beginnings, from August 1904 all conjecture ends. Peter Dawson's recording career can now be divided into five periods; 1904–1918, 1919–1925, 1926–1939, 1940–1946, 1947–1958. Although he began work with several companies well-nigh concurrently, he became famous through his enduring association with the Gramophone Company. This began on Monday 15 August 1904, when he recorded Gramophone & Typewriter 2–2479, 'Navajo' accompanied by Fred Gaisberg. How could the twenty-two year old know that this new device would quickly become the most popular form of home entertainment in the world and his vehicle to fame? Despite the brouhaha about Red Labels 'then as now the bulk of record sales were confined to ephemeral, popular music'.[24] The young bass could not afford any delusions of grandeur; he had to sing what presented itself. 'Within a few weeks I had him making popular, comic and serious ballads, oratorio and opera arias, Gilbert and Sullivan, solos, duets, trios, quartets, chorus, etc.', said Fred Gaisberg.[25] Peter Dawson was in on the ground floor – or to be more precise, the third floor of 'No. 21 City Road, E.C.' for the Gramophone Company had moved to more commodious premises in the summer of 1902. It may have been 'an enormous advance over the old basement room in Maiden Lane'[26] but by all accounts it was still small and cramped.

It was in this tiny recording studio on 4 September 1905 that the disparaging remark about Adelaide being the city of 'Parsons, Pubs and Prostitutes' was made, when the tyrant Melba first met the tyro Dawson.[27] According to Walsh: Dawson, Kirkby and Pike were backing Melba in 'The Old Folks at Home'; according to Fred Gaisberg: a male quartet was backing her while she sang 'My Old Kentucky Home'.[28] However, the recording ledgers show that the participants were actually Peter Dawson, Ernest Pike and Gwladys Roberts, backing Melba for 'Auld Lang Syne' and 'The Old Folks at Home'. Melba, who was used to being fêted, resented the trio crowding around her at the single recording horn. The atmosphere became so tense that Melba finally turned on Pike and shouted: 'Stop pushing! You're just one of the bloody chorus!' Poor Landon Ronald at the piano nearly had a breakdown on the spot.

By 1905 Dawson was 'Peter Dawson' most of the time, recording on disc for *G&T, Zonophone, Nicole, Neophone* and *Pathé*; but he and his contemporaries also did plenty of work with the cylinder companies. So we find the tenors Wilfred Virgo and Ernest Pike, the baritone Stanley Kirkby and the bass Peter Dawson appearing with Arthur Gilbert for Gramophone as the 'Minster Singers' and for Edison Bell as the 'Meister Singers' – just two of some fifty different groups we have listed in our discography.

Edison Bell issued two 'Peter Dawson' type songs, 'The Good Rhein Wine' and his ever-popular 'Simon the Cellarer'. He was also coupled with Virgo for that wonderfully stirring, sentimental, unequivocally Victorian duet, 'Excelsior', which can still bring an audience to its feet. For *G&T* he sang Mephistopheles in the finale to Gounod's opera *Faust;* and had his fair share of solo recording too, including the rollicking 'Down at the Old Bull and Bush'. This adaptation of the American hit, 'Under the Anheuer Bush', by Russell Hunting and Percy Krone was so successful in England that Dawson recorded it for *G&T, Zonophone* and *Nicole* for release in early 1905. In the same year he recorded repertoire as diverse as 'Tis I'; his first of seven versions of 'Bedouin Love Song'; and his first of seven versions of 'Asleep in the Deep' – that lugubrious bass song with its final descending low notes, which transport the listener into eerie, subterranean depths.[29]

All this activity is evidence of the flourishing demand for both cylinder and disc recordings. Fred Gaisberg wrote: 'Our recording studio in the City Road was a merry, carefree place in those days. We had the monopoly of a promising industry.'[30] The monopoly was yet to come, but those initial years in the cramped recording studio were the foundation of the productive years that made Peter Dawson and his mates legendary. They were allies in a revolution.

While claims of the quantity of recordings may have been grossly exaggerated, quality was not. Despite the length of his recording career, there is rarely any criticism of Dawson's vocal technique; on the contrary, analysts who compare recordings hold him up as the model singer. But because aficionados confine themselves to cylinders and discs they gain the impression that 'recording Peter Dawson marked the beginning of a new phenomenon – a career that could be made and maintained almost entirely

Charles Santley, born 1834 and regarded as 'one of the finest baritones of his era'. This portrait appeared in the programme for his Jubilee Concert, held at the Royal Albert Hall, on 1 May, 1907. Later, on 16 December, he became the first English singer to be knighted.

through recordings'. [31] Far from it. It would be a grave mistake to imagine that Peter Dawson's productive life centred round the recording studio. At its peak, recording took up less than one-third of his time and from the mid-1930s it gradually dwindled to a couple of courtesy discs.

In 1904 his principle occupations were his singing lessons and the preparation of repertoire which would establish him as a concert artist. That year he published his first composition, 'Sun and Song', [32] dedicated to Charles Santley, who had become his mentor. 'Sometimes Santley would invite me to dinner. After dinner we would smoke fierce black Spanish cigars but I could smoke anything in those days.'[33]

His domestic life was taken up with Nan and her family. In October he returned to Glasgow for concerts.[34] From Rutherglen he posted a sketch – a grinning black chef on 'HMS Mill Hill' with the message 'I hope Pete comes down soon' – to Miss Nan Noble.[35] Six months later they married. The cartoon shows his wicked sense of humour but his deepest feelings were expressed in an unpublished song, 'Woman's Love', (in $E^\flat$, common time, a comfortable range $B^\flat$–$E^\flat$). Most noticeable is the big improvement in his musical calligraphy since 1903. The song is simply dated 1905 but from the sentimental text: 'There's a gem that ever shines with pure and holy light … that gem is woman's love' we can place the composition close to the date of his marriage.

To finance his studies Peter received a renewable credit of £100 per annum from his father.[36] 'When I had failed to find engagements after I had been studying for two years my father strongly advised me to come home and rejoin the firm. Later he cut my allowance.' Elsewhere he said that the cut came after three £100 credits because his father was angry that he wanted to get married at twenty-two to a girl 'who danced and sang in theatres'.

But they married anyway. The wedding between 'the Vocalist, Peter Smith Dawson and the Spinster, Annie Mortimer Noble' was witnessed at the Registry Office in the District of Westminster on Saturday 20 May 1905 by Nan's father, her brother Harry and her sister Fan, already married to the actor Fred Groves.[37] It was destined to be a long and happy marriage. In Nan Peter found the ideal companion: she understood his style of life so well that she could support him not only in his triumphs but also in the frustrations and disappointments inevitable in their way of life. She accepted his nature and his talent and in some respects kept it under control. Peter's Australian family came to regard Nan as the power behind the throne: 'He never had a secretary', said one of his nephews, 'Nan typed. He practised a lot as I understand; Nan played for him. Nan was his guardian; no one was

The Dawsons' honeymoon: a weekend at Margate, May 1905. In the possession of
Ann Jacquet.

allowed to speak to him before concerts.'[38] Peter simply said, 'My wife goes everywhere with me. I could not do without her.'[39]

On 11 October 1905 the Gramophone Company board authorised the administration 'to enter into contracts with Peter Dawson, John Harrison, and Miss Gwladys Roberts.'[40] The same board minutes reveal that Owens had gone and the long reign of Trevor Williams had begun; that Melba could command outrageous fees (royalty: £767); that 'National and International Branches' had been established; and that the monthly budget was £200,000 (over £2 million for the year: £85 million in present-day terms). So even at this stage, when the demand for cylinders was still in the ascendancy, there must have been a huge demand for discs.

In any history of the recording industry the names which frequently occur are not only Will and Fred Gaisberg but also Alfred Clark, Louis Sterling and Russell Hunting. Alfred Clark (later Sir) became managing director of the Gramophone Company, and later chairman of the board; Louis Sterling (later Sir), a sometime business associate of Russell Hunting, became general manager when Clark became chairman; and Hunting was a key figure in many recording ventures.[41] These peripatetic Americans, pioneers from the phonograph's earliest days, ruled various sections of the English recording industry until 1939 and beyond. They knew each other so well that they entered into what Fred Gaisberg described as a 'secret understanding': 'I exchanged with them certain non-contract artists, and we worked together to our mutual benefit'.[42] Dawson was a beneficiary of this policy; he moved comfortably among the friendly companies until 1907, when the Gramophone Company finally insisted on an exclusive disc contract.

As samples of his repertoire will show, Peter Dawson, like his fellow artists, was a sort of musical Man Friday contracted for 'Solo, quartette or part-songs'. According to Walsh, Dawson had a retaining fee of £25 and earned £72 on his 1906 contract.[43] There was other income from concerts such as the full *Messiah* in Woolwich on Good Friday, 13 April 1906.[44] Nevertheless he was not yet earning enough to survive 'the dead-summer season for vocalists in those early days'.[45] The solution? Hector Grant.

Dawson used many false names for both recordings and compositions. The use of pseudonyms was clearly common practice. These *noms de disque* may have occurred to allow the singer to sing for another record company; but record companies also changed artists' names to make their catalogues appear more varied or to allow singers to indulge in music outside the 'normal' repertoire associated with their names.[46] Peter Dawson certainly had quite a collection: Leonard Dawson, George Welsh and C. Adams have

A 1907 Star Artistes collectors' card of Hector Grant with words for a
parody of 'Sandy, You're a Dandy' on the back; plus a 1930s Wills' cigarette
card, in their Radio Celebrities series, with a biography on the back
describing Dawson as 'one of the greatest living baritones'.

been noted. For his 1909 'Simon the Cellarer' and 'The Deathless Army' he used James Osborne; we have mentioned Will Danby – with Yolande Noble; other sources cite Arthur Walpole and Walter Wentworth[47] but there were more, including: Victor Graham, David Peters, Will Strong, Charles Handy, Robert Woodville.[48] Why Dawson chose these names remains an enigma;[49] he only admits that he saved his own name for concert material and hid behind false names to sing 'pop music'. Leonard was cosmetic; Will Danby allowed him free reign as a comedian; some names were used for lighter repertoire or group work; others appear to have been used to avoid breaking contractual obligations. But Hector Grant was more than a *nom de disque*: Peter actually created the Scottish music-hall comedian.

Hector has enjoyed the embellishment of years of anecdote. Knowing Peter's Scottish background and his inclination 'to pull your leg all the time',[50] it comes as no surprise to read that one day he amused his colleagues in the studio by imitating Harry Lauder. Both Fred Gaisberg and Dawson claim that the prank occurred in the Gramophone studios in 1904:

> One day I gave an imitation of Lauder singing 'I love a Lassie'. Fred Gaisberg came up to me excitedly and said: 'Peter, can you do any more like that? I mean, can you sing Scottish?' I was amused at the way the little American put it, and answered, 'Yes, of course. I can sing all his songs, including "Stop Yer Ticklin', Jock" and "We Parted on the Shore".'

Gaisberg then persuaded Dawson to record all Harry Lauder's songs for *Zonophone* hidden behind a phoney name – and Hector Grant was born.[51]

In fact, the label was not *Zonophone* nor was the year 1904. Harry Lauder (later Sir) was 'a youngish Scot who had recently come into the limelight with his inimitable combination of balladry and Highland parody'.[52] Lauder's own 'I Love a Lassie' had been a hit in the pantomime, *Aladdin* in Glasgow in the summer of 1905. On 26 August he recorded it for the Gramophone Company. It was so successful that he was quickly established as an Edwardian superstar.[53]

As the companies soon ran out of Lauder numbers to pirate, the logical next step was for Peter Dawson to compose some Hector Grant numbers himself. The published song, 'Sandy, You're a Dandy', 'Written, Composed and Sung by Hector Grant' and the manuscript, 'My Hee'lan' Fairy' signed 'Hector Grant' belong to this brief interlude between 1905-07.[54] Then, kilted, bearded and with a thick Scots accent, 'Hector wi' th' curr-rly stick & terrific red tartan tammy … toured the Moss & Stoll circuit'.[55] Large posters confirm that the support artist, 'Hector Grant Comedian', appeared from one end of the country to the other 'twice nightly and during the week Matinee'.[56]

Shortly after, in November 1905, Dawson adopted his comic *alter ego* to record 'I Love a Lassie' – not for the Gramophone Company, not for Edison Bell, but for the grand master, Edison. Hector Grant cylinders hit the market about January 1906, among them: 'Lassie, Dinna Sigh for Me', 'Foo the Noo', 'Tomorrow Will be Friday', 'Ticklie Geordie' and 'I Wish I Had Someone to Love Me'. As musical piracy was rampant in those early days, 'Hector' was soon working for the other companies. He could be heard on Edison Bell cylinders with 'Lassie Dinna Sigh for Me', 'Ticklie Geordie' and 'Saftest of the Family'; on *London Popular* cylinders with 'I Love a Lassie'; on *White* cylinders with 'Lassie Dinna Sigh for Me' and 'We Parted on the Shore'. Hector's first recording for *Zonophone* discs was 'I Love a Lassie' in January 1906.

Hector Grant certainly recorded and toured but it seems strange that such a lucrative character survived only the summer of 1906. In one report Peter claimed that he was broke when he married in 1905 because his father had withdrawn the £100 credits;[57] in another that he only took on the music-hall tour because he needed an income to tide him over 'the dead-summer season for vocalists' of 1906.[58] At that time Dawson's only substantial income came from recording so, if his father had withdrawn financial support he could well have been broke. However, the statement is contradicted in a letter to Nan during his 1909 Australian tour:

> I have had a great chat with Mum & Dad, and they will not hear of us ever returning a farthing of money. They declare that I have barely had my share out of the business which is worth £6000. I think, Nan dear, that altogether I have had £900 since leaving home 8 years ago.[59]

In later life Peter confided that he had adopted the successful disguise for 15 weeks at £15 per week, but when offered another 50 weeks at £25 he had declined manfully: 'No, I'm sorry. I can't do that because originally my father sent me over from Australia to study for the concert platform.'[60] This may have been Dawson's view; but Edison's is likely to have been that they needed a temporary replacement for Lauder that summer to cash in on the craze for his songs.

One of Hector Grant's most successful cylinders was the 1907 release, 'John, John, Go and Put your Trousers On', which Dawson said he recorded continuously for a week.[61] Melbourne comedian Billy Williams, the composer of 'John, John', had recorded it for Edison and it was sweeping the United Kingdom like an epidemic.[62] It was then pirated for Hector by Edison Bell:

'Everybody did it', said Dawson. 'Billy Williams once threatened to punch me in the nose but never quite got around to it.'[63]

The evolution of the talking machine covered several stages. By the late 1890s Edison recording engineers could make 'five master cylinders at each performance' and each master would 'produce at least twenty-five duplicates before the original impressions wore out' wrote J. N. Moore, [64] that is, 125 cylinders per take. In 1907 it still took a lot of time to produce a large number of cylinders. Dawson's 1933 account reads: 'A song had to be sung over and over again to twelve machines, grouped in fours on three shelves. Thus twelve records were made ... One mistake and twelve records were spoiled.[65]

In 1951 the details had varied:

> Making the old Edison Bell records you needed lungs of leather. You did eighteen records at a time with a row of six machines, with another row on top of those and another on top of those – and if you made a mistake eighteen records went west and they didn't like it. So they put up a blackboard with the words on it – it didn't matter how well you knew the song – you had to repeat it so many times – you'd sing the one song for at least a week. They had to have as many as 200 moulds going if a thing was popular – night and day they worked – they had three shifts in the Edison Bell works.[66]

No wonder Peter remembered 'John John'.[67] To produce sufficient cylinders which had 'a playing time of two minutes', he bellowed into the recording horns hour after hour, from 10am–1pm, then 2pm–5pm for five consecutive days – for which he earned £75. As the going rate was 5/– a round, he must have made 300 rounds in the week, that is, between 3,600 and 5,400 cylinders.

As everyone, including Fred Gaisberg, had been cashing in on Hector's success since the beginning of 1906, why did his records stop so suddenly? It might be thought that Dawson dropped the character because he felt the role of comedian might damage his career as a serious singer, but, in fact, the decision was the Gramophone Company's. Lauder, a canny businessman, had worked primarily for the Gramophone Company, but after he skyrocketed to fame protracted negotiations must have ensued because suddenly all recording stopped. Hector Grant stepped in to fill the breach. But when Lauder re-entered the Gramophone studios, on 16 August 1906, Hector Grant virtually disappeared, along with most of his titles.[68]

The escapades of Hector Grant, however, had not interrupted the development of Dawson's normal recording career. The general managers of the talking-machine companies clearly believed that the real money was to be made in music for the masses.[69] They needed bulk sales: to steadily increase their market share; they not only needed to improve quality but to identify repertoire which would sell. One altruistic firm, British Sonogram, sought to couple a popular song with a classical piano piece, causing Walsh to observe that it had 'such a poor grasp of the average record buyer's psychology that it obviously wasn't long for this world'. British Sonogram folded within a few months.

Purveyors of talking-machines delved into every nook and cranny in an effort to determine what was popular: hymns, Gilbert & Sullivan numbers, music-hall songs, popular American songs, patriotic ballads, hackneyed arias, marches, comedy sketches, recitations and a vast array of instrumental solos. American advertising was now in full flight, inferring that the performers of numbers like 'Navajo', 'The Bandolero', 'In the Shade of the Old Apple Tree' or 'Down at the Old Bull and Bush' were as exceptional as celebrated opera singers. The rise of Peter Dawson and his colleagues to national icons was the product of the power of this blatant new advertising.

Once the public had chosen a favourite, a career was assured. From the beginning Peter Dawson had the natural ability to produce what the talking-machine companies and their listeners wanted to hear. Fred Gaisberg summed it up: 'the velvety quality of his well-produced voice, his ability to throw pathos, tears, laughter and drama into it, his quickness at reading, musicianship and contagious good humour made him a recorder's dream.'[70]

The cosy arrangement between Gaisberg and his friends must have continued until 1907 because Dawson appeared on cylinder labels during 1906. In January 1906 'The Redemption' recorded for Edison was reviewed as 'an impressive sacred song ably rendered in Peter Dawson's rich bass voice'. Although he sang anonymously, he is recognisable on a *Colonial* cylinder singing the sentimental 'The Singer was Irish'. For Edison Bell he sang the 1864 American Civil War song 'Tramp Tramp Tramp'; his first recording of the duet, 'The Moon Hath Raised Her Lamp Above'; and 'the raging hit of the year', 'In The Shade Of The Old Apple Tree'.[71]

The Gramophone Company's serious label, *Gramophone & Typewriter*, featured him in 'The Admiral's Broom' and the beautiful 'Sincerity', which encapsulates all those qualities associated with his name. He also embarked on his first solo operatic venture, Wagner's 'O star of eve' and was able to indulge a lifetime predilection for sacred songs with six hymns in duet with

Ernest Pike. On 21 August 'Sullivan's Operatic Party' crowded into the City Road studio to record 'The Complete Mikado'. Dawson sang solo: 'A More Humane Mikado'; sang duets with Amy Augarde: 'Miya Sama' and 'There is beauty in the bellow of the blast'; and bass in the ensembles 'Here's a how-de-do' and 'The Criminal Cried'.

But the bulk of his work was for *Zonophone*: numbers as diverse as solid ballads like 'The West's Asleep' and 'Bantry Bay'; the duet 'The Singer was Irish' with an anonymous soprano; and the maudlin cowboy songs, 'Wrap Me Up in My Old Stable Jacket' and 'The Place Where the Old Horse Died'. Edison Bell retaliated with the best-forgotten cylinder 'Beautiful Bird, Sing On' complete with appropriate bird noises by the well-known whistler Alfred Holt.

In his autobiography Dawson does not mention that he recorded for *Pathé* discs ('That Old Sunny Window') and the White Cylinder Company. On *White* he could be heard on a mixed series of cylinders as Peter Dawson in 'The Punch & Judy Show' and with the bird imitator – who also did animal impressions – in 'A Barnyard Serenade'. As Hector Grant he joined Arthur Gilbert in 'Jingles, Jokes & Rhymes'. As Will Danby he recorded 'It's A Different Girl Again', 'Waltz Me Around Again, Willie'; and with his sister-in-law, 'Their First Quarrel', a comic confrontation between newlyweds.[72]

The day of reckoning came in April 1907 when Dawson was offered an exclusive contract by the Gramophone Company. On the one hand he would lose his freedom, on the other he would enjoy some guarantees. By good luck – or more likely on the advice of his brother-in-law who understood the market – Peter Dawson aligned himself with the Gramophone Company for the length of his extraordinary career.[73]

Reports about Dawson's rates of pay are conflicting. To Walsh it appears that he signed exclusively with a company that offered one third of what Edison would have paid him. Other accounts maintain that he was given a choice between a flat rate and one shilling royalty on each disc. As the cheapest disc – which carried the bulk of his early recordings – sold for 2/6, the 1/– rate is obviously exaggerated. In fact, it was many years before he even considered a royalty contract. The source of this fallacy appears to be the retail price of *Edison* cylinders. These were reduced to one shilling when the cylinder market began diminishing; other companies tried to sell at a lower rate and went bankrupt. In 1908 Edison introduced its successful four-minute wax *Amberol* cylinder – double the playing time – but it only survived in England until 1912 when it was replaced by the unbreakable blue *Amberol*. Despite a downturn in sales after World War I, the blue *Amberol* survived until 1929.

Peter Dawson's first extant registered agreement is a renewal contract for three years from April 1907.[74] The agreement begins by repeating the terms of the 1906 retainer and recording fees, but at this point Tom Noble appears to have intervened to point out that Peter's popularity was increasing, and the Gramophone Company would need to be more generous if it wanted his services exclusively. So the retainer that begins as a typed £50 per annum, becomes a handwritten £80 and finally £100. Similarly the recording fees are doubled: solos increased from one guinea to two and 'each Quartette' from 10/6 to one guinea, with an overall guarantee of 'a minimum of £100 work each year'. At twenty-five Peter Dawson was now guaranteed at least £200 per year from 1907 until 1910 – about half a reasonable living wage from disc recording alone.[75] To justify £100 he would have needed to record only 48 solos, but we know that he sang in many ensembles and could have sung double that number.

All that singing into a single horn was no doubt good practice in the recording technique for which he was renowned. The Gramophone Company's methods did not change significantly until 1925. Whereas cylinders were recorded through rows of horns, discs were recorded through a single horn. Photos show the horn, the focal point for all recording artists, protruding into the studio. At his audition Peter Dawson 'Sang into the little funnel and someone laid a hand on his shoulder and pushed him closer to or farther from the horn'.[76] Melba's irritation with her chorus had arisen because she and the trio had had to crowd so tightly around the one recording horn and bellow into it. Gerald Moore recalled that many years later, even after the company had moved to a larger studio at Hayes, Middlesex, there was still a constant tussle to be closest to the horn. The studio was 'in the uttermost interior of the building, completely shut off from daylight and outside noise'. It was wooden, bare and too reverberant. The 'pianoforte was harsh and metallic', 'had the brazen splendour of a brass spittoon' and could make an impression only by being belted loudly. When Peter Dawson was recording he would naturally stand in front of the huge horn, 'nay, more … he would have his head halfway down the trumpet; his buttocks were all I could see of him'. Moore complained that he could never hear Dawson properly 'and my difficulties under these conditions can be imagined since his sounds were not emanating from the end of him nearest me.'[77]

The sounds made through the horn were collected on a wax master disc in the control room on the other side of the wall. The wax, too, was temperamental. Even though the music might occupy no more than one side of a record, it could sometimes take a whole day to get a good impression. Often as many as six 'master discs' were made before the artists and technical staff agreed that there were no imperfections in the performance. 'Each copy on wax had to be frozen, so it would shrink and come out of its matrix, and there would probably be a hundred matrices working at the same time on a popular record', Dawson recalled.[78]

Studio technicians certainly regarded their vocation as an art and a science. As Fred Gaisberg explained, the human ear could hear a range of musical sounds between 60 and 8,000 vibrations per second. But on early discs the top frequencies were triple C at 2,088 vibrations per second, the lowest at E at 164 vibrations per second, while 'voices and instruments were confined rigidly within these boundaries.'[79] The richness of a voice or the complexity of the tone, was dependent on 'overtones' or upper partials, those vibrations which occurred above the principal note in all sounds. As triple C (c''') would not be the highest notes possible for singers like Patti or Melba, their highest upper partials would disappear, giving a tinny sound; while the highest notes of violins could not be recorded at all. Men's voices, however, fitted comfortably into the middle of the recording range. Peter's bottom note was Fred's low E; his consistent high note the baritone F (f').

The singers who got the most work were those who adapted quickly to acoustic recording techniques, possessed a voice with a sympathetic recording quality, were capable of working long hours and made few errors. Peter's personal attributes and musical abilities fitted the infant industry like a glove. No wonder that Walsh thought that 1907 was 'perhaps Peter Dawson's busiest year as a recording artist'.

Early in the year 'the jovial basso', Hector Grant, could still be heard on Edison, but for the Christmas market it was Peter Dawson who sang 'That's Why I'm Santa Claus'. 'The well-known bass singer' could be heard on *Sterling* cylinders; on the unfortunate British Sonogram's double-faced *Sovereign* discs – with material appropriated from 1904/05 *Nicole* tracks;[80] and quite a handful of typical Peter Dawson songs on *White* cylinders: including 'Calvary', which he had already recorded for the Gramophone Company.[81] His first recording of 'Glorious Devon', a magnificent ballad which remained in his repertoire, was among ten Edison Bell cylinders.

But from now on the bulk of his famous songs would be recorded by the Gramophone Company. The earliest were 'A Jovial Monk Am I', 'The Bandolero' and 'Tommy Lad', which 'every young man did his best to sing like Peter Dawson.'[82] His pronounced affinity with oratorio now came to the fore when he was allocated the baritone solos in Mendelssohn's *Elijah*. A review of the 1906 hymns recorded by Ernest Pike and 'the hard-working young man from the Antipodes' considered them 'in splendid style'; another praised Dawson's version of 'that greatest of all drinking songs', 'Little Brown Jug' and a song that every Scout has since sung around the campfire: 'Oh, My Darling Clementine'. Hector Grant was now claimed as a *Zonophone* artist. Two Harry Lauder numbers were reviewed in January; 'four rollicking records' including 'John, John' in March; in May four 'never done anything better' records including 'I Wish I Had Someone to Love Me' ('a master-piece' of its kind); and in July, his own 'Sandy, You're a Dandy'.

In October *Zonophone* recorded the much-parodied 'Christmas Eve in the Barracks' and the equally entertaining 'Christmas Eve in an Australian Miner's Camp'. It is easy to imagine the lighthearted mood in the recording studio: the stock quartet, most members using false names: talking, singing, cheering loudly, a violin squeaking away until finally a hearty toast is raised to the King and Queen led by a rousing (carousing) National Anthem.

'The Wreck of a Troopship' was in similar vein – and thereby hangs a tale! Try to imagine the singers and an orchestra crowded into the tiny City Road studio and the gabble of yelling, shouting, blowing, bowing. Random bugles pierce the din. Lightning zaps through the chaos. Thunder rumbles and explodes. In his enthusiasm to sink the ship, the shaker of the thunder machine, a large, heavy, flexible sheet of metal, loses control; the sheet flies through the air, hits Peter on the head and knocks him cold. 'It wrecked me,' said Peter, 'but it saved the troopship.'[83]

We can only marvel that one man could be employed to sing such a wide range of music: if Dawson ever had any qualms about the repertoire, he never voiced them. These examples project a feeling of youthful exu-berance coupled with opportunism and lack of direction, but, though it is difficult to believe that the same voice suited every style of song he sang, the pattern repeated itself continuously throughout his life. 'Peter Dawson' quickly became an established name. Magazine reviewers at that time pre-ferred to praise recording artists rather than offend advertisers; neverthe-less the consistency of excellent reviews for Dawson's recordings was proof of his innate empathy with the medium. No surprise then that by the end of 1907 he was being touted as '*Popular record maker No. 11: Mr Peter Dawson*'.[84]

At this time, when he was under contract to the Gramophone Company, White Cylinders were claiming that he was exclusive to them. Dawson never referred to the matter but the explanation lies in Dawson's 1907 contract: James H. White, another American who had set up a cylinder company in

London, had an understanding with the Gramophone Company.[85] While Peter Dawson had agreed to work exclusively for the Gramophone Company *on disc*, he was permitted to record for the White Cylinder Record for reproduction on cylinders only.

These claims of exclusivity are confusing. Despite his 1907-1910 contract with the Gramophone Company, Dawson's name still crops up in other catalogues. During 1907 he appeared on a 10in. double-face 'hill-and-dale disc' for Pathé; at the beginning of 1908 he appeared with two ballads in the first listing by *Clarion*, a new wax cylinder label;[86] and in November 1908 he recorded one of the greatest sentimental favourites, 'The Volunteer Organist', for Edison's new premier four-minute *Amberols*. This 'old fashioned sob song', as Walsh called it in 1962, was a Peter Dawson specialty: a ragged old man appears mysteriously in church, sits at the organ and has the congregation in tears as he accompanies tales of his own misfortunes. The old man stops playing and disappears. Spooky. The reviewer of the song was ecstatic: 'the glorious, expressive voice of this eminent artist is heard in all its grandeur and dramatic force'.

Trying to recover ground lost to Edison, in 1908 Edison Bell brought out an elaborate version of another favourite, 'The Village Blacksmith', which occupied two cylinders 'in the new (gold moulded) process at 1/– instead of 9d'.[87] When White went bankrupt in 1907 Dawson was permitted to sing for other cylinder companies; but when he was heard on an alien disc the Gramophone Company sought legal advice. In the opinion of the solicitor, if Peter Dawson had sung 'into any instrument so that Disc-records of his voice can be reproduced by anyone but yourselves, he will have committed a breach.' As it turned out the recording in question had been pirated.[88]

At the beginning of 1909 Peter Dawson was one of thirty-five artists who had contracts at the 'London Branch', among them Amy Castles, the Coldstream Guards, Harry Lauder, Adelina Patti, Maggie Teyte and Luisa Tetrazzini.[89] Technically speaking, it was incorrect for Dawson to say that he had recorded for *His Master's Voice* any earlier. There can be little argument that *His Master's Voice* is the most famous trademark in recorded music, so much so that it is easy to forget that it is simply a trademark. In the original painting by Francis Barraud (1856-1924) his dog, Nipper, was depicted listening to an Edison phonograph. When Barraud could not sell the picture to Edison, he approached Owens at the Gramophone Company to obtain a more modern machine to substitute. Owens provided him with the 1898 model and purchased the touched-up painting and the copyright; but he did not immediately use it to replace his current trademark, an angel using a quill to write on a disc. Early in 1900 Emile Berliner visited Owens and was so taken with the painting that he asked if he could use it as his trademark in the United States. Owens agreed. In May 1900 Berliner registered the trademark as 'Nipper and the Gramophone' but assigned it the following year to Eldridge Johnson, who had founded his own Victor Talking Machine Company. Nipper began his long career as 'The RCA dog' when he appeared on Victor's paper labels in February 1902. The British company continued to feature the 'Recording Angel' for its 'G&T' discs until it 'added the Trademark *His Master's Voice* to its label' in February 1909.[90]

The wild extremes of repertoire in 1907 were repeated by Dawson thoughout 1908 and into 1909, but he was only one of Fred Gaisberg's stable of young singers who became famous: others were Amy Augarde, Eleanor Jones-Hudson, Florence Venning, Ernest Pike and Stanley Kirkby, kept in control by the company conductor, Geo. W. Byng. As Gaisberg recalled: 'this high-spirited company, crowded into the small recording room of those days, made a Roman holiday of this work. Peter Dawson was invariably the ringleader of the pranks that kept everyone seething with merriment.'[91] But however busy the catalogue makes him appear, the terms of his Gramophone Company contract tied him down to 'at least two calls in each month'; that is, two three-hour sessions, the equivalent of one day if everything went smoothly. More time was obviously required for his prodigious output, yet on this evidence even in his hey-day, disc recording sessions would rarely have totalled more than one month in any year.

On tour with Amy Castles, 1909. Above: in flood waters on the Victorian/South Australian border, with Amy riding shotgun and Peter tipping his hat. Below: on the road between Casterton and Mount Gambier, showing (left to right), Anderson Nicol; the 75-year-old driver; George Castles; Peter Dawson and Colin Campbell (J. & N. Taits' manager).

The first Australian tour

As Peter Dawson made some of the definitive recordings of operatic standards in English, the question has often been asked, why didn't he become an opera singer like Melba?[1] His grandniece Beverley knew the reason: 'I can tell you why Uncle Peter did not become involved in opera. He married Nan Noble whose family were producing gramophone records in London. They persuaded him to make records and give concerts.'[2] Dawson, too, never lost an opportunity to affirm that he had made a deliberate choice not to follow the glamorous, élitist path through the opera houses.[3] Yet when he first saw opera at Covent Garden he was filled with wild enthusiasm. The idea of 'standing centre-stage' must have appealed to him.[4] The real reason for his not following that path was that, unlike Melba, Dawson did not have an operatic voice or temperament.

Recordings give a false impression. During the successful 1931 Australian season a critic wrote: 'The Dawson voice is not big, but beautiful in texture, smoothly produced throughout an exceptional range, and so flexible that it could negotiate the Figaro patter song from "The Barber" without trouble – in English.'[5] This view was supported in latter years by Kenneth Neate, the Australian tenor who made his international career in London and Munich. He confirmed Gerald Moore's view that 'the voice was not huge, but it was not small either. It was exactly focussed and marvellously modulated according to the text.'[6]

Dawson's entire operatic career consisted of four performances in English of a minor bass role, Schwarz the Master Stocking-Maker, in Wagner's *The Mastersingers* at Covent Garden in 1909.[7] Looking back over his life, these four performances between 25 January and 13 February were insignificant. Schwarz is just one of a dozen Masters who form, in effect, a semi-chorus between the principals and the very large chorus. *The Mastersingers* (*Die Meistersinger*) is an unusually long opera: four-and-a-half hours without cuts, so the minor-role Masters have substantial longeurs. 'Let me say at once that I was not very impressed with operatic work,' wrote Peter. 'It struck me as too much work for too little pay.'[8] He could have said, 'Too much time for too little pay.'

After that opera appears to have held no further interest for him. Perhaps he simply recognised that while the dramatic arias of Rigoletto or Tonio or Iago were his forte on recordings, he lacked the dramatic voice and heroic stature required for such roles on stage.[9]

Some believe that Dawson considered recording a mere supplement to his concert work;[10] others that concert appearances always remained secondary.[11] Certainly concerts took up far more time than recording sessions. Because there is little detail available about his concert activities prior to 1909 there is a tendency to ignore them. We have only Dawson's word that he appeared in a Queen's Hall Promenade Concert as early as September 1904 and on five later occasions had sung with 'Santley, Plunkett Greene and others at the Crystal Palace'. A 1911 *Talking Machine News* interview added appearances at the Alexandra Palace and Chappell Ballad Concerts.[12] We do know that Dawson shared a Prom with the English operatic and concert soprano, Caroline Hatchard, on 22 August 1908, and 'in the Fall of 1908' they joined Palgrave Turner and Albert Watson on a concert tour of Britain organised by the soprano and composer, Liza Lehmann, and conducted by her husband, Herbert Bedford.[13]

In July 1909 Dawson returned to Australia for the first time, as part of the Amy Castles' tour organised by J. and N. Tait – 'Australia's only recognised Agents'.[14] The tour was scheduled to begin in late August so negotiations must have taken place in late 1908 or early 1909. The supporting artists contracted were the Scottish tenor Anderson Nicol, the 24-year-old Australian pianist Victor Buesst, the flautist, Adrian Amato and the 27-year-old Peter Dawson.[15] News of the impending tour caused a flurry of last-minute activity with publishers making suggestions to the Gramophone Company and the Gramophone Company recommending advertising methods to its Australian agent.[16]

Dawson claimed that he took the Australian job on the spur of the moment to escape the wrath of the dominant concert entrepreneur, William Boosey. The Booseys had promoted concerts since the mid-nineteenth century when Chappell & Co. and Boosey & Co. had centred their publishing activities on the increasingly popular drawing-room ballad market. The Victorian ballad – any 'song with sentimental text' – was big business. As far back as 11 April 1857 William Boosey's Uncle John had hit on the idea of presenting promotional Ballad Concerts 'for the performance of the Choicest English Vocal Music by the Most Eminent Artists'. A year later Arthur Chappell started his Saturday and Monday 'Pops' in his purpose-built St James Hall. In 1880 William Boosey took over from his uncle and from 1894 ran Chappell's concerts too.[17]

The programmes had a specific pattern: 'The finest specimens of Old Songs and Ballads; A few New Compositions by the Best Modern Writers; A Selection of Glees and Madrigals; Instrumental Solos by Eminent Performers.' Famous artists associated with these concerts were legion. Publishers paid them large sums to sing new compositions. Their names dwarfed that of composer and lyricist on the garish title pages of 'royalty ballads'. No doubt, it was one of these stars, the influential Santley, who introduced his best pupil to William Boosey; though by the time Peter appeared on the scene the Victorian ballad frenzy had waned. The Monday Pops had already closed down in 1898; the Saturday Pops fizzled out in the season 1902-1903.

But Boosey's Ballad Concerts were still in vogue and the Pops had been replaced by the more popular Queen's Hall 'Promenade Concerts', which had begun in 1895 when the original instrumental sections branched off into a separate concert series. William Boosey was nicknamed 'The Emperor of Bond Street' because his publishing houses controlled the major performing venues, commissioned songs, published songs, and employed famous singers to promote these publications. But he also had the foresight to replenish his material and his artists, so new generations of composers, authors and performers were given a chance to prove themselves, including the young hopeful, Peter Dawson. In this case, Boosey had asked him to 'pencil in' a number of engagements for the Queen's Hall for 1909. Unfortunately, in Peter's experience pencilling in did not mean a firm booking, so he asked Boosey to confirm in writing. Boosey was so angry at a young upstart doubting his word that he cancelled the engagements and made certain others shunned poor Peter too.[18] While it is difficult to believe Dawson saw his career as entirely dependent on the good graces of one impresario, it does indicate that in 1909 he still believed his professional future lay in concertising.

A successful entrepreneur is one who exercises sound commercial judgement, not one who acts on sentiment. An entrepreneur uses every device to attract an audience creating a general atmosphere of hyperbole. The longevity of an artist indicates an ability to satisfy both impresario and audience. Although Dawson's career was to last much longer, at this stage Amy Castles, who was only two years older, was the celebrity in their mutual homeland.

According to Castles' biographers she 'swept over the Commonwealth like a queen in fairyland'; 'became known as The New Jenny Lind'; 'continental opera claimed her in Germany, Vienna and London'; '6000 attended the Ballarat concert held in the Colosseum'; '2000 turned away at the Exhibition Hall in 1902'.[19] At the time Thorald Waters wrote in the *Bulletin*: 'The Castles voice was endowed with almost incomparable elements of beauty'. In the *Bulletin* nearly 90 years later John Cargher wrote: 'Amy Castles was one of the best singers Australia ever produced'; and in 1989, as an old man, James Farrell recalled:

> I have heard the world's finest singers at Covent Garden, the Paris Opera House and, of course, in Australia. However, the highlight of my operatic memories will always be Amy Castles singing Mimi's Farewell at Her Majesty's so long ago. The beauty and pathos of her voice haunt me still.[20]

After such flattery a recent investigation by Dr Jeff Brownrigg of Canberra into the life of Amy Castles, and this tour in particular, has proved provocative.[21] According to his research the biographical claims were inordinately extravagant and her international career consisted of a few insignificant appearances. On the basis of criticisms of the 1909 tour and her few recordings, he suggests that Amy Castles had a rather inadequate voice, neither strong nor musically reliable.

Nevertheless Amy Castles was the focal point of the tour: the whole pre-concert razzamatazz referred only to Amy Castles 'and her party'. But we must look at the tour from Peter Dawson's point of view. Much had changed since he left Adelaide seven-and-a-half years earlier. In a formal photo we see a handsome young man with a mass of wavy hair parted in the middle, wearing a fashionable suit, a shirt with a broad turned-down collar and a huge, floppy, silk or satin bowtie. He left the *Otway* in Adelaide while Amy Castles and the others continued on to Melbourne to prepare for the first concert. The reunion with his family, choral society friends and old C.J. Stevens must have been overwhelming: 'From the speeches I learned that my concert appearances in London had been the interest of Australian journalists in that city [Adelaide]. My more or less sensational success as a gramophone artiste, too, had been hailed throughout Australia'.[22]

The first concert of the tour was scheduled for 21 August in Melbourne, with performances to follow every second or third day. In fact, Dawson missed the first concert because floods had disrupted the train line near the Victorian border. Much to his chagrin, he was docked a day's pay for the missed concert. On 1 September he wrote a long letter to Nan beginning:

> My own Darling Hannah —
> Mail day again, — to say nothing about a rehearsal at 12 o'cl & a Matinee this afternoon at 3 o'clock. These Scotch to do run a chap hard and no mistake, and you can bet your bottom dollar darling that I shall be heartily thankful to get out of it, & back to England, home, & beauty.

But Dawson's hopes of getting home for Christmas were unrealistic: 'If they hold me the six months, which by all appearances they are <u>sure</u> to do – on account of my great success – it will mean that we cannot revisit Australia until the year after next.' The contract was renewed and ran through to February so it was March 1910 before he saw Nan again.

It is a measure of the courage and stamina of both agents and artists that there was a constant flow of international performers visiting Australia. This tour, which followed one by Nellie Melba, is conspicuous for the number of isolated communities visited. The number of towns and concerts range from 'four and a half months touring 72 Australian towns'; '81 concerts many of them in the roughest and most isolated parts of Australia'; '100 concerts – all states – packed houses everywhere'; to 'in the end we anticipate that the tour will embrace upwards of 150 concerts instead of the 60 for which we originally contracted with Miss Castles when the party left England.'[24] In his September letter to Nan Peter listed 31 towns. 'This is just the towns in Vic^ia & N. S. Wales', he wrote (though some were in Queensland) and added: 'the outlying towns of S. Australia are to be visited, besides New Zealand & Tasmania & W. Australia'.

In these days of rapid communication and comfortable transport, it is difficult to imagine how arduous a concert tour could be at the turn of the century. There were long boring train journeys, broken up by games of poker: 'a week or so after the Melbourne concert we were travelling between Melbourne and Newcastle. The party consisted of John Tait, myself and three others. When the game ended and the score was added up, I had won £3. We met many times after that on railway trains, but we never had another game of poker. However, he could not resist the old challenge, "John, I'll toss you for two shaves." We tossed many times.'[25] Trains took them to major centres but there were plenty of dusty journeys in horse-drawn vehicles over rough country roads.[26]

Nor should we imagine plush concert halls out there in the bush. The population of Australia was not even five million at the time; there would have been very few country towns with halls large enough to hold 600 people, let alone 6000; many of the small towns would have been little more than railway sidings. In fact, most of the concerts took place in the local Mechanics' Halls, where, despite the heat and trying conditions, the audience expected the artists to be at their superb best. [27]

Naturally the local critics concentrated primarily on Amy Castles. The impresarios may have expected her to sweep the audience off its feet but reviewers had some reservations:

> Miss Castles is the possessor of a magnificently trained organ, and during her songs she gained the unstinted admiration of the audience … Still, in those songs calling for passionate feeling … the requisite intensity was missing. That quality that stirs the listener's inmost sympathies was absent.

She also suffered somewhat in comparison with Melba: 'Melba's concert here is looked upon as the last word. Miss Castles succeeded in realising to them some of their high anticipation and the concert throughout brought plenty of approbation.' It was her young associate who found more favour with the critics: 'In the opening number … he was not altogether at ease, but later in the evening he was magnificent. That is the only adjective to describe his singing.' [28]

The repertoire of each concert could only be partially verified from the printed programme, because the encores, which formed a substantial part of the presentation, were not included. When the company performed in Dawson's home town on 7, 9 and 11 September, the citizens of Adelaide heard Amy Castles sing: 'Caro Nome', Willeby's 'Four Leaf Clover' and 'The Perfect Way', and Tosti's 'Goodbye'.[29] Dawson began by making an impact with Mendelssohn's 'I am a Roamer', an unusual song with several long series of very low notes (F) and very high notes (E) connected by leaps that require a form of vocal callisthenics. In his next bracket he introduced the recently published ballad, 'Young Tom o' Devon', then joined Anderson Nicol for the rip-roaring duet, 'Excelsior'.

In his memoirs Dawson lists thirty encores he claims to have sung during this tour. 'Little Grey Home in the West' and 'Phil the Fluter's Ball' were not yet published, but most were great standards of the period like 'Sincerity', 'My Old Shako', ''Tis I' and 'Rocked in the Cradle of the Deep'. Others were classics, which were to crop up again and again during his career: 'She alone charmeth my sadness', 'It is enough', 'Honour and Arms', 'Why do the nations', and the perennial 'O ruddier than the cherry'.[30]

This last aria, from Handel's *Acis and Galatea* (1720), was unquestionably one of his all-time favourites. He sang it as a youth, and at his audition with Santley; and he continued to sing it in a myriad of concerts right through to his last orchestral concert. A good song captures the essence of an aesthetic idea and can be sung without any reference to any original source, so without knowing the story of Acis and Galatea or that the aria was sung by the one-eyed giant Polyphemus, he could succeed instinctively.

Dawson was obviously aware of the strong impression the aria would make on his audience. 'Adelaide, 16.12.09': 'At the second concert I sang 'O ruddier than the cherry'. I took the top 'C', and it brought the audience to its feet! But something happened in the orchestra: I don't know who won, but it was a race between the piccolo and myself.'[31] A top C is a tenor's dream. Peter Dawson could not have sung a top C: the passage should read top G, for, although the penultimate note is 'middle' G, dropping an octave to the 'low' G, Dawson moved the conclusion up an octave to put in his flashy 'top' G.

The aria describes Polyphemus' early infatuation with the nymph, Galatea. The change from ferocious giant into wheedling supplicant is apparent in the brief recitative where Polyphemus' cyclopean rage is expressed in a wildly rising coloratura passage, but soon fizzles out as he exchanges his club for a puny reed flute to fit his 'cap-a-cious mouth'. Dawson could wallow in his rich bass notes as these words descended to the featured low F – like entering some dark vocal cavern.

As Polyphemus then simpers through the bouncy aria with the awkwardness of an uncouth swain, Dawson could present the classical ambience of a Handel aria with his accurate coloratura sequences, without hindering the galloping vulgarity of the A and B sections. The inserted top G to finish the *da capo* made the aria comparable to comic opera. With his fine delivery laced with grotesque humour 'O ruddier than the cherry' warmed up his voice throughout the whole range without strain – and warmed up the audience.

In 1911 *Talking Machine News* reported:

> Everywhere they were received with open arms; in the bush townships people rode miles to hear them for there is scarcely a homestead in the

back settlements without a gramophone. Peter Dawson was astonished at the knowledge which the kindly up-country folk displayed of his favourite songs ... Give us 'Drinking!' Give us 'Shade of the Old Apple Tree!'[32]

Like the concert successes he claimed to have had before the tour, this interview should be taken with a grain of salt. The talking machine was certainly no longer restricted to the amusement parlour but it was certainly not yet as prevalent as he claimed. There was a wide choice of music on both cylinder and disc, and the price of gramophones, from large expensive ornate cabinet and horn models to compact cheaper models, varied enormously. In 1909 Dawson had been recording for only five years; his name would soon feature prominently in record catalogues, but not yet. The 1911 interview was Gramophone Company publicity and the concert successes were not reported until 1912.[33] In 1909 Dawson was still a minor support artist, not paid enough to afford travelling expenses for himself and Nan. But he did have every reason to be pleased with himself: he had completed his apprenticeship with flying colours; in the future he would lead his own companies.

The Noble family, c. 1910. Standing: Nan, Peter, Eva, Tom, Fan, Bill; seated:
Thomas senior and his wife Annie; Constance, Dora and Harry.

Nan and Peter, 1913. In the
possession of Ann Jacquet. Portrait
of the pseudonymous Leonard
Dawson, 1904, from an Edison Bell
cylinder box.

The artist is established

By April 1910 Peter Dawson was at last back in London. On 6 May Edward VII died and George V ascended the throne which he was to occupy for the next twenty-six eventful years. The effects of the losses sustained in the Boer War and the growing self-confidence of returned soldiers from the lower classes resulted in a 'mounting tide of discontent organised through the trade unions – massive strikes 1911–14 – suffragettes fighting to give women the vote – opposition to Home Rule in Ireland'. The class war had started but for the time being Parliament remained dominated by the Conservatives and Liberals. Until after World War I 'a working man was just as likely to vote Liberal or Conservative as a rich man … an Englishman largely knew his place in society and kept it, whether he was master or servant, upper, middle, or working class.'[1]

By 1910 the Gramophone Company had achieved a position of pre-eminence in the industry.[2] Branch factories had been established in Germany, Russia, Denmark, Sweden, Persia, Austria, France, Spain and India, so London was mainly responsible for the English market and the export trade. In 1908 a new factory had been opened at Hayes, Middlesex. Alfred Clark had become managing director and was to lead the company until his death in 1950.

Upon his return Dawson's contract with the Gramophone Company was immediately renewed for a 'Period of 3 years from 25.4.1910 and for so long thereafter as may be mutually agreed'. A 1910 *Talking Machine News* competition to find Britain's most popular recording artist placed Ernest Pike first, Peter Dawson second and Harry Lauder third. Despite this manifest proof of his popularity, the rate of pay was not increased, even by an inflation factor.

If Dawson had been rebuffed by William Boosey prior to the 1909 tour, the Emperor of Bond Street had soon relented, for Dawson was invited to become the principal baritone in Chappell's Ballad Concerts in 1910.[3] On recordings and on tour Dawson had been singing as a Bass. He attributed the acquisition of his reliable upper register and the baritone high notes to lessons with Professor Kantorez – a 'Russian singing specialist'. He claimed that his range had only been 'E$^\flat$' to D' until a brief training with Kantorez had extended his range from the low 'E$^\flat$' to the baritone A' – an extraordinary range for any singer. That is Peter's story.[4]

While it is not uncommon for the upper range to develop further, it is usually accompanied by some lightening of the vocal colour because there is a tendency to lose the fruity lower notes as the higher ones are attained. We have already noted that his compositions favoured the baritone tessitura and that he had adopted the habit of singing the baritone top G in 'O ruddier than the cherry'. Dawson's baritonal inclination could also be observed in earlier repertoire choices like 'It is enough' (*Elijah*), 'O star of eve' (*Tannhäuser*), or 'The Toreador Song' (*Carmen*). 'Even in the earliest recordings', wrote one modern critic, 'the high notes up to G are brilliant, easy and secure.'[5] Standing beside true basses, like Robert Radford, he may have realised that he was destined to shine in the higher register.[6]

As our initial search for information about Professor Kantorez had proved fruitless, we began to suspect the name was a fanciful pseudonym or even a figment of Peter's fruitful imagination. Such pusillanimous suspicion was confounded by the recent discovery of a programme among some Peter Dawson papers (see page 71).

During Peter's absence, it emerged, Nan had been studying classical repertoire with Kantorez so that she could join Peter on later tours. In this concert she sang Santuzza's aria from *Cavalleria Rusticana* in the first half and in the second 'Love is a slave' (Squire). Peter sang 'Prologue from Pagliacci' and 'Onaway, awake beloved!' both of which were to feature extensively throughout his career. However, on this occasion the greatest exposure was given to the 12-year-old 'English Child Patti', who dared to sing massive arias like 'Caro nome'.

On 20 January 1911 the Gramophone Company board was told: 're Pike & Dawson it is essential that we should obtain exclusive rights of all kinds from them'. And on 23 February 'the Executive agreed this day to enlarging our guarantees, so as to make their services exclusive for our Company only'. From 24 April 1911 Dawson's guarantee was increased to £200, making a total of £300 annually.[7]

Walsh notes that from 1911 to 1914 Peter Dawson 'added steadily to his Gramophone Company, Zonophone and Edison lists' and 'made cylinders

STEINWAY HALL,

LOWER SEYMOUR STREET, LONDON, W.

Programme

On Tuesday Afternoon, 1st November, 1910,

AT THREE O'CLOCK,

Professor

KANTOREZ

PRESENTS HIS PUPILS

Mr. PETER DAWSON
(The English Sammarco),

Miss Annetta George
(Soprano)   (First Appearance)

Mr. Louis Alvarez
(Tenor)

Miss Louise Arkandy

and

CATHERINE ARKANDY
(Aged 12)   THE ENGLISH CHILD PATTI.

At the Piano—
Mr. A. Lindo and Signor G. De Lucia.

Professor Kantorez guided Dawson in the change from bass to baritone. Italian baritone Mario Sammarco (1873–1930) made his English debut in October 1904 in 'Tosca'. He gained fame from his inclusion in the Gramophone Company's historic 1902 celebrity catalogue.

for Edison and other companies as long as they existed'. With the demise of White Cylinders, the cylinder clause in his contract had been modified to allow 'the Artist' to 'Sing for one cylinder talking machine concern'. In return the Gramophone Company could acquire the cylinder recording for its own purposes, so the same song might legitimately appear as an *Edison* cylinder as well as an *HMV* or *Zonophone* disc. With the cessation of Edison Bell cylinders, Edison became the only surviving cylinder company, so notionally Dawson recorded 'exclusively' for them until late 1912.

In the May 1911 popularity competition Harry Lauder was first, Billy Williams (the composer of 'John, John') second and Peter Dawson third; Ernest Pike had dropped to fifth. On 16 November 1912 the Gramophone Company acknowledged Dawson's status by improving his contract substantially. £450 for singing, a £200 retaining fee plus £100 bonus; that is, a guaranteed total of £850 over eighteen months. The previous two guineas (£2/2/–) for solos, one guinea for ensembles, became five guineas for solos, four guineas for duets, three guineas for quartettes or other part-songs.[8] To recoup this outlay the company would have needed to record a minimum of 86 solo records over the eighteen months left on the contract but, as Dawson also sang with many other singers, the total number recorded must have been in the hundreds. Some idea of the extent of his activities may be gained from the 'Peter Dawson Account, April 1910 to October 1912'.[9] During these two-and-a-half years he was paid a total of £905/11/–, of which some £500 was for 77 solos and 237 ensembles. This means he sang an average of 126 calls a year, of which only one third were for solo numbers.

On 29 May 1911 Commonwealth and State representatives from throughout the Empire, who had gathered for the Coronation festivities, came to the Imperial Institute in London, eager to see Australia's contribution, a silent history in six tableaux 'depicting the progress of Australia since its discovery', which had been devised by the painter, Tom Roberts.[10] As a prelude, Dawson sang two Edward German songs to Kipling texts: 'Kangaroo and Dingo' then 'Rollin' down to Rio', which he recorded ten days later for *Zonophone*.

The recordings he made between 1910 and 1913 were the usual conglomeration: the Coronation of George V on 22 June 1911 spawned a right royal fistful of 'God Save the King's and 'Hail King George's. Two long-term favourites, 'Boys of the Old Brigade' and 'The Arrow and the Song' appeared for the first time, on Edison four-minute *Amberols*. 'The Toreador Song' and 'I am a Roamer' – the difficult Mendelssohn song with the athletic leaps, which he had sung on the 1909 tour – also appeared as

Amberols – long before they entered the HMV catalogues.

'Notwithstanding the demands [made] on his time by concert engagements in London and almost every town in the Kingdom ... the most perfect voiced of contemporary Bassos' was 'coaxed into the recording studio' to sing Handel's pleasant, undemanding, 'Droop not young lover.' [11] However, ephemeral music was not neglected: as a member of the 'The Zonophone Concert Party' he could be picked out singing 'Little Annie Rooney is my Sweetheart', and he and Pike continued their successful partnership – there exist 'no more perfect records of male voice duets'. 'Glorious Devon', which he had recorded for Edison Bell in 1906, now appeared on *Zonophone* as did his 1910 and 1912 versions of Willeby's 'Mandalay'. *Zonophone* now carried the bulk of his material, including a host of other 'Peter Dawson ballads', among them 'The Admiral's Yarn', 'The Blue Dragoons', 'The Village Blacksmith', 'Up from Somerset' and 'The Little Grey Home In The West'. In early 1912 Dawson recorded a single-faced *HMV* piano edition of a new ballad 'with catchy accompaniment and sung in rollicking style': it was destined to be re-recorded several times and sell more than any other 'Peter Dawson' recording. It was Katie Moss's, 'The Floral Dance'.

Programmes from October 1912 indicate that Dawson was by now well and truly established in Boosey's stable. The Adelaide *Advertiser* of 18 May 1912 had already carried the news of his concert successes: the long article began: 'Without serious rivalry, the "Adelaide boy" Peter Dawson, is the foremost male singer Australia has produced.' It included quotations from London newspapers, one of which reported that the 1909 tour had been beneficial:

> ...if anything, Mr Dawson has improved since he left this country for Australia ... his usual perfect enunciation and expression, showing to full advantage his exceptional range and his thorough mastery of dramatic effect – he was always in perfect voice, deep, resonant, and strikingly musical – he has in no way forfeited his right to be the premier baritone.

'After reading such praise from the greatest press critics in Great Britain' the article concluded, 'we must realize that in Australia's gallery of fame Peter Dawson stands in a niche beside Melba.'[12] No wonder the thirty-year-old felt confident enough to plan his own tour of Australia.

Organising a substantial Australian tour relatively close to the Amy Castles' tour was risky, but Peter was itching to introduce Nan to his family, show her his country and promote her at his side as a classical singer. The

Gramophone Company supported the idea enthusiastically because audiences would see their recording artist in the flesh. In 1913 Dawson bit the bullet. Twice, as it turned out.

Because Dawson toured Australia from June to September 1913 with one company, then returned to England and brought out a second company in mid-1914, biographers have mistaken the two tours for one. He was supposed to be in England for Promenade Concerts in September 1913 and had certainly returned by October. Recording dates confirm the two-tour scenario: there was a flurry of recording activity to 5 April 1913; then a consistent flow from 26 September 1913 until 30 April 1914.

The Dawsons must have left the United Kingdom at the end of April, just after Nan's brother Harry had organised a 'Grand Farewell Concert (Prior to his Australasian Tour)' for the 'Famous Basso Cantante'. The first concert in Australia was the 'Grand Welcome Concert' in the Exhibition Hall, Adelaide, on Tuesday 17 June 1913 with 'Peter Dawson, the world-famous basso', Annetta George, soprano, the tenor Alexander Cooper and the violinist Eugene Alderman. Dawson rejected the music-hall dictum of using one or two support artists to 'warm up' the audience before 'the main act'. Confident of his own powers he generally sang the first bracket. In the *Souvenir Programmes* printed numbers followed a musically hierarchical pattern: to demonstrate his serious vocal strengths Dawson's first song was either an 'old master' or an operatic aria, which would always be followed by an unprinted encore in comparable style. As the evening progressed the quality gradually lightened. His second bracket would include art songs by British or Continental composers, in which he could again demonstrate his technical and musical abilities, but the encores would now cover serious but well-known recordings. A third bracket contained the ballads that were making him popular; and the following encores raised the hysteria to fever pitch.

This 1913 tour set the pattern for all future tours. His audiences certainly got their money's worth: 'Mr Peter Dawson was plainly out to win the favour of his large audience by a downright and vigorous appeal for popularity ... one item calling for no fewer than three extras'.[13] During the 1915 New Zealand tour Dawson claimed to have sung an 'average of 20 songs nightly';[14] and in 1931 'in Sydney alone sang no less than 125 different songs at nine concerts', an average of 14 songs per concert. Six or eight would be listed, six or more would be encores.[15] For that first concert in 1913 six numbers were printed: No.1: 'Prologue', No. 4: 'Why do the nations', and No. 6: a duet with Nan, 'Still as the Night' (Goetz). In the second half, No. 8: 'The Floral Dance'; No. 11: two Ballads by Lohr. 'Little Grey Home in the West' and another duet, 'It Was a Song You Sang Me'.

The Adelaide critic for *Australian Musical News* had hardly finished expressing enthusiasm for five concerts by Dame Clara Butt and her husband, Kennerley Rumford, when Dawson and his party invaded 'the Queen City of the South'. As could be expected 'Adelaide turned out in force'. The 'famous basso' was 'now showing pronounced baritone tendencies'. The 'Prologue' was a 'virile and altogether excellent reading [which] demonstrated his fitness for big baritone operatic roles'. ' "Why do the nations" was not quite so successful' – a little surprising as Dawson has been held up as the model for the articulation of its complex coloratura to this day.[16] His 'extras' included 'Song of the Flea' (Moussorgsky), 'The Blue Dragoons', 'The Admiral's Yarn' and 'Sincerity'.[17]

According to Dawson's memoirs one Melbourne critic complained that he had sung too many 'Smoking concert songs' during the 1909 tour[18] but it was during this tour that any number of reviews began to comment on his choice of repertoire. The Melbourne *Argus*, 9 July 1913, for example, declared 'He makes use of all that is comprised in good musicianship but he does not allow this element to obtrude itself unduly. He sings to please, and not to torment'; a view shared by *Australian Musical News*: 'If you look for a sound classical programme … give Mr Peter Dawson a wide berth. But if you want manly "breezy" singing and are not too "pernickety" – he is the man for you.'[19]

Dawson must have asked himself what the hell the critics really wanted. He always programmed classical numbers: major baroque arias, excerpts from oratorio, operatic arias and the finest art songs, yet in Melbourne his 'Prologue' was 'not a heart to heart talk', Schubert's complex *lied*, 'Der Wanderer' was 'a healthy sort of wanderer … a much less despairing figure than Schubert conceived'. These were balanced somewhat by the accolade 'very impressive' for 'Der Asra' (Rubinstein) and Schubert's short but beautiful 'To Music', which depends on absolute control of the sustained vocal line. The only numbers to win collective critical approval were Liza Lehmann's recently-published *Cowboy Songs*: 'The Rancher's Daughter'; 'Night Shepherding Song' and 'The Skewball Black'.[20] These were 'most interesting because most out of the common'; 'even if they were composed in St John's Wood they have an excellent Wild West flavour'. There was general agreement that the ballads, in particular Balfe's sentimental 'The Arrow and the Song' ('I shot an arrow in the air') had 'scored a marked success'.

The critics tried to distinguish between what Dawson was and what he purported to be, for Dawson could not disguise his tendency to sing everything as if it were a good story. His enthusiastic audiences left the concert hall satisfied with the programme and the encores, the critics felt puzzled and betrayed:

> a bluff hearty singer, with no aspirations to elevate humanity by his art. He can sing you the ordinary ballad – some which he chose were distinctly "ordinary" … and can come nearer to persuading you they are worth singing despite all your better instincts.

Reviews focussed on Peter: Nan was hardly mentioned. In Adelaide she had been described as 'a soprano of light and warm quality. [She] sang Santuzza's song and several songs by Lohr, Del Riego and d'Hardelot'. In the *Argus* she was dismissed as a 'nice clear soprano singer'; but *AMN* noted 'the capable assistance of Miss Annetta George whose "Vissi d'Art" was too fast albeit in her other numbers she showed a pleasing soprano to advantage'.

Dawson's company did not neglect the country centres. 'Owing to limited time at Mr. Dawson's disposal, before returning for his English and American Seasons' he could *only* visit some twenty-four, mainly Victorian towns.[21] He did cross the border to Corowa, where he gave fourteen encores. He could have given more if W. G. James, 'the leading pianist of the University Conservatorium of Music, Melbourne', had had the music with him.[22]

Despite this high-flown rhetoric William Garnet James (1895-1977) was only seventeen years old. He had been called upon at short notice to play for this international star. His nervousness was made worse because he had forgotten to bring Dawson's music with him so there was a mad panic as everyone chased up suitable scores from singers in the town. In this state of mind the young pianist had to transpose this conglomeration of music into the keys that suited Dawson. Halfway through the programme Dawson whispered to him, 'James, the last accompanist I had was shocking but you're bloody worse.'[23]

'The company left Corowa for Yarrawonga by drag, intending to have a little rabbit shooting and to boil the billy and have lunch in a real bushmanlike manner along the road.' By 13 August they were back in Adelaide for their farewell concert. Dawson began his programme with Rossini's cheerful 'Barber's Song', one of the arias he trotted out to good effect all his life. His baroque item was 'When valiant Ammon' 'from the Opera Amena, Composed in 1794 by Jonathan Battishill', and, although he was now tending toward the baritone repertoire, he still sang Mozart's bass aria, 'Within these hallowed halls', curiously bracketed with 'Wild Wishes' (Schrader) and

Cowen's now familiar 'Onaway, Awake Beloved!'. The success of Dawson's record sales in Australia was exaggerated, for 'The Blue Dragoons' and 'Young Tom O' Devon', (Item No. 13), were his only songs in the Gramophone Company catalogue at that time.

This time the Emperor of Bond Street could well have had grounds for a row with Dawson (rather than in 1909, as reported in Dawson's memoirs), for he expected Dawson in London for the '19th Promenade Concert Season' on 10, 16, 19 September and 11 October, 1913. Even if Dawson's company had left Adelaide the day after the farewell concert, they could not possibly have reached London on time. Yet despite his late return, the news soon reached Australia that Dawson had arrived back 'just in time to take up the running at the Promenade Concerts. He received a demonstrative welcome back, and was particularly congratulated by Sir Henry Wood.'[24] He was certainly in London by 26 September for a recording session; and he signed 'Love from Pete, 11.10.13' under a cartoon in the new autograph book of Nan's eleven-year-old sister, Constance, who was destined to become his second wife.

Banner for Dawson's Tivoli season, Adelaide December 1915 or Melbourne April 1916. Below: a 1920s English Ariel Grand Record reissue of a song originally issued on Zonophone in 1913. How many 1920s record buyers recognised the true identity of Maurice Evans?

World War I – stranded in Australia

During Peter Dawson's absence in Australia, the Gramophone Company's long-awaited recording studio at Hayes had been officially opened by Feodor Chaliapin on 5 July 1913.[1] Dawson's old recording contract ran out at the beginning of April 1914; he signed a new one, from 8 April to 7 April 1916. The overall increase of £50 per annum merely covered inflation. Peter and Nan were planning to return to Australia almost immediately and between 15 and 30 April, just before they left, he completed an intense recording schedule.

The maximum duration of 12in. discs was 4 minutes 15 seconds per side, for the cheaper 10in. 3 minutes 10 seconds. As a result, many fine works were emasculated. Opera and oratorio suffered the most: introductions, play-outs, verses, interludes were deleted or truncated. These time constraints still applied after electrical recording was introduced and the doctoring continued. When Dawson re-recorded his old 1922 acoustic version of 'Till the Sands of the Desert Grow Cold' on 3 April 1929, he was advised that 'we have made various "cuts" in this to make it a three minute record.'[2] It is no coincidence that popular songs became three minutes long.

To tour once in 1913 is understandable, to tour again in 1914 seems like carelessness. Perhaps Dawson's popularity had made him so cocky he felt another tour through Australasia would consolidate his success. Perhaps he felt the tour had been cut too short by his concert and recording obligations in London. However this may be, his departure in 1914 marked the end of the first recording period, that period of ten years from his first experiences with the talking machine industry to recognition as one of the outstanding artists in that medium. By 1914 cylinders were becoming a thing of the past:

cheaper machines and the cheaper priced *Green Label Zonophones*, which featured Peter Dawson, were aimed at the broadest market. Through his recordings Dawson was fast becoming a folk hero.

The Peter Dawson English Concert Company tour began auspiciously with three performances of *Elijah* at the Exhibition Hall, Adelaide, on Tuesday 23, Thursday 25 and Saturday 27 June. The soloists were Peter Dawson (in capital letters), Miss Annetta George and two local singers, Miss Gladys Cilento and Furness Williams. As C. J. Stevens had died three years earlier the Adelaide Choral Society and 'full orchestra', was now conducted by Prof. J. Matthew Ennis.[3]

When Peter and Nan, with 'a Welsh tenor and a London entertainer and humorist'[4] moved on to Melbourne: two concerts in the Town Hall on 7 and 8 July proved far less favourable. 'The nights were cold and the audiences sparse'; and the verdict was that Peter Dawson had 'brought with him a company of uninteresting vocal artists, generally correct in delivery, but cold and unemotional'. [5] The company moved on. 'On 4 August 1914, I was in Goulburn, N.S.W. The concert had just commenced when a message was brought to me that Britain had declared war on Germany.'[6]

The historical significance of the period 1914–1918 cannot be overemphasised. For Australia, it was arguably the most momentous and dramatic period of political turmoil, and its repercussions are felt to this day. Australian troops fought alongside troops from Canada, New Zealand, India, South Africa and other parts of the British Empire; and allies from French and Belgian possessions.[7] The infant Commonwealth of Australia still numbered less than five million; it had not known war. 'Many Australians felt a hidden discontent with the absence of battle honours, a false concept that manhood and nationhood must be proved by deeds of valour,' wrote Marjorie Barnard. War was portrayed as dramatic and exciting: death with honour, sacrifice for others, laying down one's life for one's country. But one's country meant Britain: even Aboriginals were welcome to enlist, though they had no legal rights, no identity in the eyes of white Australia and no influence and or power.

Prime Minister Joseph Cook encapsulated the mood of the time with: 'Whatever happens, Australia is part of the Empire right to the full. When the Empire is at war so is Australia at war.' Not to be outdone, the Leader of the Opposition, Andrew Fisher added: 'Should the worst happen, after everything has been done that honour will permit, Australia will stand behind the Mother Country to help and defend her to our last man and our last shilling.' Australia still thought of itself as an outpost of Great Britain camped on the Pacific rim. It was a country of immigrants or their descendants; a

Christian community of predominantly Anglo-Celtic origin: Anglicans (39.5%) and Catholics (23%) dominated, followed by Presbyterians (12.9%) and Methodists (12.6%). The assumption was that Anglicans could be found among all classes, that the working-class was mainly Catholic, that Methodists were an upwardly mobile middle class, and that the Presbyterians were retailers and solid middle-class businessmen, like Dawson's father and brothers.

The clergy, many of them from 'the old country', saw themselves as the 'wise men of the tribe', wrote the war historian, Michael McKernan. They welcomed war as Australia's 'baptism of fire, because it would have a re-generating effect on Australian society, weaning the people from material-ism and a love of pleasure'. Secular government, the sensationalist press and the Church cranked up the propaganda machine of Empire. Fit young men who had not enlisted were labelled shirkers and cowards. Honour and loy-alty became blind passions. No one gave a thought to the consequences of death or incapacitation.

Dawson's tour continued: they moved to Wagga Wagga next morning. Back in Melbourne, they 'played to good houses': the reception this time was comparable to 1913.[8] Dawson performed much the same repertoire to similarly enthusiastic audiences; critical comment, though a little kinder on the more substantial numbers, repeated that of the previous tour: 'While the singer excels in the portrayal of somewhat commonplace passions and perfervid sentiments, as expressed in the popular ballad, he can do finer things as he showed in the treatment of some better stuff.' 'Better stuff' included his admirable friends-in-need, 'O ruddier than the cherry' and 'Onaway, Awake Beloved!'. This time he stamped his authority on Handel's mighty 'Why do the nations so furiously rage together'; the critics acknowl-edged 'the fine treatment of the difficult roulades' and that 'the words came out like a feeling of indignant protest'. Most numbers, however, had an 'unfailing success even when they were on occasion musically of no ac-count'.[9]

Biographies of Dawson, including his own, give the impression that the tour disintegrated in Wagga Wagga with the outbreak of war; that Peter and Nan were stranded in Australia for the duration; that they lost all their money and were only saved from financial ruin by the intervention of 'the music hall impresario H. D. MacIntosh'. Some elements of this story are valid but the chain of events is more complex. Contrary to Dawson's memoirs, the *Theatre* of July 1915 reported that he had returned to Australia in June 1914, had appeared in Adelaide, Melbourne, Sydney, Brisbane, then Rockhampton and had worked his way back to Adelaide by the time the war broke out. He had decided to return to London, though not before giving six concerts in Melbourne, another ten in Tasmania and then on to New Zealand.[10]

Programmes indicate that J. & N. Tait had organised at least the New Zealand leg of the tour. There the support artists were Nan, the violinist Grace Newman, and the pianist Carlien Jurs. A review of the concert on 28 December showed that Peter had lost none of his usual expansive form: 'encored again and again … Mr. Dawson has a charmingly genial way of singing to his audience, and not over their heads.' Well into this 'triumphant tour' Peter wrote: 'It is hard to realise that a terrible war is in progress. Everyone seems prosperous and ride about in their motor-cars, attending concerts, theatres and music-halls, not forgetting the inevitable picture shows. Money to burn so to speak!' The Dawsons returned from New Zealand in May 1915 after giving more than a hundred concerts: they had toured for a year. They had planned to leave Adelaide on 11 June but their departure was delayed for another year.

The horrors of Gallipoli now gripped Australia. Someone had to be blamed for the catastrophe. In early 1915 a meeting of the Anglican Synod in Brisbane began to rail against German preachers and argued that Germany, using its Pacific dependencies, had long ago planned the annexation of Australia. An ethnic witch-hunt began: abandoning any semblance of religious tolerance, the Church singled out the 34,000 German residents. After 1916 these 'aliens' were required to report weekly to the police. Although there were no proven instances of enemy spying, national hysteria 'led to a strict censorship of newspapers, mails, cables, films, foreign books and pamphlets, even phonograph records'.[11]

Suddenly audiences turned their back on Peter Dawson's concerts. According to his memoirs, disaster struck the tour in Brisbane. He and Nan ran out of money and Nan had to pawn some of her jewellery to pay the hotel bill. 'But just then I found a good Samaritan. "Hugh D." offered me a music-hall tour of the Australian States.' Hugh Donald McIntosh[12] was a Sydney-born impresario, who had recently taken over Harry Rickard's Tivoli Theatres.[13] Whilst he had 'difficulty finding overseas artists during the War', wrote Frank Van Straten, the principal artists in Melbourne in 1915 did include the boxer James J. (Gentleman Jim) Corbett, the actor-comedian Leo Carrillo, the comedians Gene Gerrard and Ida Barr, the actor Julius Knight and the baritone Peter Dawson.

As there is a gap between June and November it is possible that Dawson's music-hall tour did begin in Melbourne in mid-1915, but Adelaide in December is more likely. In November 1915 the Dawsons were in Sydney where Peter sang in Haydn's *Creation* one evening; on the next Nan joined him in the Peter Dawson Popular Farewell Concert in aid of the Central Sandbag Committee.[14] On Boxing Day, 'Peter Dawson of gramophone fame' supported by 'Annette George, a celebrated English soprano', were at the new Tivoli in Adelaide.

Dawson was certainly at the 'Tiv' in Melbourne from 1–6 April 1916, for the *Argus* reported that: 'those patrons who regard song as an unwelcome and unnecessary break in a rapturous succession of knockabout turns' were won over by the 'hackneyed, "try your lungs" "Toreador"', while 'Mother Machree' and 'Where the Mountains of Mourne Sweep Down to the Sea' were 'perfectly done'.[15] The music-hall audience loved Dawson and he was no less enamoured of the music hall. As he confided to a reporter: 'I am in love with vaudeville. Compared with concert work, an engagement on the halls is simply a holiday. I do five songs a night, compared with sixteen at a concert.'[16]

Dawson's mother had died on 30 March, aged 74. Peter and Nan returned to Adelaide again but were not there long before Hugh McIntosh put a South African tour their way. On 22 May Peter wrote to composer friend, Aileen Neighbour: 'I want to make Gramophone records of your songs in London … we are leaving on Friday 26th inst per RMS Osterley. We leave the ship at Durban (S. Africa) where we commence a six weeks Vaudeville engagement under the "African Trust Ltd". After that we push on to London.'[17]

The *Osterley* sailed 'in convoy carrying troops and stores and only a few passengers'. Sailing to England in 1916 was a very risky business. Submarine attacks, especially on the Atlantic leg, were a very real danger: 'in 1916 an average of 46 merchant ships a month were being sunk. By February 1917 sinkings had risen to 98, in March to 103, and in April to 169.' Only the protection of the slow merchant ships by faster cruisers and battleships finally halted the carnage.[18]

Either the planned six-week tour of South Africa was extended or the Dawsons could not get another berth, because it was some time before the Gramophone Company board learned that he 'was due to arrive in this country on the 2nd prox. [October] and was likely to do so in a broke condition'. His absence had prejudiced his contract, which had run out on 7 April 1916. He had been paid his retainer and advances but, as he had not recorded sufficient numbers to satisfy his liability, he now owed the Company £448.12.0.[19] One director urged 'legal means to enforce fulfilment', another said he could 'snap his fingers at Mr Dawson'. The next contract did not begin until late 1919 but the directors must have come to some arrangement

with him to work off the debt because an almost frantic recording period
followed. Dawson noted that he sang '40 songs in six weeks, from October
13 to November 23' (1916). We have traced only 33 titles within this period
but 86 by 20 June 1917.[20]

Among the 86 recordings of 1917 we found one of his most short-
lived *noms de disque:* Llewelyn Morgan, warbling 'Taffy's got his Jenny in
Glamorgan'. This audio avalanche also included his second most popular
disc, the lugubrious 'Cobbler's Song', from the new musical, *Chu Chin Chow*.[21]
The Gramophone Company was so anxious to get the hit onto the market
that Dawson was obliged to record it *prima vista* [at sight]. Peter liked to tell
the story:

> When I arrived, the manager caught my sleeve very excitedly. 'Look
> here, Dawson,' he said, giving me this piece of music, 'This song is
> going to be all the rage, and I want you to record it.' I looked at the
> song. 'I've never heard of it,' I replied, 'but I'll sing it. When do you
> want me to do it?' 'Now, of course,' he replied. It was a shock, but I
> ran over the song once with the orchestra, and then made the record. It
> was one of my best![22]

The urgency of the *Chu Chin Chow* recording was repeated with *The Maid
of the Mountains*: the musical opened at Daly's Theatre on 10 February 1917
and the company recorded it on 30 March. Dawson sang the duet 'A Paradise for Two' with Bessie Jones, alias Louise Leigh, and his perennially popular
'A Bachelor Gay'. He also recorded a patriotic collection: 'Australia' (Matson),
'O Canada March On', 'Soul of England', and 'Your England and Mine',
with a curious companion, 'Down Among the Dead Men'.

However, for the majority of his '40 songs' Dawson invented (or was
allocated) a new pseudonym, 'Will Strong', and was listed as 'Comedian'.
'Will' could be heard in light-hearted, pro-Allied forces numbers like 'The
Tanks That Broke the Ranks'; in many pseudo American-Negro folksongs
like 'Where The Black-Eyed Susans Grow' and 'Down Where The Swanee
River Flows'; not to mention a South Seas repertoire: 'Hello Hawaii!, How
Are You', 'My Hawaiian Sunshine', and 'O'Brien Is Tryin' To Talk Hawaiian'.

When these songs appeared one critic wrote:

> Will Strong … a singer whose name has appeared a good deal of late
> on *Zonophone*, who is worthy of more than a passing notice, although
> he may not sing the very highest class of song is the happy possessor
> of a full, rich, and powerful baritone.

Dawson mixing with Army brass on a Queensland recruiting tour, 1918. He was soon to be in uniform himself. In the possession of the Documentation Collection – ScreenSound Australia, National Screen and Sound Archive.

And another:

> A strong baritone with a voice singularly in consonance with that of
> another 'Strong baritone' recently departed these shores.

Although the songs were recorded between late 1916 and mid-1917,
some did not appear until 1918 and a few were even held over until
November 1919, inferring that the singer was still in England, but in fact,
Dawson had long since returned to Australia.

The 1920 *Zonophone* catalogue contained 137 solos by Peter Dawson, the
1920 *HMV* catalogue contained 39. As nearly all these titles were issued on
the low-priced *Zonophone* label rather than the up-market *HMV*, it suggests
that the Gramophone Company wanted to recoup its debt as quickly as
possible. But if this move was intended as a mild chastisement for their
colonial larrikin, the idea went slightly awry. This over-abundance actually
propelled Dawson into more homes than ever and accelerated his fame
among the budget-record clientele.

At the outset of the war the Australian forces consisted mainly of young
men aged 19–21. According to one statistic, land forces alone rose from
45,645 in 1914–15 to 122,186 by 1918–19; military expenditure increased
significantly from £12,709,017 to £98,823,485.[23] In March 1917 a coded
telegram reached the Governor-General of South Africa: 'Numbers enlisted for service abroad to 31st January last 347,000 or 14 per cent of male
population Australia.'[24]

The war dragged on. The euphoria did not last. The litany of losses had
the predictable effect: volunteers no longer came forward. But Prime Minister Billy Hughes had committed Australia to providing 16,500 troops a
month to the front and forced a referendum on conscription. It split the
country in two. When finally the Military Service Referendum Bill was introduced to Parliament in September 1916 it 'aroused all the latent animosities
in the community'. The Irish-based Catholic Church with its strong working-class roots still harboured rancour against the English and vehemently
supported the opposition. The referendum took place on 28 October and
was lost by a narrow margin. A second referendum also failed.

Although the United States joined the Allied forces in April 1917 the war
still showed no signs of abating. Australian troops were still needed. The
Government had to try other recruitment strategies. Dawson was invited
back for 'a tour on behalf of the Australian Government for war loan
purposes'. However, the invitation could not have been too urgent because
he wrote: 'I arranged a short tour of South Africa on my way home.'[25]

Whether the performance contract in South Africa or the Australian Government invitation was the real reason for leaving England is a matter of conjecture. Certain is that the 'short tour' was quite substantial.

The timeframe can be pieced together: recording stopped on 20 June 1917; both Dawsons were working in Johannesburg by early August because an advertisement from the African Theatres Limited Empire Theatre, Johannesburg, showed that Peter Dawson and Annette George would commence the third week of their run on 27 August. Another programme for the same company's Rinko Vaudeville & Photo-Playhouse September 3–8, showed Annette George as Act No. 4, sharing the limelight with a mix of short films, a feature film, and 'Francis & Alfred, The Unparalleled Juggler and his clever Assistant'. The same programme advertised Peter Dawson for the following week. Peter and Nan must have stayed on in South Africa until December because Peter signed his handwritten manuscript, 'O, My Love is Like a Red, Red Rose', 'at sea in Indian Ocean, Dec 19th 1917, H. M. Transport "Militaides"'. They could have been in Adelaide in time for Christmas 1917.

The war loan project proved to be a recruiting drive. Dawson's zeal and naive patriotism was just what the Government needed. In January 1918 it sent him through the backblocks of Queensland. Talking to an old Army comrade in 1931 Peter recalled that 'we had a March to Freedom campaign through Brisbane and Toowoomba and over the stringy-bark flats with me on a lorry singing all the recruiting songs of the day'.[26] Then came the final effect, the culmination of the rabblerousing. On 13 February 1918, on the steps of the Brisbane Town Hall, the famous singer very publicly enlisted in 8th Queensland General Service Reinforcements. The announcement of the enlistment of the 36-year-old volunteer, 'was received with cheers'. The citizens of Adelaide – and probably the rest of the country – were 'proud to know he will help represent them at the front'.[27] Two Farewell Peter Dawson Concerts at the Tivoli in Adelaide on 30 March and 1 April heightened the publicity.

With World War I the Australian soldier was born: previously without battle experience, isolated by distance, Australian soldiers had come out of a void. Unfettered by military convention, they had shown skills and independence invaluable to the British Army. 'Two chapters of the myth had already been created and absorbed, the bush and its peculiar people, mateship and the religion of mateship. Now came the legend of the soldier.'[28] But who counted the cost? From its population of less than five million Australia lost 59,258 'killed, died and missing' with casualties of 226,073 – an incredible 68.5% of the armed force, 'the highest casualty rate in the Empire.'[29] Considering the cataclysmic effect the war had on the British

Dawson's NCO School, Brisbane, July 1918. Dawson is seated second from right.

Empire and Australia in particular, it is sobering to read that what we refer to as World War I 'took place in a relatively small area of Europe … the rest of the world was little affected'.[30]

In Australia the war created a peculiar monoculture: the returning soldiers banded together, glorifying in the myth that had been created. Dawson liked to be seen as one of them too and always remained actively involved with the Returned Services League. Over the years his service record was variously reported:

> • shown 'peeling spuds' before 'his voice was utilised in drilling rookies, when he was promoted to the rank of sergeant-major' (1933);
> • 'Served World War I, Qld. reinforcements, company sergt.-major' (*Who's Who in Australia*, 1933-59);
> • 'Peter Dawson will end his [singing] career in Brisbane' – 'befitting as signed up there for WW1' – 'Signed up in Brisbane because warmer than South' – 'they made him a sergeant-major. "And a pretty tough one, too", remarked a friend' (1939);
> • according to his book he was 'Battalion Orderly Sergeant', when he finally left for the European front (1951);
> • 'eventually becoming company sergeant-major. He held that rank when the ship on which he was being sent to France reached Panama, and peace was declared' (1951);
> • 'during the World War served with the Australian forces in Europe' (1951).[31]

This was how Dawson promoted his military service and until now it has not been challenged. His army service record, however, puts it slightly differently.[32] Dawson became No. 65041 *Private* Peter Smith Dawson when he 'attested' on 13 February 1918; he was not actually required to 'join' until 1 June. His address was given as 'Ruddle's Hotel in The Valley', the hotel at which the disastrous tour of 1915 allegedly ended. The story of pawning Nan's jewellery becomes a little suspect because the proprieter, Ernest Ruddle, was obviously a good friend to Dawson. When the Dawsons were to return at the end of May he wrote: 'Will meet you with the car next Thursday night – Till then Cheer Oh "Private PD". Kindest regards from all in Brisbane to self and Mrs Dawson.'[33]

Dawson had no sooner joined than he was off again. He was issued 'Special Leave Pass A78972' available for '348 hours from 12.30pm 1.6.18 to 11.59pm 15.6.18' in order to undertake a propaganda tour to Sydney. He recollected driving 'around Sydney on a lorry singing recruiting songs' and turning up in Martin Place singing his famous 'Blue Dragoons', with emphasis on the lines 'Come along boys and join us, too' and 'I don't want to lose you, but I fear you'll have to go'.[34] On 11, 12 and 13 June, he sang 'Three Farewell Concerts to Private Peter Dawson'[35] at the Sydney Town Hall 'prior to his departure for the Front with the A.I.F.'. Back in Brisbane, Private Dawson 'passed examination for the rank of Corporal, Standard V.G.' on 21 August 1918 and shortly afterwards was promoted to 'Acting Sergeant'; but he lost any rank when his company embarked on the S.S. *Carpentaria* from Sydney on 7 November.[36]

In the European summer of 1918 the war still seemed deadlocked: some of the fiercest fighting on land and in the air took place that August; then almost without notice the German war machine ran out of supplies and collapsed. On 11 November, four days after the *Carpentaria* had left Sydney, the Armistice was declared. The troops were 'transhipped to Riverina, in New Zealand, on being recalled to Australia upon the signing of the Armistice' and were back in Sydney on 20 November.[37] Nan was waiting at the dock in Sydney when Peter returned 'from overseas',[38] then stayed at Ruddle's Hotel until Private Peter Smith Dawson received his discharge in Brisbane on 28 December, 1918.

The embellishments to his army career evolved later. Although he was officially Private Dawson, he could honestly say he had been a sergeant and although he did not reach Europe or even Panama, he did leave Australian waters. Attesting might have been a publicity coup but he received no special benefit – such as extra money or an honorary rank – so his enlistment appears to have been genuine. The Army certainly profited from his unequivocal patriotism for he was a morale builder, an expert communicator and a top-class entertainer.

After his brief stint in the army he and Nan returned to Adelaide where they stayed with his aging father. According to Peter's memoirs, he had nothing to sing so he worked for his brothers. But he soon got so bored that he arranged for a phoney cablegram to be sent saying that the Gramophone Company needed him in England urgently. To his surprise, the next day he received a genuine offer: six weeks in Melbourne 'at £85 per week, followed by another for twelve weeks in South African tour at £75', which stretched into 20 weeks at an increase of salary.[39]

We have not been able to verify this version of events but he certainly performed in Melbourne on Saturday 25 January 1919. Among items mentioned in a review of the concert that evening were his familiar 'Largo al factotum', the dramatic aria from *Rigoletto*, 'Pari siamo', Handel's bubbling 'Droop not young lover' and the gentle 'Drink to Me Only with Thine

Eyes'. Dawson's technique was praised: 'He showed all his former beauty of tone coupled with a power of moulding the tone that was little short of remarkable ... he makes every word and syllable beautifully musical' – but his understanding of the arias was damned.[40]

A new driver's licence confirmed that Peter was back in Adelaide in early April[41]; but after that we lose track of him. Though both Dawson and the Gramophone Company reported that he had been entertained by the Savage Club in Melbourne prior to his departure, no date was given.[42] No confirmation of a South African tour that year could be found; but as the Dawsons were not back in London until the end of the year this tour cannot be discounted.[43] On the other hand, in August Chappell was advertising a Melbourne season in which 'The Famous Baritone', would feature Hermann Lohr's 'Little Grey Home in the West', and 'Away in Athlone'.[44] As no review of any Dawson concert at that time could be identified, we have no evidence this event took place either.

Old Tom Dawson died on 10 November, at the age of seventy-seven. By that time Peter and Nan were probably back in London because the Gramophone Company entered into a new contract with its prodigal son on 1 December 1919.

Edward, Prince of Wales, with Sir Joseph Cook (right), High Commissioner for Australia, hears Peter Dawson broadcasting from Australia House during the Australia Day reception, 26 January 1923. *Daily Sketch*. In the possession of the Documentation Collection – ScreenSound Australia, National Screen and Sound Archive.

The dazzling heights: radio begins

The war had changed Australian society irrevocably. Government leadership had fallen to Billy Hughes (1864-1952), 'Welshman, socialist, ex-trade-union secretary, Labor politician, lawyer, an ardent nationalist and imperialist', whose implacable opponent was Melbourne's Archbishop Daniel Mannix, leader of the strong Irish Catholic minority. The return to peace was not easy; it was marked by continued political conflict and industrial unrest. The country was exhausted and grieving the loss of a generation of young men. But the absorption of those who returned led to such a demand for services and commodities that there was full employment and a buoyant economy right through the 1920s.

The far-seeing Hughes, who objected to Australian foreign policy being controlled from London, took advantage of the wartime achievements of his small nation to obtain the participation of Australia in the Peace Conference at Versailles. In 1919 the British Dominions became completely independent, setting up their own embassies and acquiring seats at the League of Nations.[1] At home, however, Hughes soon came to be seen as too authoritarian and was replaced in 1923 by Stanley Melbourne Bruce (1883-1967). Bruce was 'a dyed-in-the-wool Liberal, a Cambridge man with an Australian accent, an athlete, a returned soldier and a business man', who held on to the reins until 1929 and carried through the plans for independence initiated by Hughes.

In England the pattern was reversed: Lloyd George, elected in 1916, led the Liberals until 1924 when Labour leader Ramsay MacDonald defeated him. This first Labour minority government survived only nine months, and was replaced by the Conservatives led by Stanley Baldwin. This in turn gave rise to the first General Strike (1926), a showdown between the Government and the labour unions. In Britain the 1920s 'was a period when hopes of post-war reconstruction were quickly dashed by depression.'[2]

During the war Dawson's career had lost both continuity and direction. A fresh start was needed to strike a balance between the practical reality of bargaining for a living and the exaggerated expectations caused by the prolonged excesses of publicity. Peter and Nan had not made those peripatetic journeys through Australia and New Zealand for altruistic reasons, but the fortunes they had hoped for had proved elusive. Nevertheless, his management of the groups, the audiences' reaction and the resolution of his economic worries further matured Dawson and firmly established him as an international concert artist.

That he still wanted to be considered a classical artist is apparent from the titles which appeared most often in his programmes: Handel's 'O ruddier than the cherry' and 'Why do the nations'; the arias: 'Largo al Factotum', 'Toreador Song' and 'The Prologue from Pagliacci'; and the 'serious' songs: 'I am a Roamer,' 'Onaway, Awake Beloved!' and the four 'Cowboy Songs'. Despite adverse criticism of most of these numbers, he persisted in singing them before the lighter music his public had come to hear.

The growing political turmoil in England had little effect on the entertainment industry; on the contrary, the public wanted to celebrate the end of the war and Peter Dawson personified the best of England's glory. Dawson had made no recordings during 1918 and 1919 but now he was back in London and back in favour. The boom of the 1920s made him the golden boy of the Gramophone Company and rocketed him to absolute stardom.[3] His new exclusive contract now became: a retaining fee of £300; solo fees £10, duets £5 and other £4, with a minimum £900 worth of work; a guaranteed total of £1,200 ($70,000 in year 2000 terms) from recording alone.[4]

Nevertheless, this contract was initially for one year only, which suggests a certain caution on the part of his employers; but this was not reflected in the brash publicity. In March 1920 he was heavily promoted in the new Gramophone Company in-house magazine, *The Voice*.[5] A photo showed the thirty-eight-year-old still with a full head of hair and wearing the wing collar he always favoured. After his 'long absence in Australia … his voice is better than ever. Perhaps the tropical sunshine may have helped.' 'I owe more to the gramophone than I can possibly express,' said Peter, joining in the spiel.

The November issue was careful to extol his universal competence and popularity: 'Peter has long been a favourite at the "Proms", the ballad concerts at Queen's Hall and the Albert Hall and the leading choral societies all over the kingdom'. It also mentions a concert to which Dawson refers in his memoirs as: 'My first engagement after the war ... at the Albert Hall to sing at Mme Tetrazzini's Farewell Concert.'[6] This titbit however, cannot be reconciled with any of her biographies. Charles Gatty, author of *Luisa Tetrazzini – The Florentine Nightingale* (1955) assured us that she did not sing any 'farewell concerts' at that time; the only 1919 concert was on 20 September, when she was supported by the French violinist, Madame Renée Chemet and the English tenor, Frank Mullings. Peter could have replaced the tenor at the last minute, of course, but we believe the Dawsons were not back in London by September. The only time we can be sure Dawson sang with Madame Tetrazzini was in 1933.

After the serious prelude, the *Voice* continued: 'There is no artist whose voice is more suitable for recording; the numbers made by him are as popular as any in our catalogue'. These numbers included several operatic arias: 'Now your days of philandering are over' (in the now-outdated English); 'The Toreador's Song' (with its awkward beginning: 'Sirs! A toast'); 'Room for the Factotum' (difficult in Italian, a tongue-twister in English);[7] and that model of truncation, 'The Prologue from Pagliacci', beginning 'A word allow me, sweet ladies and gentlemen', which is still the favoured English version, although the translation dates from Weatherly in the late nineteenth century.

Dawson's working year probably began on 4 March 1920 with *The Yeomen of the Guard*, part of a series of Gilbert and Sullivan recordings, which were not completed until October, when the *Voice* carried a photo of the 'Principals of our Light Opera Company'. Geo. W. Byng was still the conductor; the singers were now: Violet Essex, Bessie Jones, Sarah Jones, Edna Thornton, Nellie Walker, George Baker, Peter Dawson, Walter Glynne, Edward Halland, Derek Oldham, Ernest Pike, Robert Radford and Harold White.[8] With Nellie Walker, Bessie Jones, Ernest Pike and Edward Halland, Peter recorded four titles from Fraser-Simpson's *A Southern Maid*, just eleven days after the show had opened at Daly's Theatre.[9] He and Pike also reverted to their scallywag characters of 'Courtland & Strong' to record heady material like 'Take your girlie to the movies, if you can't make love at home'.

Most of Dawson's recordings were accompanied by what was euphemistically referred to as an 'orchestra'. The notoriously confined space at Hayes allowed only a small combination of instruments. According to Dawson, it was so cramped that on one occasion a trombonist, who was forced to move his slide between the violin and cello caught the ear of the violinist and toppled him over onto others in the band.[10] In one photo he is seen in shirtsleeves surrounded by instrumentalists 'recording at the Gramophone Company in 1920'.[11] Two cornets, a cello and a clarinet are

The HMV Gilbert & Sullivan recording party in 1920, listening to their *Pirates of Penzance*. Standing (left to right): George W. Byng (conductor), Derek Oldham, Walter Glynne, Ernest Pike, Edna Thornton, Peter Dawson, Edward Halland, George Baker, Nellie Walker. Seated: Bessie Jones, Violet Essex, Sarah Jones, Harold Wilde, Robert Radford.

recognisable in the photo, and there would also have been a tuba, a trombone and kettledrums. It was an odd combination, like an enhanced brass band, the cornets being substituted for violins. As Fred Gaisberg said, 'There was no pretence of using the composer's score; we had to arrange it for wind instruments ... and all nuances were omitted'.[12] However, a quick look at the files shows violins and violas were indeed used during the 1920s acoustic recording period. Most sessions employed ten to twelve musicians – two first violins, one second violin, one viola, one cello, one tuba, one flute, one clarinet, two cornets, one trombone, kettle drums – although on occasion these could be augmented to twenty-one.

According to the conductor Sir Adrian Boult, the studio was so small 'it would hardly have held a full-size billiard table' but the recording horn was enormous, 'three or four times the size of the one we know from the HMV picture':

> I sat high up on the wall near the great horn; the concert master, surrounded by a few strings, had his fiddle nearly inside the mouth of the horn; other instruments were at varying distances and the French horns looked into a mirror so that their sound faced the recording horn, [which] was the centre of our world, immovable.[13]

Arthur Clarke sat in the machine-chamber on the other side of the wooden wall, handling the huge discs of heated wax which were 75–100mm thick. The indentations could not be touched until they had hardened, so the moment it was finished the master was placed in a special container – and 'the performance was perpetuated warts and all'.

'The gala days in the recording studio were those on which Chaliapin, de Pachmann or Peter Dawson recorded. Peter Dawson looked upon recording as a relaxation and a holiday,' wrote the *Daily Chronicle*.[14] The mood in the studio can be imagined. While the technical personnel were busy with their preparations, the assembled musicians would be waiting restlessly:

> Dear old Peter would keep everyone quite helpless with laughter till 'the cake was on the table'. Up to that moment he would play the fool outrageously, and sing every sort of parody, rude or otherwise; then Arthur Clarke, the head recorder, would stick his head through the little window and plead with him to be sane.[15]

Dawson would then drop into recording mode as if nothing had happened.

On 20 May 1920 Dawson recorded his own rollicking wine-and-kiss song, 'Chant of Bacchus'. His own vocal range is marked by a high F added as an 'effect note' on the final dominant chord, leading into a descending coda-like cadence. The original manuscript bears the signature 'composed by Peter Dawson, London, 1914' and his orchestral arrangement suggests that he sang it then, possibly at a Prom concert.[16] The 1920 recording, however, names the composer as J. P. McCall. Although Dawson occasionally composed under his own name or other pseudonyms, for the bulk of his songs he favoured 'J. P. McCall'.[17] J. P. McCall, sometimes J. Petter McCall, appeared in print for the first time on a setting of a Fred Weatherly lyric, 'Friend For Me', published by Boosey in 1920. This *nom-de-plume* became effectively an alter ego. Although Dawson let the cat out of the bag on the 1935 recording, *Peter Dawson's Christmas Party*, many continued to believe in the existence of J. P. McCall. As late as 1957 the Misses Molly and Jessie Robarts of Ormond, Victoria, requested:

> In these days of such calamities as the H. Bomb and Elvis Presley …
> would it be possible to make your final programme one of the songs
> by that very close friend of yours, Mr McCall?[18]

Asked where this pen-name came from, Constance Dawson replied: 'Oh, just out of the blue. He was a doctor of Nanny's. He used to come to see Nanny and he took a fancy to the doctor.' In fact, J. P. McCall was the family doctor in Adelaide.

As the name first appears in 1920 Nan must have been taken ill while they were in Australia. Her recurrent bad health (which might explain why the Dawsons had no children) has been attributed to a mid-life car accident in 1925[19] but Constance confirmed that Nan had already had bouts of illness from the time of her marriage. She had not gone with Peter to Australia in 1909 because she had to have her first operation, said Constance. In 1921 she accompanied Peter on their tour of India but 'declined to participate due to medical advice'. We do not know what this medical condition was, but we did learn that she was a diabetic in her old age.[20]

At the beginning of 1921, Dawson dutifully advised the Gramophone Company that he had been invited to tour India and signed a letter of agreement for a new contract on his return.[21] Before he left he recorded one of his all-time favourites, the poignant 'Mountains o' Mourne' but the last recording before his departure was the ominous pairing, 'The Sea Road' coupled with 'Hurricane am I', on 3 February. The next recording session was on 9 September, a neat seven-month absence from London.

Among Dawson's papers an album of small, slightly faded sepia photos shows members of the party – 'Self, Nan, Dorothy Treseder (Pianist), Winifred Small (Fiddler)' – 'Outside our bungalow at Corstorpheus Hotel,

Simla, 7500' above sea level', 'On the way down to Kalka from Simla' and 'under The Great Banyan Tree, Royal Botanical Gardens, Sibpur, nr Calcutta' on 15 May.[22] Dawson's own chapter about this tour of 'India, Burma and Straits Settlements' is very general;[23] information in an article about Winifred Small is a little more specific.[24] The impresario, Edgar Warwick, could reasonably have expected that the home of the British Raj would welcome 'Peter Dawson England's foremost baritone'. The party arrived in India on 2 March 1921 and gave 96 concerts in six months. From a Madras programme we see that Winifred opened with the 'Slow Movement from Mendelssohn's Violin Concerto' and was to appear later in the programme. Mr Selwyn Driver gave 'A humorous Pianoration'.[25] 'Overall the tour was a success', but there were pockets of bad luck. In Madras Mr. A. W. Price had replaced 'Miss Dorothy Treseder the solo pianist and accompanist who has a serious indisposition'. At another stage Winifred developed an abscess under a tooth; but worse was to come – in the heat her valuable violin began to fall apart.

The Madras programme shows that Dawson was singing his usual repertoire: 'O star of eve', 'Don Juan's Serenade' (Tchaikowsky), 'One Lone Star' (McCunn), 'The Sands o' Dee' (Frederick Clay), 'Songs of a Rover' (R. Conningsby Clarke), 'Sea Fever' (Ireland), 'Vagabond' (V.Williams) and 'The Golden City of St Mary' – a hefty programme even without encores. One encore led to an incident at the Excelsior Theatre, Bombay, on 24 June. When he had finished singing 'Annie Laurie' someone threw 'five rupees and one anna' onto the stage. The discomforts of the hot weather and the intolerable superciliousness of the English civil servants must have been getting to Peter, for he lost his cool and shouted, "This is the second time I've come under attack since I started on this tour!" – and stomped off the stage. But as soon as it was explained that the paltry sum was intended as a sign of appreciation, he relented, and returned to an effusive reception.

In his diary Peter kept a note of the box-office receipts for one week:

Saturday	Rs 1263.88
Monday	258.25
Tuesday	367.75
Wednesday	448.75
Thursday	451.75
Friday	620.25
	Rs 3410.63
55% =	Rs 1875.84
Incidentals (taxis) absorb Rs	71.00
[Nett	Rs 1804.84]

The percentage of the total and 'incidentals' suggests that Dawson was keeping a record of his personal income. It also shows that the company performed six days a week when they were not travelling – pretty heavy going. Saturday was clearly the popular night: assuming it was a full house the other nights were depressingly scanty.

From Dawson's biography it could be assumed that the party got no further than Penang, although in 1926 he talked about the fine concert hall in Singapore as if he had sung there. By 1935 his account of the exotic journey had extended to China and Japan, [26] but this also appears to be poetic licence. At least he came home with a first-hand knowledge of the heat and sweat of the jungles, a healthy aversion to malarial mosquitoes, bats and a myriad of other tropical insects, and a vivid picture of his Burma gal a-setting on the steps of that old Moulmein pagoda.

Back in London life returned to normal. Dawson renewed his annual recording contract to 8 September 1924. The proposed nett sum, £1,200 per annum, remained the same and he had to repay a £200 debt on the old contract by accepting £1,000 the first year – a gradual reduction in real terms. There may have been some initial disagreement about the terms because, although Dawson began recording on 9 September, he did not sign the contract until 17 October. [27]

Walsh aptly categorises him as 'a sort of handy-man' during these years. Although he is remembered for his solo numbers, ensembles remained part of his contract as well. [28] The selection was as catholic as ever, ranging from opera to nonsense; many still remembered, many relegated to the sin-bin. He recorded two beautiful Tchaikovsky songs, 'Don Juan's Serenade' – which he had just sung on tour – and 'To the Forest', with its long cantilena, dramatic climax and gentle vocal postlude. Both were to feature in many concert programmes. Another was Landon Ronald's unusually heady English art song, 'The Lament of Shah Jehan', the story of the potentate who built the Taj Mahal in memory of his dead wife.

Dawson had a particular affection for Landon Ronald (1873-1938), 'composer, conductor, accompanist, coach', who had been associated with the Gramophone Company as musical adviser since 1901 and had been the pianist for the fraught recording with Melba in 1905. [29] In the meantime he had risen to become the Principal of the Guildhall School of Music, one of the largest music institutions in England, and was knighted in 1922. Perhaps it was to acknowledge that honour that Peter recorded 'Shah Jehan', 'one of the finest that Landon Ronald has yet given us. Few singers could give it with such effect as Mr Dawson'. Dawson retained it in his concert repertoire all his life but it was one of the few discs that sold poorly.

More in the expected style was the aqueous bass song, 'Rocked in the Cradle of the Deep', and the rousing, maritime duet, 'Larboard Watch' in tandem with the tenor, Sydney Coltham. He could be heard in repertoire as diverse as 'Dancing Time' (from Jerome Kern's *The Cabaret Girl*); the ever popular waltz, 'Peggy O'Neill'; the zippy, shimmying 'Sheik of Araby' (as Robert Woodville) or on six 10in. sides of spoken *HMV Physical Culture Exercises* – for which he remained discreetly anonymous.

Occasionally the *Voice* gave some idea of Dawson's out-of-town commitments. The February 1920 issue listed fourteen venues between 2 and 27 February: the November 1921 issue listed nine venues between 2 and 30 November, some of which were operatic concerts, for, despite the negative reviews in Australia, Dawson persisted in his enthusiasm for this genre. On his return to England he joined forces with a group of recording associates to present opera concerts throughout Great Britain. The critical reception proved no better this time: 'a dozen excerpts ... whose stories have neither beginning nor end'; 'one is at a loss to understand why a concert of this nature should be more popular than ... more natural songs'.[30] Dawson's memoirs are not date specific but we found one programme, a Grand Operatic Concert in Preston on Monday 23 January 1922, which was billed as 'a repetition of one of the most enjoyable concerts of the last series'. This particular group, described as 'British Artists of International Fame' were: Rosina Buckman, Edna Thornton, Maurice D'Oisly, Peter Dawson and William James, who was now working in England.

For the Preston concert each artist was allocated an aria and some ensembles:

Aria	*Madamina* (Don Giovanni)	Mozart
Aria	*Joan of Arc's Farewell*	Tchaikowsky
Aria	*Suicidio* (La Gioconda)	Ponchielli
Aria	*O Paradiso* (l'Africaine)	Meyerbeer
Aria	*Addio terra nativa* (l'Africaine)	Meyerbeer
Aria	Delilah's *O Love from thy power*	Saint-Saëns
Aria	*Jewel Song* (Faust)	Gounod
Duet	Madame Butterfly Act 1	Puccini
Quartet	*Presto, presto andiam* (Marta)	Flotow[31]

Despite the seriousness of the programmes a travelling group like this could act like kids out of school, especially when one of them was Peter Dawson. As William James remembered: 'during a spinning song he was providing the 'thrum thrum thrum'. I was at the piano. At each 'thrum' he would knock me with his elbow … and he made the pace so fast that the soprano threatened him after with "if you ever do that again …".[32]

These singers were not an isolated group. In another programme Dawson was to be found with Stella Power and Katharine Goodson. They were part of an impressive undertaking, the International Celebrity Subscription Concerts Season 1921-22, under the direction of Lionel Powell & Holt, whose celebrity roster also included Tetrazzini, Dinh Gilly, Josef Hofmann, Florence Austral, Fritz Kreisler, Jan Kubelik and Landon Ronald.

At the end of 1922 a new player entered the entertainment industry in England: the British Broadcasting Company. The first radio station had been established in Pittsburgh, Pennsylvania, in 1920. In England prior to 1922 radio programmes had been broadcast from London, Birmingham, and Manchester under the auspices of the Marconi, Radio Communications, Metropolitan Vickers, British Thomson-Houston, General Electric and Western Electric companies. In 1922 they joined forces to form the British Broadcasting Company Limited. The first broadcast, 'the London regular service', was opened on Tuesday 14 November 1922 and 'the first programmes were transmitted from Birmingham and Manchester on Wednesday November 15th'.[33]

Dawson had his first encounter with this startling new technology just two months later, on 26 January 1923, when a group of Australian artists celebrated Australia Day with a broadcast from Marconi House. It was a right royal affair. Dawson, who was photographed with the Prince of Wales, recalled 'a big Australia House party, with Melba, Percy Grainger, and other celebrities present.'[34] Melba and Grainger may have been there but they did not perform. The broadcasters were nevertheless the Australian élite in London: the sopranos Stella Power, Gertrude Johnson and Rosa Alba; contraltos Clara Serena, Ada Crossley; the tenor Alfred O'Shea; the baritone Harold Williams; basses Malcolm McEachern and Peter Dawson; together with Lauri Kennedy (cello), Daisy Kennedy (violin), Albert Whelan (entertainer), and the pianists Anne Williams, Irenon Asdaile, W. G. James, and L. Stanton Jefferies.

Malcolm McEachern sang three of William James' *Six Australian Bush Songs*, accompanied by the composer.[35] At 9.45pm it was Dawson's turn:

> 'They hauled me out, shoved a microphone into my hand and told me to start singing!' he said. 'There wasn't a piano, so I sang "Ships that pass in the night" unaccompanied. We had a lot of enquiries from ships at sea, all wanting to know what had happened to the piano, and if it had been lost on the way!'[36]

In her diary Nan wrote: 'Australia House, 9 o'clock – very fine night – bed 5 am'.

William James had composed the *Six Australian Bush Songs* in response to a challenge from the Anglo-Australian actor, Oscar Asche (1871-1936), who had asked Dawson why he did not sing any dinky-di Australian songs. 'The "Bush Songs" set to the poetry of Adam Lindsay Gordon were the result,' said James.[37] The flavour is distinctly Australian, in character somewhere between a good English art song and a Peter Dawson style ballad. Today, No. 6: 'The Stockrider's Song', with its galloping rhythm and Ya-ya-yipees, is a popular concert piece for anyone from baritones to children's choirs. To judge from the range, tessitura, style and the editing marks on Dawson's personal copy of the songs, they seem to have been tailored to his taste and abilities.[38] The fact that Malcolm McEachern broadcast three of them and recorded four in January 1924 might suggest that the songs had been written for him; but Dawson had already recorded five of the six new songs on 25 January, 1923, the day before the Australia Day broadcast.

A flattering review of Dawson's recording appeared in Compton Mackenzie's new magazine, *The Gramophone*, the following December; but this acoustic recording had a very short shelf life. Dawson re-recorded the songs electrically in 1927, but because the set was too long for a 12in. disc, again omitted 'King Billy's Song' (No.3).

The establishment of the BBC put an end to the last remnants of promotional ballad concerts and the Victorian drawing-room culture. From the outset gramophone records provided a high proportion of broadcast material but there were also live relays and studio recordings;[39] so it is curious that, despite his high profile, there were few BBC broadcasts by Dawson for nearly eight years.[40]

Meanwhile, during 1923 and 1924 he took part in a number of memorable concerts. One was the Payling Concert at the Royal Albert Hall on 14 April 1923, which featured some of the Australians who had broadcast on Australia Day. However, the focus was on Madame Lily Payling (1880-1967), 'The Famous Australian Dramatic Soprano', whose subscription concerts at the Royal Albert Hall were a highlight of the musical year during the 1920s and 1930s.[41] Madame Payling claimed that she had introduced more young musicians to the public than any other singer. On this occasion 'the young musicians' were: Peter Dawson, 'The World-Famous Australian Baritone'; Lauri Kennedy, 'The Celebrated Australian 'Cellist'; and Adela Verne, 'England's Greatest Lady Pianist'. The accompanists were L. Stanton Jefferies and Herbert Dawson, both of whom were to have a long association with Dawson.

Another noteworthy concert took place in Ireland in early 1924. Dawson devoted a chapter of his book to 'My Irish Tours' but he does not make it clear when these tours took place.[42] In fact, they were spaced out throughout the 1920s, a period when Irish politics were particularly turbulent. Ireland had long been a thorn in the side of England, and the demands for home rule had culminated in the formation of Sinn Fein and the modern Irish Republican Army.[43] This in turn had brought on the Easter Rising of 1916 and the War of Independence (1919-1921). The peace treaty signed in July 1921 split the IRA. For his part in the 1916 rising William Cosgrave (1880-1965) had been condemned to death; but the sentence was commuted to life imprisonment and he was released in December. Cosgrave subsequently became an Alderman and was elected President of the Provisional Government in 1922. A 'New Irish Republican Army' immediately took arms against the Provisional Government. A number of these die-hard extremists were arrested in September and executed in December. On 10 April 1923 the Chief of Staff of the New Irish Republican Army, General Liam Lynch, was 'killed in action' and shortly after the leaders, Eamon de Valera and Frank Aiken, surrendered. They were pardoned but remained active political opponents of Cosgrave.

One might have expected a singer of Dawson's empire style to have been unwelcome in Ireland but there is no evidence that this was the case. It comes as something of a surprise to find Peter Dawson as the featured artist in the politically-sensitive General Liam Lynch Commemoration Concert at the Theatre Royal, Dublin, on Sunday 30 March 1924. Though he might have sung Irish songs as encores, his printed programme stuck to his perennial opener, 'Hey For The Factotum', followed by *Three Shakespeare Songs* by Quilter and Godard's 'The Traveller' – very apolitical. However, a local performer, Miss Daisy Bannard Cogley, rendered 'When the Praties are Dug' by P. J. [sic] McCall.

Although Dawson's concert programmes had musical substance, by now he had become stereotyped by the popularity of his recorded ballads and encores. 'His *métier*,' wrote Gerald Moore, 'was the ballad – 'Songs of the Sea', 'The Open Road', 'The Floral Dance'. I do not think anybody could sing such songs better than he, for he possessed a voice of fine manly quality … straight-forward songs came to him naturally without having to think about them or spend any time on their study'.[44]

To counter this Dawson finally felt compelled to prove that he could sing the best art music. In May 1924 he advertised three Wigmore Hall lieder recitals with Gerald Moore: 'Professionally,' wrote Moore, 'he startled everyone by stepping out of the channel where he was distinguished by giving three recitals, each of a different programme'.[45]

There are several versions of events leading to Dawson's decision to give these recitals. In one the Canadian singer Dixon Ryder said it was about time Dawson did something worthy of his voice, so Dawson undertook three years' study with him before giving four recitals of German lieder at the Wigmore Hall and another four at the Aeolian Hall.[46] In his autobiography Dawson gives the impression that Dixon Ryder was not in London but 'at that time chorus master at the Met'. He claims to have organised the Wigmore series because Ryder had asked him to try out a young Canadian accompanist: 'the first real chance Gerald Moore had of showing his remarkable ability. ... I gave him the chance to accompany me at three recitals I was to give at the Wigmore Hall of German lieder and a number of French and English classical songs.'[47]

The 'Canadian pianist', Gerald Moore, was actually born in Watford, Hertfordshire, in 1899. His family had migrated to Canada in 1913 but he returned as a twenty-year-old to study with Mark Hambourg, a long-time friend and colleague of Dawson's. Moore dates his association with Dawson from 1921 when they made a concert tour through the British Isles during which they 'became good friends and he engaged me on every possible occasion'. In fact, Moore's name does not appear as Dawson's tour accompanist until late 1923.[48]

Some clarity may be gleaned from Nan's 1923 diary. Many entries give an insight into the Dawsons' domestic life: late nights after concerts ending 2am, 3am, 4am; many visits from Mum, Fan and Fred, Con, and Lil; went to the theatre, went motoring, much ping pong and spaghetti suppers; Pete often absent, home late, tired, bad foot, feeling queer, visited several doctors. Their hectic professional schedule can be judged from a sample:

August 24:	Promenade – poor Pete – Flea Song – H. Wood drowned him, fine second half;
October:	[Nan and Peter] very busy all over England: Shrewsbury, York, Scunthorpe ... Cardiff, Plymouth, Exeter. Comments on hotels, food, dresses. [Nan] recital Haverford West, Oct 3; Newport; Oct 4;
November 14-16:	[Nan and Peter] Palace Hotel, Southport, black dress, Aida Lament, Ecstasy, What's in the Air, Springs Singing;
November 17:	Royal Choral Peter Elijah – Mum, Fan, Con, Evelyn tea & supper after Mrs Smith;

November 19:	Pete's Queen's Hall;
December 14:	Oldham – Pete, Gerald & I at Midland Hotel, Manchester – nice concert – Austral – came home in her car – saw Vera Pearce;
December 15:	Liverpool Peter Messiah – wonderful show – me a great success – jolly supper we two alone.

The diary entries confirm that Dixon Ryder was a London voice teacher. Nan has noted lessons both for Peter and herself and that 'Rider's young accompanist, Gerald Moore, was always in attendance'.[49] Nan's first lesson was on Monday 2 July 1923; Peter's on 30 July, her sixth. They paid six guineas per lesson; there were 36 lessons in three lots of 12, ending on 9 November. Nan had a 'bust up' with Ryder on 16 November but it was quickly resolved for she had her next lesson three days later. Dawson's 'lessons' were twenty-five coaching sessions in preparation for the recitals.

The programme for the first recital on 9 May 1924 read:

I

(a) Sei mir gegrüsst	Schubert
(b) Erstarrung	
(c) Wasserfluth	
(d) Die Krähe	
(e) Ungeduld	

II

(a) Die Mainacht	Brahms
(b) Botschaft	
(c) Ständchen	
(d) Der Tod, das ist die kühle Nacht	
(e) Blinde Kuh	

III

(a) Nun wandre Maria	Wolf
(b) Verschwiegene Liebe	Wolf
(c) Frühlingsnacht	Schumann
(d) Du bist so jung	Eric Wolff
(e) Traum durch die Dämmerung	Strauss

IV

(a) Down by the Sally Gardens	Herbert Hughes
(b) Must I go bound	Herbert Hughes
(c) White in the Moon	Arthur Somervell
(d) The Last Revel	Julius Harrison
(e) In Prison	Julius Harrison

(f) Four Elizabethan Lyrics set to music by   Quilter
    (i) Weep ye no more
    (ii) My Life's Delight
    (iii) Damask Rose
    (iv) The Faithless Shepherdess[50]

Peter Dawson had recorded many art songs in his time but this random selection of German songs was indeed a daring step. The importance of their addition to his repertoire cannot be overestimated: he could now demonstrate that he had the technique for substantial, impulsive songs, ('Sei mir gegrüßt'), lyrical songs with beautiful cantilena ('Traum durch die Dämmerung'), the exalted, extended E^b climaxes of 'Die Mainacht', or the delicate humour of 'Ständchen'. In retrospect Dawson tended to downplay the significance of these concerts for fear of being labelled a musical snob. 'It was very nice but when I added up the accounts for the three concerts I found I was 90 quid out of pocket so I decided there and then that what my mates had been telling me was right. People want me to sing in English.'[51]

Although Dawson did on occasion sing some foreign songs in their original language, in public he made a fetish out of singing in English. 'Singing in English' was a popular catchcry: it was argued that works in foreign languages in translation would be understood and therefore accessible to a broader audience. Some might argue that the true character of the original was destroyed; that German lieder, French art songs or Italian arias depended on the marriage of words and music to give true expression. But Dawson would disagree. He was well aware of the élitist affectation of presuming that a piece by Schubert, Schumann or Brahms was better than any by an English composer but British songs for Britain was his motto: 'an Englishman likes to understand the words of a song. I have sung in German and Italian but am unhappy when I know that nine-tenths of my audience has no idea what I am singing about!'[52]

Contemporary English art songs became fertile ground: 'Why trouble to learn all these foreign songs?' he asked. 'We have British lieder every whit as good.' If English composers needed a champion they certainly found one in Peter Dawson. The art songs he chose ran the gamut of emotions: they ranged from the dramatic and lyrical: 'Speak, Music!' (Elgar), 'Rann of Exile' (Bax), 'Lovely Kind and Kindly Loving' (Holst), *Five Ghazals of Hafiz* (Bantock), 'Loveliest of Trees the Cherry Now' (Somervell), and *Songs of Travel* (Vaughan Williams); to the light-hearted and amusing: 'Rolling Down to Rio' (Edward German) and 'Five Eyes' (Armstrong Gibbs). Reviewing his 1939 recording of 'Speak, Music!' one critic expressed the hope that Dawson was 'reverting to the far-off days when he recorded good music': he thought he should like 'Rann of Exile' too, but it was so difficult he could not make out what it was all about. Some of the other serious songs might have been over the head of his audience too, but to his credit, Dawson persistently fitted these songs into his concert programmes.

In May 1924, after the Wigmore Hall recital, Dawson made a rare recording in German, the 50-second vocal in 'Jokanaan is summoned before Salome' from Richard Strauss's 1905 opera, *Salome*. This essentially-symphonic excerpt was conducted by Albert Coates, who on one occasion became the object of one of Dawson's practical jokes. Having perspired freely in the warm recording studio, the famous conductor had retired to the artists' room to change his underclothes. 'When I saw Albert's underwear hanging on a line in the dressing room, well, my hands itched to "have a go", and of course I did,' said Dawson. He borrowed stencil plates from the despatching department then diligently stamped the underpants *Passed Wear Test* and the vests *Technically Rejected*. The conductor was not alone in his embarrassment; his wife washed the underwear herself instead of sending it to the laundry.[53]

According to some sources, Dawson's income from recordings and other sources peaked in 1923;[54] in fact, it was somewhere between 1926-29. In November 1923 he needed an advance of £200; he eliminated this debt in April 1924. In September 1924 he extended the 1921 contract for a fourth time to 8 September 1925. In these final years of acoustic recording the Gramophone Company seems to have decided to give their star baritone an improved and more dignified profile: 'Will Strong' and 'Robert Woodville' were last employed in 1922 and he appeared much less as a support singer. From 1922 to 1925 there was a concentration on the mid-range *HMV* label (80 titles) instead of the budget-priced *Zonophone* (only five).

Gerald Moore claimed that he arrived at the Hayes studio in 1921 to make his first recording with Renée Chemet, the French violinist, then 'with Peter Dawson, the baritone, whom I next accompanied'.[55] But the recording ledger shows that from 1921 to 1924 most of Dawson's records were with orchestra; if a pianist was needed, it was usually Madame Adami. Gerald Moore's turn was yet to come. The beginning of their recording association appears to be 19 February 1925, just before the introduction of electrical recording, when they recorded Tchaikovsky's 'Summer Love Tale'.

Dawson's last acoustic session was on 3 June 1925. He recorded 'Wood Magic', 'The Fiddler of Dooney' and 'The Kerry Dance'. Only 'The Kerry

Dance' (HMV C-1212) was issued, which makes it his last acoustic recording. The release of two virile duets, 'The Lord is a Man of War' (Handel)
and 'Sound, Sound the Trumpet' (Bellini: *I Puritani*), with the highly-re-
spected bass, Robert Radford, produced another ecstatic review: 'the effect
is electrical!'[56] No pun was intended, for electrical recording was still under
wraps.

Bell Laboratories (Western Electric) perfected electrical recording in 1924
as a 'side-line to their research in telecommunication' – a logical sequence
from the use of microphones for broadcasting. When Russell Hunting played
a pirate copy of an electrical recording to Fred Gaisberg in the autumn of
1924 he remarked: 'Fred, we're all out of a job!' Fred understood. 'There
were many technical secrets in recording and matrix-making which were
known only to me', he said.[57] These old skills suddenly became obsolete;
trained electrical sound engineers would now be needed. The new method
could catch every vibration of every human voice and every instrument, it
could record a whisper, some said, it could even record the atmosphere of
the studio.

An era had come to an end. How would the old guard, who had built
up a recording technique based on loud sounds and few nuances, adjust to
the new technology? In particular, how would it affect Peter Dawson?

A studio rehearsal at Abbey Road, August 1932, with musical director Ray Noble (far left), Clarence Greenwood at the Steinway, and a chorus of leading London singers, working on 'The Veteran's Song'. In the possession of the Documentation Collection – ScreenSound Australia, National Screen and Sound Archive.

Electrical recording arrives

In July 1925 at Caxton Hall, London heard the first public demonstration of electrical recording: 4,850 voices singing 'Adeste Fideles' and 'D'ye Ken John Peel', which had been recorded by the Columbia Graphophone Company in New York's Metropolitan Opera House on 31 March.[1] Because of its enormous range and sensitivity the microphone revolutionised gramophone recordings overnight, but record companies colluded to keep silent about this development because they believed the better quality electrical recordings would threaten the sales of stocks of acoustic records. As the new records looked just like the old ones, a few were sneaked secretly onto the market; but astute critics soon noticed the difference and the cat was out of the bag.

The Gramophone Company wasted no time getting Dawson back into the studio to try out the new recording system. His first electrical recording was made on 19 August: he re-recorded two of his last acoustic titles, 'Wood Magic' and 'The Fiddler of Dooney', and added 'House of Mine' and 'Molly of Donegal'. Gerald Moore was at his side to farewell the acoustic horn and welcome the microphone.

Dawson's concert season had also begun. He was scheduled for the 31st Promenade Season on 8 August, 2 September and 18 September;[2] and, as the Sparrow's Nest Concert at Lowestoft on 30 August indicates, he was busy in the provinces too. On Sunday 4 October he and Nan were returning 'from Glasgow to Newark in his big Renault saloon', when they collided with 'a gay party returning from a football match at a crossroads about seven miles from Leeds'.[3] Their car overturned. Peter was not hurt, but Nan was nearly killed. Pinned underneath the car, she 'suffered several broken ribs, deep lacerations to one leg, a broken left shoulder, and her head was almost scalped. A few days later gangrene was discovered in the leg and it was only saved by a daring operation'.

The injury to his beloved Nan was the most traumatic experience in Peter's life. He carried the ghastly hospital record with him as a permanent reminder of the terrible accident.[4] The expensive hospitalisation and Nan's slow recuperation in a nursing home added to Peter's emotional stress. The accident left Nan debilitated for the rest of her life: she remained Peter's constant companion and adviser but she never sang publicly again.

Dawson's recording contract had been due for renewal on 9 September, but negotiations were protracted until 14 November.[5] Whether the Gramophone Company had decided to alleviate Dawson's financial problems or whether Tom Noble, who 'knew the gramophone business from the inside', had talked the Company into it, Dawson's new contract included an unexpected bonus of £4,000 for past services. That was not all. Finally, after twenty years service, Dawson switched to a royalty agreement. He calculated that sales of his records had rocketed from 5 million in 1920 to over 8 million by 1925, so 'it was obvious I was not getting the fee commensurate with my enormous sales'.[6] Times had changed from 'an order for 100 records [of one title] by Peter Dawson meant a few days work' to 'to-day he can record half-a-dozen in a couple of sessions'.[7] Dawson believed he would be disadvantaged if he were still paid under the old system. The two parties agreed on the standard royalty of 5%:

(a) in the case of a single-sided record reproducing a song (solo) sung by the Artist alone … 5% of the English selling price

(b) song with

1 other singer	5% of $^1/_2$	[= 2.5%]
2 other singers	5% of $^1/_3$	[= 1.67%]
3 other singers	5% of $^1/_4$	[= 1.25%]

(c) in the case of double-sided records royalties shall be calculated and paid on each side of such records at half the rates agreed for single-sided records above.[8]

'A royalty of 5% on retail may not sound a lot,' said Peter, 'but when it runs into hundred of thousands it becomes a very respectable total.' At the time, the cost of records were:

Label	Size	Cat. No. Prefix	Price
Plum	10"	(B)	3/-
	12"	(C)	4/6
Black	10"	(E)	4/6
	12"	(D)	6/6
(Celebrity records)			
Red	10"	(DA)	6/-
	12"	(DB)	8/6

The bulk of Dawson's recordings were 10in. *Plums*, on which he would earn 1.8 pence for each solo record, so the company would need to sell the equivalent of 1.2 million to recoup its advances over the five years of the new contract. During this period, Dawson's earnings were protected by a guarantee of £1,000 per annum, any loss to be carried by the company. If sales exceeded the projection, Dawson would earn more than the cumulative £5,000; plus the £4,000 bonus. At this stage both parties were optimistic, but the loss clause was to become a thorn in their sides in the future.

'Peter Dawson' had become a by-word in every household even before the advent of electrical recording; now the microphone showed his skills to even greater advantage. 'The difference in the tone quality was a revelation,' he wrote, 'So much so, that the company decided to remake most of my important records on their list.' Thirty years later the journalist Gale Pedrick could still remember Dawson in shirtsleeves, collar loosened, recording 'with equal skill and imperturbability, a solo from *Elijah* or a rollicking re-issue of "The Bandolero".'[9] In 1926, he recorded a new version of the oft-revived 'The Boys of the Old Brigade', coupled with a new song in comparable parade-ground rhythm, 'When the Sergeant Major's on Parade'. He re-recorded 'The Floral Dance'. 'One of the most noteworthy of his early electric recordings', wrote Walsh, was yet another 'Prologue', a 12in. version requiring both sides of a record. And the critics waxed just as lyrical about the remake of Vaughan Williams' 'The Vagabond': 'Our famous bass-baritone Peter Dawson is in fine form, but when is that incomparable singer out of form?'[10]

Aware of Dawson's publicity value the Gramophone Company even constructed a special glass studio so that the public could see him at work during the 1926 Ideal Home Exhibition.[11] Gerald Moore wrote that 'vendors in gramophone shops up and down the country would sell a machine by playing Peter Dawson's rendering of "The Floral Dance".'[12] The tenor Webster Booth recalled that 'in those days, to me, Peter *was* recording, and all it meant! I was familiar with music-shops whose shelves were full of his records on a Saturday morning and empty at night.' [13] Dawson's drawing power was not restricted to Gramophone Company products: he endorsed anything from Saronys cigarettes to Horlicks malted milk.[14]

'Everyone loved Peter,' wrote the Australian musical comedy star, Gladys Moncrieff (1892-1976). 'The Peter Dawson I knew was a wonderful singer, and a sincere, kind person. I first met Peter in 1924 in London when we were guests at the Grosvenor Square home of the Australian contralto, Ada Crossley. Peter immaculate in morning suit and striped trousers, looked tall, slim, and handsome. He sang divinely.' With respect, Glad, it was 1926;

Peter at home with family dog Toby, Mill Hill, London, 1930. In the possession of Ann Jacquet.

Gertrude Johnson and May Brahe were also there: the gala event was reported on 8 April under the banner: '*Australian Singers*, Famous guests of
Madame Ada Crossley'.[15] 'Our Glad' also recalled Dawson's story of his
visit, at the height of his fame, to the eminent singing teacher Madame
Blanche Marchesi (1863-1940). To be received at Madame Marchesi's home
was an awesome event, but our suave, sophisticated baritone was used to
making an entrance. As he was ceremoniously ushered into her huge, highly
polished hall he skidded on a rug and went flying. 'That was his entrance!'
said Moncrieff. 'But it's no good when I tell it. You had to hear it from Peter
himself.'[16]

Dawson's busy concert schedule included yet another patriotic concert in
Dublin: the Tenth Anniversary Easter Week Commemoration of the 1916
uprising on Sunday, 4 April 1926. Padraic Pearse's Oath, printed at the
beginning of the programme in both Gaelic and English, set the mood:

> In the name of God
> By Christ, His Only Son,
> By Mary, His gentle Mother,
> By Patrick, the Apostle of the Irish,
> By the loyalty of Colm Cille,
> By the fame of our race,
> By the blood of our ancestors,
> By the murder of Aodh Ruadh,
> By the pitiful death of Aodh O'Neill,
> By the fate of Eoghan Ruadh,
> By the desire of Sarsfield at the point of death,
> By the groaning of the oppressed Fitzgerald,
> By the dripping wounds of Tone,
> By the noble blood of Emmet,
> By the corpses of the Famine,
> By the tears of the Irish exiles,
> We swear the oath our forefathers swore,
> That we will burst the bondage of our nation
> Or fall side by side. Amen.

A harpist performed 'The Jacobite Ballad' and the Republican Players
performed *The Gaol Gate*, a one-act play set outside Galway Gaol. Dawson
stuck to his stock repertoire: 'Now your days of philandering are over', 'She
Moved Thro' the Fair', 'When the Lights Go Rolling Round the Sky'. As a
concession to the occasion he sang Stanford's setting of an old Irish text,
'The Fairy Lough' (1901). This led to an encore: 'And now for all the little

ones here tonight, Mr Dawson will sing "The Kerry Dance".'

On 25 August, 10 September, 23 September and 9 October 1926 Dawson
sang at the Proms. As usual Sir Henry Wood conducted.[17] The Queen's Hall
in Langham Place could seat 3,000 people. During the promenade season
there were ten weeks of nightly concerts and each Prom lasted two-and-a-
half hours.[18] The most expensive seats cost 7/6; the promenade 2/–: although mainly standing, it filled up first. The lighting was always increased
dramatically just before the concert began and never lowered during the
performance. Sir Henry never left the platform except, in a mixture of
courtesy, efficiency and warm encouragement, to bring on the lady soloists.

Conductors do not always kowtow to the egos of soloists: for them,
conducting is a job. Apart from their own ego, which has sustained their
drive to this position of power, conductors are more concerned with con-
trolling their large orchestra than pandering to the foibles of artists who
claim the spotlight for a fraction of the time. So it is not entirely surprising
to read that the 'mercurial' Sir Henry's 'strange brusque way of quashing
artists' led to a confrontation with Dawson on 'the last concert before the
BBC took over the Proms' (1926).[19] The fracas, according to Dawson,
occurred when he responded impromptu to audience demands by singing
his own new setting of the Kipling poem, 'Boots'. The crowd responded
with 'tumultuous applause' but Sir Henry damned it as rubbish. Dawson's
dander was up: he retorted by calling Sir Henry a philistine for not admiring
Kipling's words. It's a good yarn, but hard to accept that neither Sir Henry
nor the orchestra had seen the music before it was performed.[20]

Dawson tells us that Chappell's offered to publish 'Boots' immediately
after the concert so he sought Kipling's permission: 'Yes, Mr Dawson', replied the poet, 'sing the song with my best wishes for a success… There is
no one I should like to hear sing one of my verses more than you.'[21] 'Boots'
was published in 1928 and recorded in mid-1929. It became the most popular number Peter Dawson ever composed and, as he trotted it out on most
occasions, it was obviously his idea of an excellent song.[22]

Rudyard Kipling was the poet laureate of the British Raj.[23] For Peter and
his peers words like 'the King', 'patriotism' 'empire', 'commonwealth',
'dominion', were emotive. Every citizen of the Commonwealth was a British
subject and had free access to Britain: loyalty to the Crown was unqualified.
No formal occasion in Australia began without the singing or playing of
'God Save the King'; the entire audience stood, the men bared their heads.
Australians probably knew more about British history and literature than
their own. Australian schoolchildren assembled first thing on Monday
mornings to salute the flag: they might have sung a hymn, they might have

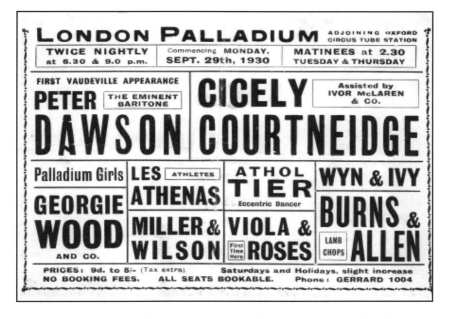

Peter topping the bill at the London Palladium, 1930, supportd by Cicely
Courtneidge, Athol Tier and American comedians George Burns and Gracie Allen.

sung 'Advance Australia Fair', but they certainly sang the National Anthem.[24]
'Boots' epitomised this ethos: it stirred the heart. When it was sung, listeners
identified with the common soldier, the powerhouse of the mighty British
imperialist system.

'Boots' was born one day when Dawson was travelling by train: in his
imagination the regular click-click-clicking of the train wheels became
footsoldiers marching. Curiously, the expected 'plod, plod, plod' of boots
is introduced by three bars of galloping triplets. 'Too agitated' said Nan
when she first heard it. Perhaps the officer in charge of the weary infantry-
men was on horseback. But after that the listless, repetitious, monotonous
fall of heavy boots pervades the entire piece. No one who has worn army
boots could fail to identify with those soldiers 'foot-foot-foot-foot-sloggin''
over Africa'; with the pointless 'boot-boots-boots-boots movin' up an' down
again'. There was 'no discharge in the war!' for the poor aching soldier
imprisoned in this wall of motion.

Each of the two verses has the same construction with 'no discharge in
the war' as a refrain, repeated at the end of each verse with the same awkward musical phrase. Dawson did not compose any vocal effect at the
conclusion and there is no piano postlude so the song ends abruptly. Nan's
reaction was: 'It's – well, it sounds a little ordinary'. Despite her reservations
the song tapped into the nostalgia for old comradeship, the sharing of the
same mesmerising meaningless tedium. 'Try-try-try-try to think o' something different – Oh my Gawd keep me from goin' lunatic'. The indestruct-
ible bond between old soldiers was formed less in the heat of battle than in
the shared boredom, symbolised by those essential, reliable, inescapable –
boots.

The juxtaposition of Dawson's concerts and recording sessions continued
throughout those prosperous pre-Depression years. In June 1926 a rave
review appeared for Schubert's 'Erl King', 'perhaps the best dramatic ballad
ever written … sung in a manner which thrills', but the pianist who played
the difficult accompaniment was not mentioned: it was Gerald Moore, who
was now a regular partner. In October 1927, for example, he accompanied
the remake of five William James' *Australian Bush Songs*; in September the
following year he accompanied Bantock's 'Captain Harry Morgan',
d'Hardelot's 'The Curtain Falls' and 'Hinton, Dinton and Mere'.[25]

Both names appear on 9 June 1927 in a British Music Industries Convention Concert at Folkestone, along with an impressive array of stars: Arthur
de Greef (piano), Isolde Menges (violin), the sopranos Mavis Bennett and
Elizabeth Pechy; and the huge Russian bass, Feodor Chaliapin (1873-1938),

generally regarded as the greatest operatic singer and actor of his generation. He features in a number of Peter Dawson stories.

> Chaliapin was furious when at [this] Trade Convention … Peter
> followed him on the platform before hundreds of gramophone dealers
> and, imitating the Russian's mannerisms of waving his arms and
> striding along, smiled sweetly and announced in broken English in a
> deep voice 'Number Fifty-Five', and … waved to the pianist to carry
> on.[26]

Another incident occurred in the recording studio. In order to sing into
the single horn Dawson was obliged to stand on a stool and sing over the
giant's shoulder. To get closer to the horn he leant further and further forward until he suddenly lost his balance, fell off the stool, grabbed onto the
big man to save himself, and finally ended up on the floor with Chaliapin's
watch in his hand. Chaliapin's reaction: 'You don't have to go to that much
trouble to find out the time, Peter.'[27]

The first of three recitals at the Aeolian Hall with Gerald Moore, which
Dawson coupled with the Wigmore Hall recitals in his memoirs, actually
took place on 30 October 1928. The centrepiece was Arthur Somervell's
setting of Tennyson's *Maud*, a cycle of twelve songs published by Boosey in
1898 but re-worked for these recitals. *Maud* has a similar story to *Lucia di
Lammermoor*: aristocratic daughter and handsome but unwelcome neighbour
fall in love – discovered at forbidden tryst by brother – brother killed in
duel – protagonist flees: in this case though, it is the hero who goes mad, not
the heroine. The music was redolent of late Victoriana: quality music with
saccharine sentiment. On 25 October Somervell wrote to Dawson: 'Here is
a précis of Maud which I am told (& I think I agree!) is rather good. Will
there be time to get it printed for Tuesday?'[28]

Dawson's score gives an insight into the care with which he looked after
his music. The pages have been sewn together; the text, which he recited to
set the scene before singing each song, was typed and pasted in. To begin,
he introduced Maud and her lover, Lancelot, before singing the first number,
'I hate the dreadful madness'. He then proceeded to the next monologue,
which ended with: 'She was tall and stately, and although as children, they
had played together, they had never spoken since the feud. One day he
heard her singing: "A voice by the cedar tree".' He then sang the number –
and so on until the last number: 'Finally this song shows him sane but shat-
tered, "My life has crept so long".' At this point Dawson noted: 'Finish up
quickly.' It is a pity that the cycle is rarely performed nowadays. Each number,
particularly 'Birds in the High Hall-garden', 'Go not happy day' and 'Come

into the garden, Maud', is an excellent English art song, well worth singing.[29]

In June 1929 the *Voice* carried a photograph of Dawson lunching with 'President Cosgrave of the Irish Free State and his family'. "'I have sung," said Mr Dawson, "before many audiences but in that home at Templemore where I sang one little song at the special request of Mr. Cosgrave, I think I met one of the most pleasing in the President, his wife and two children".'[30] Cosgrave was still President but the internecine war had not been resolved. When Eamon de Valera proposed a constitutional role for Sinn Fein in 1925, the New IRA dissociated itself from him. It now regarded the prisoners executed by Cosgrave in 1923 as martyrs. The remaining prisoners were not released until de Valera superseded Cosgrave as President in 1932.

Dawson may have sung for President Cosgrave, but he also sang in a requiem concert for the murdered IRA volunteers. The heading of the programme gave an inkling of the mood of the evening: 'In Memory of Richard Barret, Joseph McKelvey, Liam Mellows, Roderick O'Connor, IRA members executed in Mountjoy Prison 1923". Extracts from prisoners' letters were added, including the last letter from Liam Mellows, dated 8 December 1922.[31] As on the previous occasion, none of Dawson's programmed songs – 'Largo al factotum', (again), 'The Smugglers Song' (MacFadyen), 'Invictus' (Huhn) or 'The Spirit Flower' (Tipton) – seem particularly appropriate. But he must have added specifically Irish numbers because he wrote that he got tired after singing more than his fair share of encores. Finally, to show that he had sung enough and the concert had ended, Dawson sent his accompanist out alone to play 'God Save the King'. Fortunately the pianist, Hubert Bath, was more sensitive than Dawson: he simply closed the piano and bowed.

With the advent of electrical recording, symphony orchestras, which had until then been difficult to record well, 'suddenly moved into the spotlight'. In 1925 the Gramophone Company had begun making new G&S recordings to replace the 1920–21 acoustic versions. To ensure they were 'authentic' these recording sessions were supervised by 'Carte & Sullivan', descendants of the original impresario and composer.[32] At the end of 1928 Dawson was contracted for *The Yeomen of the Guard*; in February 1929 for *The Pirates of Penzance*.[33]

As Hayes was too small for such a large undertaking, the more spacious Small Queen's Hall was rented. Many of Peter's famous colleagues – Derek Oldham, Leo Sheffield, George Baker, Dorothy Gill, Elsie Griffin – plus a full chorus, had gathered for the recording of *The Pirates of Penzance*, which the young Malcolm Sargent was conducting from Sullivan's original score. The strings had a microphone to themselves; the wind, brass and percussion

'Invictus' (Huhn) score in his own handwriting, from the Dawson collection, the
Documentation Collection – ScreenSound Australia, National Screen and Sound
Archive. He recorded this work in both 1917 and 1937.

another; a third was set up for the soloists, who were 'penned off in the central space with the chorus', which had a fourth. From a high rostrum Dr Malcolm Sargent 'controlled his scattered forces with the most admirable spirit and patience'. [34]

That was not how Dawson saw it, however. For him the sessions were unnecessarily long and irritating. Sargent wanted the singers to sing full voice all the time, which was very tiring, especially with many niggling interruptions by the conductor and the fussy D'Oyly Carte agents. Dawson had no intention of wearing his voice out before the actual recording, so he sang his role quietly. Exasperated, Sargent accused him of not knowing his part and a row erupted. It was quickly quashed by the producers, well used to dealing with volatile temperaments. [35]

By now the first sound movies were appearing; Dawson began to show a serious interest in motion pictures. In correspondence dating from June 1929 to a Mr Javal, Dawson wrote:

> I have an offer to start on two films lasting about 10 weeks at Elstree for a firm who are renting space at B.I.P. starting Aug 6th. I have accepted provisionally but as I understand you are starting at B.I.P.'s sometime in September, if my taking this offer will jeopardise any chance of my being able to join your firm, I shall cancel this offer. I have heard that your firm is going to synchronise The Feather? if so can I lend a hand. That was my last picture with the Strand Film Co. as Assistant. [36]

Around this time silent films were phased out as British International Pictures (BIP) began to produce the first English 'talkies' (with musical scores by Hubert Bath, Dawson's accompanist in the Irish concert story.) [37] However, no evidence has been traced of Dawson taking part in any movie. EMI archives advised that:

> I. C. Javal was Sales Manager in the HMV Shop in Oxford Street. His connection to the film industry could not be explained. 'The Feather' was dubbed with music by the Company but there was no clear indication that Peter Dawson played any part in this or if his film career did amount to anything. [38]

In America the phonograph industry was not looking healthy: in 1923 sales figures for Victor had peaked at about 40 million; in 1927 and 1928 sales were over 37 million; but by mid-1929 collapse was imminent. In 1929 Edison finally discontinued the manufacture of phonographs and records; RCA bought out Victor and converted its plant from phonographs

Song sheet, 1931, in his familiar open road vein, with Peter 'tramp, tramp, tramping along'.

to radio production; in October Wall Street crashed. American Victor sales, which reached 34,493,447 in 1929, plummeted to 17,710,520 a year later: by 1931 sales were down to 7 million and bottomed at 3 million in 1932. The 1928 figure was not exceeded again until 1941.

England was not spared. For a time the Depression did not appear to affect Dawson directly; nevertheless, his career was locked into the fortunes of the Gramophone Company, which would soon have a battle to survive. A 1929 photo of the forty-seven-year-old shows a confidant man, still wearing the high wing collar which he affected long after it was out of fashion; head held proudly, the hair, brushed and greased back flat in twenties style, getting sparser. For the same photo session he added a trilby and nonchalantly held a smoking cigarette.[39] When he endorsed the new Gramophone – 'the latest machine' – and a portable wireless set, Dawson saw the chance of a *quid pro quo*:

> Undoubtably a good deal of publicity will be involved anent my picture
> & Testimonial in connection with the <u>portable</u> wireless set, and in
> return I shall expect in all fairness to be given one. I travel greatly by
> motor car throughout the country & I should never be without it.[40]

About this time Peter and Nan moved to their most permanent address, 10 Evelyn Grove, Ealing Common, which is stamped on much of Dawson's music. Here Aunty Nan looked after 'Jeff aged 9, Joan aged 12', while the youngest Noble daughter, now Eva Gilbert, awaited her third child, Ann.[41] Nan had not yet decided to quit the spotlight. On 1 January 1930 the Adelaide *Advertiser* flagged another tour of Australasia: 'Peter Dawson will probably come here in 1930,' said Mr Gus Cawthorne, the concert manager yesterday. 'His wife, Madame Annette George, soprano, will again accompany him on the tour, and assist in his programmes.'

Meanwhile, Dawson took time out to watch one of the most important events of the year: Don Bradman hitting his double-century at the Oval. When he was 80 Bradman remarked: 'I was a friend of the late Peter Dawson and in fact on one occasion played the accompaniment for him to sing at a private function at Bertie Oldfield's house.'[42] The 'Don' was also a skilled amateur musician. In 1930 Columbia even enticed him into the studio to have a 'friendly chat' and record a couple of light pop numbers.[43]

Dawson's association with Gerald Moore was far more extended than either of their memoirs imply. We find Moore as his accompanist for the Channel Isles Celebrity Concert of 25 September 1930 in a programme that ranged from Rigoletto's dramatic aria, 'Yon assassin is my equal' (Verdi) to 'Boots'.

A few days later Moore was again his accompanist in a broadcast from the Palladium. Dawson's memoirs suggest that the Palladium broadcast was in March 1931, just prior to the tour to Australia, but in fact, his long association with the new British Broadcasting Corporation began on 29 September 1930.[44]

The Palladium was a far cry from the Queen's Hall or the Wigmore Hall. The famous 'High-Speed Variety Theatre' had long been the pinnacle of the music-hall circuit[45] – hardly the place one would expect to find a classical concert singer on the crest of his wave of popularity. Dawson claimed that although he had dissociated himself from vaudeville since the days of Hector Grant, his brother-in-law and manager, Tom Noble, was able to persuade him that it was time to appeal to a broader public. The programmes and the substantial fee of '£250 per week' were sorted out over lunch at the fashionable Frascati's Restaurant in Oxford Street.[46]

In true music-hall fashion, items as diverse as jugglers, comedians, acrobats, singers, variety of every kind, were programmed together. Dawson's co-stars included Sydney-born Cicely Courtneidge; Wee Georgie Wood; the lanky eccentric dancer from Adelaide, Athol Tier; Burns & Allen from the United States; the monologist Billy Bennett; and Power's Four Dancing Elephants.[47] The audience was enveloped in a smoke haze, star-dotted with the red ends of lighted cigars and cigarettes. When Dawson stepped onto the stage he was blinded by spotlights. The orchestra played the entry to 'Largo al factotum' and confused, Dawson started to sing in Italian; but switched to English so quickly that the gaffe only endeared him to his listeners.[48] 'Concert audiences,' he said, 'often have no real love of music, but a music-hall audience is full-blooded and knows exactly what it wants. Tastes are not low. Sing good stuff to them in the right way and they will like it.' And so they did: on 2 December 1930 the BBC picked up Mozart's aria 'Now your days of philandering are over'. It is so teasing and balladesque that it made a fitting introduction to 'The Lute Player', 'At Santa Barbara' – and, inevitably, 'Boots'.[49] Constance told us he sang 'Boots' so often that the comedians Flanagan and Allen plotted to drop a lot of stinking old footwear onto Dawson next time he sang it. Fortunately, management caught them in the nick of time. 'Of course Peter would have joined in,' Constance concluded, 'but whether the audience would have liked it is a different thing. If you go to hear someone sing you don't want it buggered up, do you?'

Appearances at the Palladium were interrupted by the foreshadowed tour of Australia and New Zealand. To exploit his mounting popularity, the Australian entrepreneur Hugo Larsen had organised what would arguably prove to be Dawson's most successful international tour, but not with Nan:

WORLD'S GREATEST GRAMOPHONE PERSONALITY

During his career as a singer, Peter Dawson has made more than three thousand different gramophone records, the greatest number ever sung by one artist. It is computed that during the last twenty years no fewer than

TEN MILLION OF HIS RECORDS

have been sold—a great tribute to his popularity with the public.

HERE is probably no living artist who can sing a robust song, a song of the sea or open air—a song of life, like Peter Dawson. Born in Adelaide in 1882, he began his vocal studies at an early age in his native town with the late J. C. Stevens, and later continued them in London under Sir Charles Santley. His first chance came when he appeared in London with Madame Albani, whose name is still cherished by concert patrons of a generation ago. Many important engagements rapidly followed, and in 1909 he made his first appearance in Grand Opera at Covent Garden. He has been acclaimed with extraordinary success throughout the English-speaking world, and is universally recognised as the finest baritone ballad singer of the day.

Apart from his magnificent voice, Peter Dawson has a wonderful charm of manner, breezy as the plains of his native Australia, and with that extraordinary gift of anecdote which places him in the front rank of raconteurs. He is a great favourite with the Prince of Wales and the Duke and Duchess of York, who have heard him sing frequently, and have personally complimented the famous baritone upon his wonderful singing.

SOME RECENT ENGLISH PRESS REVIEWS.

QUEEN'S HALL CONCERTS—A CAPITAL SINGER.

"No need for a programme when Mr. Dawson sang—his diction was superlative."
—*Morning Post*, London.

"Peter Dawson enraptured the huge audience with his delightful singing, and well maintained the reputation he has obtained as one of the leading masters of his art. He had his hearers completely at his feet."—*Daily Telegraph*.

"Peter Dawson, the famous singer of ballads, proved last night that he is an equally accomplished artist when dealing with an altogether finer type of song. His vocal beauty has never been denied, but on this occasion he convinced us that he might be numbered among the finest lieder singers of the day."—*The Star*, London.

PRELIMINARY BOOKING.

Applications for Reserved Seats (price 7/6, plus tax; total 8/9) are now being received, and should be addressed to Box Office Manager, Nicholson's, 416 George Street, Sydney, accompanied by remittance and stamped addressed envelope.

Grand claims made in the programme for the 1931 tour of Australia and New Zealand by Mark Hambourg and Peter Dawson.

Peter was coupled with the high-profile pianist, Mark Hambourg, his next nearest competitor in the Gramophone Company's longest-service stakes. In March 1931, at the height of the Depression, they took the plunge.

As a consequence of the disastrous downturn in record sales, the Gramophone Company and the Columbia Graphophone Company merged at the beginning of March to form EMI – Electrical and Musical Industries Ltd. Alfred Clark was promoted from managing director to chairman and the chief executive of Columbia, Louis Sterling, took over as managing director. A little later the Parlophone Company was also absorbed into this group making EMI the largest recording organisation in the world at the time.

By 1931 Dawson was enjoying exclusive HMV status. He was being employed only for solo work and was being dealt songs of a better musical quality, with better arrangements and better accompaniments. No pseudonyms. No 'el cheapos'. Between 1926 and 1931, EMI released about 130 Dawson titles, which compared favourably with any other HMV artist. His fame was at its zenith: he was touted as the most recorded artist in the world. The public willingly believed the tour publicity: 3,000 titles and sales of 10 million records.[50] Ignoring minor hiccups, it could be said – and Peter and the Gramophone Company said it very loudly – that Peter Dawson had recorded exclusively for HMV for twenty-five years. In fact, about half Peter's output had been on *Zonophone* recordings, but twenty-five years was certainly an achievement. To celebrate, the Gramophone Company arranged an elaborate Bon Voyage luncheon at the Savoy on Thursday 19 March 1931.

To amuse the guests, Dawson's first version of 'Asleep in the Deep' was played on the trademark 1898 Berliner/Johnson phonograph: 'Its battered, but highly polished horn projected the thin wheezy tone into the room. "Many brave hearts are asleep in the deep, so beware, beware!" sang the voice, wobbling with the turntable.' His 'superior new' version was then played on an up-to-date Gramophone to everyone's satisfaction. Good wishes flooded in; Peter sang some old favourites; old times were remembered – until he had to rush off for an afternoon gig at the Palladium.[51]

As the company fell over itself to honour him, one might assume the event was the company's idea. An office memo, however, reveals that 'this matter was first raised by Peter Dawson'.[52] His capacity for self-congratulation is further endorsed by the fact that the same achievement – twenty-five years service, 3,000 records – was celebrated a few months later by his colleague, the British baritone, George Baker. Dawson had won on a technical knockout.[53]

On 27 March 1931, the evening before they sailed, Peter and Nan threw an intimate family party at 'Restaurant Frascati Oxford St W.' Scribbled on the menu was:

> A great evening full of most charming episodes. Oh for another such in November. Palladium Pete.
> To fit in ninety minutes the night's eve of departure is just the sort of handshake we would expect. Gawd bless. Dora & Tom.
> And he's got 14 pairs of pyjamas!! Love Nan.
> Not forgetting one pair you wore last night – Much love and heaps of happy days. Dale.
> As a male friend of Peter's I think the ladies are – shall we say – near the knuckle – but why wear pyjamas at all? Tom.[54]

During the twelve years since Dawson's last visit Australia had matured as a nation. Its relationship to England had changed as an outcome of recommendations from the Imperial Conference of 1926, which became law with the 1931 Statute of Westminster.[55] This gave the dominions complete autonomy: all were of equal status; allegiance to the Crown was not compulsory. Dominions could appoint high commissioners; governors-general would be appointed on their advice. Australia's ties with England appeared to have been finally cut, but the statute was not actually ratified by an Australian Parliament until 1942.

In preparation for the tour a stack of new Peter Dawson titles was sent to Sydney: by now an urgent package could be sent by aeroplane. The package reached the agent on 15 May, the day before the tour commenced.[56] Included were serious works like 'Rolling in foaming billows' from Haydn's *Creation*, and 'Through the darkness' from Rossini's *Stabat Mater*, and excellent remakes of two of his popular arias, 'Yon assassin is my equal' (*Rigoletto*) and 'Tempest of the heart' (*Il Trovatore*). There were quality English art-songs like Amy Woodforde-Finden's 'Jhelum Boat Song' and 'Kingfisher Blue'; plus a stack of the old stalwarts commonly associated with his name: 'The Cobbler's Song', 'The Mountains o' Mourne', 'I Travel the Road', 'Shipmates o' Mine' , and the aforementioned 'Asleep in the Deep'.

Also included were two local numbers, which the Australian agent believed would be successful if sung by Peter Dawson: one had a hymn-like character, the other was a jaunty melody not unlike Dawson's 'Will Strong' numbers. The Gramophone Company was cautious, only releasing them on the limited Australian series (*HMV EA*), but the agent knew his market: their success was immediate.[57] One, 'Advance Australia Fair', was to become the national anthem; the other, Jack O'Hagan's 'Along the Road to Gundagai', has remained one of Dawson's most popular recordings. With all its elements of Australian folklore – the bushman, loneliness, the faithful dog guarding its master's tuckerbox till death – it has been recorded by a variety of artists about 150 times since it was first waxed in 1923.

The tour itinerary can be traced from various sources: 16 May Brisbane; 2 June Sydney, to Melbourne later in June, back to Sydney in July, July/ August across to New Zealand, back to Melbourne in August, over to Tasmania early September, late September Adelaide and finally Perth in October.[58] It was a daring undertaking: the Depression was at its height and unemployment was acute. But impresario Hugo Julius Larsen and the Gramophone Company exploited the popularity of both touring artists at every possible outlet. Peter Dawson, the great favourite of 'the Prince of Wales and the Duke and Duchess of York', returned in triumph. He unashamedly accepted praise for 'his magnificent voice', his 'wonderful charm of manner', his 'extraordinary gift of anecdote', and modestly stepped into the role of 'the world's most popular singer'.[59] Larsen knew his craft: no virtuoso could find more stops on the publicity organ.

Mark Hambourg was no stranger to Australia either, nor to Dawson's company.[60] The two shared a self-confident rapport that spilled off the stage into their personal lives. It was a memorable tour. Their photos were in every newspaper. In Brisbane they were photographed with the aviator, Charles Kingsford-Smith; in New Zealand they were received at Government House by Lord and Lady Bledisloe.[61] They were treated like today's superstars, albeit more soberly.

Dawson was the centre of attention when they finally arrived in Adelaide in September. The local newspapers had a field day: 'Plumber Turned Baritone Still Adelaide Boy', 'he has no fads, and he likes a rollicking good song. He loves the limelight, and does not care who knows it. Receptions, the plaudits of big audiences, and making speeches are the spice of life to him, and he never wants to drop it.'[62] At a Commonwealth Club luncheon, it was reported, Peter responded to the question: 'Has the advent of the wireless and the gramophone affected audience attendances?' with 'No! After having heard records, people wish to see the artists in the flesh.' 'And be disappointed!' remarked Mark Hambourg.[63]

Many men of substance, like the Lord Mayor, J. Lavington Bonython, and the famous leg-break bowler, Clarrie Grimmett, together with his friends, the singer Fred Williamson and the cartoonist Kerwin Maegraith, were present at an urbane dinner arranged by the Good Companions Society. The four panels of the amusing menu provide an insight into the atmosphere, taste and humour of the times. Panel One lists a series of toasts: 'His Majesty the King', each of the guests, 'South Australia'. Panels two and three boasted

Four celebrities meet, Brisbane 1931: Mark Hambourg, the aviator Charles Kingsford-Smith, the entrepreneur Hugo Larsen and Peter Dawson. *Brisbane Courier*, May 16 1931.

Maegraith caricatures of Dawson and Hambourg with a doggerel verse under each:

Here's to Peter Dawson, Back in Adelaide, his home. To every fine function Our Peter lends "tone."	We drink to Mark Hambourg, Pianoforte lord; In the hearts of good fellows He strikes the right chord.

The fourth panel, the menu, was titled *The Joyful Journey*. Each course had a name related to an automobile: 'Petrol' – Consommé au Vin de Port; 'Sparking Plugs' – Oyster Cocktails; 'Engine Feed' – Roast Turkey and Ham; 'Scenery' – Cauliflower, Green Peas, Boiled and Baked Potatoes, Asparagus au Beurre. After many speeches, many songs and many a glass they ended the evening standing in a circle, hands joined, singing 'Auld Lang Syne'.[64]

The media frenzy continued. When they left Adelaide a photograph of 'Peter Dawson, Mark Hambourg, Alan Richardson, accompanist, on Grand East-West Railway Port Augusta to Kalgourlie' appeared. Also in Perth Peter was good newspaper fodder: 'He holds the floor when he gets going. There is an enthusiasm about him that is infectious', wrote the reporter. In his lighthearted way Peter Dawson could brag about anything: the mammoth number of songs he had sung, that he had sung them all from memory (as if that were a singular achievement) and that he had never sung better. He could brag about his impeccable preparation, and – casually – brag about his fame.

Such charlatanism is endemic to the industry but, fortunately, the extravagant publicity was matched by the performers' abilities. Each had a comfortable empathy with the audience. Dawson applied his impeccable vocal technique as carefully to a banal ballad as to the most demanding art song – which pleased the severest critics. There was no more carping this time.

With so many songs to his credit it could be expected that the programmes for different tours would vary considerably; on the contrary: he knew his own abilities, knew his audiences and stuck to what had proven successful. As always he began his programmes with the most serious songs, moving gradually to the light numbers. The first bracket, the most demanding songs, were his 'old masters' of which the most substantial was the Bach recitative, 'Ah, shall not this great day of wrath', leading to the air, 'Thou most blest, all quickening day'.[65] But he also used his old friends, 'O ruddier

Caricature by Kerwin Maegraith used for a Good Companions Society dinner, Adelaide 1931.

than the cherry', 'The Prologue' and 'The Barber's Song'. Certainly he added or expended material: the superb aria, 'Vision Fugitive' (Massenet), and Beethoven's elegant 'Adelaide' made brief appearances on this tour, but the other songs soldiered on through many campaigns.

The second bracket were mainly culled from his Wigmore Hall and Aeolian Hall recitals: Somervell's *Maud* cycle; Brahms' 'Die Mainacht', 'Nicht mehr zu dir zu gehen', 'Blinde Kuh' and 'O liebliche Wangen'; Fourdrain's 'Marins d'Islande' and 'Promenade à mule' and Godard's 'The Traveller'. The third bracket headed toward lighter musical quality: 'House of Mine' (Stewart), 'A Sea Gypsy' (Michael Head), 'The Fairy Lough' (Stanford), 'The Donkey' (Besley), 'Kangaroo and Dingo' (German); and a random collection of Shakespeare songs: 'Autolycus's Song' (Greenhill), 'Crabbed Age & Youth' (Parry), 'Hey, Ho, the Wind and the Rain' (Walthew) and 'Come Away Death' (Arne). Among these 'English songs' were three excellent foreign songs sung in English: Moussorgsky's 'Song of the Flea' – made famous by Chaliapin, Schubert's 'Erl King' and a German composer's setting of the Scottish ballad 'Edward'.

'Song of the Flea' is a setting of a comic passage from Goethe's *Faust*, in which he lampooned the nepotism of late eighteenth-century courts by likening sycophants to fleas. When one flea found such favour with the King that it became the most senior royal functionary, it immediately granted positions to all its relations. These fleas bit the Empress and the courtiers, who endured the pain because they feared the King. Peasants, however, squashed their fleas and laughed at the folly of the court. The text was ideal for Dawson, who could react to the mounting musical itch and indulge in the raucous, ribald *ad libitum* laughter at the conclusion.

'The Erl King' is quite different. Over Schubert's relentless accompaniment of galloping triplets, a father bearing his fevered son flogs his horse through the bitter night while the hallucinating child keeps seeing the Erl King, the spirit of death. The distraught father tries to calm the boy, dismissing the visions as a wisp of fog, an old tree. At first friendly, enticing, the evil Erl King finally loses patience and kidnaps the screaming child. The desperate father gallops to a safe haven, but too late: 'in his arms – the child – was dead!' Schubert's harmonic progressions, the mounting intensity, the compounding of the insistent theme leading to a frightening dissonance when the child is taken by force, make this one of the most powerful songs ever written.

Carl Loewe's setting of Sir Walter Scott's melodramatic poem *Edward* can also chill the marrow. Needled by his mother, Edward, a Scottish nobleman, reluctantly reveals, strophe by strophe, that the blood on his sword

is not from an animal but the blood of his father, whom he had murdered
on his mother's order. Each phase of the abomination grows with musical
intensity. Each strophe concludes with an agonised 'Oh!' 'And what will ye
do now, Edward?' asks his mother. Revolted by his deed, Edward flees
from his beloved family, his inheritance and his country. As he goes, he
shrieks a last, desperate 'Oh!' as he thunders a curse upon his mother. It is a
gory story with dramatic music, requiring histrionic power and vocal
stamina.[66]

There were, of course, extended encores: a listener in Sydney on 6 June
noted: 'Barber's Song' and 'Who is Sylvia?' in the first half, 'Boots', 'Song of
the Flea', 'I Travel the Road', 'Floral Dance', 'Sincerity', 'Simon the Cellarer'
at the end. On 14 September a Hobart listener noted the encores after each
bracket: 'Botschaft Brahms, Take those lips away, Measure for Measure';
'Largo al, Diaphenia'; 'Boots – Kipling, A Banjo Song – Bendana'.[67]

Headlines like 'Peter Dawson Comes Home and Proves an Artist, Huge
Audiences in Sydney' were the overriding tenor of the season. The critics
agreed that he had 'certainly catered for the most catholic tastes'; 'in every
concert, Dawson has dispensed good music, and enhanced the first impression as a gifted interpreter'.[68] His vocal maturity was now admired: he gave
'the full measure of dignity and power to a recitative and aria from the
cantata *Wachet Betet*' delivering 'a lengthy scale passage with perfect legato,
and on one breath'; 'his preservation of tone-quality over the wide range
was remarkable'. 'Die Mainacht' was 'as good as a lesson'. 'Leowe's [sic]
setting of the tragic ballad, Edward, where his Scottish accent was that of a
native, was not only great singing – it was also elocution of the highest
order of art; each exclamatory "O!" was given a different shade of intensity'.

Many of the critics – not all – now regarded the lighter material as an
acceptable indulgence: 'the inevitable "popular" encores have delighted lovers
of the obvious and familiar', wrote one: 'a jolly lot of encores in popular
vein, which no one could deprecate who properly appreciated the substance of the actual programmes', wrote another. One of the less indulgent
critics was Dr Keith Barry, an organist, who later rose to a position of power within the Australian Broadcasting Commission:[69]

At the matinee given by Dawson-Hambourg the performance was
mediocre. Dawson was the star of the combination, being the
possessor of an excellent resonant bass-baritone of wide range. His
breathing and phrasing was first class and his sincerity of delivery
undoubted. He chose both ballads and art songs, an action to which

he had a perfect right when one considers that his object in singing at all was to attract an audience. Where he fell down was in languages, his German being very ordinary.

When Dr Barry turned his pianistic sights on Mark Hambourg he peppered the page with words like 'banging', 'crashing', 'bad playing', and 'depressing'. His review of a radio broadcast was just as caustic: he did praise Dawson's technical abilities but 'one would have preferred a more cultured selection of items. Hambourg was Hambourg, and I think we will let it go at that'.

But Peter Dawson and Mark Hambourg were not performing for the Dr Barrys of this world – those so musically educated that they had had the common touch knocked out of them – they had a broad-spectrum audience in mind, an audience which knew them from popular recordings. This tour was the most successful of all Dawson's tours both artistically and financially. In the rosy glow of retrospect he remembered that 'in spite of depressed times, the pair averaged £400 houses in 60 concerts in Australia and New Zealand'.[70] Hugo Larsen was so satisfied with his enterprise that he had already cabled the Gramophone Company on 8 July: 'Dawson Hambourg tour successful beyond expectation.'

Nan and Peter are met at Euston Station, London, on their return from their 1931 Australasian tour by Tom Noble (left) and others.

Post-Depression blues

'On our return voyage to England my wife and I between us won the daily sweep on the ship's run 56 times. That was an unusual series of sucesses, and because we sat at the captain's table our fellow passengers hinted at collusion,' Dawson told reporters when they arrived at Euston Station on 2 December 1931.[1] The trip from Perth had lasted some seven weeks. 'A gossipy Christmas letter from Capetown'[2] and the following yarn indicate that they had travelled home via South Africa and stopped off to perform: 'When Hambourg and I were giving a recital in South Africa on a very hot evening, Hambourg left the stage sweating after one bracket. I remarked to a native stagehand that playing piano was hard work to which the stagehand replied: "Yes boss, but did you ever try to lift one!".'[3]

During Dawson's absence EMI had overcome the vagaries of hiring halls for large orchestral works by converting No. 3 Abbey Road, St John's Wood into a 'studio on the scale and with the acoustics of a concert hall, with smaller studios and offices integrated'. The complex was officially opened by Sir Edward Elgar on 12 November 1931.[4] Dawson began recording at Abbey Road on 5 January 1932 with 'Bells and Hobbles', followed on 24 February by 'Song of Australia'.[5] Peter's mate, the South Australian tenor, Fred Williamson (1893–1992), had occasion to remember that recording session very well. He had just arrived in London; he was penniless; but by good fortune he met up with his famous compatriate the night before the recording and Peter insisted that Fred turn up at the studios next morning. When he arrived Peter told one of the chorus that he was not required that day, then gave his Adelaide mate the wink, and Fred stood in alongside some of the best studio singers in London.

It is a fair indication of the plight of performers at that time that the male choruses backing Dawson regularly included his old colleagues George Baker, Edward Halland, Walter Glynne, Stuart Robertson and Sydney

Coltham and the newcomer, Webster Booth. They backed some 'really fine marching songs':[6] 'El Abanico', 'Sons of the Brave', 'With Sword & Lance' and 'Punjaub March' — and a new recording of one of Dawson's favourite cycles, Stanford's *Songs of the Sea*.[7]

On 24 February, Dawson had also re-recorded 'I Travel The Road', this time with Lawrence Collingwood conducting. His old friend and mentor, George Byng, who had made the popular 1931 recording for the Australasian tour, had died while Dawson was away.[8] Little has been written about George Byng, yet for Dawson he was an unsung hero. An Irishman, he had started life as a violinist but came to prominence conducting theatre orchestras. He must have been about fifty-five when he joined the Gramophone Company. Between 1915–1931 he conducted more than a thousand titles for *HMV* and *Zonophone*, as well as making arrangements and supervising purely orchestral light music and band music. Fred Gaisberg, recalling successful G&S recordings, wrote:

> George Byng was our house conductor, whom we took from the old Alhambra Theatre, where for many years he conducted those elaborate ballets for which that house was famous in the nineties. Dear old George was steeped in the Gilbert & Sullivan tradition and was a meticulous drillmaster who rarely smiled.[9]

Earlier Byng had been associated with Edison and would have produced about thirty two-minute or four-minute cylinders with Dawson between 1910–12, but their finest collaborations were the Gramophone Company recordings of the 1920s. Although Byng conducted about 300 titles for Dawson, for most of them he received no credit on the label.

When Dawson sang his first BBC studio recital on 11 May 1932, accompanied by Gerald Moore, he had the opportunity to use serious material from the recent tour: 'Die Mainacht', 'Botschaft', 'Marins d'Islande', 'Le Manoir de Rosemonde', 'Hear me, ye winds and waves' (Handel), 'A Sea Gypsy' and 'King-fisher Blue'. However, listeners were not denied the perennial encores: 'I Travel the Road' and 'Boots' concluded the broadcast. Dawson swung from one artistic extreme to the other as demand arose. In the first week of June 1932 he was the main attraction at the Manchester Hippodrome;[10] but on 28 July he and Gerald Moore broadcast 'Adelaide', 'O liebliche Wangen', 'La Caravane', 'Chanson de la Touraine', 'Promenade à mule', 'Speak Music' and 'Rann of Exile'. On 15 November, accompanied by the BBC Symphony Orchestra, he opened with the noble 'Wachet Betet', followed by 'Largo al factotum'. He then slipped into nautical mode with Sanderson's 'Shipmates O' Mine' and no prizes for guessing the last two numbers.

In a broadcast shared with the pianist Arnaldo Tapia-Caballero in January 1933, Dawson concluded a recital of Schubert lieder with the première of a new McCall composition, 'The Pirate Goes West or Westward Ho!', an excellent ballad with considerable musical variety, far more complex than 'Boots'.[11] As the title suggests, it is a sea-faring song of the 'Give me sails and masts and spars, buccaneers and pirates bold' variety, lyrics by Lockwood Moore.

The cut and thrust of text development detailed in correspondence between Lockwood Moore and the publishers had left us with a conundrum: who exactly was Lockwood Moore? Was she the wife of Gerald Moore? In his memoirs Moore refers to only one wife, Enid, his English cousin whom he met in 1919 but did not marry until the 1940s. However, a letter from Swan & Co. dated 11 January 1933 is unambiguously addressed to 'Dear Mrs Gerald Moore'[12] and the writer signs off: 'With kindest wishes to you and to Mr Gerald Moore'. Dawson assigned the copyright of the lyrics to Gerald Moore and later wrote that Gerald Moore's 'first wife was a beaut Yank'.[13] Research shows that she was indeed his first wife, although omitted from Moore's biographies until after his death in 1987. In 1996 Joseph Cooper, relying on 'family information, personal knowledge', divulged that 'Moore had a previous marriage, in Canada in 1929, which lasted only three or four years and which ended in divorce.'[14]

Dawson's detailed diaries and his singular tidiness with his music suggests an ordered mind, but when it came to money: 'Hopeless businessman,' said Constance, 'Didn't know one penny from another as you might say. Anyone could hand him a sob story and he'd say, "Oh here's fifty for you." That was his whole trouble. If he had had a good business manager as singers do today he'd have been a millionaire.'[15] Despite a lucrative income over many years he was constantly borrowing from the Gramophone Company and had continuing problems over taxation. Much to his surprise and anguish, in February 1933 the Department of Inland Revenue pounced on him, claiming he had not declared the £4,000 he had received as a bonus in 1925. Dawson's argued that it was a non-taxable gift, but the tax inspectors insisted that it was a bonus for services rendered from 1904 to 1924 and back tax must therefore be paid pro-rata for those twenty years. Dawson dug his heels in. 'Peter Dawson vs Income Tax Inspector' dragged on for the next sixteen months.

Meanwhile, despite the risky experiences of 1913–14, Dawson signed for another tour of Australia on the back of the last one. This time it was with the Tait brothers, who had taken over J. C. Williamson Ltd.[16] The contract stipulated that, unless the parties mutually agreed to extend, the tour was to last four months from the first concert, to be not less than 40 concerts but with no more than four in any week.[17] Gross receipts per concert were set at a minimum of £200, of which Dawson would be paid one-third. This guaranteed him a substantial £66/13/4 gross per concert.[18] The last clause revealed that Dawson's associate artist was to be the 26-year old Chilean pianist, Arnaldo Tapia Caballero.[19]

The tour publicity machine went into in top gear. 'Old Father Thames' was recorded just in time to catch the Australian market.[20] The music publisher, Chappell, cashed in with two collections of favourite baritone songs, the *First* and *Second Peter Dawson Albums*. Dawson contributed a gossipy, optimistic article in the February *Australian Musical News*. 'Australians could be proud of the success of many other Australians in England,' he wrote. Foremost was the hero of the day, Don Bradman, 'the Victorian monarch of the MCC'; there were also Amy Johnson, the flying woman who was trying to break the London to Cape Town record; and Charles Kingsford-Smith, who had been knighted. This was Dawson's cue. 'As Kingsford-Smith encircled the world in his plane so somebody said my output in Gramophone records would encircle the world's crust', he modestly concluded.[21]

Originally the tour was to begin in Melbourne or Sydney but in fact it began in Perth on 15 April.[22] On 27 April 'the eminent bass-baritone' and his wife were greeted with customary affection in Adelaide, albeit with the photo and biography from the last tour. He was again 'welcomed by the Good Companions Society, a body of which he is world patron'; and on 28 April opened the 1933 football season at Unley Oval.[23] In Sydney he was welcomed by the RSL and promoted to Sergeant-Major. Though his army career had been negligible, his service became an important aspect of the way he wanted to be perceived. To be a returned soldier was proof that you had been prepared to make the ultimate sacrifice for your country, was proof that you proudly shared in egalitarian Australian mateship. Though his official rank had been 'Private', Dawson preferred to remember his time as 'Acting-Sergeant', as reported in the RSL newspaper, *Reveille*, during the 1931 tour:

> On enlisting in the AIF in Brisbane, he was handed out a suit of dungarees, and started his soldiering days at the potato tub. However, in due course he rose to the rank of sergeant, and took 250 troops on the train journey between Brisbane and Sydney without a single casualty – that he achieved by withholding their pay.[24]

An immaculate Peter Dawson at the Valley State School, Brisbane, on 18 May, 1933, teaching students how to sing Carl Linger's anthem 'Song of Australia'. Eddie Cahill is at the piano.

However, 'At a smoke night on July 11' [1933] the Sydney RSL President 'divulged' that Dawson had risen 'from potato peeler to sergeant-major in the AIF'. There is no explanation for the promotion. It could well have been a slip of the tongue, yet Dawson used it consistently from 1933 onwards.

The programmes for this tour stuck closely to the successful formula of the previous tour. The critics found no fault, one saying he was 'deliberately doing fine work in the musical education of those who regard "Drum Majors" and "Floral Dances" as fine songs', another that 'he [could] afford to disregard their preferences and make them listen to a lot of good music'. At the same time it was admitted that Dawson 'had the knack of bringing to the feeblest of musical twaddle such a wealth of understanding and vocal address as to make it almost endurable to people who prefer good music, and enormously satisfying to those who don't'.[25] The advertisers had no such quibbles. *HMV* promoted the 'new song' 'Old Father Thames', and the old favourites, 'Room for the Factotum', 'Cobbler's Song', 'The Floral Dance', 'I Travel the Road' and 'Boots'. The most popular can be judged from the State Savings Bank of Victoria's advertisement: 'You need more than "Boots" When You "Travel the Road".'

Despite this ostensibly enthusiastic welcome, something must have stuck in Dawson's craw because in August he abruptly ended the tour in Melbourne. There is no clear explanation: the Depression might have affected audience attendances; the Tait brothers, experienced concert managers but a feisty bunch, might have been too pragmatic or interfering; the young pianist might have been less of a drawcard than the inimitable Mark Hambourg.[26] Whatever the reason, on 16 August Dawson sent a letter on elegant Hotel Windsor notepaper to 'Mess' J&N Tait, Comedy Theatre, Melbourne' – a block away:

> In accordance with the Contract existing between us the time limit expired yesterday (August 15th). At the close of the Four Concerts to take place at the Kings Theatre Melbourne on August 19th, 22nd, 24th, & 26th respectively I have decided to discontinue the present tour.

If trouble had been simmering Claude Kingston, the concert manager, was unaware of it. He rushed round to the hotel but Dawson refused to see him. Dawson remained adamant: this was the end of the tour.[27]

On 24 August Dawson wrote to the Australian composer, Edith Harrhy

(1893-1969), advising her that he had featured her song, 'The Mallee Root' in some concerts and added that: 'I have to get back to Sydney for a sound picture.' While we could find no evidence that a film eventuated, it is a possible explanation for the blunt conclusion of the tour.[28] He did, however, sing a Grand Charity Concert on 9 September, but not for the Taits. The programme exuded all the old flair; in particular, patrons were given a choice of an amazing 45 possible encores:

Peter Dawson, according to requests, will choose his encores from the following songs:-

1. O Ruddier than the Cherry (Handel)
2. Largo al Factotum (Rossini)
3. The Glory of the Sea (Sanderson)
4. Garden of Allah (Marshall)
5. Trumpeter (Dix)
6. Shipmates o' Mine (Squire)
7. Glorious Devon (German)
8. Cobbler's Song (Chu Chin Chow)
9. Song of the Highway (May)
10. Border Ballad (Cowen)
11. Chip of the Old Block (Squire)
12. Admiral's Yarn (Ruben)
13. Green Hills o' Somerset (Coates)
14. If I Were King (Eyton)

15. Kingfisher Blue (Finden)
16. Lute Player (Allitson)

17. Ole Man River (Leoncavallo)
18. Santa Barbara (Russell)

19. Banjo Song (Homer)

20. Who is Sylvia (Schubert)

21. Erl King (Schubert)

22. Mandalay (Hedgcock)

23. I Travel the Road (Thayer)
24. Floral Dance (Moss)
25. Bandolero (Stuart)
26. Love Could I Only Tell Thee (Capel)
27. There is a Green Hill (Gounod)
28. O Star of Eve (Wagner)
29. Droop not Young Lover (Handel)
30. Hear Me, Ye Winds (Handel)
31. Lake Isle of Innisfree Love (Travers)
32. An Old Garden (Herbert)
33. The Kerry Dance (Molloy)
34. Bonnie Earl o' Moray (Hope Temple)
35. The Kerry Dance (Molloy)
36. The Bonny Earl o' Moray (Lawson)

Boots; Shipmates; Cobbler's Song; Drum Major; Rolling Down to Rio; Kingfisher Blue; Danny Deever; Trumpeter; Trees.[29]

Back in London Dawson put a positive spin on the tour, although he did admit that record sales had been hit badly. This was confirmed by an internal EMI memo, '…partly due to broadcasting, partly due to general business conditions', Peter Dawson's Australian sales had dropped from 12–14% of his English sales to 7–9%. The memo concluded: 'Dawson's recent Australian tour was not nearly so successful as previous one with Mark Hambourg.'[30]

In the light of future developments this memo was ominous. While Dawson sought to blame the economy, the ramifications were much wider: the power and influence of the United States was growing at the expense of Britain. Taste in popular music was changing: American music, with its pervasive Negro rhythms, was invading Europe and gradually replacing the Dawson-style English ballads. In retrospect, the 1931 tour had been his finest hour. Before long there would be questions about the appropriateness of his repertoire, his stamina, his impending retirement. However, Dawson could only continue to play the cards in his hand as best he could. On 26 October friends joined Peter and Nan at Frascati's to celebrate their return;[31] on Sunday 12 November Dawson sang his only concert with the fabulous Luisa Tetrazzini: her 'Farewell Concert' at the Royal Albert Hall.[32]

During his absence the taxation saga had been put on hold but no sooner was he back in London than he was embroiled in it again. The revenue department had changed tack: instead of spreading £4,000 retrospectively over twenty years it had added it to the years 1925–30. Finally, in June 1934, Dawson settled by paying back tax at four shillings in the pound, plus compound interest, a claim of more than £800.[33]

Another controversy arose when he began negotiating his new recording contract. He could reasonably have expected his agreement to be renewed on the old terms at least, because *HMV* catalogues carried over 200 entries bearing his name: 174 solo titles and a myriad of ensemble entries. But the Depression had drawn an economic line in the sand: *HMV* sales in 1933 were less than those of the Gramophone & Typewriter Company in 1907. This downward spiral had had its inevitable effect on all recording artists.[34] Dawson's royalty losses had been accumulating under his contract for some time:

	10in.	12in.	£ Royalty Earned
30/31	158,417	104,453	2,364/8/11
31/32	138,521	43,617	1,348/7/1
32/33	100,257	35,587	1,017/13/4
	397,195	183,657	£4,730/9/4

We have already shown that the Gramophone Company needed to sell the equivalent of 1.2 million *Plum* label records to recover their guarantee: Dawson's total sales were only 580,852. As his guaranteed income was £7,750, the company had lost £3,019/10/8, which led to a new offer on dramatically reduced terms. Faced with the facts, Dawson said he would sign up with the opposition and take his good name with him. The directors were forced to compromise:

> Having regard to the prestige and wide popularity still enjoyed by Peter Dawson, and the fact that, for recording and broadcasting purposes, his voice and style are as effective as ever, it is considered advisable to make a new contract with the artiste on the above terms rather than lose his services to a competitive company.[35]

The above terms were a guaranteed £1,250 per annum for three years, and a write-off of the unearned balance as at 31 December 1933.[36] At one blow Dawson's contract was reduced by one-third. His pride might have been hurt but he was also realistic – at least he did not have to work off the £3,000 loss. On 14 December he grudgingly signed the new contract – but for two years, not three.

The Gramophone Company did not intend to squander its money either, so Dawson was again given anything and everything to sing. From this period came Allison's 'Tramping Through The Countryside' (one of his own compositions); he also recorded the nightmarish duet, 'Watchman, What of the Night' – with himself; re-recorded his grand old 'The Lute Player' and yet another version of 'The Floral Dance': 'the original must have sold in thousands and this new one is magnificent ... the sheer artistry is overwhelming'. 'Trees' was touted as 'one of the best Dawson has made in a long time and should have a big sale'. On the flip side was Alba Rizzi's 'Little Prayer I Love', her new setting of the old Saxon prayer, 'God be in thy head and in thy understanding', for which Dawson developed a great affection. It became a firm favourite in future programmes, and in compliance with the composer's last wish he sang it at her graveside in April 1950.[37]

Dawson claimed that he learned a salutary lesson about broadcasting German lieder in his first BBC broadcast. Immediately after, his brother-in-law had complained they were the wrong songs for a Peter Dawson audience; but Dawson countered: 'I wanted to show I was capable of singing these beautiful German songs, and I must say I enjoyed singing them'. He cited this programme as: 'Sei mir gegrüsst', 'Die Mainacht' 'Botschaft', 'Blinde

Kuh' (Brahms) and 'Du bist so jung' (Wolff). In fact, 'Die Mainacht' and 'Botschaft' were included in his first studio recital (5 May 1932) but 'Blinde Kuh' and 'Du bist so jung' do not appear in any broadcast programmes.[38] The programme in question was actually on 7 October 1934.

Die Mainacht (The May-Night)	Brahms
Botschaft (The Message)	Brahms
Sei mir gegrüsst (Greetings)	Schubert
Am Meer (By the Sea)	Schubert
Wood Magic	Martin Shaw
Lights Out	Ivor Gurney

In *Once a Jolly Swagman*, J.D. Vose embellished on the reprimand:

> Artistically, it was successful and deeply satisfying to Peter. The B.B.C. postbag was not, however, a source of comfort. Such letters as 'What the devil is Peter Dawson doing singing German rubbish!'; 'Has Dawson lost his head? What about the good old ballads of the open road? I don't even mind a bit of opera if it's got a good tune to it, but this German stuff is beyond my scope'; 'Leave German to the Germans, I say, and let's have "Boots" and the rest of 'em.'[39]

Vose argued that Peter had to 'come to terms with the fact that he was branded as a "Popular" singer. It was a bitter pill but he knew in his heart that he had to swallow it.' Whether it was such a bitter pill is questionable but Dawson did drop these songs from his repertoire and never recorded them. Industry disc sales had dropped 90 per cent in three years. Dawson was in need of a new 'Floral Dance', not critics' bouquets.

Despite the parlous state of the economy, Dawson was still in demand for concerts. From 'The Tenth Finchley Group Annual Concert on Friday May 4th 1934' we become aware that he was an active Rover Scout. The final item was a selection by Rover Scout Peter Dawson accompanied by Rover Scout Herbert Dawson.[40] A. W. Sharpe of Newcastle-under-Lyme, who was 'Rover Scout Leader when Peter Dawson was enrolled' remembered that 'Bertie Dawson was a close friend but not a relative, who, when I knew him, was organist of St Margaret's, Westminster'. D. S. A. Gardner of New Milton, who was twelve at the time, confirmed this piece of trivia:

> Our scout group was the 10th Finchley Scottish Scouts. Peter Dawson looked a fine figure in his Gordon kilt and scout uniform and as you can imagine was a tremendous draw at our annual scout concert ... he

Dawson as a wandering vagabond in a British Pathé Picture musical short made to promote his 1934 HMV recording of 'The Winding Road' (Arale & Andrews).

and the Group Scout master acted a competition to see who could sing the lowest note, each going down the scale one by one. You can guess who won.[41]

Dawson's engagements continued to swing from one extreme to the other: the *Grand Theatre Derby* poster for the week beginning 10 September 1934 ('at enormous expense') was infinitely more flamboyant than the modest Scout programme. The poster was three feet long and nine inches wide (90 x 22.5 cm), in bold black and red, with 'Peter Dawson' in by far the largest print.

Back in London the 62-year old composer Herman Lohr heard Peter at the Proms.[42] 'My dear Dawson,' he wrote,

> I have just got back from The Albert Hall, where I had the great pleasure of hearing you sing those two songs of mine – 'The Grey Home' was beautifully given – see, how truly they loved it! – You held on that end as I like it – & 'The Song You Sang' – Well! Sube-nous. That's the first time I've heard it as I intended it – Thanks for your top note there too – but hold it for ever !!

At the beginning of 1935 Peter and Nan sent out invitations to a cocktail party 'prior to their South African Tour':

> We haven't enough chairs to seat
> But plenty of stuff to eat
> So come along chums
> If no room for your elbows
> There's plenty of room for your feet.[43]

The tour, arranged by Bowker Andrews Concert Direction, was scheduled from 19 February to 19 March in Cape Town, Johannesburg, Pretoria, Bloemfontein, Durban, Pietermaritzburg, East London and Port Elizabeth.[44] The reception proved so good that the tour was extended for another three weeks and another ten concerts. Dawson was billed as the 'World's Greatest Baritone and Personality Singer'; his faithful accompanist, Hubert Greenslade, was named in very small type; his associate artist was simply called Niedzielski.

When Dawson was interviewed for *The Natal Mercury* after the Durban concert of 9 March, the reporter enthused: 'It is doubtful if anyone has enjoyed such a reception as this singer … he is as delightful in company as he is on the concert platform'. Dawson is quoted as saying: 'Twenty, or even 10 years ago good music was regarded as "high brow" or "tabu" at music-halls. A few years ago, however, I sang at the Palladium, heading the bill in a variety programme, and I have never had a more attentive audience. Years ago the same audience would have given me the bird...' – and much more in this vein. The article also reveals that: 'the palm for Thursday night's concert must go to Stanislas de Niedzielski, the brilliant young Polish pianist, who stepped into the breach when Peter Dawson sensibly applied the soft pedal to his voice, when he was affected by a slight cold.'

Dawson kept a copy of his earnings. The nett receipts ranged from £590/17/4 in Johannesburg to a modest £15/16/11 in Brakpan on 2 April. The total nett receipts were £3,663/10/10 of which Dawson's share was one third, from which he had to subtract the booking commission of £105/10/6. So he netted £1,115/13/1 – nearly as much his recording guarantee for a whole year.[45] The wild fluctuations in receipts reflect vastly different audience attendances and expectations. Dawson had stuck to his old programme formula: serious classics tapering gradually to popular numbers. But as Nan complained that 'in many other places my husband had been asked for songs of a lower standard musically than those he had prepared,' provincial audiences had probably expected him to stick to gramophone favourites.

In later life Dawson wrote that 'singers must always remain non-political' and indeed he had sung on both sides of the political fence in Ireland.[46] But in 1932 he and Nan had committed themselves to the Conservative cause by joining the Imperial Chapter of the Primrose League.[47] As they were now accepted by the circles around the British Prime Minister, Stanley Baldwin, Dawson responded as only he could: by setting the 'Patriotic Song', 'We'll Stand by the Primrose League' to words by the Dowager Countess of Jersey.

In May 1935, about the time King George V celebrated the twenty-fifth anniversary of his accession to the throne, Dawson was co-opted a member of the Primrose League Grand Council 1935-36.[48] We may assume that Peter and Nan attended an anniversary reception, because the Prince of Wales had autographed Dawson's Jubilee Procession programme.[49] As part of these Jubilee festivities, Dawson sang in the Primrose League concert at the Royal Albert Hall and also starred in the BBC *Jubilee Gala* on 11 May, where he sang Besly's 'England' and Edward German's 'Glorious Devon'; and kipling along behind them, 'Boots'.

By now, Dawson was in his fifties. Although his concerts still attracted large audiences, he was becoming a liability to the Gramophone Company because his large disc royalties were excessive for the depressed record market. Yet this had to be balanced against his publicity value. Newspapers would attach any sort of nonsense to his name. In December 1933, for example, the *Star* carried an article with photo: 'Peter Dawson on carpentry for women';[50] the *Daily Sketch* offered 'Things I Hate by Peter Dawson'[51] and a story about Dawson replacing the dead pony of a disabled ex-serviceman horse-and-cart man. 'I reckon you're a slap-up gent – one o' the proper ones,' exclaimed the grateful Robert Cooper.[52] As Dawson had recorded 'Dark-Haired Marie' in April 1935 the *Daily Express* even sneaked his name into the case of Alma Rattenbury, the composer, who was on trial for murder.[53] At the end of the year he earned a couple more lines: 'Mr. Peter Dawson, the singer, was fined ten shillings at Marylebone for failing to conform to traffic signals at Orchard-street.' Any publicity is better than none!

The silly season was far from over: the recording industry was still trying every ploy to revive its sales. In September 1935, 'Peter Dawson and Friends' – consisting of a male quartet and the dapper English comedian, Leonard Henry, acting as a Jeeves-style butler – recorded *Peter Dawson's Christmas Party*. The only Christmas number was 'Good King Wenceslas': the rest was a curious muddle, which included 'Mai Pahi Aipo', the 'Gendarmes' Duet' and Dawson fooling around on tin whistle and mouth organ. Though not memorable, this recording is remembered because here he revealed that he was the mythical J. P. McCall. The following November he could be heard singing 'Oranges and Lemons', 'Old King Cole' and 'A Frog He Would A-Wooing Go' on *Uncle Peter's Children's Party*.

Such nonsense did not augur well for the upcoming contract negotiations.[54] A review of earnings may well have been routine for all recording artists, but questioning Peter Dawson's contract was like touching a taboo. However, the cost-cutters had already rolled up their sleeves. They had produced tables and graphs that again proved he was 'earning about half his guaranteed advance'. Officially the 'unearned' amount from the previous contract had been buried, but they dug it up again, showing that since 1930 the company had paid him £9,000, and he had earned only £5,500. Negotiations were torrid and finally provoked a major confrontation over royalties for the broadcast of recordings.[55]

As early as August 1927 the British Broadcasting Company had been broadcasting a daily *Gramophone Hour*. In April 1933 'a much more enlightened policy of two hours a day from any one station' had been agreed with the gramophone industry – for which it would receive a royalty for every record played.[56] Artists received nothing. Dawson had resented this practice for a long time but now he loudly blamed radio for loss of sales on his recordings and demanded redress. Memo 23 November: 'he insists that the broadcasting fees should be mentioned'; memo 5 December: 'refused to sign; objects to broadcast clause'. When agreement was finally reached on 18 December; broadcasting royalties were included in the new two-year contract. Although the new contract was expressed differently, his total income had not changed. Peter had won the day.[57] Today, we take for granted performance contracts, percentages for residuals or royalties for repeats of performances; but we should not forget our debt to artists like Peter Dawson, who had to fight for them.

George V died on 20 January 1936. Edward VIII reigned from 20 January until 11 December, when he relinquished the throne in favour of marriage to the divorced American, Mrs Wallis Simpson. His abdication forced the unwilling accession of his quiet brother Albert, who became George VI, and was destined to face the mounting turmoil in Europe. On 13 October 1936 Peter Dawson, backed by the Wireless Singers Quartet, had recorded a pantheon of 'magnificently sung' patriotic songs, many of them still favourites: 'Hearts of Oak', 'We are the Boys of the Old Brigade', 'Soldiers of the King', 'Private Tommy Atkins', 'The British Grenadiers', 'Red, White and Blue', 'The Lads in Navy Blue', 'Here's a Health unto His Majesty' and 'Rule Britannia'. This recording was no doubt intended to honour the coronation of Edward VIII but was held over to celebrate the coronation of George VI.

In a further effort to increase sales, the Gramophone Company hit on the idea of using their patriarch to record hillbilly songs, cowboy songs and tin-pan alley pops, many from current films. This crop included 'We Saw The Sea', 'There'll Be No South' and 'Saddle Your Blues To A Wild Mustang', 'With A Shillelagh Under Me Arm' and Harry Richman's rollicking showstopper 'We All Go Rollin' Along'. One faithful reviewer still believed that 'Mr Dawson could not make a dull record if he tried'; but when 'There's A Bridle Hanging On The Wall' appeared on the reverse of the ballad, 'Song of the Grateful Heart', another gave up: '"Song of the Grateful Heart" – Here is hope; "There's a bridle hanging on the wall" – Here is despair.'[58] 'I received hundreds of letters abusing me for singing such songs', wrote Peter,[59] but he soon 'emerged unscathed from the prairie' with 'Mother o' Mine', 'Danny Deever', 'Hybrias the Cretan', and two new McCall ballads, 'The Jolly Roger' and 'Fret-Foot'.

But Dawson's sales had plateaued. He was now in direct competition with popular American artists:[60] in the record catalogues the new musical categories, 'Swing' and 'Crooner', appeared. The trend was reflected in an Australian commercial radio poll: the tenor Richard Crooks, who was touring

Australia, received by far the greatest number of votes; next came Richard Tauber, Gladys Moncrieff, Gracie Fields, Peter Dawson, Paul Robeson and Nelson Eddy; Bing Crosby, 'the founder of the crooning craze', was eighth. Older women voted for 'Our Glad' or 'Gracie'; older men voted for Peter Dawson; and the young people voted for Bing.[61]

In June 1936 Peter and Nan set out by car on an extensive tour of England and Scotland. Dawson's meticulous diary is headed: 'Round Tour: 2223 miles by road 8th – 20th'. [62] They drove up to Bowness, through the Lake District and over to Edinburgh, they circled Scotland and returned via Harrogate. On the way to Edinburgh the 'run-away couple' got 'married' at the traditional trysting place:

Marriage Certificate
Gretna Green 10th June 1936.
Peter Dawson & Ann Mortimer Noble of Ealing Middlesex.
Witnesses: William Trapp of Scrubs Lane
Charlie Olsen of Norway[63]

BBC television broadcasting began in England on 26 August 1936: 'From Aug 26 until Sept 5 1936 high definition Television programmes, specially arranged for reception at Radiolympia were transmitted from BBC Television station at Alexandra Palace, London, on week days.' Two days later, on 28 August, Peter Dawson was the first live performer.[64] Constance remembered the occasion: 'Peter actually opened it. He sang into a sort of mike – but you could see him, singing – in full evening dress – I've forgotten what song he sang then – we just stood and listened.'

Between August 1936 and October 1937 Dawson attempted to arrange a concert tour of the United States and the Gramophone Company generously did whatever it could to help. The American saga began with an optimistic exchange of programmes, photographs and biographies. As the right to record for American Victor was written into Dawson's contract the Gramophone Company executives assumed that he was featured in Victor's catalogue. But it turned out that 'we cannot trace that the Victor Company have ever listed Peter Dawson in the USA. All they have done is to import pressings of his various records to a total of about 200 a year average.'[65] Dawson was virtually unknown there. In the end his attempt to arrange a tour was abortive. America had its own genuine cowboy and hillbilly singers and film music belonged to the new breed of microphone singers. Whether Dawson would have had a chance before World War I is a matter of conjecture; now it was far too late.

Such attempts to keep a career buoyant were and are simply part and parcel of any performer's life. Another might have succumbed to despondency, but not our ebullient hero. At the invitation of old Palladium friends, including Flanagan & Allen – those scallywags from the 'Boots' episode – Dawson took part in a motion picture, *O-Kay for Sound*, at the beginning of 1937. *Halliwell's Film Guide* summarises the movie as: 'The Crazy Gang runs amok in a film Studio. Patchy farce'. However, in a big, flag-waving production number, 'The Fleet's Not In Port Very Long', Dawson had acquitted himself quite well.[66] Around the end of 1937 he appeared in another film, *Chips*, which used the 3rd Poole Sea Scouts, in which 'Peter Dawson (Salty Sam) hands two Sea Scouts a clue leading to the discovery of the place where the smugglers imprisoned Chips.' Of course, he sang with the boys who joined in the chorus of J. P. McCall's 'Song of Salty Sam'.[67]

The general perception of HMV as a company was one of dignity and good taste. Great pride was taken in their mandate 'By Appointment to His Majesty' and the extensive annual catalogue contained sections titled 'Connoisseur', 'Classical Societies' and 'Historic Records'. This 'serious' side of the catalogue was subsidised by the popular music. With a foot in both camps, Dawson had dominated the catalogue for two decades, 1919–1939. As sales went down, the hype went up: publicity – initiated by the Gramophone Company or by the singer himself – never stopped. But the public eye was one thing, the balance-sheet another: long before he signed his next contract, internal forces were being marshalled against him.

Despite their undoubted goodwill HMV's directors could not ignore the facts: under the current contract Peter Dawson sales were 22,082 10in. *Plum* at fivepence plus 3,589 12in. *Plum* at 1/3; a miserable total of £694 against costs of £3,117, giving a loss of £2,423. The conclusion was inevitable: 'As it is becoming increasingly difficult to find suitable repertoire for Dawson, the renewal of his contract is not recommended.' However, the directors did make him an offer – at less than half the current contract. His reaction was predictable: 'In the circumstances I have decided to cut the painter and give recording a rest', he wrote. A few days later he relented: in March a truculent Peter Dawson finally signed the contract of 27 January 1938, which obliged the company to pay him for 20 titles at £25 each, without any obligation to make the recordings or issue them.[68]

At the same time, despite the dispute, the Gramophone Company loaned Dawson another £500 to help him out of financial difficulty.[69] But further financial problems were in the offing: like an avenging Fury, the Taxation Department descended on him again. The Inspector of Taxes was of the

Scenes from

"CHIPS"

THAT WILL COME TO LIFE ON THE SCREEN

HEAR PETER DAWSON SING
THIS ROUSING SONG

in

"CHIPS"

THE ONLY WAY TO MAKE SURE OF
SEEING THE PICTURE IS TO—

ASK YOUR CINEMA MANAGER TO SHOW IT

Send the names of your local cinemas where you have asked for " Chips " and receive details of the Great Scout Competition. Postcards should be addressed to " Music," British Fine Arts Pictures Ltd., 25 Haymarket, London, S.W.1.

Mutual promotion for the movie and the Boy Scouts with the *Chips* sheet music. The film's theme song was Rover Peter Dawson's own composition, 'The Sea is the Life for Me'.

opinion that the £1,500 advance on royalties against his 1935 contract could not be spread over the two years 1935–37, but related only to the 1935-36 return.[70] The matter went to court. Dawson lost his case in November. Newspaper headlines proclaimed: 'Income-tax claim against Mr. Peter Dawson' (*The Times*); 'Peter Dawson must pay tax on £1,500' (*Daily Telegraph*); 'A Tax On His Voice' (*News-Chronicle*).[71]

During the final throes of this turmoil Dawson had recorded two songs which eventually made rocketing sales. As they were not released for six months, the company probably recorded them to pacify Dawson and without much faith in their market value. These two recordings were 'Waiata Poi' ('Little ball on end of string') and 'Waltzing Matilda', recorded on 3 March 1938. The initial reception was indeed rather cool: Dawson wrote that the reaction of the EMI Manager in Sydney to the matrix of 'Waltzing Matilda' was a brusque: 'don't send me any more of that sort of rubbish!'[72] The English review merely glossed over 'Waltzing Matilda' and dismissed 'Waiata Poi' as 'exceedingly noisy … [the] general racket not mitigated by the exuberance of the chorus'.

Exceedingly noisy they were. As Dawson tells the tale, four Maori singers were to sing the chorus, but at 11am the recording equipment broke down, so the manager told the singers to come back at three o'clock, which they did – but after a liquid lunch. The inebriated Maoris were off key and their singing was wild – but the effect was marvellous.[73] Nice yarn, Peter, but not backed up by the recording ledger. 'Waiata Poi' was recorded in Abbey Road Studio No.2; the conductor was Walther Goehr, the chorus was the BBC Male Voice Quartet.

'Waltzing Matilda' was recorded on the same day as 'Waiata Poi'; same chorus, no slurring of diction. As it is now so well known it is hard to believe that 'Waltzing Matilda' became popular only during World War II. It was first recorded in London in 1927 by the tenor John Collinson, but sales were abysmal. The next recording, by Colin Crane in Sydney in 1930, fared better and an April 1937 recording by a British group, the Hill Billies, was moderately successful; but it was Dawson who guaranteed the world-wide popularity of 'Waltzing Matilda'. [74]

The accepted wisdom of the origins of 'Waltzing Matilda', as reported in newspapers covering the centenary of its première, was that 'Banjo' Paterson wrote 'his catchy lyric at Dagworth Station' near Winton, Queensland. A fellow guest, Christina Macpherson, then set the words to an old Scottish brass-band melody, which she had heard at a race meeting at Warrnambool.

Paterson did not regard his poem as a very great literary achievement but he did like the little Scottish tune. Winton tradition holds that 'Waltzing Matilda' was first sung at the local pub on 6 April 1895. True or not, the haunted waterhole has been significant for Winton tourism.[75]

Other sources, however, say that the tune was edited by Marie Cowan (1855–1919) for the *Billy Tea* advertisement made by the Inglis Tea Company of Victoria.[76] This fits with Dawson's own 'authentic version', based on an extract from Thomas Wood's *Cobbers* used in the preface to the music he recorded.[77] Marie Cowan, he writes, had heard an old British Army marching tune at Warrnambool, Victoria 'and played it over on her piano; 'Banjo' Paterson was struck by its rhythm, and in a few hours they were collaborating in the setting of words to the tune'. There is no clear explanation for these differing versions. Dawson appears to have confused Warrnambool in Victoria with Warrnambool Downs, which is close to Winton. But the debate does not end there: the origins of the tune have been questioned and there is no consensus on whether both Christina Macpherson and Marie Cowan used the same tune. Australians like the vision of their most loved song having been written in the outback, but it might well have been cobbled together by Banjo Paterson and Marie Cowan when they both lived in Sydney. Whatever the background, it is the Marie Cowan version that we know, and more significantly, it was Peter Dawson's 1938 recording which made 'Waltzing Matilda' famous.

There had been a hiatus in Dawson's BBC television engagements because a squabble about fees had arisen after his original appearance in 1936. He stubbornly insisted on his radio broadcast fee of 49 guineas. The contretemps was not resolved until he accepted 25 guineas for BBC TV's *Music Makers* on 25 May 1938.[78] When he returned to Australia in 1939 interviewers were agog to hear his opinion of this new medium. His comments were not sanguine: motion pictures were losing customers, the plight of performers was worsening, and young aspirants would have a battle to survive because there was 'only room for a few supreme artists at the top'. Personally, it had been the 'most awful experience he had ever suffered':

> You are being photographed and at the same time have to be letter
> perfect, conscious the whole time of glaring lights and many technicians
> on all fours around you. The heat is enough to boil you. The band is
> a little distance away, but the conductor cannot hear you, and has to rely
> on lip-reading. It is dreadful, and I hope I do not have to go through
> it again.[79]

Music Makers was his last BBC engagement: even radio contacts dried up.
Until he left for Australia in April 1939 Dawson relied principally on forays
into the far-flung corners of England, Wales and Scotland, where he took
the opportunity to introduce three new settings of J. Francis Barron lyrics
by J. P. McCall: 'Old Kettledrum', 'Fret-foot' and 'The 'Prentice Lads o'
Cheap'.[80] Because Dawson tailor-made the songs for himself they provide
a further insight into his musical taste and vocal competence. Clearly he still
liked a good story set to a good tune. The artistic horizon was not set too
high, the text not too poetic. 'Old Kettledrum' was a military song, 'Fret-
foot' a sea-faring song, 'The 'Prentice Lads' a light-hearted peasant-to-peer
song. All were in simple keys, within similar ranges (low G – high F), in
simple four-square rhythms. The lyrics of each story were in straightforward syllabic settings introduced by a wisp of melody.[81]

The inner title page of 'Old Kettledrum' carries this note from 'J. F. B.
(Late 'Queens' Bays')': 'A small and inadequate tribute to that fast disappear-
ing body of four-legged veterans, and to one companionable old troop-
horse in particular!' In this ballad, the gun-carriage horse personifies mateship
welded in war. The nostalgic singer, growing old and feeling neglected himself, hopes that his old comrade is receiving better treatment for the sacri-
fices he made for his country. 'Fret-foot' has some musical similarities to
'Westward Ho!' but on the whole it is much more direct. With a touch of
Mandalay sentiment, the singer watches ships at Stepney and dreams of the
sea, of palm-lined shores, 'brown shapen shoulders of maidens of Mom-
basa' and 'the Peter at the fore with the square of blue a-showing'. This was
a lively number which allowed Dawson to change vocal character several
times; but he could change character even more in 'The 'Prentice Lads o'
Cheap'. Using a continuous melodious patter it follows an East End apprentice working his way to the top of the social ladder. We can imagine
Dawson adopting various poses and vocal qualities as the lively mercer
dances, marries, grows 'middle-aged and staid' until:

> Then a shiny pate and a portly gait
> With a shrew of a wife to keep, sirs!
> And the Wig and the Chair of a plump Lord Mayor,
> For your 'prentice lad o' Cheap, sirs!
> For your 'prentice lad o' [top f] Cheap, sirs!

A programme for 1 March 1939 – one of his last provincial concerts
before his return to Australia – contains a surprising number of Peter
Dawson's compositions under various pseudonyms: 'The Three Souls' and

'Westward Ho!' (J. P. McCall), 'Heart o' the Romany Rye' (Charles Weber), 'The Dreamer' (Evelyn Bird).[82] In his memoirs Dawson also admits to 'Peter Allison', 'Denton Toms', 'Charles Webber', 'Arnold Flint', 'Gilbert Munday', 'Geoffrey Baxter', and 'Alison Miller'. We were able to find Peter Allison, 'Tramping Through the Country Side' (1934); the signature 'Arnold Flint January 1939' on a clean copy of the setting of Hugo Bolton's 'The Soul of a Ship', and a manuscript of 'Song of the Road' signed 'Gilbert Munday January 1939'. The signature, 'Denton Toms February 1939', appeared on a manuscript of 'The Chant of Bacchus', and both Charles Webber and Charles Weber signed 'Heart o' the Romany Rye' on 'April 5th 1938'.[83] As Dawson also wrote songs under his own name, the reason for the use of these *noms-de-plume* is elusive. Perhaps he felt a programme looked better with a variety of composers, or thought that being a composer would jeopardise his fame as a singer; perhaps it had a bearing on royalties. But most likely it was merely an outlet for his teasing humour.

As things were getting tough in England, Dawson reasoned that he might be better off in Australia – especially if someone would ask him back. In 1939 he let it be known that the Australian Broadcasting Commission had been chasing him for a tour. ABC files, however, reveal that an agent acting for him had contacted the relatively new Australian Broadcasting Commission as early as 15 June 1936: 'Have had several talks with Dawson in regard to a tour through America and Canada next year. D. has much more to offer than just his grand and inimitable repertoire of ballads. He is still the Unquestioned Ballad singer and singer to and of the people.'

In 1936 the ABC was still in swaddling clothes. 'Licensed' radio had been established in November 1923; the first of the commercial radio stations – those that earned their income from advertising – began broadcasting in January 1925. In 1932 the Australian Government followed the motherland in setting up an independent, national radio broadcaster. The Australian Broadcasting Commission soon began establishing an orchestra in each state. In Peter Dawson's home state, 'when the depression reached its nadir in 1931, musical life in South Australia was hit particularly hard' and did not recover until the Australian Broadcasting Commission formed an orchestra there in 1934. The influence of the ABC on the development of serious music in Australia has been significant. Studio recitals and orchestral performances by local and overseas artists activated a musical culture that was singularly fruitful.

When Charles Moses, general manager of the ABC, approached Dawson in 1938 a new chapter in Dawson's life began. Charles Moses, 'tall, powerful, handsome, charming and English', ex-soldier, ex-car salesman, ex-federal talks organiser of the ABC, was appointed general manager on 30 October 1935.[84] He was a strong man physically – 'a champion axeman'[85] – and equally strong and ambitious as chief executive. He was an excellent administrator: he built the ABC from its infant beginnings in radio and the development of its orchestras to the introduction of television and the ABC's partnership in the drive to build the Sydney Opera House.

Moses instituted a strictly centralised administrative hierarchy into the ABC. In the case of serious music, an idea was *recommended* by the federal director of music – Peter's old friend, the composer, William (W. G.) James. It was then *endorsed* by the federal controller of programmes – Dr Keith Barry, organist and critic, (who as a reviewer had already shown little respect for Dawson); and finally *approved* by the general manager. Everything passed over Charles Moses' desk.[86] With the exception of an absence on wartime service – November 1940 to February 1943 – it was Moses Dawson had to reckon with during his entire association with the commission.

Publicity from 1943 infers that the relationship between singer and entrepreneur was amicable and mutually rewarding. It was not. ABC files show that the relationship was in fact a torrid one.[87] Moses was an autocrat and had such a commanding personality that he was bound to run foul of other strong characters. Ken Inglis' *This is the ABC* (1983) gives an insight into Moses' administration, his political manoeuvring and his falling out with a number of personalities, including his mentor, ABC Chairman W. J. Cleary. Another who fell out was the bandleader, Jim Davidson (1902-1982), a feisty Sydney-sider, who, like Moses, had returned from the war with the rank of Lieutenant Colonel. He had expected Moses to fulfil a promise to appoint him 'Director of Variety' but Moses reneged. This gave rise to a long dispute over appointment procedures, which was finally settled by the Attorney-General, who sided with Moses.[88] In 1948 a bitter Davidson took up an appointment with the BBC as assistant head of variety and became director of light entertainment before retiring in 1964. In original form his autobiography was: 'Dedicated to my three Broadcasting Bosses: Sir Lindsay Wellington, who encouraged me in the BBC; Sir Charles Moses, who forced me out of the ABC; and Sir Talbot Duckmanton, who endeavoured to bring me back.'[89]

Peter Dawson's association with the ABC began on 17 June 1938, when his response to a 'letter just received from Mr Moses in reference to 1939' was tabled at a music sub-committee meeting chaired by William James.[90] Using his old ploy of letting others speak for him, Dawson had directed his demands via Ernest Lashmar, the Sydney manager of Chappell. As he intended to remain in Australia indefinitely Dawson required steamship fares only one way. For a comprehensive fee of £300 per week in English currency he would sing two radio performances and one public concert a week for a minimum of twelve weeks.[91] Predictably, the music sub-committee found Dawson's fee excessive. It countered with an offer: 'for public concerts £50 sterling per or 40% of the gross takings whichever is the larger'; studio: £25 sterling per appearance'. Alternatively, he could sing four public concerts a week at £50 per. Ernest Lashmar wisely withdrew and left negotiations to Moses, who made the offer directly to Dawson at the end of August. But again it was Lashmar who advised that Dawson would accept the offer, which suited the ABC because 'negotiations with John Charles Thomas for 1939 have fallen through.'[92]

The ABC decided that Dawson would be the ideal person to fulfil its commitment to country areas 'such as Kalgoorlie, Broken Hill, Wollongong, Lismore'. His tour would start in Perth in March so that he would not clash with the German soprano, Lotte Lehmann, on the eastern seaboard. Before sending off his final offer, Moses wrote: 'Our artists for 1939 do not include any Australians, and for this reason, apart from the fact he would undoubtably be a popular success, it is right that Peter Dawson should be engaged.'[93] The substantial offer of 31 solo recitals plus one orchestral concert within twelve-and-a-half weeks was contained in the fateful letter of 10 December 1938.

However, if the tour was to begin in March, the ABC needed a decision before the formal offer was either written or received, so the general manager cabled Dawson: CABLE IF ABLE COMMENCE TOUR SECOND WEEK MARCH. Peter replied: CAN COMMENCE TOUR SECOND WEEK MAY. Moses' responded on 8 December: MUST BEGIN SECOND WEEK MARCH OTHERWISE IMPOSSIBLE. Peter Dawson riposted: CAN ARRIVE SYDNEY MARCH SIXTEEN. Three weeks later Dawson sent another cable: ITINERARY IMPOSSIBLE. He had accepted a better offer: a tour of Australia with Greater Union Theatres.

While the cables were flying back and forth Dawson's impending EMI contract renewal was also being discussed. Only fourteen of the 20 titles from the last contract had been recorded and the financial wizards now proved to the directors that since 1930 the company had accumulated a loss of £6,877 on Dawson's account.[94] This revelation produced two divergent views: one, 'from a commercial point of view we are not particularly anxious to continue'; the other, 'we would not like Dawson to leave H.M.V. at the present time'.[95] In the event on 21 April, a few days before the Dawsons finally left for Australia, Peter signed a contract for £300 – for 12 titles he had already completed.[96] No orchestra, no conductors, no special arrangements, no fuss; just Peter and two old friends, the pianist Hubert Greenslade and organist Herbert Dawson. 'Drink to me only with thine eyes', which he had first recorded on cylinder in 1904, still drew the familiar, perennial praise: 'Mr Dawson can still knock 'em cold when he likes'. Although Dawson's Gramophone Company contracts had been reduced from their peak in 1933 to this sad 'not less than 12 titles', the publicity now read, 'continuous recording contracts for 35 years'.

Before he could escape, Dawson was asked to sing at Fred Gaisberg's retirement dinner.[97] 'When Fred Gaisberg's retirement was announced, the entire gramophone industry stood to attention' wrote Moore: those invited were 'a virtual encyclopedia of the world of music'.[98] Gaisberg did not retire any more than Dawson, but their paths diverged for some years. Peter and Nan threw one last extravagant family party and were gone.[99]

Nan and Peter, 1940s. In the possession of Ann Jacquet.

World War II: stranded in Australia again

To say that Dawson had blotted his copybook with the ABC was putting it mildly. By the time he and Nan had docked at Fremantle on 23 May 1939 a war of words was already in full swing. It had begun with Dawson's excuse in his letter of 6 January: 'I understood that your cable dated 8th December [i.e. 'dates impossible'] held good. During the interim I made other commitments on this side, and then your letter arrived.'[1] Dawson pointed out that the timing of the proposed tour was bad and the itinerary outrageous and suggested that the ABC offer him a tour for the following year more in keeping with his status.

Moses was angry. 'We are frankly surprised…', he replied. Neither he nor his advisers believed Dawson's version of events; they believed he had weaseled out of the ABC contract after he had received a more lucrative offer. Moses rebutted Dawson's objections, arguing that he was not being asked to do any more than Elisabeth Rethberg (1936), Lotte Lehmann (1937) or Alexander Kipnis (1938) had already done,[2] and told him bluntly that there was no possibility of a 1940 season.[3]

Had it been anyone else the matter might have ended there, but the ABC had reckoned without a tetchy Peter Dawson. Moses' letter had hardly reached London when an article appeared in *Radio Call* headed: 'Why Dawson is not coming'.[4] Whenever Dawson was interviewed he repeated the same litany:

> I was expected to sing in all sorts of out-of-the-way-places, such as Kalgoorlie and Broken Hill. … Naturally I objected. It would have been too strenuous. Besides the tour would have begun before Easter,

which is a bad time for concerts. I suggested that I should come in 1940, but the Commission replied that it had already filled its programme for that year. Next, I learned that a member of the Commission had told a newspaper that the Commission did not want Peter Dawson on any terms in 1940 or any other year. Naturally, I was not pleased.[5]

Moses was stung into defending the ABC and may well have thought that was the end of the matter, but three months later Dawson attacked again. The *Herald*, *Telegraph*, *Weekly Times*, and *Mail* carried an aggressive response to Moses and Cleary: 'Dawson has flatly denied the statement by the Chairman of the ABC that he broke his contract: "There never was a contract. It wasn't finalised. I objected to the itinerary".'[6] Dawson accused the ABC of announcing the tour before contracting him and wanting to run him 'up and down the country like a smoothing iron'. He could not have done the tour anyway, he said, because he was booked up for the next couple of years. As Lotte Lehmann was the major celebrity artist for the season the *Bulletin* weighed in with an article headed, 'Does A stand for Austrian?': Peter Dawson was back, it said, 'but the ABC prefers foreigners'; 'the ABC can put up with a certain loss, for it lives off the proceeds of an excessive impost.' (These phrases sound suspiciously like Dawson's language.)

All the more surprising to find that Basil Kirke, 'Manager for New South Wales and a devout admirer of Moses',[7] had forwarded to the general manager an enquiry from Greater Union Theatres, asking whether the ABC might like to broadcast some of its Peter Dawson concerts and take over his return fare to England. Moses' response was less surprising: he had 'no interest in any proposal to engage Peter Dawson'.[8]

For all that, the confrontation with the ABC was a sideline to Dawson's main commitment, the Greater Union Theatres tour. This commercial company ran a chain of cinemas, known in the major cities as the State Theatres, and owned the subsidiary Cinesound Productions. Dawson's arrival in Australia was not only publicised in the press but also on Cinesound newsreel.[9] As usual the Adelaide *Advertiser* carried all the news about him: on 24 May it referred to Nan's failing health and made the mistake of highlighting Dawson's impending retirement. A few days later it carried his forceful contradiction. 'I love the life, and until my voice begins to show signs of wear I am not going to think of retiring,' said 'the world's "best-selling" baritone', who was 'under contract to Greater Union Theatres until

Window display to welcome 'The World's Most Popular Baritone' at Begg's Music Store, Christchurch, New Zealand, August 1946; and below: recording 'Swinging Along the Road to Victory' at the Columbia studio, Homebush, NSW on 11 July 1940, with Brian Lawrance and his orchestra.

the end of October, before returning to England via New Zealand and the United States'. 'If I do not catch the first available ship after my tour finishes, my contract with Greater Union Theatres provides for a fine of £75 a day as long as I remain' he said. He was contracted for eighteen weeks and Adelaide would hear him in September, 'in the new State Theatre now being built in Hindley Street.' Dawson could not resist a parting swipe at the ABC: 'I have often thought that, wonderful as wireless is, the little switch that turns it off is even more wonderful.'[10]

En route to Sydney, Norman Banks, one of Melbourne's best-known commercial radio personalities, caught up with Dawson on board the *Oronsay*.[11] Banks could not resist baiting Dawson with a question about the latest singing style, crooning. This was certain to raise Dawson's hackles because the rise of the crooner, personified by Bing Crosby, was cutting into his territory. Although Dawson still had a slight edge in the 1939 EMI catalogue – Peter: 178 titles; Bing 152 – 'the singer's reply was short and to the point, "They're two distinct types," he said, "a first-class singer can never be a crooner, and a crooner can never be a first-class singer".' Dawson later got his come-uppance for such remarks in a letter to the editor of the *Radio Times*:

> Some Cheek
>
> It is just like Peter Dawson's impudence to refer to Bing Crosby's crooning as mooing. It should be very interesting to hear Bing's opinion of Peter Dawson's singing. It might by a strange chance coincide with mine. I can't stand a bar of Peter Dawson. No doubt there are people who like Mr Dawson's voice, but I'll guarantee that if Mr Dawson was broadcasting from one station and Bing from another, Bing would have a decidedly larger listening audience.[12]

Although Dawson had signed exclusively with Greater Union Theatres, that company had hedged its bets with a 2UE radio deal.[13] The *Radio Times* announced that Dawson had been sponsored by a cigarette manufacturer to sing twice weekly for at least three months from a Sydney commercial radio station. The 'cigarette manufacturer' turned out to be McWilliams Wines, which 'saw in his appearances at the State Theatre and at the 2UE studios an excellent opportunity to boost another all-Australian product, Yendarra old sherry.' 2UE broadcast programmes alternatively from the State Theatre and its studios. One week the latter included listeners' requests: within three days 400 had been received, by the end of the week nearly a thousand. Another gimmick was a search for the oldest Peter Dawson recording: which 'will be played over the air and the noted baritone will then sing the song as he would today. The possessor of the historic record will receive a large framed portrait of Mr. Dawson.'

When the State Theatre in Sydney was refurbished for its tenth anniversary in June 1939 it fulfilled a vision of the future Peter Dawson had described in a letter to the *Australian Musical News* back in 1932.

> Imagine those gloriously appointed picture theatres, seats such heavens of comfort compared to the hot-cross-bun chair of ye concert hall! No draughts, beautiful soft light, acoustics nigh perfect, stage lighting...plus an all-time orchestra.[14]

The comfortable cinemas in which he now appeared fulfilled his predictions. He had also foreshadowed that the only way for the talkies to survive would be to intersperse live appearances between films. Stages were now large enough to hold performers and a sizeable band so that live entertainment could be presented between the B film and the main feature – in this case, *The Mikado* – in the new-fangled technicolor.

As presented at 2 p.m. and 8 p.m. sessions.

At the Wurlitzer Organ: Mr. Manny Aarons

Δ

STATE NEWS REVIEW
Compiled from Universal and Cinesound Newsreels

OVERTURE—"Gems from Gilbert and Sullivan"
Hamilton Webber and State Symphony Orchestra

"HUNTING DOGS"
A Fox special sports feature related by Ed. Thorgersen

Walt Disney All-color Silly Symphony Cartoon —
"FARMYARD SYMPHONY"

Δ

The Directors of Greater Union Theatres are proud to present
PETER DAWSON
The Eminent Australian Bass-baritone
In a Programme specially selected from his extensive repertoire
At the piano: John Douglas Todd.

Δ

Before the opening newsreel, the Wurlitzer organ rose from the depths with the organist playing; as the picture screen appeared it descended again with the organist still playing until the newsreel began. Then came a live orchestra before Walt Disney's *Farmyard Symphony*, in which Mickey Mouse, Clarabelle Cow, Horace Horsecollar and others clucked, brayed, mooed and cackled the *William Tell Overture*. While the audience was still chuckling at the cartoon the screen disappeared into the flies, curtains opened and 'Peter Dawson was seen advancing round the curve of a great black and white staircase with long windows at the back'. After he had sung his favourite introductory number, 'Largo al factotum', 'lights in the windows changed to soft red and blue for a more sentimental song "The Forest Prays". A Kipling ballad, a song by John Ireland and the famous "Boots" completed his program.'[15]

This pattern was repeated in other states but before the tour had ended, World War II was declared. 'Australia went to war by wireless,' wrote Inglis: 'At 8p.m. Eastern Standard Time on Sunday 3 September 1939 listeners heard Neville Chamberlain's announcement … that the British Government was at war with Germany. The government of R. G. Menzies accepted the broadcast as authoritative evidence … and declared that as a result Australia was also at war.'[16]

In England BBC television screens suddenly went blank: without any announcement BBC–TV closed down for the duration. The world wondered how Germany, which had been defeated in World War I, had once again become the aggressors, but the depressed economy of the 1930s had spawned a nationalist leader, Adolf Hitler. He had begun his rise to power by initiating constructive employment programmes: Europe watched as he built up Germany's military strength and raised patriotic fervour to fever pitch. But the thought of warfare was so abhorrent to England and her allies that they ignored Hitler's annexation of Austria but finally confronted the threat when Germany attacked Poland. Twenty-one years after 'the war to end all wars' another conflagration broke out in Europe.

In Australia, Joseph Lyons had led a United Australia Party government for most of the 1930s: he died in office. An 'unwilling Menzies [was] elected on 26th April 1939. With him it was axiomatic that if the United Kingdom went to war Australia went with her',[17] and the majority of Australians, still with their heads in the sands of Empire, agreed. Every Australian was affected by the war. The 2nd Australian Infantry Force were volunteers, but every other physically and mentally fit adult up to 45 years of age had to register and work in some capacity. Men and women of retiring age worked on; many women 'entered fields where they had never been before', such as

LASSETER'S LAST RIDE

WORDS: EDWARD HARRINGTON   MUSIC   J.P. M°CALL.

Lasseter rode from his camping ground,
In search of a golden lode.
But no one knows what Lasseter found,
Or the track that Lasseter rode.
He fared alone to the great unknown,
And followed a phantom guide,
For only God and the stars looked down
On Lasseter's last long ride.

Now Lasseter sleeps in the great North West,
Where they say that the dead sleep sound,
But what was the end of Lasseter's quest
And where is the gold he found?
Others will go where the fierce winds blow,
And die as Lasseter died.
But only God and the white stars know
The end of Lasseter's long ride.

Some may jest at his fruitless quest,
Or murmur his name in grief;
But somewhere out in the great North West,
Lies a track to a golden reef.
And men will go to the great out-back,
And try as Lasseter tried,
But only God and the stars looked down,
On Lasseter's last long ride

PUBLISHED BY:- ALLAN & C°

A page from one of Peter's 'immaculate' song books.

operating machines in munitions and aircraft factories; looking after young families was also considered essential war work for mothers.

Peter and Nan were stranded in Australia – again. The declaration of war had made it impossible for them to leave in October as planned; now, by working for the war effort, Dawson could very publicly retire from professional singing without losing face. After the death of their father in 1919, Peter's brothers, Thomas, David and William, had relocated the family business to the inner-city Sydney suburb of Camperdown[18] but by 1939 William was the only one living ('Will was very straight. Uncle Peter used to call him old money bags'). Peter now joined his brother: 'I have been included on the Board of Directors of Messrs T. Dawson & Sons Pty Ltd. Canister & Drum manufacturing', he wrote to an old mate. He called his job 'No. 1 Handshake' and said he had to survive on 'the princely sum of £12 per week'. However, his income tax return for 1939/40 shows that as well as £2,250 from Greater Union Theatres plus £200 in lieu of his return fare to England, he received £400 from T. Dawson and Sons for the rest of the financial year.[19]

During 1940 Peter, the passionate imperialist, gave singing a rest and turned his attention to composing songs with Australian themes, some of them outright jingoistic. His first song that year was titled: 'Australia', (since 1842 sixteen other songs called 'Australia' had already been published). 'It is a stirring thing in slow time, and it took me two hours to compose,' he said when his 'new anthem' was premiered with the NSW Police Choir at a carnival on 24 February.[20] Despite this fanfare, 'Australia' was actually just a simple rewording of Maurice Besly's 'England' – which Dawson had often sung – transposed down a tone to E♭, to a comfortable range for the average voice: B♭–D.

Arguably the best from 1940 were settings of Edward Harrington's 'Lasseter's Last Ride' and 'The Bushrangers', and Louis Esson's 'Whalin' Up The Lachlan'. Dawson had already played with the theme of the bushranger as folk hero in a fragmentary manuscript signed 'J. P. M. 11.7.30'. On this setting he had pasted a newspaper picture of Ned Kelly with a pencil note: 'Ned Kelly, Joe Byrne, Dan Kelly and Steve Hart descended on the bank at Jerilderie NSW, capturing the police, borrowing their uniforms, holding up the bank.' Dawson's empathy with the poets' characters and their feeling for the landscape inspired quite substantial compositions. 'Lasseter's Last Ride' and 'The Bushrangers' are in minor keys, the former in a slightly pretentious 9/8 riding rhythm, the latter in 3/4 – a change from Dawson's usual marching or walking rhythm, which he used again for 'Whalin' Up the Lachlan'.

Some of the unfamiliar words of Esson's 'Whalin' Up the Lachlan' were explained when it was included in Allan's collection, *Songs of the Peter Dawson Era* (1950): 'whalin' = wandering'; 'B-Bows = old-fashion shears'; 'Sundowner = a swaggie who would arrive at an outback station at sundown on the chance of getting tucker and a shake-down for the night, and disappear next morning.' The poem deals with a swaggie on a less confrontational course than his Warrnambool Downs ancestor:

> Whalin' up the Lachlan
> Done with axe and plough,
> Whalin' up the Lachlan
> The billy's boiling now.
> We'll fill our pipes an' yarn there
> And watch the world roll by,
> Whalin' up the Lachlan,
> Under a starry sky.[21]

The 'virile, swinging quality' ascribed to Harrington's poems could be as aptly applied to Dawson's compositional style. The *Australian Musical News'* assessment was headed: 'Three songs with life, A budget from Allan's'. 'Here is typical Australian verse, music with a sturdy sweep to it'. The *Bulletin* commented on the settings: 'The tunes are original and phrased to the words, and there are dramatic qualities in both ditties. Any baritone could sing them and any pianist of any pretensions could play the accompaniments.'[22]

From the time he became known as a songwriter Dawson was inundated with verses of all kinds and widely varying quality. At this time most reflected the chauvinistic spirit of a country at war. Among them were four verses from Dame Mary Gilmore: titled 'No Foe Shall Gather Our Harvest'. In June 1940 these verses were published in the *Australian Women's Weekly* surrounded by a collage of horses and riders, a bullock wagon, sheep, and ANZACs landing at Gallipoli. The magazine commented:

> At 75, Australian poet and writer Mary Gilmour [sic], Dame of the British Empire, has written one of her finest Australian songs of the war. It appears above. 'I'm too old to do many things I would like to do to win the war,' she said, 'but I can still write. Here is a song for men and women of Australia.'[23]

Dawson was as keen as Dame Mary to do his bit for the war: 'Retirement,' he said, 'does not mean that I am giving up singing, My voice might still do a bit of good for charities.'[24] Because he had left England, EMI (Hayes) would not permit him to record for *HMV* labels; but EMI (Sydney) managed to recruit him for four patriotic compositions – 'The AIF is Marching' (Lane), 'Swinging Along the Road to Victory' (Cohan), 'We Shall Prevail' (Bowden & Gerity), and 'Song of Australia' (Jackson) – on the lower status *Regal-Zonophone*.[25]

From Dawson's acidic press comments about the ABC it would appear that the two parties were irreconcilable: he was certainly not in the 1940 ABC 'business as usual' orchestral season, which included Sir Thomas Beecham, Harold Williams and Gladys Moncrieff.[26] Charles Moses remained understandably obdurate, but in March 1940 Dr Barry – who always maintained a healthy mistrust of Dawson – wrote to Moses:

> I know what your own feelings are on this matter and although … he has acted unfairly towards us I somehow feel that it would be unwise politically to refuse to consider him as an artist we might use. Dawson was a digger [so] an appropriate night to affect a reconciliation would be Anzac Night. He would be a great feature in our Camp Concerts and on the popular side of our programmes. I think he will listen to reason. James and he are very friendly, James being his accompanist from the age of fourteen and Dawson being intimately linked with his Bush Songs.

Gradually – between March and May 1940 – Dawson was reinstated. As usual he could only be approached through another person, this time Kerwin Maegraith. The ABC found Dawson's opening gambit, twelve studio broadcasts for £1000, exorbitant.[27] They countered with a combination of studio recitals, celebrity concerts, community concerts and public recitals for a total of £700, or a 13-week tour for circa £800. Negotiations were protracted beyond Anzac night so the next suitable date suggested was Empire Day. Dawson claimed he had a better offer from a commercial broadcaster, but the ABC stuck firm. Just as Charles Moses concluded that further approaches were pointless, William James advised him that Dawson had agreed to ten studio broadcasts between May and September at £40 per broadcast (i.e. a total of £400).

When Dawson had completed this contract Maegraith put forward another proposal: a tour of North Queensland, then across to the AIF in Darwin at £40 per show; and on completion a further tour of concerts and broadcasts through Western Australia and South Australia, which would include many country centres.[28] Internally, the ABC was still smarting from Dawson's earlier rejection of its 'country centres' offer, but the official reply was that it had insufficient funds for such tours. If Mr Dawson wanted to make the tours under his own steam they would be prepared to broadcast some of the concerts.[29] Dawson declined.

In November 1940 Moses departed for the front and T. W. Bearup, an Australian who had been manager for Victoria,[30] became acting general manager until his return. Bearup received an enquiry from the New Zealand Broadcasting Commission about the appropriateness of Dawson's broadcast fees as he had proposed a tour there: one month, twelve broadcasts, for £1,000 plus travelling costs for himself, his wife and his agent.[31] Nothing came of this proposal either.

As Peter Dawson could sing any patriotic song with absolute conviction he had been a mouthpiece for martial sentiments for decades. Now, the fervour of World War II gave rise to a spate of patriotic songs 'Sung by Peter Dawson' like 'Bravo, Sons of the Sea' and 'Bravo, Sons of the Air'. He also composed many himself: 'The Blamey Boys', 'The Flag That Will Never Be Furled', 'God Bless Australia Fair', 'Dreaming of England', 'The Spirit of Britain', 'The Spirit of England', 'Wake Up Australia', 'Sons of the Southern Cross', and 'V for Victory'.

'V for Victory', 'Words and Music by Peter Dawson' is typical of the style. What better title for propaganda purposes than the sign made famous by Winston Churchill. On the garish cover a wreath encircling the initials *A.C.F.* is superimposed over a large V with the words: 'Adopted for the "V for Victory" Drive, sponsored by The Right Hon. The Lord Mayor of Sydney (Alderman Stanley S. Crick). Full proceeds given to the Australian Comforts Fund.' Dawson recorded the number on 14 August backed by Jim Gussey and the ABC Dance Orchestra:

> ANNOUNCER: V for Victory it sweeps Australia – V for Victory it sweeps Europe – V for Victory it sweeps the world. The Australian Victory Song written and composed by Peter Dawson himself. The proceeds are to swell the funds for you fellows overseas. Here is Peter Dawson himself.
>
> MR. DAWSON: You're doing a great job, diggers, a job we in Australia are proud of. This Victory song was in my heart so I did my stuff and put words and music to paper. And now to sing it. I hope you like it, you blokes. Cheerio. Good Luck.
>
> (*sings*)
>
> Verse:
> > The letter V is going round the world today,
> > Everybody knows it;
> > Everybody shows it.

A little symbol to repeat in every way
V for Victory all the way.
Chorus:
       Say it, sing it,
       Play it, swing it
       V for Victory.
       Write it, talk it,
       On walls chalk it,
       V for Victory.

       Tho' we've taken hard blows on the chin, chin, chin,
       In the end we are bound to win, win, win.
       So say it, play it,
       Sing it, swing it,
       V for Victory.

Its optimistic 2/4 marching rhythm and restricted range, C–E, indicate that it was meant to be sung by anyone – and it was: 'This song was sung all over Australia – in the theatres, music-halls, picture houses, concerts, schools – and played by all military bands' wrote Dawson.[32]

December 1941 proved a turning point in Australian history. Menzies' United Australia Party, uneasily supported by two independents, had lost the balance of power in the Coalition and in August Menzies resigned the leadership. When the independents withdrew the Governor General called on the opposition to form a government; and it fell to Labor legend John Curtin to lead Australia through those troubled times. Australians had seen the war as essentially another war between Britain and Germany. Although the Japanese had occupied China and were moving south, they were not considered a danger to Australia until they bombed Pearl Harbour in December 1941. Suddenly Australia itself was under threat. The attack on America had mobilised 'an ally with untapped potential and the greatest standing resources in men and material in the world'. America looked to Australia as a major Pacific base, and John Curtin, realistically assessing the situation, redirected the focus of the nation. 'Without any inhibitions of any kind, I make it quite clear that Australia looks to America, free of any pangs as to our traditional links of kinship with the United Kingdom'.[33] By the time Singapore capitulated on 15 January 1942, Britain had still not responded to Australia's call for help. Whether it could not or would not is still debated; but the day after the surrender of Singapore the ABC gave Australian news precedence over overseas bulletins for the first time and substituted 'Advance Australia Fair' for 'The British Grenadiers'. [34]

Lae fell on 24 January; Darwin was bombed on 19 February; Japanese submarines entered Sydney Harbour in May and June. The Minister for External Affairs, Dr H. V. Evatt, told ABC chairman Cleary that 'news, talks and other programme features would all have to carry subtle propaganda for "Australia first".' Subtle it was not. One programme, aggressively supported by the Government, assailed listeners with such a diatribe against the Japanese that it split Australian opinion down the middle. The frenetic atmosphere was exacerbated early in 1942 by the arrival of (well-paid) American soldiers.

Peter Dawson's version of 'Waltzing Matilda', released in April 1939, was now beginning to earn its destined place. Australians who still had memories of swagmen wandering the country during the Depression of the 1930s could identify with the wartime correspondent, who explained the meaning of 'Waltzing Matilda' to his American neighbour during a Peter Dawson recital:

> Waltzing Matilda means sleeping under the stars; having your bath in a stream and using the sun for a towel: it means walking from one sheep station to another, and not seeing a human soul for days at a time. We've waltzed Matilda up and down Libya and Greece and Syria and before we've finished we'll waltz Matilda all over the great and glorious Reich and right up Unter den Linden! So look out, Hitler, for the Wizards of Aus![35]

Rocketing sales of Dawson's 'Waltzing Matilda' were stimulated by American soldiers looking for something identifiably 'Australian' to take home, prompting Victor to issue it in the United States and Canada. Even the Dum Dum factory in Calcutta hurried it out on Indian HMV. At last count the 'Waltzing Matilda' craze had produced about 550 different recordings in an endless range of musical styles. It has become our unofficial national anthem, the song that reminds expatriates and travellers that they can 'Still call Australia home'.

Dawson had smoked all his life and by now it was beginning to affect his health: after a serious attack of bronchitis he was forced to stop.[36] He was now sixty, but gave no indication of slackening pace. He could be often heard broadcasting, live or on recordings, from the commercial radio stations favoured by most Australians.[37] They could listen to the 'the top eight' sung by Judy Garland or Bing Crosby or the new boy, Frank Sinatra, or ingest a diet of popular Strauss waltzes, Chopin études and operatic overtures from Rossini, Verdi or Mozart. They heard famous tenors singing

'Digging for Victory'. *ABC Weekly* promotion for Dawson's radio
appearances on *Out of the Bag* and *Peter Dawson's Ballad Album*. In the
possession of the Documentation Collection – ScreenSound
Australia, National Screen and Sound Archive.

'Your Tiny Hand Is Frozen' and 'Girls were made to loff and keess'. Sand-wiched between these two extremes were copious quantities of 'Open Road, Open Sky', 'The Green-Eyed Dragon', 'Wandering the King's Highway', 'The Road to Mandalay' and ballads of that ilk.

For many listeners the ABC had the reputation of being too highbrow or boring, yet Dawson kept knocking on the door: 'It is high time that I did some broadcasting, in order to hearten the denizens of our beloved Australia,' he wrote to William James.[38] This led to an ABC offer of a minimum of ten engagements over a six-month period at a fee of fifteen guineas – instead of the previous £40.[39] This so angered Dawson that he wrote directly to the Prime Minister. Curtin had more serious worries at the time but, such was Dawson's name, his letter was passed to the Postmaster-General, who wrote to the ABC giving him the Government's support. The response ended up on Bearup's desk. Bearup did not cave in. He retaliated by giving the whole history of Dawson's unreliability; but ended by advising that the ABC would certainly engage him if he went to the bother of contacting them.

A month later Peter sought an appointment with Bearup who was, un-fortunately, genuinely ill. In the morning Bearup's secretary noted: 'D. seemed fairly reasonable, but stressed that he must see you;' but by afternoon Dawson was uptight:

> At approx 3 o'clock rang – tone had changed considerably – in fact, manner most objectionable – told Bearup ill & no time for appointment … Mr D then said that he 'was not going to be put off by the Commission as he had been in the past and that if he didn't get satisfaction, he would go straight to the PM'.[40]

The real thorn in the side was Dr Barry, who referred to Dawson as 'a popular vocal artist probably considerably older in years than Harold Williams who has never achieved Mr. Williams' eminence in the musical world… I see no reason at all for offering Peter Dawson any larger fee than offered to Harold Williams or Heddle Nash, both of whom received 15 guineas for studio recitals.'[41] There may have been genuine budget constraints but the fact that other important artists accepted these fees did not make them adequate; rather it indicated that they regarded broadcasting as important for their public profile.

The distinction between fame and eminence dogs Peter Dawson to this day. He and Sydney-born Harold Williams (1893-1976) had been good friends since their days in England.[42] Though some musicians considered Williams the better singer he never achieved Dawson's notoriety. He had stuck primarily to the more classical repertoire and had a long and fruitful recording career with Columbia; but the public appeal of his superb recordings never matched those of Dawson. Williams, who became a prominent teacher at the New South Wales Conservatorium of Music, is remembered for 'his ringing baritone … its firmness and richness and effortless production'. Yet, though classified as a 'classical singer' he also sang plenty of 'Peter Dawson' style ballads and lighter music, especially during his long reign as 'Orpheus, who sang the songs the Argonauts requested as well as the theme' on the ABC's popular children's radio programme, *The Argonauts*.[43]

Acting as if nothing had happened, Dawson dropped Bearup a note in March 1942 suggesting 'a series of dates either here in Sydney or throughout our Sister States'. Although a Mr McCall argued on Dawson's behalf for the BBC fee of £50 per recital, Dawson himself agreed to '6 weekly recitals commencing Wednesday 20 May 8:15–8:30 pm in the series *Great Australian Baritones*' – at 15 guineas.[44] Once the contract had been approved by Central it was up to Basil Kirke, the NSW manager, to arrange the programmes; but Dawson had vanished. Then one evening he telephoned Kirke at home, saying the series 'could be later – any time at all'.[45] He had received a better offer and was off to New Zealand.

The approach to New Zealand in 1940 had finally paid off. The press reported that he was 'to star in a series of big patriotic Liberty concerts'. The open-air concerts were to be accompanied by the Royal New Zealand Armed Forces Band; the recitals by the London-born accompanist, Henry Penn, who pronounced his name in the French manner (Peter pronounced it 'Pong').[46] One collage photograph, signed 'Peter Dawson 18/5/42' shows him shaking hands with the New Zealand Prime Minister, crowds in the city square, and a newspaper cutting headed:

WELLINGTON RALLY
New £1 Bonds On Sale

The presence of the famous Australian baritone, Peter Dawson, at the lunchtime liberty rally in Wellington yesterday drew an unusually large crowd to the rally headquarters at the corner of Hunter St and Featherstone Street. There must have been fully 4000 people filling the pavement and roadways when he sang 'The Changing of the Guard'.[47]

Later Peter wrote to his brother-in-law: 'Such is fame! £1000 + all expenses … £15 million War Loan was filled in 3 weeks'.[48]

Despite his unreliability the ABC was still interested in pinning Dawson down to a series of broadcasts – for the same fee he had accepted prior to the New Zealand sortie. Dawson protested to the Postmaster-General:

I do not think, as an Australian, I have been offered a fair deal by the Australian Broadcasting Commission and especially in consideration of the services rendered by me in connection with the flotation of War Loans since their inception. The Australian Broadcasting Commission has made me an offer of £15 each for a series of ten recitals. This is unreasonable considering their previous payment to me during 1940 was £40 for a similar engagement.[49]

In a long, detailed explanation, which went back to the gripes of 1938, Bearup again accused Dawson of being intractable.[50] At the end of August: stalemate.

Meanwhile other work had not flagged, for Dawson was much in demand for national commercial radio programmes. However, in April 1943 he agreed to consider a ten-week contract with the ABC at '23 guineas per week covering two performances per week', which the ABC gingerly sought to verify: 'It is understood that you are available for these engagements without interruption'. Acting as his agent, Mr McCall tried to negotiate a better rate but Dawson advised that he was 'agreeable to accept and abide by the terms'. The agreement coincided with the return of Moses, who advised the Commissioners that: 'These terms are very good from our point of view – the fee being lower than usually paid to artists of this standard such as Harold Williams.'[51] For the rest of the war Dawson was kept busy with programmes like *Out of the Bag*, *Peter Dawson's Ballad Album* and *Comrades in Arms*, a series dedicated to a different battalion each week.

In 1943 Chappell's published Dawson's composition, 'The Aussie Spirit', to words by Leslie Davis.[52] The manuscript was written out on the back of a Carl Loewe ballad, 'The Clock', which, like 'My Grandfather's Clock', accompanies the protagonist from birth to death. Dawson had first programmed 'The Clock' in 1933 and it remained a favourite all his life. The note on this manuscript, 'The copy mislaid, this one written out from memory, Sydney 6.11.43, Peter Dawson', not only dates 'The Aussie Spirit', but also indicates the extent of Dawson's excellent musicianship.

During August-September 1944 the Returned Services League of NSW launched a mammoth fund-raising appeal to build and furnish Anzac House, a returned servicemen's rehabilitation centre in Pitt Street, Sydney. The theme song, 'The Anzac House Song', – music by Peter Truman, words by Kerwin Maegraith – was appropriately patriotic, beginning 'When the boys come home again' and leading to the chorus:

Be a brick, buy a brick, wear a brick!
In your best good-hearted way.

Anzac House will be there for the lads,
When they're home again some day …
So be a brick, buy a brick, wear a brick
To build up Anzac House.

Dawson sang the song and, as it was very much in his style, it seems likely
that 'Peter Truman' was our hero, then playing a major role in the Appeal.[53]
A flyer sported a Maegraith cartoon of Peter, rotund, bald, in evening dress,
holding 'Boots' under his arm.[54]

News of the appeal was in the papers every day: 'Button sellers wanted,
buttons 6d-£5'; '1600 sellers on duty in City'; 'Bob Hope drew the first prize in
the Motion Picture Industry raffle'; 'Miss Sydney to be crowned at the
showground on 9th September'; 'Anzac House now assured'. The appeal far
outstripped the target of £150,000; nearly £400,000 was raised. When 'Miss
Sydney' was crowned at the Royal Agricultural Society's Ground, the gaudy
souvenir programme announced that Marjorie Lawrence would start proceed-
ings 'with the American and British National Anthems'; however, she was ill, so
Gladys Moncrieff, who was there to sing 'Land of Hope and Glory', probably
sang them. Dawson's turn came after the crowning, with:

> *The Romance of the Swag*: a descriptive adaptation of 'Waltzing Matilda'
> and its origins during which Mr Peter Dawson, supported by the Police
> Choir will render the song 'Waltzing Matilda' to the accompaniment
> of the NSW Police Band.

As the words were printed on the back page, we may assume that the
audience was invited to join in.

When Victory in Europe was declared on 8 May 1945, attention focussed
completely on the Pacific. Japan was being repulsed but remained obstinately entrenched in the islands and refused to surrender until America
brought the war to an abrupt halt by dropping the first atom bomb on
Hiroshima on 6 August: the war ended nine days later (15 August 1945).

During this period Dawson continued to make recordings. Sacred melo-
dies dominated among eight titles recorded in late 1944.[55] In late 1945 he
spliced together four settings of the Kipling's 'Mandalay' – by Willeby,
Hedgcock, Cobb and Speaks – to make his 'Mandalay Potpourri'. In early
1946 he recorded more sacred music; and in December 1946 four titles
including his own 'Bushrangers'.[56] 'I worked with him between 1940 and
1951,' recalled EMI artist and repertoire manager, Ron Wills. 'He was very
critical of his own work, was never satisfied with anything but perfection.

ANZAC HOUSE APPEAL
PIN-UP MAN CONTEST

A

GREAT

SINGER

IN

A

GREAT

CAUSE

ANZAC

HOUSE

WILL

CONTAIN

A

FINE

MUSIC

ROOM

PETER DAWSON, the world's most famous Baritone, nominated by Music Trade,
5 Barrack Street, Sydney.

Be sure to Vote PETER DAWSON [1]
Buy a Peter Dawson Button

Like that mosquito, the Music Trade people know when they are on a good thing, and are sticking to it. Their pin-up runner is the most celebrated Australian singer since the great Melba. His recordings sales are stated to far exceed those of Caruso, John McCormack, and all the other noted singers of his day. His singing of "Anzac House Song" alone is worth many bricks.

BUY A BUTTON — BUTTONS FROM 1/- TO £1

Crows Nest News Print, XB4491

Publicity brochure, August–September 1944.

At that time we used to record on wax not tape. I remember our engineer calling, "We're running out of wax" as Peter kept making one recording after another.'[57]

After his 1945 series *Music of the British Isles* the ABC files about Dawson fall silent for nearly two years.[58] However, he was active on commercial stations. From 1945 he appeared on Colgate-Palmolive variety shows and Jack Davey's *Calling the Stars*, where he introduced new local compositions like 'Let Us Sing Of The Wheatlands' (Lionel Shave & Iris Mason), and patriotic favourites, like 'There'll Always Be An England'. He also broadcast *Song Hits of Two Wars* on the *Big Parade* and returned to Radio 2UE for a series of 52 quarter-hour sessions, under the sponsorship of the distributors of *Purr-Pull Motor Oils*. These ran until shortly before his 1946 tour of New Zealand.

By 1946 the tide of wartime rationing was receding. As Dawson wrote to his brother-in-law, Tom:

> There is everything here that mortal man desires. Over and abundance. Shops groaning with all the commodities. Money by the bag. Don't know what to do with it – other than throw it away on gambling – bon chance.

The letter concluded: 'I have appeared and sung for all factions in Sydney over six years & until they must regard me as a piece of wall paper but there is still money in the concert business'.[59] Concert business included the *Dominion Tour* of New Zealand between 9 July and 5 September 1946 with the twenty-nine year-old Adelaide accompanist Clarence Black.[60] Talk of Peter Dawson's retirement was now never too far from reporters' pens and the old maestro used it to flatter his potential audience: ' 'Peter Dawson may retire to New Zealand: Peter Dawson, the Australian singer, told reporters today that he was likely to retire and live in NZ after completing engagements in England and America.'[61] From this successful tour Dawson netted £1,853/17/–.

Tax had been deducted in New Zealand but in Australia another tax saga began. Dawson's returns from 1940 to 1944 reveal that his income had come from a steady core of about £600 from T. Dawson and Sons, £400 in EMI royalties, and broadcasting fees ranging from £200 to £600. However, between 30 June 1939 and 30 June 1945 he had also received royalty cheques from Hayes amounting to £2,486/16/5.[62] The Australian Taxation Department was unable to reconcile his Australian and English royalty earnings, because they were uncertain about the country in which tax was payable. Dawson was worried that both countries might demand tax on the same earnings. He argued that he was an English resident, stranded in Australia by the war. This did not satisfy the Australian authorities. Fortunately, a double taxation treaty between the two countries came into effect in June 1946, before the matter had to be settled.

Toward the end of 1946 Dawson approached the ABC again with the old idea of a country tour – at the same fee as in 1944. William James thought it a good idea; Dr Barry did not: 'I cannot say that my immediate reaction is favourable … if he thought he could make money he would go off by himself and make more profit.' Moses however needed someone to fulfil the ABC's obligations to regional Australia so he made an offer – to which Dawson did not reply.

Yet again a project died in the water. In November 1946 Dawson went to the papers again: he complained about the inadequacy of ABC fees, asserting that commercial fees were far better. This time even William James was stung into replying. He countered that commercial stations only employed 'certain "names" for a few sessions', whereas the ABC employed hundreds of artists: 'Serious ones would have little scope for their talents over advertising stations.'[63] Because the commercial networks provided more career openings for lighter and popular music, under its charter the ABC had been given the responsibility for 'Serious' music. The ABC did employ a large number of local artists: many established Australian singers made their first broadcasts on programmes like *Young Australia*; and the ABC sought to be equitable by grading artists. Problems only arose when certain artists, especially those returning from overseas, felt that their status exceeded the top level.

Nevertheless, nine months after this outburst Dawson agreed to a country tour of thirteen weeks, with accompanist Clarence Black: three concerts per week, one for 'Young People', at a minimum of £40 per week. Despite Dr Barry's justifiable reservations, Moses endorsed the venture.[64] 'The Bradman of the Baritones' had already been bannered across a two-and-a-half page spread when Dawson informed the Commission that he could not complete the tour as he would soon be returning to England. The ABC obliged by reducing it to New South Wales, Queensland and South Australia. On 8 April Dawson informed the Commission that he would 'fly in May' so the ABC reduced his appearances to studio performances in NSW. Dawson then confined his commitments to 'Sydney only' on account of Nan's poor health. In July Peter and Nan set out for England. The war was over. The sixty-five year old gypsy was about to travel the road again.

The Gramophone Company's farewell party for Peter Dawson at the Savoy Hotel, London 1948. Oscar C. Preusse, Fred Gaisberg; general manager Sir Ernest Fisk, and Dawson; and Fred Gaisberg reminding Peter not to overwind the newfangled spring motor on his presentation of a 1898 Trade Mark Gramophone.

The sunset of a glorious career

Oppressed by years, the Human Organ grows
Less pleasing – as the Primo Uomo shows –
The gramophone escapes our common curse.
Bad to begin with, it becomes no worse.[1]

The atomic bomb dropped on Hiroshima had cataclysmic results for the world. Like Damocles' sword, fear of a nuclear holocaust has hung over humanity ever since, a constant threat to a fragile peace. Britain had not fully recovered from World War I or the Depression before it was engulfed in World War II; by the end of the war she had used up most of her resources and authority over her Empire had become tenuous. Commonwealth countries began to seek independence. The first to leave was India: independence was granted in August 1947, in January 1950 it became a republic. South Africa, unwilling to acknowledge the basic tenet that all Commonwealth countries were equal, regardless of colour or creed, stuck to apartheid and withdrew. Gradually smaller member countries that could support themselves broke away too.

It took a long time for Britain's economy to regenerate: destruction had been horrific, rebuilding was urgent. Germany, whose industries had been razed, purchased modern machinery with American rehabilitation loans and in a surprisingly short time regained its position as a leading industrial power, whereas Britain, whose industries had remained relatively intact, remained anchored in the past. By providing much of the capital for reconstruction, the United States strengthened its grip on world economic power, and American troops still stationed in the major battle areas of both Europe and the Pacific gave new impetus to the spread of American culture and its capitalist philosophy.

In Australia the Labor leader, John Curtin, had died in office in 1945 and was succeeded by Ben Chifley. The political pattern of World War I repeated itself worldwide: wartime leaders were no longer in favour. In 1949 the Labor Government was defeated by a Liberal-Country Party coalition led by Robert Gordon Menzies, who retained power until his retirement in January 1966, becoming Australia's longest serving Prime Minister. Like Peter Dawson, Menzies belonged unequivocally to the old imperialist school. Despite the post-war shift of world economic power away from Britain and the growing need for Australia to play a major role in Asia and the Pacific, Menzies stubbornly strove to retain Australia's allegiance to the Crown during Dawson's autumn years.

Many performers – politicians, sportspersons, business leaders and others accustomed to public adulation – find it difficult to leave the stage. Dawson was no exception. Wherever there was an opportunity to sing he took it. Although he 'retired' a number of times, he still took umbrage if his performance diary was not full. He was 74 before he declared there would be 'none of the Melba business!'[2]

But, just when the Dawson repertoire appeared to be dead in the water, he enjoyed a revival for another seven or eight years. This renaissance began with the 1947 tour of the English provinces arranged by the impresario, Harold Fielding. Fielding believed there was still a core of the British population that held fast to the old values Dawson personified. And there was. In Colombo on his way back to the United Kingdom he told the press that he had 'a six-month contract for 70 concerts in the British Isles with the option of extension of the tour for another six weeks for another 70 concerts'.[3]

The tour opened at the Opera House, Blackpool, on Sunday 7 September 1947 with:

Peter Dawson	The World's Most Famous Baritone
Steve Conway	Britain's Singing Star of Radio & Columbia discs
Adele French	Bringing Melodies to you
Tommy Reilly	Canada's Harmonica Virtuoso
Radcliffe & Ray	Radio's Two in Harmony
Winifred Atwell	The Famous West Indian Pianiste[4]

Note the hierarchy: Britain – Canada – West Indies – The World! Music-hall presentation had not changed. Other colleagues during the tour included Anne Ziegler and Webster Booth, Albert Sandler, and Mark Hambourg. Mrs Doris Walker of Swanage, Dorset, wrote: 'I saw him soon after the war at Sandown on the Isle of Wight, Pier Pavilion – Associate artist Eileen Joyce, I think – the temperature was in the 80s. Peter Dawson stripped off his jacket, mopped his brow, and said, "Lummee, ain't it 'ot" which set the scene for an hilarious performance – encore after encore.'[5] After 66 concerts, the tour ended at the Empire Theatre, Cardiff, on Sunday 4 April 1948 – but Peter and Nan stayed on in London until the end of the year.

Dawson's adoring audiences were not the only ones awaiting his return. H.M. Inspector of Taxes was also hovering in the wings. During his absence Dawson had accumulated earnings of £2,277/5/10 plus interest on which English tax was due. He complained to the press: 'Spent the intervening years in Australia, New Zealand and elsewhere singing to the troops. Got back here in '47 to be greeted on landing with: "You owe £1,665 in income tax. Pay, or ...".'[6]

More pleasant was the renewal of his association with Fred Gaisberg and the Gramophone Company. Though this twilight recording period was merely a tentative recapitulation based on the aura of his past, it prolonged the Peter Dawson recording legend to its mythical length. With the habit of a lifetime Dawson had approached the company. After checking that he was 'still capable of making good commercial records', the practical Gramophone Company showed its goodwill by contracting him for a year's supply of six record sides from 15 September 1947, with the option of a further year.[7] Dawson wrote to his old colleague, Bessie Smith:

> There is life in the old dog yet. My goodness how the dreadful war has changed everybody or is it that we have grown older? The HMV has not the slightest resemblance to what it was ten years ago. There is not the fun in the sessions. One is 'Stood over' by a recording manager and the Orchestra must not do any more than 4 titles at any one session of 3 hours duration.[8]

As a result of these sessions Dawson's new recording of 'Wandering the King's Highway' – an English 'Waltzing Matilda' without the ghostly ending – gave the song a new lease of life: it became the staple of every budding bathroom baritone for decades. The opening lines: 'I've always been a rover, summer and winter too, Wandering the wide world over, Tramping my whole life through...' could have been Dawson's epitaph. Similar sentiments can be found in many songs, including Vaughan Williams' musically superior 'Vagabond'; but 'Wandering the King's Highway', with its rambling rhythm, comfortable range, and that never-to-be-missed *tenuto* on the last high note, was the quintessential drawing-room ballad.[9]

Dawson also renewed his association with BBC radio and television.

When television ceased in September 1939 there had been no announcement: television screens simply went blank. In September 1946 – at the
same hour of the same day – the screens flickered again and an elegant
voice said: 'We apologise for the break in transmission caused by unfore-
seen circumstances and return you now to your programme.' The same
Mickey Mouse cartoon continued from the point where it had been interrupted in 1939.[10]

A year later Dawson appeared on the television show, *Music Makers*. It
heralded a flurry of BBC activity that was dovetailed into his touring and
recording commitments:

1947
Sept 4: *Music Makers*[11]
Oct 2: Peter Dawson – 7 songs.
Oct 22: *Around and About* with David Martin – Interview
Nov 30: *Grand Hotel* – 4 songs with Albert Sandler's orchestra
Dec 22: BBC Theatre Orchestra – 4 songs including an arrangement of
    'The Twelve Days of Christmas'.
Dec 26: George Melachrino Orchestra and the Luton Girls' Choir.[12]

1948
Mar 1: *Puzzle Plate*; host Ronnie Waldman. Peter sang 'Walk Down the
    Road' supported by Kenneth Horne and Richard Murdoch from *Much
    Binding in the Marsh*.
May 17: *Favourites from his Repertoire* BBC Variety Orchestra, BBC Chorus,
    Doris Arnold at the piano. 7 Peter Dawson songs including 'Simon the
    Cellarer'.
Aug 27: BBC Theatre Orchestra.
Sept 7: *Tuesday Pop*, BBC Theatre Orchestra – 4 songs including Handel's
    'Droop not, young lover' [Handel a 'pop' composer?]
Dec 12: *Sunday Evening Popular Concert* – BBC Theatre Orchestra.[13]

Dawson's diaries also mention social engagements with a range of
personalities including Harold Fielding, Fred Gaisberg, Kenneth Neate, actor/
comedian Stanley Holloway, Sir Louis Sterling, Thomas Playford (Premier
of South Australia), and Robert Menzies. One notable social event was the
bon voyage party the Gramophone Company hosted at the Savoy a few
days before Peter and Nan left again for Australia. Sixty-five signatures of
recording company associates were scribbled on a farewell card; Peter sang
'The Kerry Dance' and told all those in-house stories again; and the general
manager, Sir Ernest Fisk, presented Peter with the 'Model 2000 Reproducer'
and an 1898 'Trade Mark Model Gramophone'.[14] The EMI press release

updated the old superlatives: 'The British Empire's King Of The Ballad'; 'has travelled 250,000 miles'; 'has recorded more than 3500 songs'; 'consistent best seller for HMV for 40 years'. On his departure Peter told the press that he was making his '10th tour of Australia and New Zealand'.[15]

On 14 December 1948 Peter and Nan sailed on the *Orcades,* which was making its maiden voyage to Australia. They arrived in Sydney on 14 January 1949. They had hardly landed when it was announced that Dawson was under exclusive contract to the ABC for 'a long tour', which would begin in Sydney on 7 February and take him throughout the country. 'He will give studio recitals in all States on the mainland, and in NSW, Victoria, West Australia and Queensland he will give public recitals; he will also appear with the Sydney, Melbourne and Queensland symphony orchestras'.[16]

The official announcement came at the end of another contract saga, which was finally resolved during Dawson's journey home. Bill Bearup, now ABC representative in London, had advised Sydney in November that '[Dawson's] agent says he has not had a concert tour of Victoria and Queensland for ten years, of South Australia and Western Australia for fifteen years & Tasmania for seventeen.' Despite the short notice Moses cabled an offer at Dawson's wartime rate: 15 guineas studio, £40 public recitals. In Colombo Peter wrote in his diary: 'Tues 28 wired Broadcast – nothing doing.' Like two old bulls, Charles Moses and Peter Dawson locked horns again. Cables, telegrams, teleprinters churned out offers and counter-offers as Dawson battled obstinately for a return to pre-war fees. He and Harold Williams might have accepted 15 guineas for studio engagements as part of the war effort, he said, but times had changed.

Finally, Peter signed a contract for a minimum of 25 appearances in studio recitals and variety programmes, at 40 guineas studio, 35 variety; 11 public recitals at 60 guineas and eight orchestral concerts at 50 guineas, as well as fares for himself and Nan when travelling out of Sydney.[17] It had been a long haul. On the front page of his diary he commented: 'Never in the history of human endeavour have so many been buggered about by so few – for bugger all. John Citizen.'

On 28 February Dawson met the young winner of that year's ABC Instrumental and Vocal Competition: Geoffrey Parsons, who became his 'Associate Artist' and 'self-effacing accompanist'.[18] Parsons received a fee of £15 per week, plus a travelling allowance of 25/- per diem when absent from Sydney.[19]

On 7 March Peter, Nan and Geoffrey Parsons flew twelve hours by Trans Australian Airlines to Perth to begin the tour. How times had changed. In 1939 Dawson had complained: 'I was expected to sing in all sorts of

Peter with his new young accompanist, Geoffrey Parsons, 1949 winner of the ABC's Instrumental and Vocal Competition, in concert in Dunedin, New Zealand, October 1949.

out-of-the-way-places, such as Kalgoorlie and Broken Hill. Naturally I objected!' He listed this itinerary in his diary: Perth, Kalgoorlie, Adelaide, Melbourne, Bendigo, Melbourne, Mildura; on 10 May they reached Broken Hill. The following day the 67-year-old stopped off at the radio station where he 'was linked to 138 two-way wireless sets within a radius of 500 miles [and] the air was soon filled with gales of laughter as impromptu funny stories were exchanged.'[20]

The diary continued: Ballarat, Horsham, Mount Gambier, Geelong, Wollongong, Sydney, Armidale, Tamworth, Newcastle, West Maitland, Bundaberg, Rockhampton, Townsville, Mackay, Brisbane, 'Sydney Sat 2 July end of tour'.[21] At the end of the tour Dawson boasted that he had travelled 'over 12,000 miles by air'. Some 9,000 customers had paid to hear him, and he had netted £1,690.[22]

Comments on the strength of Dawson's voice began to surface: 'obviously saving his voice, and employs what might be described as a "microphone" technique, whether singing over the air or in the hall'. [23] In Brisbane, however, the young music reporter for the *Courier Mail*, Roger Covell, was enthusiastic: his article was headed 'Peter Dawson First Lord of the Gramophone' and sub-headed 'Croon-happy teenagers, fed on milk-and-water songs flock to his concerts to hear that robust hearty voice.' Another Queensland critic was more circumspect: 'Peter Dawson is in danger of becoming a legend during his own lifetime.'[24]

Dawson did not rest: he and Geoffrey Parsons soon set off for New Zealand to perform '26 concerts in 19 centres' between about 1 September and 3 November.[25] Dawson used four different programmes, each with a total of eleven of his classical numbers. If he sang his hits – which he surely did – then they were encores. This tour grossed over £5,000 and netted almost £4,500. As could be expected, the best box-office receipts were in the larger cities – Auckland, Christchurch, Wellington and Dunedin – with small top-ups in Napier, Blenheim and Oamaru. Dawson left Auckland for Sydney by flying-boat at 8am, Saturday 5 November, arriving at Rose Bay at 2 pm.

Ten days later he and Nan set off for England again. Harold Fielding had been able to arrange 'over 60 concerts' through the provinces. 'Fielding has signed me on for 10 months exclusive for concerts and broadcasting – I wonder who Fielding will couple up with me. I hope neither the Booths or Rawicz & Landauer blokes – I've had them', wrote Dawson to Arch Kerr, recording manager for EMI in Sydney.[26] Mr and Mrs Dawson settled into their first-class cabin with bath on the *Dominion Monarch* (cost £360) to sail from Sydney to Southampton via the Cape; they arrived in London on

17 December. H.M. Inspector of Taxes had again had news of Dawson's return and felt sure that Dawson would like to drop into the office to discuss his 1948–49 tax liability.[27] Dawson confided his plight to the press: 'At 69, Peter Dawson ("A Gipsy am I") is to travel the road again. After 50 years as a concert singer, he says: "I am so near broke that I cannot afford to do anything else".'[28] It could have been this taxation burden which necessitated this final 'final' tour of England.

The first concert took place again at the Opera House, Blackpool, on Christmas Day 1949; in the end there were about 40 concerts.[29] In the new year he was joined by Geoffrey Parsons: 'It was a six-months concert tour that turned into permanent residence,' said Parsons later.

> Showbiz, smiles and endless performances of 'The Road To Mandalay' lasted until Dawson came home and handed me over to fellow variety stars Anne Ziegler and Webster Booth, the intensity of whose shimmering love duets was equalled only by the bitterness of their backstage rows.[30]

An invitation to sing 'Waltzing Matilda' on Australia Day was the beginning of a substantial number of BBC engagements for Dawson.[31] At one of his weekly commitments to *Rainbow Room* an EMI executive heard him singing 'Waiata Poi'.[32] 'We enjoyed [the concert] immensely', she wrote, 'particularly the Maori song, during which I was strongly tempted to jump up and "whoop" with you.'[33] But for Dawson 'the greatest and most pleasing success I achieved … was the series in 1950 called "Our Pleasure to Present". The first programme was on Sunday, 4 July, and the twelfth on 19 September.'[34] These programmes gave him particular pleasure because he sang a sacred song in each, and he could enjoy the company of old friends Doris Arnold (piano), Herbert Dawson, Hubert Greenslade and Walter Goehr, still conducting the 60-piece BBC Theatre Orchestra.

To keep their share of the home entertainment market, the record companies strove continually to improve their product. 'High fidelity', which had seemed elusive in the 1930s, became a reality in 1944.[35] Magnetic tape, a new recording medium developed by the Germans during the war, came into limited commercial use in Europe and America in 1947 and finally forced the introduction of 'fine thread', better quality, microgroove recordings. In June 1948 American Columbia introduced the first successful 33$^{1/3}$ rpm LP. In January 1949, RCA Victor announced the release of a 45rpm 7in. vinyl disc, designed to compete with the 10in. 78rpm. When Decca introduced 33rpm records to the British market in June 1950 a battle of the speeds began. Sales of 78rpm declined dramatically and became obsolete in 1959. Recording on tape came into general use as the new recording method for the production of discs, spelling the death of the time-honoured but temperamental wax-master method.[36]

Dawson got in touch with EMI again. To 'find out whether he still has a public' the Gramophone Company signed him up to record two modern pop numbers, 'The Cry of the Wild Goose' and 'That Lucky Old Sun'.[37] These ballads, closely related to the dross he recorded in the early 1920s, were more suitable for the current crop of crooners, whisperers and shouters. Tennessee Ernie Ford, Vaughn Monroe ('The Mellow Bellow'), Frank Sinatra, Sarah Vaughan and Louis Armstrong were among those who recorded these songs; and Frankie Laine, who earned a gold record for both in 1949–50. So, despite the *Gramophone's* enthusiastic review – 'sounding as young as the best of them' – it was clearly mission impossible.

The BBC, however, stuck with Dawson's tried and trusty repertoire. He put forward the idea for 'a series of 10 programmes under the title "Songs I Have Sung – from 1900-1950", which was developed into the series *Fifty Years of Song*, for release during the Festival of Britain the following year.[38] 'The average cost [was] £155 per programme.' Costs for the artist, the accompanist, the conductor and the orchestra reveal the hierarchy:

Peter Dawson	52/10/0
Freddy Grisewood	12/12/0
Louis Voss Orchestra of 22	70/10/0
+ orchestrations	6/ 0/0
	141/12/0[39]

The variable factor was the 'number of new orchestrations required for some of the old-fashioned songs he sang and for which music was not available'. Much of Peter's music had been out of circulation for at least two decades, so the decision to proceed must have been strongly supported by someone with the power to authorise such a substantial outlay. That person was none other than L. Stanton Jefferies, the 'Head of Light Music', who had been one of the accompanists for the Australia Day broadcast in 1923.

Dawson pre-recorded all the programmes between 22 August and 4 October.[40] Sometimes the old warhorse would record three days in a row and he retained his policy of interlacing anecdotes among the songs: ('He told us scores of rattling good stories in his broadcast series, *Fifty Years of Song*.')[41] Unwittingly, Peter was building a monument to himself: BBC administrators might have thought the music old-fashioned, but the large listening audience in 1951 did not. Here were the songs indelibly associated with Peter Dawson: here was the Peter Dawson they had always known.

Two days after the last BBC recording Peter and Nan sailed once more for Australia on the *Orcades*. On the way – 'Indian Ocean, 19.10.50' – he dropped a note to Stanton Jefferies:

> Dear Jeff,
>
> Do you think you could possibly lend me the score of 'Lament of Shah Jehan' as used. It has never been done over there with orchestra & yours being such a beaut, I would deem it an everlasting favour Etc Etc and minza brown sherry. … and then again Jeff – a copy of that lovely song 'Your Voice Beloved'. I will reimburse you most significantly Jiffy old pal.
>
> Poor Nan has had a bad fall and injured herself badly … The weather is Hell with the lid off. The ladies are quite bare from the arse to the ground, but it is nice & refreshing even after my 50 years of song to see the dear things at play with tiny balls and coyly laughing and tittering. The latter game is played where there is least light & it is most uplifting for the deaf and short-sighted. I will drop you a line from time to time just to let you know 'how's things'. Both Nan & I trust this finds you well and that Sheila is enjoying the same blessings – please give her our love. We arrive in Sydney on Nov 6th & shan't be sorry with poor Nan crocked up. My very kindly remembrances to Marjorie.
>
> Cheers & Beers
> Your old Cobber
> Peter Dawson

The boat arrived in Fremantle on 28 October; on 5 December the *Advertiser* titillated its readers with the news that Adelaide's favourite son would begin another ABC tour beginning in Melbourne on 9 December. Back in May Dawson had written a gossipy letter to Charles Moses: he referred to the Festival Hall which was 'quickly taking shape', expressed his 'unbounded enjoyment' at watching the King and Queen on television, and mentioned that he intended to leave England in November.[42] Moses took his cue: 1951 was to be a year of celebration for the fiftieth anniversary of Australian Federation. So, on William James' advice: 'I think Dawson would be well worth using. He is an Australian figure and we must <u>not</u> overlook him', cables again began to fly back and forth. Dawson suggested 'one weekly studio from Sydney as from week commencing 12 November until end of year and at £50 per appearance': the ABC had offered £40. Dawson refused, so Moses agreed to £50 if he would throw in the three orchestral appearances at the same price; but Dawson wanted £100 for each orchestral. In the end both parties agreed on £60.

The Dawsons arrived in Sydney on 6 November: on 19 November Peter sang an open-air concert at Cooper Park, Woollahra. The concert, under the baton of the famous English conductor, Eugene Goossens, drew huge crowds.[43] The newspapers had a field day:

> to most of his fellow-countrymen a favourite record-and-radio voice rather than a living person ... in the flesh they saw and heard a short, bald, but heavily handsome man ... he is unmistakably a man with a great gusto for life, who has had and still has lots of fun.[44]

The *Sydney Morning Herald* carried a photo of the aging monarch of the ballad, sub-captioned 'Peter Dawson besieged by autograph hunters at Cooper Park.'; the *Daily Telegraph* was headed: '20,000 listened to two arias' – our old friends 'Largo al Factotum' and 'Now Your Days Of Philandering Are Over'. With the former Dawson could always hit his target: about a year later, in Mildura, he again opened with this aria and 'in three brief minutes 68-year-old baritone Peter Dawson last night stole the show' – but 'was not allowed to sing anything except the two items programmed.'[45]

Prior to the major tours of the jubilee year there were about a dozen miscellaneous concerts. One in particular must have given him a great deal of satisfaction: on 7 December 1950 Dawson sang a 'Special EXTRA Performance' of *Messiah* in the Adelaide Town Hall, to honour the golden jubilee of 'his first performance under the baton of the late C. J. Stevens'.[46] He had fulfilled the destiny predicted by his mentor at the turn of the century. The critic praised the conductor, the choir, tenor Fred Williamson, and, of course, Peter Dawson: 'The rich, sweet timbre of Mr Dawson's voice, and the artistry with which he made his climaxes, in the recitative 'For Behold Darkness' and the following air 'The People Who Walked in Darkness' make his singing here memorable.' The orchestra, however, was not praised: it was blamed for drowning 'the finer nuances of the singer's quiet, but eloquent, interpretation'.

For some time, other critics, too, had been worrying about his 'saving his voice' or 'singing quietly', and rumours were floating around about memory lapses. Memory lapses are quite common among singers; Dawson recalled an occasion he had blacked out while singing 'The Erl King': he could not even remember the beginning again so he turned the embarrassing moment to his advantage by singing 'The Floral Dance' instead.[47] But that was some 20 years earlier; now he always had the text in front of him for studio sessions and admitted he had 'bother learning new songs'.[48]

A member of the South Australian orchestra recalled a recording session when Dawson had become completely lost several times and was suspected of being drunk. Although there is no documentation corroborating excessive drinking, another source reported seeing him a more than trifle merry on one occasion. Later diary entries and comments in interviews suggest that in old age he did not always adhere to the abstinence of earlier days.

Dawson's own jubilee in 1951 did not go unnoticed. A Melbourne Town Hall programme at the end of May proclaimed him as 'the world's most popular baritone'.[49] His associate artists included the soprano Marjorie Lawrence and the young Aboriginal tenor, Harold Blair (1924-1976). Blair had hit the limelight in March 1945 by winning the annual final of Australia's *Amateur Hour*, one of the most popular commercial radio competitions, with a record number of votes. Although audiences loved him he was unable to sustain the rigours of a concert career. In later life he worked for the Moral Rearmament movement in Europe and was an activist in the cause of his neglected people. Blair remembered the concert vividly:

> [Dawson] was a wonderful man, a really fine old chap ... but unfortunately he was well past his best when I met him, little wonder after 50 years of singing! We all learnt much from being associated with him for whilst his voice had almost gone at this stage there was still the fine technique and authority of style.[50]

Some were now commenting that Dawson's old zing was missing, others that he had used up his vocal capital and was living off the accumulated interest. But Dawson had invested a lifetime in his voice and building his popularity. Now, even without the physical capability of his prime, he still had so much concert and broadcast charisma that his public was apparently prepared to adore him forever.

For a moment, however, Dawson's attention was diverted by the Korean War: 'He is now singing for a new recruiting drive. "I'm too old to join up myself but if I can do anything to help build up our defences – then I'm in it, boots and all".'[51] In one song, 'Now or Never', 'the patriotic sentiment was so vigorous that it aroused the anger of pacifists and others.'[52]

As part of the ABC's obligation to the Commonwealth Jubilee Celebrations William James had organised a series of tours for Dawson beginning in April. Now that he was re-established in the ABC's good books, Dawson enthusiastically endorsed radio: 'He thinks that the phonograph has been the greatest means in the world of musical education, bringing the best into homes', wrote one staff member; 'radio he rates as the phonograph's worthy successor.'[53] However, when the South Australian ABC tried to contact him at the end of May, they were surprised to discover he was touring

Tasmania for the Red Cross. In the packed Hobart City Hall he sang 16 songs and 13 encores. 'Those which appealed most to the audience were ... "Green Hills of Somerset", "Boots" and "Snowbird". After singing another favourite, the "Cornish Floral Dance", Peter Dawson commented: "That must be the 7000th performance!"'[54]

Dawson's set programmes were the old familiars; the only relatively new material being 'Gentleman Jim' (Oliver), Pat Thayer's haunting North American Indian ballad, 'Snowbird' and his own 'Mandalay Potpourri'.[55] He was sent from one side of the country to the other, especially into the provincial centres and into schools – a nice way of reminding parents of the concert that night. A note in his diary sums it all up: '28 October: 14th wear of dress shirt'.

In England *Fifty Years of Song* was broadcast each Sunday afternoon from 6 May–8 July. It was an instant success:

> Peter Dawson's first big radio comeback, which proves (a) that he is still in magnificent voice; (b) that the old ballads still have the power to bring a blink to the eye; (c) that here, if anywhere, is a singer worthy of a regular series. *More of Mr Dawson please.*[56]

It was the right time for the English publishers Hutchinson & Co to bring out Dawson's memoirs, also titled *Fifty Years of Song*. Despite his celebrity status, no one had yet written a biography of Dawson, so he had done it himself. Geoffrey Parsons recollected him preparing notes during their 1949 New Zealand tour: 'Peter certainly enjoyed my company – and I enjoyed his probably ten times as much – I think he was in the process of writing his book at the time and reminding himself of stories as we were going along in the bus.'[57] When Dawson returned to Australia in 1950 he left his manuscript and notes in England where 'Tom Noble was to edit & publish them'.[58] The autobiography was released in Britain in October 1951. Dawson had had a hand in the drafting but it was left to his English connections to see it through to publication, so the rumour that it was ghostwritten was partly true.

Peter Dawson fans still regard the contents of *Fifty Years of Song* as gospel. But as the London music critic and broadcaster, L. A. G. Strong, wrote: 'His memory is not always accurate, and it is a pity he did not get someone to read the proofs.' Strong noted a long list of errors, but concluded: 'these are trivial flaws in a lively, interesting, often valuable book, the life-story of a fine singer and a warm-hearted, fearless, and likeable man.'[59]

The fateful year 1951 set in train a change in Dawson's domestic life. Since 1945 photographs of Nan had shown a frail, grey-haired, genteel lady dressed in sober elegance. Her poor health since the early days of their marriage, exacerbated by the dreadful car accident in 1925, was taking its toll. Her diary, full of depressing entries, reveals why she had been too ill to accompany her husband on the 1949 New Zealand tour: 'bad back – pain in side – pains all over me – ill all night – ray lamp, all day treatment.' In early 1951 a reporter commented: 'Nowadays she is far from robust, and her white hair and soft, slow voice give an impression of frailty and of a person who has suffered much physical pain.'[60]

On 10 June 1951 Nan's youngest sister, Constance – the little girl for whom Peter had drawn that cartoon in 1913 – made a note in her diary: 'Wrote to Nanner, asking if they would like me to come out to Australia'. Nan accepted Con's offer: 'Arrived Australia on the "Orcades" Sat 20th – Ruby Staton met me, we went home to Nannie's. 31 Wolseley St Haberfield.'[61] Constance was a shy person and her life had not been easy. She had not married but remained at home to look after her mother until she died. Constance immediately became part of the Dawson household where she found herself fulfilling much the same role.[62]

Another matter also came to a head in 1951: the question of a knighthood. Despite his fame, Peter Dawson had never received any public honours. 'Australia had Melba, Malcolm McEachern and it has you – and you three have carried the name of Australia everywhere. But while you have gone everywhere the two others went, you have gone into the hearts they never reached,' wrote Dame Mary Gilmore.[63] He was accustomed to accolades, he was constantly named as one of Australia's musical ambassadors: he had every right to believe that the Commonwealth Government might treat him as one of Australia's honoured sons.

An Australian Archives file: 'Peter Dawson – Civil Honours (1949-58)' shows that the matter had been raised.[64] In December 1949 a Mr G. C. Ghys of Haberfield had written to the newly-elected Prime Minister, Robert Menzies, suggesting that Peter Dawson be honoured in the New Year's List. No particular honour was suggested. Mr Ghys was advised that the proposal had been noted.

In February 1949 Stan Staton[65], trading manager of the New South Wales Returned Services League, had lobbied the South Australian Premier, Thomas Playford, on Dawson's behalf. Playford had already successfully recommended another South Australian, Don Bradman, for a knighthood, yet he responded that honours were a Commonwealth prerogative. Then in November 1950, at Staton's prompting, Jim Beveridge, OBE, general manager of McClaren and Co., Printers, of Fitzroy, Victoria,[66] approached his friend Prime Minister Menzies. Menzies and Beveridge knew Dawson well: they had been connected for some years through the Caledonian Society,

Melbourne Scots, and Dawson had lunched privately with Menzies from time to time in Australia and England.[67] To support the efficacy of this nomination Staton and Beveridge had included a cutting about Sir Donald Bradman, because there had been some question whether a sportsman could qualify for such an honour.[68] As Bradman had been successful, they felt sure Menzies would see no objection in extending the honour to an outstanding singer. Menzies acknowledged receipt of the nomination on 24 November.

Another nomination from a Reverend Broughton of Sale in Victoria crossed Menzies' desk the following May (1951):

> Peter Dawson has delighted millions during a long and tireless life. He is a true son of Australia. A native troubadour if ever there were one. We honour cricketers and others of less account than they. Might it not help to dispel the creeping cynicism in the matter of 'honours' if we could have Sir Peter?

In June Menzies contacted Jim Beveridge, who immediately supplied 'the details which you requested regarding our mutual friend', adding, 'I am sure that if Peter is knighted the bestowal of this Honour would have universal approval, not only in Australia, but all over the English-speaking world.' This last letter suggests an agreement between the two, but no decision was made in Dawson's favour.

Another three proposals for a knighthood also fell on deaf ears. In theory Dawson knew nothing of these attempts but the style of the biographical material suggests that he had been consulted. Unfortunately, the assessments of unsuccessful applicants are destroyed so we shall never know why Dawson's nominations failed. The last entry in his file is dated 1958: the Governor-General's Secretary wrote to the Prime Minister's Department: 'I am enclosing some biographical notes and would like to suggest for your consideration that he be recommended for an O.B.E. in the next List. I am sure that such an award would be wildly acclaimed.' Wildly? Not as wildly acclaimed as a knighthood. Having ignored the man for so long it would have been a pitiful reward.

King George VI died on 6 February 1952 after a reign of sixteen years. He had hoped to see Britain rejuvenated after the Depression but had witnessed only war and the gradual devolution of the British Empire. Post-war rehabilitation was still underway when the mood of hope for continued peace and prosperity became vested in his daughter, Elizabeth II, as she accepted orb and sceptre.

Although Dawson's performance cupboard was not bare, 1952 was comparatively quiet: there were 26 country recitals – as far flung as Warren

(Western NSW), Burnie (Tasmania) and Charleville (Queensland) – for which
he received £1,620. He also sang four recitals in New Guinea.[69] On 18
October he and Clarence Black flew to Port Moresby for two recitals, then
on to Wau and Lae, and were back home by 29 October. But it was Nan's
failing health which now preoccupied Peter.

Con's diary read: 'Year not a very happy one. Nannie's health seemed to
be getting worse. Nannie taken to Masonic Hospital Ashfield 7pm suffering
from coronary occlusion paralytic seizure, 6th Sat Dec: 1952.' Old trouper
that he was, Peter sang in the ABC *Australia Day Concert*. A few days later, on
31 January 1953, Nan died. Peter's diary continued the story:

> Monday 2 February: Bill, Con, Matie & I went to Ch of Eng Summer
> Hill, 8 pm. Nan in her coffin lay before the altar. The organist played
> 'Evensong'. Tuesday 3 February: Funeral Service, 10am Ch of England,
> Summer Hill. Archdeacon Hume Moir. Then to Rookwood
> Cemetery.[70]

On the bereavement acknowledgement he had printed:

> Now in her green mantle blithe nature arrays
> And listens the lambkins that bleat o'er the braes
> While birds warble welcome in ilka green shaw;
> But tae me it's delightless, my Nannie's awa'
>   Robert Burns

Nan died on Peter's 71st birthday. Tragic as it was for him, her death was
not unexpected. 'Don't go back. Stay on and look after the old boy,' whispered the dying Nan to Constance.[71]

Con stayed. Left alone with a sister-in-law seventeen years his junior
Peter's attitude towards her changed completely. He took on a new lease of
life as Con became his new confidante. A fortnight after Nan's death Con
wrote: 'Pete & I left for Adelaide on the 13th Feb, 1953, my first plane trip,
from Mascot'. From now on, as contracts show, Con became Peter's travelling companion. They sold the house in Haberfield and moved to Hal-
cyon Flats, Darling Point.

As there had been no EMI recordings for more than two years, Dawson
flirted with the idea of making private recordings for both Rex Shaw's
Prestophone and Stuart Booty's *Vitavox* labels. Three 10in. 78rpm titles exist
on *Prestophone* for 1953 but three noted in Booty's 1951 diary do not.[72] Rex
Shaw was a recording engineer; Booty was a man of parts, had invented
film cameras, film biograph machines and X-ray plants. In 1921 he had
produced his Vitavox gramophone; and during the mid-1920s had recorded

many Sydney artists. He still continued to make private recordings in his Leichhardt studio. However, Stuart Booty appears to have entered the Dawsons' lives as a practitioner of homeopathic medicine to whom Nan had turned for support. She and Edith Booty became good friends and Dawson and Booty developed the idea of founding their own recording business. As Booty wrote to a cousin:

> Mr. Peter Dawson is also throwing his weight into the concern. He has done a great amount for the HMV, but he told me they have treated him rather shabbily. Naturally we must use caution, as the big influence of Columbia and HMV would try to put a spoke in our wheel and prevent us starting if they could.

The idea came to nothing. Dawson was reinstated by EMI and the embittered Booty believed he had been misused:

> Peter Dawson let me down over the recording. I made out a rough prospectus for a company, showing him equal sharing with myself. I was to be in charge and he musical director. He took my rough copy to HMV and used it for his own benefit. They paid him a large sum to keep him with them, so I cut him out altogether, and it is fortunate I found out before we got started. I have been told since that he's done similar things to other people here and has got himself disliked in consequence.[73]

1953 was marked by occasional engagements but generally things were now slack, partly due to Dawson's miserable health during the winter. A few entries from his diary tell the melancholy tale:

> 3 JUNE: bronchitis & influenza – Dr called in by Con – Dr Blake Greaves, a charming man & a pleasure to be sick with him. He's 'bout my age & full of knowledgeable musical data – feeling lousy.
> 4 JUNE: Dr visited 10am Examined bronchial tubes – said the organ was playing 'Roses of Picardy' with 40ft Stop. Whistling in the bronchials. Still feeling lousy.
> 5 JUNE: Dr visited 10am Hell of a hurry – thousands on his round suffering from Influenza – I know – I must have spread it per his overcoat. Weather terrifically cold – wind from Blue Mountains – train whistles and barking backfires – feeling bloody awful – Blue Heaven for me!
> 6 JUNE: Dr visited 10am he said he was satisfied & going alright – him or me? Blimey, a lady visitor collided with my gouty toe-end – gurgling like a sink plug. Blimey

16 JUNE: First day up, much better
17 JUNE: Down again – feeling very old and burned up.
18 JUNE: Up again.

That year Gerald Moore came to Australia to accompany the German soprano Irmgard Seefried; but the ABC had also contracted him to give a number of public talks about his career. 'Bill, Pete & I, Frank & Maddie Halls went to hear & see Gerald Moore at the Conservatorium', wrote Con. It was the last time Gerald Moore saw Peter:

> We spent several evenings together and he always turned up like the good friend he was at my lectures in Sydney. By this time he had lost his first wife Nanny to whom he was devoted and he had retired from the public platform. He had a new wife, Conny … I spent the evening prior to my departure at dinner in his house and we laughed and chatted over old days. He came to the airport with his friend Harold Williams to see me off. My final glimpse of him was his cheery face as he waved me goodbye.[74]

The year 1954 was more productive. The most intensive undertaking was the ABC studio series, *Fifty Years of Song* – not a BBC transcription but a new series in the same style. (The BBC and ABC programmes for these series are listed at the end of the chapter.) The idea of re-creating the BBC series in Australia had been in Peter Dawson's mind ever since he wrote that letter to Stanton Jefferies in 1950. Now it was reality. The BBC format was repeated: five years in each segment starting with 1900. The series was scheduled for ten weeks beginning 8 March.[75] Jack McNamara, a fine trombonist, remembered Peter interlacing stories when prompted by the celebrated announcer, Bryson Taylor:[76] 'Bryson Taylor, who had a very plummy ABC-type voice, asked him, "When you knew you were going to London to be a singer, what went through your mind?" Peter the Plumber replied: "Hooray! No more dunny diving!"' Peter Dawson's repertoire and anecdotes proved so popular that the series was repeated each week from 4 January 1955. But by then Peter had married Constance and they were on tour in England.

Dawson's diary entry for 29 April 1954, 'our wedding day', was illustrated by a heart pierced by two arrows. When the last episode of *Fifty Years* had been completed the 'young couple' set off to Queensland on their honeymoon. But why marry at his age? As Constance tells it: after Peter had suffered a mild heart attack, she had moved another bed into his bedroom to be near at hand should anything happen. 'One day, out of the blue Peter said, "Connie, I think we'll have to get married, people are beginning to talk." I said, "Well, please yourself" – and we got married.' On 8 November Peter and Constance boarded the *Iberia* for England via Suez for a final, final, 'final' tour of England. Harold Fielding believed they had 'arrived for a year's stay';[77] but Peter and Constance left again at the end of May 1955 because Fielding's promised concert engagements had proved almost nil.[78]

Although concert audiences had disappeared, there was still a large audience for BBC radio and television. Dawson's first television appearance on the David Nixon Show, *Home & Dry*, to celebrate Australia Day, was not auspicious. At the rehearsal he fell down the entrance stairs. He tried to hold the corporation culpable for his injuries but they said it was his own fault.[79] Despite this, Peter later told an Adelaide newspaper that 'a highlight of his seven-month English tour had been his appearance in the Australia Day show'.[80] During his stay he also pre-recorded four recitals under the title *Peter Dawson Singing*, which were broadcast later in the year. In October a friend wrote to Peter:

> the BBC series ended last night … programme before included 'Waltzing Matilda' and 'Snow Bird' … last night 'Boots'. Dollie said, 'He has not sung "Boots" in any of the series' and lo and behold 'Boots' came through as the last number, as only Peter can sing it.'[81]

When the Gramophone Company executives learned that Dawson was in England they graciously invited him and Con to celebrate his 73rd birthday at Hayes.[82] This goodwill generated a final recording: 'Clancy of the Overflow' coupled with Dawson's own curious potpourri, re-named 'Mandalay Scena'. At Dawson's request the young Australian conductor, Charles Mackerras,[83] who had conducted for *Peter Dawson Singing*, was employed for the take with the London Symphony Orchestra at Abbey Road on 4 May.[84] On this last EMI disc Dawson's recording abilities have hardly diminished. Albert Arlen's setting of Banjo Paterson's 'Clancy' (pub. 1948) is musically a little more adventurous than Dawson's own ballads. The overall rhythm is designated 4/4 but it varies throughout and uses some quasi-recitative sections. For vocal comfort Dawson sang from an edited version, transposed 'down one tone' – into F major, with a range, A–E. Con was present at the recording:

> I'll never forget Charles Mackerras – they had been through it twice – I sat at the back and just listened – it was a lovely orchestra and everything like that – and the producer said, 'Oh that'll be alright.' But Charles Mackerras came up and said: 'Oh, you can't do that! You see you've played a messed tape, Peter. You've said "dirty city" instead of "dusty city".' Now the most difficult song to sing is 'Clancy of the Overflow'.

I've never heard anybody sing it like Peter did. Very, very tricky. And
Peter was singing it so quickly – that it wouldn't be noticed. So Peter
said, 'You can go to buggery as far as I'm concerned I'm not going
through that another time.' So the producer said 'Oh no. Just let it go.
You couldn't better that.' [85]

Those of us who think that 'On the Road to Mandalay' is the ultimate
drawing room ballad, the acme of a Peter Dawson programme; those of
us who feel ourselves striding out when the bold opening measures are
played, only to be pulled back by the sudden, repeated, *rum-tiditty-tum-tum* in
the dark minor key when we are confronted by the Old Mulmein Pagoda;
we show that we are mere youngsters in the business of ballad singing.
Because Oley Speaks' setting of 'On the Road to Mandalay' was the last of
four settings of Kipling's poem which Dawson made famous.[86]

Those familiar with Dawson's 'On the Road to Mandalay' might assume
the poem had three verses, of which the second was often cut. In fact, the
poem has six verses which begin:

- By the old Mulmein pagoda
- 'Er petticoat was yellar
- When the mist was on the rice fields,
- But that's all shove behind me
- I am sick o' wastin' leather
- Ship me somewhere's east of Suez

Each verse ends with a repetition of the phrase: 'On the Road to Mandalay...'.

'Mandalay Scena' gives a brief insight into changing styles during the
span of Dawson's career. In it he has combined sections of the four
settings he knew: Speaks, Hedgcock, Willeby and Cobb. The product is
not a clever fusion of the four songs, it is merely a hotch-potch: Dawson
has taken one section from each setting and tied them loosely together.
He obviously liked Speaks' robust music to catch the audience attention
but, surprisingly, favoured Cobb's waltzing finish, which has no elaborate ending.

The disc of 'Clancy of the Overflow' and 'Mandalay Scena' was released mono-aurally in February 1956 as one of the first extended-play
45rpm versions. However, the veteran critic W. A. Chislett noted that '"Mandalay Scena" was recorded bi-aurally (in effect, stereophonically) and heard
by visitors to the Radio Show last year'.[87] Some may consider 'Mandalay
Scena' dated but Chislett selected it as one of the six outstanding records of

the year, in fact, he thought that it was 'one of the most remarkable of all time'. Vintage Peter Dawson.

If the BBC producers were treading on eggshells after the Australia Day incident, they need not have worried: Dawson's last BBC television performance, *Music for You* on 25 April 1955, was the hit of the season:

> OLD FATHER DAWSON PUTS LIFE IN TV
>
> It took the 73-year-old Australian baritone Peter Dawson to put life and vitality into last night's TV programme 'Music for You'. Until he appeared it had threatened to die of a palsy brought on by a series of old English songs presented against a phoney Olde English background. On came Peter Dawson with 'The Floral Dance' and the inevitable 'Road to Mandalay'. Straightforward, bustling, honest-to-goodness stuff, bringing red blood to what, until then, had been an anaemic programme.[88]

The *News Chronicle* bannered with: 'A Hot Sausage, Caruso and Melba', for Dawson could not resist taking a crack at Melba. In his book he admits to her talent as a singer but deplored her manners:

> For years Melba was referred to by musicians as 'Madam Sweet and Low.' A sweet voice, but low language. There is no doubt that she possessed a glorious voice. The trouble was that she was unable to 'get down to earth' again after her rave notices. From the nice Australian girl she became the spoilt social snob of the music world.[89]

The newspapers recounted that during the television show, 'his eyes twinkled like a naughty schoolboy as he told an outrageous story of Caruso pressing a hot sausage into Melba's palm as he sang "Your Tiny Hand Is Frozen".' Dawson's co-star that evening, the renowned soprano Elisabeth Schwarzkopf might well have felt like extending the old adage 'never appear on stage with children or animals' to 'or with Peter Dawson'.

Shortly after the television success Dawson told reporters that 'the sudden death of my brother, an industrialist in Sydney, has meant my return to clear up the estate … but I will be back here for a farewell tour lasting most of 1956'. The virile septuagenarian and his 'young' wife boarded the *Himalaya* on 12 May 1955.[90] They could leave England satisfied and optimistic; for Peter's broadcasting and television appearances had created a sensation and his last recording contract had extended his association with the Gramophone Company of London to fifty-one years. Fifty-one years! The stuff of true legends.

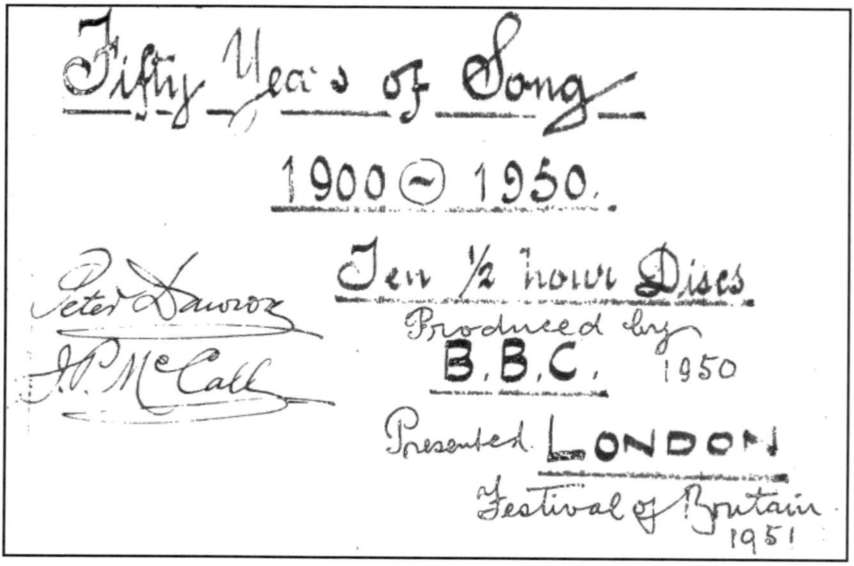

Fifty Years of Song
1900 — 1950.

Peter Dawson
A.P. McCall

Ten ½ hour Discs
Produced by
B.B.C.   1950

Presented LONDON
Festival of Britain
1951

Fifty Years of Song
1900 – 1950

From Peter Dawson's self-made handwritten booklet. The cover is signed *Peter Dawson* and *J. P. McCall*. The booklet has columns for Time, Key, Title, Composer, Publisher; and for ABC also Date of Publication. (BBC and ABC made minimal changes to order)

BBC 1950		**ABC 1954**	
Programme 1: 1900-1905		**Programme 1: 1900-1905**	
The Bandolero	Stuart	O ruddier than the cherry	Handel
Bid me to Love		An Old Garden	Herbert
Out on the Deep	Lohr	Blow Blow thou Winter wind	Sergeant
'Tis I	Pinsuti	The Trumpeter	Dix
Glorious Devon	German	Nazareth	Gounod
Programme 2: 1905-1910		**Programme 2: 1905-1910**	
Bedouin Love Song	Pinsuti	Bright is the Ring of Words	V. Williams
The Arrow and the Song	Balfe	Glorious Devon	German
Trumpeter	Dix	Sincerity	Clarke
Sincerity	Clarke	'Tis I	Pinsuti
Shipmate o' Mine	Squire	The Holy City	Adams
Programme 3: 1910-1915		**Programme 3: 1910-1915**	
Anchored	Watson	The Arrow and the Song	Balfe
Green Hills o' Somerset	Coates	Greens Hills o' Somerset	Coates
My Old Shako	Trotere	My Old Shako	Trotere
Shipmates o' Mine	Squire	Shipmates o' Mine	Squire
At Santa Barbara	Russell	Floral Dance	Moss
Programme 4: 1915-1920		**Programme 4: 1915-1920**	
The Blind Ploughman	Clarke	The Glory of the Sea	Sanderson
Roses of Picardy	Wood	Roses of Picardy	Wood
The Traveller	Godard	The Blind Ploughman	Clarke
Admiral's Yarn	Ruben	Little Grey Home in the West	Lohr
The Floral Dance	Moss	A Sergeant of the Line	Squire

BBC 1950		**ABC 1954**	

Programme 5: 1920-1925

Silent Worship	Handel	The Arrow and the Song	Balfe
The Lute Player	Alltison	The Lute Player	Allitson
The Fairy Lough	Stanford	By the Side of the Road	Thayer
The Bonny Earl o' Moray		A Bachelor Gay	Tate
	HopeTemple		
Mandalay		Boots	McCall
Speaks, Willeby, Hedgcock,Cobb			

Programme 6: 1925-1930

Now your days	Mozart	Kerry Dance	Molloy
Sherwood	Dear	Bless this House	Brahe
Tam I' th' Kirk	Barclay	Up from Somerset	Sanderson
Song of a Sailor	Peal	A Smuggler's Song	Mortimer
Boots	McCall	Westward Ho!	McCall

Programme 7: 1930-1935

The Air Pilot	Garrett	The Snowbird	Thayer
Coronach	Barrett	Wanderthirst	Fordell
The Snowbird	Thayer	Waltzing Matilda	Cowan
Dark Haired Marie	Lozanne	Dark Haired Marie	Lozanne
Route Marchin'	McCall	Route Marchin'	McCall

Programme 8: 1935-1940

Lament of Shah Jehan	Ronald	Anchored	Watson
I Heard a Forest Praying	de Rose	Gentleman Jim	Oliver
Turn ye to me	arr Lawson	I Heard a Forest Praying	de Rose
Little Prayer I Love	Rizzi	Fret-Foot	McCall
Changing of the Guard		Changing of the Guard	
	Flotsam & Jetsam		Flotsam & Jetsam

Programme 9: 1940-1945

Westward Ho!	McCall	If Music be the food of love	Travers
Gentleman Jim	Oliver	The Spice of Life	
Dream one more Dream	Rizzi	Cells	McCall
McPherson's Farewell	McCall	Wandering the King's Highway	Coward
Factotum	Rossini	The Drum Major	Newton

BBC 1950		**ABC 1954**	
Programme 10: 1945-1950		**Programme 10: 1945-1950**	
Fret-Foot	McCall	The Vagabond	V. Williams
Your Voice Beloved	Jeffries	Waiata Poi	Hill
Cells	McCall	Drake	Hewlett
Nut-Brown Ale	Murray	Lassaters [sic] Last Ride	Dawson
Waltzing Matilda	Cowan	The Lords Prayer	Malotte

Constance and Peter at the Grande Hotel, Coolangatta, Queensland, August 1955.

The closing years

The *Himalaya* arrived in Sydney on 12 June 1955 in the middle of a particularly cold winter, so Peter and Con headed off to sunny Cairns and Coolangatta until early August. Back in Sydney Dawson paid a number of visits to Dr Holmes à Court in Macquarie Street, but that did not stop him working. An idea for a new series, *Peter Dawson Sings Again* had been floated upon his arrival, then approved and pre-recorded, but the public announcement was held over until 3 December. The programmes were broadcast over 2BL on Saturdays from 10 December until 14 January.[1] Dawson was accompanied by a small studio variety band – like those used by commercial radio – conducted by a young Hungarian pianist, Tommy Tycho. Dawson introduced the songs himself and signed off with 'on behalf of Thomas Tycho & his players I bid you goodnight'.[2] All the items were pure nostalgia: no arias, no old masters, no oratorio. 'Today', said Peter, 'People like me to sing songs of the open air, of the country, sea and travel like "The Road to Mandalay" and "Boots". But the song that has remained the favourite of most people is "The Floral Dance".'[3] The six programmes were repeated between 21 January 1956 and 25 February and then sold on to the New Zealand Broadcasting Service. As was customary in broadcast agreements, residuals attracted half the initial fee: Peter Dawson signed for £20 per programme, Thomas Tycho signed for £20 per – for himself plus the whole band.[4]

In December, after the recording was completed, Peter and Con visited relatives in Adelaide, then spent 'Christmas day in Melbourne with Marjorie & Norman Shepherd'.[5] While he was in Melbourne Peter fitted in some work on the ABC's *Village Glee Club* and a guest spot on 3DB's *Variety Show* at the South Melbourne Town Hall – where he wowed them with 'Simon the Cellarer' and 'Snowbird'.

The following April (1956) he was guest-of-honour on *The Gladys Moncrieff Show* in Sydney which his old friend Ernest Lashmar (of Chappell's) had arranged.[6] Among the all-star cast was Max Oldaker, best remembered as the handsome hero in J.C. Williamson shows like *The Desert Song*. Oldaker's biography dwells on his own success that evening: 'The hall was packed, and it really was a thrill to walk out into that great barn to a big reception … my first ballad was noisily received but "Sparkling Eyes" really was a rouser. I walked off in the tumult, bowing and scraping …'. But Dawson and Moncrieff did get a mention: 'old Peter Dawson is a wonder, and still sings beautifully at 75 years. Glad was in good form. Her voice and range are not what they were, but the old luscious quality is still there.'[7]

Dawson and Gladys Moncrieff, some ten years his junior, were great mates and shared a common problem. Their critics equated popularity with lack of quality. Clearly, Dawson had sung his fair share of classical and esoteric music throughout his lifetime, but Gladys had stuck exclusively to musical comedy. Asked why she had avoided lieder and the coloratura repertoire, Gladys replied, 'What's the use? All who know me only want to hear me in the songs they know, and like to hear me sing.'[8]

The week after the Moncrieff concert Dawson was back in Adelaide for a Memorial Concert in honour of the long-serving ABC concert manager for South Australia, Athol Lykke, who had died a year earlier. Like the other artists, Dawson had volunteered his services (while also taking the opportunity to record two programmes for the ABC). In this concert he repeated some of his serious ballads: 'Wanderthirst', 'Speak Music', 'The Lake Isle of Innisfree', 'If Music Be The Food Of Love' and 'Crabbed Age and Youth'. Here, as in London, he could now make good capital out of his age: 'The veteran Peter Dawson displays only one weakness but refuses to be beaten by it. In fact, in one of his Shakespeare songs he shook his fist in its face crying "Age, I do defy thee!"'[9] When one of his fellow artists, the coloratura soprano Glenda Raymond, asked him the secret of his clear enunciation, Dawson demonstrated the exercises he had been using for 40 years. 'The vowels and consonants were so mixed it sounded rather like a rapid exercise in Chinese,' she said, 'but the speed gave flexibility to the muscles of the mouth, giving great clarity of expression.'[10]

Nevertheless, the frailties of age were manifesting themselves. In Sydney, Dawson began recording another six programmes for the ABC; but on 7 May, the day after pre-recording programmes 3 and 4, he was admitted to Lewisham Hospital for four weeks. However, he must have escaped the matron's eye on 13 May for he was in the ABC studios to pre-record programmes 5 and 6, which went out on 21 July. Charles Buttrose's article, advertising the final programmes, was headed 'Last Song of Peter Dawson'.[11] He may well have believed these broadcasts would be Dawson's swan song, but reckoned without the tenacity and persuasive power of the old artist.

It might have been the minor car accident Constance had on 2 November 1956 that prompted Peter to formalise certain aspects of their life. Just before they left the hurly-burly of the city for the beautiful seaside suburb of Newport, he drew up a new will favouring Constance and, if he survived her, members of her family.[12] To pay for their new house at 14 Beaconsfield Street he sold 2,900 Container shares for a net return of £3,275. Household accounts at this time are full of the bric-à-brac of setting up domestic life – plumbing, laying carpets, making curtains, buying furniture and a washing machine, and remodelling Nan's furs to fit Constance.[13]

That year television was introduced to Australia just in time for the Olympic games in Melbourne. Like radio before it, the new kid on the block upset the balance of the neighbourhood. Television quickly became the dominant medium: families stayed at home, eyes and ears transfixed by the glimmering box, to the detriment of films, radio, musicals, and live entertainment of every kind. The rising post-war generation, tagged 'the baby-boomers', was beginning to dictate taste. There was little room for those famous Peter Dawson ballads. They were a memory for a few, forgotten by most. But as the Emperor of Bond street was wont to say: 'One curious point in connection with our artistes is the loyalty of our public to old favourites. Once they have established a reputation, they can go on singing until there is not a musical note in the box.'[14] The final curtain was slowly falling but Dawson still found a few fleeting opportunities to perform.

On 28 January 1957 he had appeared with Dame Mary Gilmore on the first televised *Australia Day Show*,[15] but further appearances were put on hold when Constance was taken to hospital. After she had recovered from surgery at Mater Misericordiae, North Sydney, Dawson joined Tommy Tycho again for three *Peter Dawson Anniversary Shows*, which went to air between 27 April and 11 May. Probably his last stage appearance was between films at the Prince Edward Theatre [Sydney] on 2 June 1957: the theatre sent a car to pick him up at 11am, in time to sing 'The Floral Dance', 'The Road to Mandalay' and 'Snowbird' between 12 and 1pm. In July 1957 he returned to Sydney's Gore Hill television studio. After a five-hour delay and the frustrations of early television studio technique the old artist put down a lack-lustre 'The Arrow and the Song' for *Twenty-Five Years of Broadcasting*.

His sunset years passed in the comfort of trivial domestic events: Peter and Con had minor wins in the State Lotter; Brandy, their first-born puppy arrived; and the budgie, Cherry, was born. Dawson's nephews recalled

> Peter with his budgie on his shoulder. He always carried a shanghai around to keep the property free of cats. He overlooked the water and had field glasses to watch the boats and to watch what his nephew Frank was doing. Pete always said he was king in his castle.[16]

Now he had time to enjoy painting and watching television, but he also continued composing. On 25 November, the *Pictorial Show* carried a large photo of Peter 'busy in his Newport home writing a new ballad "My Mine of Memories".'[17]

Despite this brave front, in early 1958 Dawson's restlessness drove him and Con to visit Adelaide again where he was able to turn the visit into a working holiday. He was in his element: on 3 April he broadcast 'Non piu andrai'; on 13 April 'Changing of the Guard', 'Old Father Thames', 'Up from Somerset' and 'Glorious Devon'; on 17 and 18 April he pre-recorded eight songs for *Melody Land*; and on 21 April the 'old soldier' sang the Anzac hymn 'Australia, Rise to Glory' (Ford) 'with the old forcefulness'.[18]

An 'Extract from Minutes of the AGM' shows that Dawson was guest-of-honour at the Adelaide Savage Club on 29 April. He was 'called on to do his stuff and he did so in no uncertain manner';

> He regaled us with rich reminiscences of the fabulous years of the golden age of song – stories about Caruso, Melba, Tetrazzini, Landon Ronald, Malcolm Sargent, etc. etc. … At about 11.30 p.m. he was wheedled into singing the famous 'Floral Dance' with all members joining in around the piano.[19]

James Glennon's biography of Dawson in *Australian Music and Musician*s appears to recall the same meeting: 'He told many good stories that night. He sang, told more stories, then sang again till midnight. At nine o'clock next morning he was at the ABC studios to record two groups of songs for future broadcast.'[20] That broadcast was *The Composer Speaks*, which went out live on 30 April between 12.30 and 1pm. Dawson spoke about J. P. McCall, sang McCall's 'Waratah and Wattle', premiered McCall's latest composition, 'My Mine of Memories', and finished with – wait for it! – 'Boots'. For a time it was believed that this was 'the very last recording we have of his voice, exactly 60 years after Dawson commenced accepting professional engagements in his home city'.[21]

Dawson was so elated by this generous reception that it made the return to Sydney anticlimactic: he and Con were back in Adelaide by December. His diary note reads: 'Bill, Elsie, Frank, Santa, Ann, Ida, Con & me' had Christmas dinner at the Esplanade Hotel Brighton. But by 3 January they were back in Sydney again where there was no shortage of social occasions: among them his birthday at Ushers; the Winifred Atwell show at the Tivoli;[22] and Gladys Moncrieff in *Many Happy Returns* at the Empire. Yet something was rankling. Aging and in poor health though he was, Dawson decided to shift back to Adelaide permanently. In his letter to James Tierney in March 1961 he described the move as *The Ad'de debacle*:

> Fed up with inconsistent people including A.B.C. & Chappel & Co & Etc felt I was being by-passed – decided to sell our house at Newport & move lock stock & barrel to Adelaide, my lil home town.
>
> Put house in hands of big Estate Agent, at Newport, and got a marvellous bite £5250, clinched it 25.7.59.
>
> Ducked over to Adelaide to find a place to live in 9th Aug. purchased a fine old brick and stone house £4250 at Goodwood Road, Westbourne Park, just 3 miles out.
>
> 16th Aug, all set & flight back to Newport 7am dep Adelaide 10.50am arr Sydney, 11am home & dried, colossal luck. We were given to Mon 28th Sept to move out our goods and ~~chattels~~ chatells from No 14 & on that day Grace Bros loaded up & away for a run of 1000 miles by road to the Holy City, accomplished in less than 2 days non stop. 2 drivers.
>
> Feb 8th departed Ad for Sydney 7am arr Syd 10.5 am Motel Mona Vale 'Sunset Strip': £99

When the Dawsons arrived in Adelaide, everything seemed to run smoothly. They liked the house and in letters to their Adelaide solicitor and their old Newport neighbours they sounded cheerful. But this Christmas there was no jolly family get-together. Dawson noted in his diary: 'Just Con & I Xmas. Weeded garden'; Con's diary: 'December 24: By our selves – the loneliest Christmas we ever had; December 25: Pete & me, by ourselves – had dinner on our own; December 26: did not go out anywhere.' A month later they sold the Adelaide house. They had been there only four and a half months. There is no clear explanation. In the opinion of Dawson's Adelaide nephews 'most of his contacts had gone and he had no transport and neither did his sister Jessie'.[23] Certainly Con was virtually a stranger in Adelaide, while in Sydney they both had friends. Among these were Alice and 'Mac' Macfarlane, their Newport neighbours, who often feature in diary entries about social outings followed by champagne and sandwiches at 157 Walker Street, the flat the Dawsons had rented in North Sydney.

Two Australian icons: Peter Dawson with Gladys Moncrieff, the Queen of
Australian musical comedy, at her radio show, April 1956.

Dawson's life was now punctured by regular injections by Dr Bernard and radium treatment in Macquarie Street. It was another bitter winter. 'Gladys' wrote to Con: 'every State seems to have copt the cold this year, it would freeze the balls off a brass monkey over here. Hope you have found a little home for yourselves although where you are is central.' Peter was approaching seventy-nine. Con replied that 'Pete had been ill since first week of Christmas', in fact all year round since leaving Adelaide:

> now have semi-furnished flat at Collaroy, 2 bedrooms, quite large, sunroom looks out on to the beach 200 yards away so Pete sits at the window and watches all the goins on. Did you see the cricket match, it was wonderful on Television, we saw it all, such a thrill. Pete nearly dived down the Tele set.[24]

An old English friend, James Tierney, had been writing gossipy letters to Dawson regularly since 1955. Dawson had kept them all but for some reason had not answered them. Finally, In March 1961 he listed all the letters and prepared responses to the highlights. He began cheerfully by mentioning that he had celebrated his 79th birthday with the Macfarlanes: 'we had a very happy night, got me singing and talking', – but other remarks were bitter. None of his records were being re-issued: 'Many people complain and naturally enquire – "Where is our Peter Dawson?"' It seems that Dawson still could not accept that the world of music had moved on. Small wonder that his pen became acerbic.

In commenting on the destructive effect of public opinion, Tierney referred to Florence Austral, whom Dawson knew well, as an example.[25] Dawson explained that 'Florence Austral was banned from all big musical Festivals especially Worcester on account of Divorce & her assoc with John Amadio flautist who deserted his wife and kiddies. Her mother Mrs Fawez died of a broken heart.' Tierney had also reported an inane story by Harold Fielding, claiming that on one occasion Dawson had forgotten to bring his dress shirt, so he had to borrow one from a waiter, which turned out to be several sizes too small. Dawson's hackles went up: 'Damned idiotic nonsense anent my careless packing of my own bag for a concert. Fielding was a funny pedantic fop – too much money of Mothers.' Gerald Moore got a good swipe too:

> Gerald Moore left me like a shag on a rock for bigger fish & not until recent years did he even mention my name. A pinch-penny pianist if ever there was such an one? He was 62 last Dec. He married his cousin, the daughter of a Norwood grocer. His first wife was a beaut Yank ~~capable of every~~ knew all the answers.

Toward the end of his book *This Is The ABC* Ken Inglis wrote: 'The biography charged with most interest for ABC listeners was perhaps Nellie Melba's, in which the interwoven voices included celebrity artists Peter Dawson...'.[26] In his book Vose wrote: 'The last programme I know of took place on 23 May 1961'.[27] ABC Spoken Archives advised that the 'programme about Nellie Melba in which Peter Dawson and others reminiscence about the great diva is dated 19 May 1961'. This evidence suggests that Dawson made one final broadcast, as one of a panel of speakers on *Portrait of Melba*. He did not. John Thompson, ABC senior features producer, had recorded 24 interviews over several years. Dawson's segment, which retells the Melba/Caruso/hot sausage story, had been recorded on 30 June 1959. The one-hour documentary was edited on 16 May 1961, broadcast in Australia on 19 May, then on the United Kingdom Home Service on 23 May.[28]

So this was not Dawson's final performance. In his diary he noted two ABC recordings in Adelaide in January 1960. His last professional engagement was the second, on 17 January, comprising 'Lute Player', 'Glorious Devon' and 'Boots'.[29]

There were, however, still occasions – like 19 July 1960 – when he could be persuaded to sing for his supper – or rather his lunch. Diary note: 'Pickwick Club – Jim Macdougall – sang Mandalay'. Jim Macdougall, famous for his entertaining column in the Sydney *Mirror*, was at Dawson's last birthday:

> Peter Dawson, 79 on Tuesday last, dined that night at the Journalist's Club. For kicks after dinner dear old Pedro sang some of his old ballads with touching purity of voice. If you want to get the picture, it's just 61 years since Peter won his first prize at Ballarat's South Street Eisteddfod.'[30]

Eight months later, on 20 September 1961, the press reported that Peter Dawson was in a private hospital in Sydney with 'a malignant growth'. At his bedside was another Dawson, the famous country and western singer, 'Smoky' Dawson. Smoky and his wife Dot had been firm friends since the two singers had sung together in May 1951. In his autobiography Smoky wrote:

> I need a special paragraph to record that singing a duet with Peter Dawson in Adelaide was the greatest experience of the whole tour. We did Hal Saunders' marvellous favourite 'Old Cockatoorali' and the house tried to lift the roof. From that day Peter became my 'Uncle' and I his 'illustrious nephew.[31]

Smoky, now well into in his eighties, remembered that Dawson had cancer of the spine:

> One morning, near the end of his time, I went to see him in hospital. He was pale and drawn with pain. Then he looked up at me and sang in that warm, rich voice with all its old-time beauty, 'Clancy of the Overflow'. I like to think he, too, went a-droving to some pleasant place.[32]

Peter Dawson 'went a-droving' on 27 September, 'in his eightieth year'. Obituaries were published in Australia, New Zealand and Great Britain. Condolences rolled in. Charles Moses' letter to Constance summed them up:

> Dear Mrs Dawson,
> I should like to offer, on behalf of the ABC, very sincere sympathy on the loss of your husband. All of us who had the pleasure of knowing him personally were truly grieved to hear the news.
> Your husband's long association with the ABC will be gratefully remembered by our organisation. His personality endeared him to all those who were privileged to work with him, and his great talent has given pleasure to countless concert audiences and radio listeners. During his long singing career he certainly did a great deal to enhance Australia's musical reputation, and I know that many people throughout the world will hear of his passing with very real regret.

Peter Dawson was buried at Rookwood Cemetery, Sydney. He would have been pleased that 'a police escort led the way' and 'more than 200 mourners followed'.[33] The flag-bearer had fallen. An era had ended.

Communing with nature, Currumbin Bird Sanctuary, Surfers Paradise, Queensland,
August 1955.

The song is ended, but the melody lingers on

Constance Dawson survived her husband by another 26 years. She was pleased to get a pension when she turned 75, for, although Dawson's royalties had reverted to her on his death, after 1963 this stream practically dried up.[1] In 1959 there was only one 10in. LP of Peter Dawson in the shops; record companies were now preoccupied with catering for the younger clientele in the rapidly expanding LP market. Constance did not live to benefit from the 'best-of-yesterday' market, which now offers consumers some 200 titles on a dozen CDs. During his last years Peter's income had never fallen below a comfortable £A3,000 to £4,000 per annum,[2] of which at least £1,700 came from royalties; yet when probate was granted in 1962 his estate was not liable for death duty because 'the Australian baritone Peter Dawson who sold more than 13 million records, left only £1,555'.[3] Dawson may not have left a fortune but he left a name, which has become an integral part of Australian musical history.

Central to his success was his voice. Despite the extent of his live performances, it is the recordings by which he is best known. In 1979 Michael Scott sized up the conventional perception accurately:

> at one time there could hardly have been a home throughout the entire British Empire which boasted a gramophone that did not have at least one title of Dawson's – his preference for translating everything into English, and his appearance on the cheaper Plum Label records encourage the idea that he was somehow second class ... but there is not an infirm note throughout his compass ... his singing is of classical excellence – the ease of it is the art that disguises art.[4]

When Peter Dawson died two old colleagues were asked for their views. One was 'Mr. Joseph Hislop, the international operatic and lyric tenor':

> Peter Dawson was one of those singers who could get right into the hearts of the people because he could put the words of any ballad over so distinctly and so well that they were all with him immediately. There is no doubt he was an excellent singer.

The other, Norman Allin, professor of singing at the Royal Academy and principal bass at Covent Garden, said:

> Peter Dawson was always a fine singer. Peter had a lightish baritone voice, but he had perfect technique. That was one reason why he was able to make such fine records. In the early days very big vocal sounds would damage a recording, but Peter was always a good recorder.[5]

Today Dawson's much-praised vocal technique may seem old-fashioned to purists who like more resonance and sonority and are irritated by too many diphthongs in the vowels. Dawson consistently darkened the top of the voice and changed the colour of the vowels throughout the range, especially when making large musical leaps into higher registers. But his innate ability and the techniques he learnt destined him to sing in this style. As he said in one interview: 'You can't really sing English. One has got to use a special way of singing. An operatic Italian uses all the open tones, where we close at the top – and when you close on the top notes, when you've covered 'em, then that conserves the voice. As my Russian professor told me once: "you will sing until you are a hundred. You are singing, Petro; you are singing the right way".'[6]

In his recent *A View of Peter Dawson* (1997), Wayne Turner, an English bass, joined those who believe that the avoidance of operatic 'open' notes led to the longevity of his career.[7] However, Dawson's rigorous life of concerts, constant travelling and intense recording schedules was just as punishing as any operatic career. Turner included Dawson's opera recordings in his choice of Dawson best recordings:

> The <u>very</u> finest, the <u>very</u> best are Il Balen (Trovatore), Evening Star aria (Tannhäuser), <u>any</u> of his Handel arias, especially those from Samson and Acis and Galatea – though he didn't possess a Polyphemus voice (McEachern did!) – O My Warriors (Caractacus), the Stanford Songs of the Sea (perfect for his voice and style), Little Admiral, the Australian Bush Songs, Waiata Poi – yes, AND Waltzing Matilda!

This extraordinary spectrum points to the dilemma: how to classify Peter Dawson. Trained musicians admire his opera, oratorio and the lesser-known art songs, but at the same time admire the popular ballads. How can one singer excel at such a range of music? The answer lies in Dawson's consummate vocal technique which, combined with his presentation skills, satisfied both a general audience and the professional. Yet, behind this admiration lies a wily intelligence, for despite the hype about his extraordinary vocal prowess, Dawson never strayed from his vocal 'comfort-zone': he stayed firmly within a range that did not strain his voice at all. The proof is abundantly clear in his own compositions, which he wrote unashamedly for himself. The consistent top note is the comfortable baritone E; while the baritone F is only reserved for the resounding effect notes. Other composers' songs were rigorously transposed. He *always* sang 'The Barber's Song' ('Largo al factotum') a tone lower than the opera score, so his highest note was $G^{\flat}$ ($F^{\sharp}$), not the alternative $A^{\flat}$ affected by operatic baritones. Similarly, he transposed down 'The Prologue from Pagliacci' and other famous baritone arias, such as 'Eri tu', 'Pari siamo' and 'Vision Fugitive'. The number of songs transposed down is legion. The much-vaunted low notes, too, only occurred in one or two early arias: on recordings his sound was not significant below G, so his publicised range, $E^{\flat}$–A, stretches belief somewhat. In reality, Dawson's consistent range was a low G to a top F, like most baritones.

Drawing-room ballads had already reached the height of their popularity in the nineteenth century: they might have faded into obscurity if the talking-machine industry had not produced the recording colossus, Peter Dawson, who granted the ballad a new lease of life. Dawson's musical horizon, determined in his youth by the morals and customs of expansionist, imperialist Christianity, remained true to this Victorian music, whose sentiments were reflected in all those 'Peter Dawson ballads' about Tommy Lads, Drum Majors, Trumpeters, Sergeant-Majors and other Christian soldiers marching onward through the Empire.

Considering the ties of colonial Adelaide to the 'homeland', Dawson's family ties to Scotland, the duration of his life in London, his marriage into an English theatrical family and his fame throughout Great Britain, 'the Motherland' could have claimed him as her own. But Australia claimed him by right of birth: he never became 'Pommyfied', but remained, as William James said, 'typically Australian in spirit, speech and attitude.'[8] Emigrant parents may have to fight the hold of mother country and mother tongue, but their children 'belong' where they are born. Third-generation Australians need never question their national identity;

for earlier generations, like those of Peter Dawson's era, had developed those characteristics which define 'an Australian' today. In the words of the historian, Marjorie Barnard:

> An Australian is an individualist. He likes the image of tall and lean, silent, sardonic and brave without show; from the bush; an Anzac, who goes to the dawn service on Anzac day, Ned Kelly and a bonfire in Trafalgar Square. His speech betrays him. In truth, the average Australian had always lived in cities, and yet he carries the print of great distances on his eyelids and on his mind ... in smaller lands he has the feeling that he will fall over the edge ....[9]

Peter Dawson enjoyed being identified with this idiosyncratic figure; he flaunted his few moments of soldiering and gradually took on the mantle of an achiever from Down Under. At the beginning of his career he toured as 'the English basso'; by the end of his life he was the 'Australian baritone'. Although Gerald Moore had accompanied Dawson's most ambitious musical programmes, he wrote: 'With a more mature outlook, with industry, he could have become a serious artist, but as it was he settled down as a star turn in Variety where he had an easy and instantaneous success'.[10] Peter Dawson did not analyse what he did; he needed to sing and simply followed (or fabricated) demand.

We have described the events surrounding his personal and professional life, observed the machinations of the recording, concert and broadcasting industries; and taken into account the media manipulation that created his image. But in the end, we cannot explain the indefinable charisma of a small, rotund, good-humoured, loquacious man who became the best-known Australian baritone of his era. In advertising, concert programmes, radio promos and newspaper reports he was called 'The World's Most Popular Baritone' and, although this appellation may seem exaggerated, it was not contested by either critics or other singers. Dawson himself had no qualms about sporting it, for he had learned through the recording industry that there was no basic difference between Jimmy Sharman's Boxing Troupe and the most highbrow music: if you wanted a paying audience you had to go outside, beat the drum and use all the superlatives you could think of to coax them into the tent. Peter Dawson was a born spruiker, who had something genuine to sell. Those who complained about his scatter-gun approach to vocal literature were right, but they could not deny the success of a man who had the natural gifts and good wit to enjoy both ends of the musical spectrum, a man who could sing his way into the heart of an audience in

1900 or in 1960; in the Albert Hall, the music-hall, the Town Hall or the Mechanic's Institute; in Durban or Dublin or Dubbo. Some may not believe he was *The World's Most Popular Baritone* but millions did.

Sung by
PETER DAWSON.

"BOOTS"

Words by

RUDYARD KIPLING

Music by

J. P. Mc CALL

Copyright MCMXXVIII.
by SWAN & Cº
(Music Publishers) Ltd.

The Words of this Song are
reprinted from MR KIPLING'S
"THE FIVE NATIONS"
by permission of the Author.

Price
2/- net.

SWAN & Co.
(Music Publishers) Limited.
24. Great Pulteney Street. Golden Square.
LONDON. W.I.
(Printed in England)

Recording summary

Although Peter Dawson's recording output was phenomenal, he probably spent no more than one-tenth of his fifty-year career in a studio. For most of his professional life he was resident in London but was continually on the move performing throughout the British Isles or touring to South Africa, India, Ceylon, the Malay States, New Zealand and Australia. He was stranded in Australia during both world wars but did not return to settle permanently in his homeland until after World War II. Following the introduction of radio in 1923, he was in constant demand for broadcasts, was the first singer on BBC television when it opened in 1936 and was a pioneer of Australian television in 1956.

Nevertheless, his elevation to mega-stardom came through recording. The bulk of his recordings were made in England on either the HMV or Zonophone labels of the Gramophone Company of London, later known as EMI. A study of Peter Dawson's recording career reveals the following highlights, sidelights and insights.

1. *Longevity*
His recording career started in 1904 and ended in 1958, making it one of the longest on record.

2. *Sound Mediums*
Dawson's voice was captured on a wide range of sound carriers, from phonographic cylinders to stereophonic LP. He could also be heard on motion picture and television soundtracks and radio broadcast discs.

3. *Output*
About 1,500 song titles were issued under Dawson's name or pseudonyms. In an anonymous role in choirs and support groups he is estimated to have recorded another 300 or more songs. With private recordings and unissued masters, his final studio tally is likely to approach 2,000 titles. This is about the same number of songs recorded between 1926 and 1977 by Bing Crosby, who had the benefit of LP releases. The size of Dawson's output is shown by comparison with other major recording artists of his era:

Feodor Chaliapin	480 titles recorded	1901–1934
Enrico Caruso	265 titles	1902–1920
Nellie Melba	168 titles	1904–1926
John McCormack	1,300 titles	1904–1942
Beniamino Gigli	310 titles	1918–1954
Richard Tauber	760 titles	1919–1946

4. *Repertoire*

Dawson sang a more diverse repertoire than that of any other artist in recording history. He was at ease with ballads, evergreens, ragtime, opera, military airs, Gilbert & Sullivan, pop, comedy, sacred, novelty, patriotic, operetta, folk, song cycles, art songs, choral works, nursery rhymes, sea shanties, musical comedy, monologues and dramatic and humorous sketches. Composers ranging from Verdi, Tchaikowsky and Elgar to Kern, Romberg and Berlin were all treated with the same respect.

5. *Vocal Groups*

Dawson's recordings often feature a vocal support group of which he is also a member. Thus 'Peter Dawson & Vocal Quartet' may consist of Peter Dawson (soloist), plus Peter and three other singers as quartet.

6. *Credits*

On early discs and cylinders (pre-World War I) Dawson is usually credited as Mr Peter Dawson, bass. On many of his two-minute cylinders he announces himself & the song sometimes using a false name.

7. *The Piano*

This instrument was difficult to record before the introduction of electrical recording with its microphone. The problem was exaggerated when other instruments were involved. For this reason most of the orchestras which accompany Peter Dawson prior to 1925 do not include a piano.

8. *Popularity*

Dawson resumed his recording career after the end of World War I on 4 January 1920. At this time he had 266 titles in the *HMV/Zonophone* catalogue, trailing Ernest Pike, who had 340 songs listed. Dawson quickly exceeded Pike & proceeded to dominate the Gramophone Company catalogue for the next two decades. The following tables show titles for major artists in the *HMV/Zonophone* catalogue over a 25-year time span.

1925

1.	Peter Dawson	346
2.	Ernest Pike	286
3.	Enrico Caruso	199
4.	John McCormack	174
5.	Sydney Coltham	89
6.	Alma Gluck	83

1937

1.	Peter Dawson	248
2.	Enrico Caruso	227
3.	John McCormack	171
4.	Paul Robeson	102
5.	Derek Oldham	93
6.	Beniamino Gigli	86

1947

1.	Webster Booth	154
2.	Paul Robeson	112
3.	Beniamino Gigli	104
4.	Peter Dawson	82
5.	John McCormack	74
6.	Richard Crooks	72

1951

1.	Beniamino Gigli	144
2.	Webster Booth	100
3.	Paul Robeson	72
4.	Richard Crooks	64
5.	Peter Dawson	58
6.	Donald Peers	54

9. *Australian Compositions*

It was Peter Dawson who popularised four of Australia's most cherished compositions: 'Waltzing Matilda' (Marie Cowan), 'Advance Australia Fair' (Peter McCormick), 'Song of Australia' (Carl Linger) and 'Along the Road to Gundagai' (Jack O'Hagan). In fact, Dawson recorded more Australian songs than any other singer of his time. As well as recording about forty of his own ballads, Dawson introduced the songs of many other Australian composers, including A. Emmett Adams, Albert Arlen, Werner Baer, May Brahe, Vera Buck, George Clutsam, Horace Gleeson, Alfred Hill, Dulcie Holland, William James, Horace Keats, Lettie Keyes, Henry Krips, Jack Lumsdaine, Iris Mason, Aileen Neighbour, Hal Saunders, Reg Stoneham, Oscar Walters and Alfred Wheeler.

10. *Namesakes*

During Dawson's lifetime 'Peter Dawson Scotch Whisky' was well known and the signature on the label could be taken for Dawson's own. But despite Dawson's Scottish heritage there was no connection & no sponsorship deal. Only one other recording artist called Peter Dawson crops up in the catalogues: a Canadian Country and Western fiddler appeared on an LP disc in the 1950s.

11. *Recognition*

The 1984 *Guinness Book of Recorded Sound* chose ten singers for its all-time Hall of Fame. Elected were: Enrico Caruso, Peter Dawson, Bing Crosby, Frank Sinatra, John McCormack, Perry Como, Fats Domino, Elvis Presley, Andy Williams and The Beatles. In 1991 Peter Smith Dawson was elevated to the Australian Record Industry Hall of Fame, the first pioneer accorded this honour.

The authors acknowledge the contributions of many researchers but specifically express their gratitude to the English discographers, Mike Comber & Timothy Massey, for their long-standing cooperation and generous assistance.

Peter Dawson Song Title Discography 1904-1958

An alphabetical listing of solos, duets, trios & specific ensembles

This discography consists primarily of original releases under Dawson's own name or under a pseudonym. Anonymous recordings in ensembles or choruses (eg. a church choir) are not included. LP, tape or CD releases are only included where they are the initial issue.

Disc recording dates are mainly from record company ledgers. In general, cylinder recording dates are estimates, calculated at two months prior to the release or marketing date, but variations are common. Some two-minute wax cylinders appear to have been re-recorded more than once, at later dates, replacing earlier recordings, but keeping the same catalogue number.

Songs are listed under title: author and composer are noted where possible and stage show or song cycle added if relevant. Recording information: date, pseudonym (if used), type of ensemble & fellow artists (if not solo), accompaniment, label and catalogue number, disc or cylinder. Unless otherwise specified, all songs were recorded in London.

The major source for the preparation of this discography was the comprehensive collection of Dawson recordings held by the Australian Institute of Recorded Sound. Any fresh information, corrections or comment on titles recorded by Peter Dawson, as soloist, in small ensembles or vocal groups, may be sent to PO Box 1660, Port Macquarie, NSW 2444, Australia.

Abbreviations

acc = accompaniment
orch = orchestra or instrumental group
cyl = cylinder phonograph record
EB = Edison Bell (2-minute wax cylinder)
Edison = Edison (2-minute wax cylinder)
Edison Amb = Edison Amberol (4-minute wax cylinder)
Edison BA = Edison Blue Amberol (4-minute celluloid cylinder)
G&T = Gramophone & Typewriter Company (disc)
HMV = His Master's Voice (disc)

RZ = Regal-Zonophone (disc)
Zono = Zonophone (disc)
7", 10". 12" or 7in., 10in., 12in. = disc diameter in inches (cm 17.8, 25.4, 30.1)

HMV 'B' (10") & 'C' (12") disc series originated in England: after the opening of an HMV pressing plant in Sydney in 1925 many issues in these series were pressed in Australia (issues in these series were also pressed in India). The HMV EA (10") & EB (12") series are both Australian as is the Regal-Zonophone G (10") series. Cylinder recordings were manufactured in England unless otherwise indicated (eg. USA).

Dawson in vocal group recordings

Identifying the presence of Peter Dawson in vocal groups & choruses is often difficult. Although he is not present in all groups, on many occasions his voice can be identified, even taking solos within an ensemble. A range of experts suggest that he can be heard in the following groups:

A Church Choir	Minster Singers
Alexandra Choir	Mixed Church Choir
Ariel Glee Party	Mixed Quintette
Choir	Old Ludgate Singers
Choir of 20 Voices	Orpheus Quartette
Chorus	Quartette
Dollar Princess Operatic Party	Sacred chorus
Dorian Singers	Salvation Army Processional
Empire Glee Party	Sextette
English Christy Minstrels	Special Zono Quartette
Festival Chorus	Special Zonophone Quintette
Festival Quartet	Sullivan Operatic Party
Georgia Glee Singers	Sullivan Quartette
Gramophone Concert Quartet	Twin's Male Quartet
The Grigs	Vocal Chorus
Hampstead Church Choir	Vocal Quartet
Holy Trinity Church Choir	Vocal Sextette
Light Opera Company	Zonophone Concert Party
London Church Choir	Zonophone Concert Quartette
Male Chorus	Zonophone Glee Party
Male Quartet	Zonophone Operatic Party
Male Quintet	Zonophone Quartet Party
Male Voices	Zonophone Quartette
Meister Singers	Zonophone Quintette

Pseudonyms

Peter Dawson also sang under a large number of pseudonyms. A list appears below. In the early days of the talking machine it was common practice for companies to issue recordings, even by well-known artists, under fictitious names. This allowed artists to sidestep contractual obligations and record for a variety of labels. Many singers preferred a *nom de disque* when recording material outside their usual repertoire or style.

Both cylinder and disc publishers dreamt up some intriguing aliases for Peter Dawson, as the following list shows. The most-often-used pseudonyms were: Hector Grant (78 recordings); Will Strong (62); Robert Woodville (24); and Will Danby (20).

Mr. C. Adams	Mr. C. Handy
Robert Baxter	Charles Handy
James Bell	Mr. Miles
Percy Clifton	Llewellyn Morgan
Peter Clifton	James Osborne
Percy Dalton	David Peters
Will Danby	Sydney Reeves
Fred Davies	Will Strong
Leonard Dawson	Henry Tucker
(Mr.) Derby	Uncle Peter
Maurice Evans	Arthur Walpole
Victor Graham	George Welsh
Hector Grant	Walter Wentworth
Henry Grant	Robert Woodville

Associate recording artists

Peter Dawson was primarily a recording soloist. However, in the acoustic recording period (pre–1926) he often shared the studio with leading London vocalists both on cylinder and/or disc, either in duet or in vocal groups. The singers with whom he recorded include:

Essie Ackland (Aust)	Sarah Jones
Perceval Allen	Eleanor Jones-Hudson
William Anderson	Lillian Keys
Amy Augarde	Tom Kinniburgh
George Baker	Stanley Kirkby
Pamela Baselow	Nellie Leach
Thorpe Bates	Alfred Lester
Webster Booth	Bertha Lewis
Nellie Briercliffe	Mary Lewis
Ethel Cadman	Tom McNaughton
Feodor Chaliapin	Nellie Melba (Aust)
Hope Charteris (Aust)	Alice Moxon
Tom Child	Browning Mummery (Aust)
Sydney Coltham	Annie Mortimer Noble (probable)
Edward Davies	Yolande Noble
Tudor Davies	Derek Oldham
Violet Elliott (Aust)	Violet Oppenshaw
Violet Essex	Denise Orme
Alice Esty	Ennis Parkes
Clara Evelyn	Elisabeth Pechy

Harry Fay
Carrie Gaisberg
Fred Gaisberg
Stewart Gardner
Arthur Gilbert
Dorothy Gill
Gilbert Girard
Walter Glynne
Leonard Gowings
Sydney Granville
Elsie Griffin
Alfred Groves
Edward Halland
Winifred Harbor *
Evelyn Harding
John Harrison
Leonard Henry
Ruby Heyl
Alfred Holt
Barrington Hooper
Arthur Hosking
Leonard Hubbard (NZ)
Walter Hyde
Ben Ivor
Bessie Jones

Gladys Peel
Ernest Pike
Robert Radford
Annie Rees
Stuart Robertson
Leo Sheffield
Gertrude Shrimpton
Leonard Stanley
Leonard Sydney
Edna Thornton
Harry Thornton
Helen Trix
Carrie Tubb
John Turner
Palgrave Turner
John Van Zyl
Florence Venning
Wilfred Virgo (often as Wilfrid)
William Waite
Nellie Walker
Albert Whelan (Aust)
Harold Wilde
Constance Willis
Fred Williamson (Aust)

* Winifred Harbor is probably an alias of Yolande Noble.

Discography

A.I.F. IS MARCHING, THE (Lane)
   1940, July 11: acc orch. Sydney RZ G–24078 (10")
ADMIRAL'S BROOM, THE (Bevan & Weatherly)
   (1) 1906, August: acc orch. G&T 3–2466 (10")
   (2) 1912, July: acc orch. Edison Amb 12481; Edison BA 23338 (cyl)
   (3) 1929, June 6: acc orch. HMV B–3186 (10")   *Feb 1929 Bb16290-3*
ADMIRAL'S YARN, THE (Rubens)
   (1) 1912, November 19: acc orch. Zono 1005 (10")   *acc. Gerald Moore*
   (2) 1928, February 20: acc piano. HMV B–2661 (10")   *Bb12558 -1*
ADVANCE AUSTRALIA FAIR (Amicus = P. D. McCormick)
   1931, March 24: acc orch & chorus. HMV EA–889 (10")
AFTER YOU GET WHAT YOU WANT YOU DON'T WANT IT (Berlin)
   1921, February 2 (as Will Strong): acc orch. HMV B–1205 (10")
AH! MIMI, TU PIU NON TORNI (Puccini *La Bohème*)
   1909, February 12, duet with Ernest Pike: acc orch. Zono X–44119; Zono GO–13
      (10")
AIR PILOT, THE (Morrison, Webster & Garratt)
   1935, July 11: acc orch. HMV B–8373 (10")

AH, COULD I BEHOLD THE GLANCES (Il Balen) Verdi – (Cammarano)
('IL TROVATORE' Act 2) c Geo Byng
1922 July 19 Bb1692 HMV B1393

ALADDIN
1907, September (as Percy Clifton): monologue. Edison 13658 (cyl)

ALAS, I WAVER TO AND FRO (Gilbert & Sullivan *Yeomen of the Guard*)
(1) 1907, January 29: trio with Florence Venning & Ernest Pike: acc orch. G&T 4423 (10")
(2) 1920, March 4: trio with Ruby Heyl and Ernest Pike: acc orch. HMV D–482 (12")
(3) 1928, October 29: trio with Nellie Briercliffe & Walter Glynne, acc orch. HMV D–1551; Victor (USA) 11222 (12")

ALBION ON THY FERTILE PLAINS (Braham)
1910, April 5: duet with Ernest Pike: acc orch. Zono Z–044002; Zono A–73 (12")

ALL'S WELL (Braham)
(1) 1906, October: duet with Wilfred Virgo: acc orch. EB 10075 (cyl)
(2) 1910, April 14: duet with Ernest Pike: acc orch. Zono X–44159; Zono 527 (10")
(3) 1922, September 30: duet with Sydney Coltham: acc orch. HMV B–1453 (10")
(4) 1923, June 15: duet with Browning Mummery: acc orch. Zono 527 (10")

ALLAH BE WITH US (Towne & Woodforde-Finden *A Lover In Damascus*)
1930, September 22: acc orch. HMV C–2097 (12")

ALONG THE ROAD TO GUNDAGAI (O'Hagan)
1931, March 24: acc orch & chorus. HMV EA–889 (10")

ALWAYS (Horwitz & Bowers)
1908, January: acc orch. EB 10492 (cyl)

AMAPU (Gideon *Co–optimists*)
1921, November 8 (as Will Strong): acc orch & chorus. HMV B–1290 (10")

ANCHORED (Cowan & Watson)
(1) 1906, July 26: acc orch. G&T 3–2467 (10"); matrix 8576b
(2) 1906, August 17: acc orch. G&T 3–2467 (10"); matrix 8709b
(3) 1907, acc orch. Zono X–42626 (10")
(4) 1910, September: acc orch. Edison Amb 12239 (cyl)
(5) 1912, February 21: acc piano. HMV 02393; HMV C–437 (12")
(6) 1923, March 16: acc orch. HMV C–437 (12")
(7) 1929, August 15: acc orch. HMV C–1816 (12")

AND SO DO I! (Rosse)
1917, June 19: acc piano. HMV B–1057 (10")

ANNIE LAURIE (William Douglas & Lady John Scott)
1933, February 28: acc orch & chorus. HMV C–2597 (12" medley)

ANZAC MEMORIUM (Ford)– see 'Australia, Rise to Glory'

ARMOURER'S GIFT, THE (Barrie)
1916, October 23: acc piano. Zono A–230 (12")

ARMOURER'S SONG , THE (Smith & de Koven *Robin Hood*)
1916, November 23: acc orch. HMV B–785 (10")

ARRAH WANNAH (Drislane & Morse)
1907, January 10 (as Hector Grant): acc orch. Zono X–42556 (10")

ARROW AND THE SONG, THE (Longfellow & Balfe)
(1) 1910, May: acc orch. Edison Amb 12186 (cyl)
(2) 1912, January 16: acc orch. Zono 852; Ariel 831 (as Maurice Evans) (10")
(3) 1923, May 7: acc piano. HMV B–1750 (10") *Bb2949-2*
(4) 1932, April 27: acc orch. HMV B–4350 (10")
(5) 1957, July 1: acc piano. HMV PD–1 (12" LP set), television soundtrack, Sydney

AS GOD THE LORD (Mendelssohn / *Elijah*)

1907, January 29: acc orch. HMV C–481 (12")

AS I STAND BY THE OLD CHURCH DOOR (Murphy)

1906, December: acc orch. Edison 13559 (cyl)

ASLEEP IN THE DEEP (Lamb & Petrie)

(1) 1905, February 21: acc orch. G&T 3–2580; Zono 42353 (7")

(2) 1905, May: acc orch. G&T 3–2224 (10")

(3) 1907, December (as George Welsh); acc piano. Zono X–42732; Zono 520 (10")

(4) 1908 possibly: acc orch. Clarion 489 (disc)

(5) 1913, April 4: acc piano. HMV C–423 (12")

(6) 1923, November 19: acc orch. HMV C–423 (12")

(7) 1930, June 16: acc orch & chorus; HMV B–3542 (Parts 1 & 2) (10")

ASTHORE (Trotère)

1905, December: duet with Ethel Cadman: acc orch. Edison 13420 (cyl)

AT FINNIGAN'S BALL (Weston & Lee)

1916, November 6: duet with Ernest Pike (as Strong & Murray): acc orch. Zono 1740 (10")

AT LOVE'S BEGINNING (Campbell & Lehmann)

1912, August 29: duet with Eleanor Jones-Hudson: acc orch. Zono A–89 (12")

AT SANTA BARBARA (Russell)

(1) 1912, October 3: acc piano. HMV 02412; HMV C–437 (12"); matrix Z6644F

(2) 1922, January 9: acc piano. HMV C–437 (12"); matrix Cc 871–1

(3) 1928, February 20: acc piano. HMV B–2261 (10")

AT THE BOTTOM OF THE DEEP BLUE SEA (Petrie)

(1) 1904–1905: acc orch. Nicole 5698; Sovereign 51; Pelican P–34; Britannic-Record 2346 (10")

(2) 1905, February 21: acc orch. Zono X–42327 (10")

AUCTION SALE OF A PIANO, THE

1907, (as Percy Clifton): comic patter: acc piano. Zono X–41028 (10")

AULD HOOSE, THE (Nairne)

(1) 1906, July 26 (as Hector Grant): acc orch. Zono 70, HMV (Canada) 120131 (10")

(2) 1922, October 12: acc orch. HMV B–1462 (10")

(3) 1932, July 19: acc orch. HMV B–4338 (10")

AULD LANG SYNE (Trad Scottish Air & Burns)

(1) 1905, September 4: in chorus acc soloist Nellie Melba: acc orch. G&T 3615; Victor (USA) 94004 (10")

(2) 1923, March 7: acc orch & chorus. HMV B–1596 (10")

(3) 1930, June 24: acc orch & chorus. HMV B–3543 (10"); Victor (Canada) 120838 (10")

AULD SONGS O' HAME (Geehl), see 'Loch Lomond' & 'Annie Laurie'

AUSTRALIA (Mackellar & Holland)

1951, September 12: acc orch & chorus. HMV EA–4009 (10"), Sydney

AUSTRALIA (Matson)

1917, June 12: acc orch. HMV B–841 (10")

AUSTRALIA, RISE TO GLORY (Ford)

1958, April 21 Adelaide: radio broadcast, acc piano & bugler. ABC PR–2971 (10" LP); HMV PD–1 (12" LF set) as 'Anzac Memorium'

AWAY IN ATHLONE (Lohr)

1922, July 14: acc piano. Zono 2264 (10")

AWAY, AWAY! MY HEART'S ON FIRE (Gilbert & Sullivan *The Pirates of Penzance*)

  1929, February 19: trio with Derek Oldham & Dorothy Gill: acc orch. HMV D–1685; Victor (USA) 9614 (12")

BABY (YOU'RE THE SWEETEST BABY I KNOW) (Ayer)

  1917, March 15 (as Llewellyn Morgan): acc orch & chorus. HMV B–818 (10")

BACHELOR GAY, A (Tate *The Maid of the Mountains*)

  (1) 1917, March 30: acc orch. HMV B–805 (10"); matrix HO 3531ae

  (2) 1923, November 19: acc orch. HMV B–805 (10"); matrix Bb3860–1

  (3) 1930, May 1: acc orch. HMV B–3464 (10")

BALLAD MEMORIES – see 'God Send You Back To Me' & 'Lazily, Drowsily' (in medley)

BALLAD SINGERS, THE (Wilson)

  1914, April 30: duet with Ernest Pike: acc piano. Zono 1377 (10")

BANDOLERO, THE (Stuart)

  (1) 1907, January 29: acc orch. G&T 3–2857 (10")

  (2) 1907, April 27: acc orch. Zono X–42910; Zono 519; Ariel 798 (as Maurice Evans) (10")

  (3) 1910, October: acc orch. Edison Amb 12267; Edison BA 23084 (cyl)

  (4) 1913, April 4: acc piano. HMV 02598; HMV C–459 (12")

  (5) 1929, March 5: acc orch. HMV C–1659 (12")

BANJO SONG, A (Weeden & Homer *Bandanna Ballads*)

  (1) 1920, May 20: acc orch. HMV B–1141 (10")

  (2) 1928, September 11: acc orch & chorus. HMV B–2858 (10")

BANTRY BAY–MACMURROUGH (Molloy, Old Irish Air)

  1906, June 6: acc orch. Zono X–42426 (10")

BARBER'S SONG, THE – see 'Room for the Factotum'

BARNYARD SERENADE

  1906, August: descriptive with imitator Alfred Holt: White 129 (cyl)

BARRACK ROOM BALLADS (Kipling & Cobb) listed as 'Rudyard Kipling's Barrack Room Ballads' – see 'Fuzzy Wuzzy', 'Screw Guns', 'Route Marchin', 'Young British Soldier', 'Cells', 'Mandalay'.)

BATTLE EVE, THE (Bonheur)

  1922, December 29: duet with Sydney Coltham: acc orch. HMV B–1495 (10")

BATTLE OF TRAFALGAR, THE

  1907: member of dramatic sketch: acc effects. Zono X–49278 (10")

BAY OF BISCAY, THE (Cherry & Davy *Spanish Dollars*)

  1911, June 14: acc orch. Zono A–25; HMV (Canada) 130023 (12")

BEACON SHINES, THE

  late 1907: acc orch & chorus. Zono X–42856 (10"). Possibly unissued

BEAUTIFUL BIRD, SING ON (Howe)

  (1) 1906, August: with Alfred Holt, whistler: acc orch. EB 10001 (cyl)

  (2) 1908, June: with Alfred Holt, whistler: acc orch. EB 20116 (cyl)

  (3) 1910, September: with Alfred Holt, whistler: acc orch. EB 20272 (cyl); Little Champion (9")

BEAUTIFUL ISLE OF THE SEA (Cooper & Thomas)

  1909, May 25: quintet with Eleanor Jones-Hudson, Ernest Pike, Stewart Gardner & Harold Wilde: unaccompanied: Zono X–44132; Zono 533 (10")

BEAUTIFUL OHIO (MacDonald & Earl)

  1920, January 4 (as Will Strong): acc orch & chorus. HMV B–1080 (10")

BECAUSE OF YOU (Neighbour)
    1916, October 19: acc piano. Zono 2387 (10")
BEDOUIN LOVE SONG (Taylor & Pinsuti)
    (1) 1904–1905: acc piano. Nicole 5658; Sovereign 55; Pelican P–32; Britannic–Record
        2344 (10"); matrixes 2021 & 2168 both issued
    (2) 1905, February 21: acc orch. G&T 3–2259 (10")
    (3) 1908, January: acc orch. EB 10498 (cyl)
    (4) 1908, July: acc orch. Zono X–42856; Zono 519 (10"); matrix 8759e
    (5) 1909, June 24: acc orch. Zono X–42786; Zono 519 (10"); matrix 10347e
    (6) 1913, April 4: acc piano. HMV 02592; HMV C–423 (12")
    (7) 1929, March 5: acc orch. HMV C–1659 (12")
BEFORE THE BATTLE (Hedgcock)
    (1) 1913, March 3: duet with Ernest Pike: acc orch. Zono A–117 (12")
    (2) 1922, December 29: duet with Sydney Coltham: acc orch. HMV B–1498 (10")
BELL AT SEA, THE (Adams)
    1911, November 16: acc orch. Zono 742; HMV (Canada) 120192 (10")
BELLRINGER, THE (Greenford & Wallace)
    (1) 1904, September 5: acc orch. Zono X–42148 (10")
    (2) 1906, January 4: acc piano. G&T 3–2482 (10")
    (3) 1909, May: acc orch. Edison Amb 12047 (cyl)
    (4) 1913, January 21: acc orch. Zono A–107 (12")
    (5) 1923, June 22: acc orch. HMV C–1116 (12")
    (6) 1930, June 24: acc orch & chorus. HMV B–3541 (10")
BELLS AND HOBBLES (Gleeson)
    1932, January 5: acc orch. HMV EA–1093 (10")
BELLS OF ABERDOVEY (Dibdin, Old Welsh Melody)
    (1) 1907, June: acc orch. White 215 (cyl)
    (2) late 1907: acc orch. Zono X–42678 (10")
    (3) 1908, November: acc orch. Edison 13827 (cyl)
BELLS OF THE SEA (Lamb & Solman)
    1924, May 21: acc orch. Zono 2597 (10")
BELOVED IN YOUR ABSENCE (Towne & Woodforde-Finden *A Lover In Damascus*)
    1930, September 22: acc orch. HMV C–2096 (12")
BEN THE BO'SUN (Adams)
    1913, January 21: acc orch. Zono 1047 (10")
BEYOND THE SUNSET (Tours)
    1917, January 29: acc piano. Zono 2597 (10")
BID ME TO LOVE (Barnard)
    1904, August 15: acc piano. Zono X–42085 (10")
BIG BASS DRUM, THE (Mortimer)
    1913, April 5: acc orch. Zono 1093; Ariel 9465 (10")
BILLY BOWLINE (Royce)
    1912, January 16: acc orch. Zono 818; HMV (Canada) 120187 (10")
BLARNEY ROSES, THE (Flint)
    (1) 1917, May 22: acc piano. Zono 1791 (10")
    (2) 1922, December 20: acc orch. HMV B–1491 (10")
BLESS THIS HOUSE (Taylor & Brahe)
    1938, September 27: acc organ: HMV B–8815 (10")

BLESSED ARE THEY (Mendelssohn & Keats)

    1946, January 14: acc piano. HMV EA–3303 (10"), Sydney

BLIGHTY (Weston & Lee)

    1916, November 22 (as Llewellyn Morgan), duet with Ernest Pike: acc orch. HMV B–780 (10")

BLIND BOY AND THE THRUSH, THE (West)

    1907, November: acc orch. Clarion 74; Clarion 772 (cyl)

BLIND PLOUGHMAN, THE (Radclyffe–Hall & Clarke)

    (1) 1916, November 23: acc orch. HMV B–777 (10")

    (2) 1930, November 4: acc organ. HMV B–3691 (10")

    (3) 1954, May 3: acc orch. ABC radio broadcast, Sydney

BLOW, BLOW, THOU WINTER WIND (Serjeant)

    (1) 1904, July–August: acc orch. Lambert 5093 (cyl)

    (2) 1904, August–September: acc orch. EB 6418 (cyl)

    (3) 1904–1905: acc orch. Nicole 5790; Pelican P–32 (10")

    (4) 1905, July 27: acc orch. G&T 3–2310 (10")

BLUE BELL (Madden & Morse)

    (1) 1904, July–August (as Leonard Dawson): acc orch. EB 6399 (cyl)

    (2) 1904, July–August (as Leonard Dawson): acc orch. Lambert 5099 (cyl)

BLUE BONNETS OVER THE BORDER (Traditional)

    (1) late 1907 (as Hector Grant): acc orch. Zono 70; HMV (Canada) 120131 (10")

    (2) 1922, October 12: acc orch. HMV B–1462 (10")

BLUE DRAGOONS, THE (Russell)

    (1) 1912, September 10: acc piano. HMV 4–2229; HMV B–318 (10")

    (2) 1913, February 21: acc orch. Zono 1054 (10")

BLUE VENETIAN WATERS (Kahn, Kaper & Jurmann)

    1937, May 10: acc orch. HMV B–8576 (10")

BOM–BOM–BOM–BHE (Frisch)

    1920, December 1 (as Will Strong): acc orch. HMV B–1173 (10")

BOMBADIER (Darewski)

    1908, November 12 (as Henry Tucker): acc orch. HMV GC 3–2992 (10")

BONNIE BANKS O' LOCH LOMON' (Traditional)

    (1) 1905, early: acc orch. Pelican P–33 (10")

    (2) 1907, October: acc orch. G&T 3–2899 (10")

BONNIE JEAN (Lauder)

    1907, January: acc orch. Sterling 803 (cyl); Pathé 8025 (10" disc)

BONNIE MARY O' GLENGARY (Scott)

    (1) 1906, July: acc orch. EB 6936 (cyl)

    (2) 1906 September (as Hector Grant): acc orch. Edison 13517 (cyl)

    (3) 1906, November (as Hector Grant): acc orch. Pathé 60085 (disc & cyl)

    (4) 1907, January 15 (as Hector Grant): acc orch. Zono X–42590 (10")

BO'SUN'S LAMENT, THE (Squire)

    1913, January 21: acc orch. Zono 1047 (10")

BOOTS (Kipling & McCall))

    (1) 1929, June 6: acc orch. HMV B–3072 (10")

    (2) 1942, July 7, Wellington, NZ: radio broadcast, acc orch. HMV PD–1 (LP set) (12")

    (3) 1945?, radio broadcast, possibly Sydney, 1945: acc piano. Kingfisher STAR–16 (cassette)

    (4) 1958, April 30, Adelaide: radio broadcast, acc piano. HMV PD–1 (LP set) (12")

BORDER BALLAD (Cowen)

    (1) 1912, July 9: acc orch. Zono (India) 914 (10")

    (2) 1912 September 24: acc orch. Zono 914 (10")

    (3) 1925, December 15: acc orch. HMV B–2275 (10")

    (4) 1933, January 31: acc orch. HMV B–4467 (10")

BOY BLUE (Castling)

    1907, January 10 (as Hector Grant): acc orch. Zono X–42551 (10")

BOY'S BRIGADE, THE (Mills & Scott)

    1906, August: acc orch. White 123 (cyl)

BOYS OF THE OLD BRIGADE (Barri & Weatherly)

    (1) 1910, October: acc orch (no vocal credit). Edison Amb 12249; Edison BA 23085 (cyl)

    (2) 1926, January 12: acc orch. HMV C–1245 (12")

    (3) 1930, June 16: acc orch & chorus. HMV C–2045 (12")

    (4) 1934, January 1: acc orch & chorus: HMV B–8158; Victor (Canada) 120873 (10")

    (5) 1936, October 13: acc orch. HMV C–2866; Victor (Canada) 36200 (12" medley)

BRAVO, TERRITORIALS (Wilmott & Darewski)

    1909, March: acc orch. Edison 13846 (cyl)

BREEZE (BLOW MY BABY BACK TO ME) (Hanley, MacDonald & Goodwin)

    1921, October 17 (as Will Strong): acc orch & chorus. HMV B–1292 (10")

BRIAN OF GLENAAR (Graham)

    1920, September 24: acc orch. HMV B–1164 (10")

BRIDGE, THE (Lindsay)

    (1) 1904–1905: acc piano. Nicole D–550; Sovereign 3 (10") (D–550 is labelled as Ian Colquhoun, which could be correct).

    (2) 1909, July 1: acc orch. Zono X–42928; Zono 3040 (10")

BRIGHT IS THE RING OF WORDS (Stevenson & Vaughan Williams *Songs of Travel*)

    1922, April 22: acc piano. HMV B–1355 (10") *acc Mme. Adami Bb 1253*

BRING BACK THE SIMPLE FAITH (Simpson & Arlen)

    1944, November: acc organ. HMV EB–225 (12"), Sydney

BRITAIN'S HERITAGE (*Medley of Patriotic Songs*) – see 'Hearts of Oak', 'Boys of the Old Brigade', 'The Lads in Navy Blue', 'Rule Britannia', 'Soldiers of the King', 'Private Tommy Atkins', 'Red, White & Blue'.

BROTHERS OF THE EMPIRE (Helmore & Thayer)

    1930, September 19: acc orch. HMV B–3630 (10")

BUILDER, THE (Foley & Cadman)

    1937, July 2: acc orch. HMV B–8610 (10")

BULLDOG'S BARK (Glover)

    1912, January 16 (as Walter Wentworth): acc orch. Zono 779; HMV (Canada) 120085 (10")

BUSH NIGHT SONG (James *Six Australian Bush Songs*)

    (1) 1923, January 25: acc piano. HMV C–1125 (12")

    (2) 1927, October 12: acc piano. HMV C–1428 (12")

BUSH SILENCE (James) (*Six Australian Bush Songs*)

    (1) 1923, January 25: acc piano. HMV C–1125 (12")

    (2) 1927, October 12: acc piano. HMV C–1428 (12")

    (3) 1927–1999: Dawson 1927 London solo digitally lifted & incorporated in 1999 Sydney recording of vocal trio Tenor Australis, with orch & choir. EMI (CD) 5 20785 2 (5")

BUSHRANGERS, THE (Harrington & Dawson)

1946, December 13: acc orch. HMV EA–3462 (10"), Sydney

BUYING THE CHRISTMAS DINNER (Clifton)

(1) 1907, September (as Percy Clifton), duet with Yolande Noble: descriptive with orch. Edison 13666 (cyl)

(2) 1907, October (as Percy Clifton), duet with Yolande Noble: descriptive with orch. Zon X–41026 (10")

BY THE BANKS OF ALLAN WATER

1907, June (as Hector Grant): acc orch. White 214 (cyl)

BY THE SIDE OF THE ROAD (Homer & Rizzi)

1948, January 7: acc orch. HMV B–9634 (10")

CALL HIM LOUDER (Mendelssohn *Elijah*)

1905: acc orch & chorus. G&T 4869; HMV B–384 (10")

CALL OF THE SEA (Fraser–Simpson *A Southern Maid*)

1920, May 26: acc orch & chorus. HMV C–972 (12")

CALL, THE (Oliver)

1916, November 23: acc orch. HMV B–777 (10")

CALLAGHAN (Lauder)

1906, June 15 (as Hector Grant): acc orch. Zono X–42528 (10")

CALLING ME HOME AGAIN (Graves & Buck)

1946, December 13: acc orch. HMV EA–3461 (10"), Sydney

CALVARY (Vaughan & Rodney)

(1) 1904, August–September: acc orch. EB 6416 (cyl)

(2) 1904, September 5: acc orch. G&T 2–2496 (10") matrix 6382a

(3) 1904, September 5 (as Arthur Walpole): acc orch. Zono 42122 (7") matrix 6383a

(4) 1904, September 5: acc piano. Zono X–42250 (10") matrix 5742b

(5) 1907, c. August: acc orch. White 247 (cyl)

(6) 1907, c. December: acc orch. EB10471 (cyl)

(7) 1908, c. May: acc orch. EB 20054 (cyl)

(8) 1911, July 10: acc orch. Zono 630; RZ T–630 (10")

CAN'T YOU HEAR ME CALLING, CAROLINE? (Gardner & Roma)

1916, October, 13: acc piano. Zono 1919; Ariel 2913 (10")

CAPE HORN GOSPEL (Keel *Salt Water Ballads*)

1924, January 29: acc orch. HMV B–1799 (10")

CAPTAIN DANNY (Loughborough)

1922, November 8: acc orch. HMV B–1449 (10")

✓ **CAPTAIN HARRY MORGAN** (Masefield & Bantock)   . acc Gerald Moore

✓(1) 1928, September 26: acc piano. HMV B–2884 (10") / Bb 14550 –2

(2) 1933, January 31: acc orch. HMV B–4494 (10")

CAPTAIN STRATTON'S FANCY (Masefield & Warlock)

1927, September 14: acc piano. HMV B–2651 (10")

✓ **CARGOES** (Shaw)

(1) 1924, December 2: acc piano. HMV B–1930 (10")

✓(2) 1928, September 26: acc piano. HMV B–2884 (10")   Bb 14553–1 acc Gerald Moore

CARNIVAL, THE (Molloy)

1910, April 14: acc orch. Zono X–2–42010 (10")

CARTLOAD O' HAY (Emmett Adams)

1922, March 21: acc orch. Zono 2214 (10")

CAST THY BURDEN UPON THE LORD (Mendelssohn *Elijah*)
   1907, January 18: quartet with Ernest Pike, Florence Venning and Eleanor Jones-Hudson: acc orch. G&T 4418; HMV B–385 (10")

✓ **CELLS** (Kipling & McCall)
   (1) 1930, September 19: acc orch. HMV B–3629 (10")
   ✓(2) 1935, July 5: acc orch & chorus. HMV C–2797; Victor (Canada) 130827 (12" medley)
   (3) 1942, c. July; Auckland, NZ: radio broadcast, acc piano. HMV PD–1 (LP set) (12")

CHANGING OF THE GUARD, THE (Hilliam & McEachern)
   (1) 1941, mid-September, Sydney: radio broadcast, acc orch & chorus. HMV PD–1 (LP set) (12")
   (2) 1942, May–June: Auckland , NZ: radio broadcast, acc orch. HMV PD–1 (LP set) (12")

CHARMED CUP, THE (Roeckel)
   1910, November 23: acc orch. Zono X–2–42050 (10")

CHEER UP, MARY
   1906, September: acc orch. White 142 (cyl)

CHEER UP, MY HIGHLAND LASSIE (Scott)
   1910, June: acc orch. Edison 13990 (cyl)

CHEERILY, YEO HO! (Phillips)
   1922, January 9: acc piano. HMV B–1348 (10")

CHEERY SONG (Slater)
   1917, January 25 (as Robert Woodville): acc orch. Zono 2185 (10")

CHEERY SOULS (Burke)
   1929, April 29: acc piano. HMV B–3521 (10")

CHEYENNE (Williams & Van Alstyne)
   1907, February: acc orch. White 163 (cyl)

CHI MI FRENA (Donizetti *Lucia di Lammermoor*) – see 'Sextette'

CHILD O' MINE (MacNeil)
   (1) late 1953: acc orch. Prestophone A–55/2 (10" 78), Sydney
   (2) late 1953 (different take): acc orch. Prestophone (7" 33), Sydney

CHINA SEA (Macneil)
   (1) late 1953: acc orch. Prestophone A–55/2 (10" 78), Sydney
   (2) late 1953 (different take): acc orch. Prestophone (7" 33), Sydney

CHIP OFF THE OLD BLOCK , A (Squire)
   (1) 1916, October 13: acc piano. Zono 1736 (10")
   (2) 1929, November 17: acc orch. HMV B–3378 (10")

CHONG (HE COMES FROM HONGKONG) (Weeks)
   1920, January 15: duet with Nellie Walker: acc orch. HMV B–1087 (10")

CHOO, WHAT A SILLY IDEA (Redstone *A Night Out*)
   1920, October (as Robert Woodville): duet with Harry Fay: acc orch. Zono 2080 (10")

CHORALE (Gounod *Faust*)
   1909, May 19: duet with Harry Thornton: acc orch & chorus. Zono X–44502; Zono GO–6 (10")

CHORUS GENTLEMEN (Lohr)
   1933, February 28: acc orch & chorus. HMV B–4494 (10")

CHRIST AROSE! (Loway–Ecke)
   1908: quintet with Eleanor Jones-Hudson, Amy Augarde, Ernest Pike & Harold Wilde: acc orch & bells. Zono X–44088; Zono 535 (10")

CHRIST IN FLANDERS (Ward & Stephens)
  1932, January 22: acc orch. HMV B–4089 (10")

CHRIST IS RISEN (Merezhkovsky & Rachmaninoff)
  1934, March 12: acc orch. HMV B–8196 (10") *c. Lawrance Collingwood OB5940*

CHRISTMAS EVE IN AN AUSTRALIAN MINER'S CAMP
  1907, October (as Hector Grant): quartet with Ernest Pike, Stanley Kirkby, & Arthur
    Gilbert: descriptive with orch. Zono X–41025; Zono 693; HMV B–1570 (10")

CHRISTMAS EVE IN BARRACKS
  1907, October (as Hector Grant): quartet with Ernest Pike, Stanley Kirkby & Arthur
    Gilbert: descriptive with orch. Zono X–41024; Zono 694; (10")

CHRISTMAS EVE IN THE OLD HOMESTEAD
  1907, quartet with Ernest Pike, Stanley Kirkby & Arthur Gilbert: descriptive sketch
    with singing. Zono X–49280; Zono 693; HMV B–1570 (10")

CHURCH PARADE
  1916, November 11 & 1917, May 1; duet with Ernest Pike: acc Band of HM Coldstream
    Guards. HMV C–786 (12") (Parts 1 & 2). The duettists sing one sacred song on each
    side.

CIDER (Mullinar)
  1924, September 3: acc piano. HMV B–1914 (10")

CINDERELLA
  1907 (as Percy Clifton): monologue. Edison 13660 (cyl)

CLANCY OF THE OVERFLOW (Paterson & Arlen)
  1955, May 4: acc orch. HMV 7EG–8157 (7" EP) *c. Chas Mackerras*

CLARE'S DRAGOONS
  1906, June 6: acc orch. Zono X–42456 (10")

CLEMENTINE (Montrose)
  1906, October 31: acc orch & chorus. Zono X–42534 (10")

COALING (Helmore *Co–optimists*)
  1922, July 13: acc piano. HMV B–1394 (10")

COBBLER JIM (Oliver)
  1912, August 22: acc orch. Zono 936 (10")

COBBLER'S SONG, THE (Norton *Chu Chin Chow*)
  (1) 1916, November 22: acc orch. HMV C–756; HMV (India) M–874 (12")
  (2) 1932, February 3: acc orch. HMV B–3772; Victor (Canada) 120840 (10")

COME AND BE A SOLDIER (Nairn)
  1906, September: acc orch. Edison 13523 (cyl)

COME BACK TO ERIN (Claribel)
  (1) 1906, April: duet with Walter Hyde: acc orch. Edison 13468 (cyl)
  (2) 1909, March: duet with Ernest Pike: acc orch. Edison Amb 12013; Edison BA
    23175; Edison (USA) Amb 249 (cyl)

COME BACK TO KILDARE (Barnby)
  1911, November 30: acc orch. Zono 789; HMV (Canada) 120069 (10")

COME, SING TO ME (Thompson)
  1914, February 9: duet with Ernest Pike: acc piano. Zono 1283 (10")

COME UNTO HIM (Handel *Messiah*)
  1909, May 25: quintet with Eleanor Jones-Hudson, Ernest Pike, Harold Wilde, &
    Stewart Gardner: acc orch. HMV (India) 2–4006 (10")

COME WHERE MY LOVE LIES DREAMING (Foster)
  1909, March 2: quartet with Ernest Pike, Stanley Kirkby, & Harold Wilde:
    unaccompanied. Zono X–44120; Zono 530 (10")

COMRADES (McGlennon & Costello)
 1935, November 9: acc orch & chorus, HMV C–2805 (12" medley)
✓**COMRADES OF MINE** (James *Six Australian Bush Songs*)
 (1) 1923, January 25: acc piano. HMV C–1125 (12")
 ✓(2) 1927, October 12: acc piano. HMV C–1428 (12")
CONNEMARA (Mellor, Lawrence & Gifford)
 1909, March: acc orch. Edison 13840 (cyl)
CONQUEROR, THE See 'Thy Conqueror'
CONSIDER THE LILIES (Topliff)
 (1) late 1907: duet with Ernest Pike: acc orch & chorus. Zono X–44075 (10")
 (2) 1911, November 15: acc orch & chorus. Zono 743 (10")
CONTRABAND (Geehl)
 1914, March 20: acc piano. Zono 1345 (10")
CORNER IN YOUR HEART, A (Trotère)
 1906, March: acc orch. Edison 13448 (cyl)
CORPORAL MIKE (Bennett)
 1914, March 11: acc piano. Zono 1306 (10")
COUNT YOUR BLESSINGS (Excell)
 (1) 1907, November: acc orch. EB 10472 (cyl)
 (2) 1908, October 16: quartet with Ernest Pike, Leonard Sydney & Harold Wilde: unaccompanied. Zono X–44095 (10")
COVERED WAGON LULLABY (Freeman & Leonard)
 1936, July 21: acc orch & chorus. HMV B–8475 (10")
✓**CRUEL IS HE (CREDO)** (Verdi *Otello*)
 (1) 1921, November 7: acc orch. HMV C–1041 (12")
 ✓(2) 1927, September 1: acc orch. HMV C–1401 (12") *C R 1 4 9 4 Sept 3 1927*
T **CRUISKEEN LAWN** (Traditional)
 1917, January 14: acc orch & chorus. Zono 1841; RZ T–1841 (10")
CRY OF THE FIGHTING FORCES (Beck & Keats)
 1944, November: acc organ. HMV EB–225 (12"), Sydney
✓**CRY OF THE WILD GOOSE, THE** (Gilkyson)
 1950, April 6: acc orch. HMV B–9913 (10")
CUDDLE UP (Von Tilzer)
 late 1920 (as Robert Woodville): acc orch. Zono 2116 (10")
CUPID IS CAPTAIN OF THE ARMY (Reed)
 1906, August: acc orch. Edison 13511 (cyl)
CURTAIN FALLS, THE (d'Hardelot)
 (1) 1924, September 3: acc piano. HMV B–1901 (10")
 (2) 1928, September 26: acc piano. HMV B–2936 (10")
DADDY (Behrens)
 1908, January: acc orch. EB 10491 (cyl)
DANCING TIME (Kern *The Cabaret Girl*)
 1922, October 17: duet with Ennis Parkes: acc orch & chorus. HMV C–1087 (12")
T **DANNY DEEVER** (Kipling & Damrosch)
 1936, September 10: acc orch. HMV B–8487 (10")
DARK-HAIRED MARIE (Lozanne)
 1933, January 5: acc orch. HMV B–4405 (10")
DARLIN' GIRL FROM CLARE, THE (French)
 1929, September 4: acc piano. HMV B–3410 (10")

DAVID EVANS

1907, December (as Hector Grant): acc orch. Zono X–42726 (10")

DEAR DEVON LASSIE (Richards)

1914, January 13: acc orch. Zono 1265 (10")

DEAR HOMELAND, THE (Slaughter)

1926, January 12: acc orch. HMV C–1342 (12")

DEATH OF BORIS (Moussorgsky *Boris Godounov*)

1923, July 2: as member of the chorus (soloist Feodor Chaliapin): HMV 2–022020; HMV DB–100 (12")

DEATHLESS ARMY, THE (Trotère)

(1) 1909, July 1 (as James Osborne) acc orch. The Twin 159; Zono 159; HMV (Canada) 120256 (10")

(2) 1926, June 16: acc piano. HMV C–1275 (12")

(3) 1929, August 15: acc orch. HMV C–1805 (12")

DEEP SEA MARINER, THE (McCall)

1934, October 8: acc orch. HMV B–8343 (10")

DELAWARE'S FAREWELL, THE (Capel)

1928, March 28: acc piano. HMV B–2759 (10")

DESERT, THE (Emanuel)

1917, January 14: acc orch. Zono 1858 (10")

DEVIL–MAY–CARE (May)

1932, April 27: acc orch. HMV B–4219 (10")

DEVON FOR ME (Kahn)

1914, April 21: acc piano. Zono 1376 (10")

DEVON, O DEVON (Stanford *Songs of the Sea*)

(1) 1928, January 30: acc orch & chorus. HMV B–2747 (10")

(2) 1933, January 10: acc orch & chorus. HMV B–4483 (10")   *OB4387–2*

DEVOUT LOVER, THE (White)

1934, March 16: acc orch. HMV B–8191 (10")

DICK WHITTINGTON

1907, September (as Percy Clifton): monologue. Edison 13659 (cyl)

DINDER COURTSHIP, A (Coates)

1913, February 21: acc orch. Zono 1054 (10")

DING, DONG, BELL

1905, May: acc orch. EB 6634 (cyl)

DIVER, THE (Thompson & Loder)

(1) 1905, May: acc orch. EB 6645 (cyl)

(2) 1908, January 28 (as George Welsh): acc orch. Zono 42359 (7")

DO AS THE SOLDIERS DO (Baynes & Clark)

1909, June: acc orch. Edison 13869 (cyl)

DON JUAN'S SERENADE (Tolstoy & Tchaikovsky)

(1) 1922, June 26: acc orch. HMV C–1079 (12")

(2) 1927, March 30: acc orch. HMV C–1327 (12")   *c Lawana Collingwood Ce 10502*

DON'T GO DOWN THE MINE, DAD (Geddes)

1911, March: acc orch. Edison 14054 (cyl)

DON'T LET THE RIVER RUN DRY (Haines & Harper)

1936, March 16: acc orch. HMV B–8422 (10")

DOUGAL (*The New Aladdin*)

1907, January 15 (as Hector Grant): acc orch. Zono X–42558 (10")

T ✓ **DOWN AMONG THE DEAD MEN** (Macfarren & Phipps)
   ✓(1) 1909, April 27: acc orch. Zono X–42906; Zono 514 (10")
   (2) 1917, June 12: acc orch. HMV B–851 (10")

T **DOWN AT THE OLD BULL AND BUSH** (Von Tilzer, Sterling, Krone, Hunting)
   (1) 1904–1905 (as Mr. C. Adams): acc orch. Nicole 5717 (10")
   (2) 1904–1905: acc orch. Nicole 4458 (7"); Nicole D–158 (10")
   (3) 1904, October 25: acc piano. Zono X–42160 (10"); matrix 6168b
   (4) 1904, October 25: acc piano. G&T 3–2524 (7"); matrix 6539a
   (5) 1904, October 25: acc piano. Zono 42161 (7"); matrix 6540a

DOWN HONOLULU WAY (Burnett & Burke)
   1917, March 15 (as Llewellyn Morgan): trio with Ernest Pike & Violet Oppenshaw: acc orch. HMV B–818 (10")

DOWN IN DEAR OLD GEORGIA TOWN (Whidden)
   1920, December 3 (as Will Strong) acc orch. HMV B–1186 (10")

DOWN IN JUNGLE TOWN (Madden & Morse)
   1909, July 8 (as Charles Handy): acc orch. Zono X–42932 (10") unissued?

DOWN THE VALE (Hadath & Moir)
   1906, February: duet with Walter Hyde: acc orch. Edison 13440 (cyl)

DOWN WHERE THE SWANEE RIVER FLOWS (McCarron, Alberte, Von Tilzer)
   1917, June 8 (as Will Strong): acc orch. Zono 1797 (10")

DOWN HOME WHERE THEY SING THE DEAR OLD SONGS (Skinner)
   1917, June 8 (as Will Strong) acc orch. Zono 1826 (10")

DRAKE (Hewlett & Henty)
   1948, January 7: acc orch. HMV B–9657; HMV EA–3834 (10")

DRAKE GOES WEST (Sanderson)
   (1) 1911, June 8: acc orch. Zono 614; HMV (Canada) 120065 (10"); matrix Ab13652e
   (2) 1922, c. March: acc orch. Zono 614 (10"); matrix yy1130–1
   (3) 1922, October 27: acc orch. HMV B–1475 (10")
   ✓(4) 1929 June 6: acc orch. HMV B–3111 (10")   *July 1929 Bb 16956–2*

DRAKE'S CALL (Keats & Brandon)
   late 1943: acc piano. HMV EA–3042 (10"), Sydney

✓**DRAKE'S DRUM** (Stanford *Songs of the Sea*)
   (1) 1928, February 24: acc orch & chorus. HMV B–2743 (10")
   ✓(2) 1933, January 10: acc orch & chorus. HMV B–4482 (10")   *0B4386–2*
   (3) 1954, May 10: acc orch; Sydney radio broadcast

DREAM ONE MORE DREAM
   1951, February 21: acc orch, unissued. Test copy exists. Sydney

DREAMER, THE (Siddle & McCall)
   1948, December 10: acc organ: HMV B–9739 (10")

DRINK TO ME ONLY WITH THINE EYES (Jonson & Trad)
   (1) 1904, July–August: acc orch. Lambert 5087 (cyl)
   (2) 1913, September 26: acc orch. Zono 1179 (10")
   (3) 1922, July 14: acc piano. Zono 2264; Ariel Grand 245 (as Maurice Evans) (10")
   (4) 1939, April 12: acc organ. HMV B–8932 (10")

✓**DROOP NOT YOUNG LOVER** (Handel *Ezio*)
   1912, January 16: acc orch. Zono 852 (10")   *14818c*

DROVER, THE (Stoneham)
   1912, June 4: acc orch. Zono 3013 (10")

DRUM MAJOR, THE (Newton)
    (1) 1912, September 24: acc orch. Zono 958 (10") matrix Y15714e
    (2) 1924, c. March: acc orch. Zono 958 (10") matrix Yy4378–2
    (3) 1929, November 27: acc orch. HMV B–3280 (10")

DRUMS ARE ON PARADE, THE (Neville)
    1934, May 1: acc orch. HMV B–8267 (10")

D'YE KEN JOHN PEEL (Trad & Graves)
    1917, January 17: acc orch & chorus. Zono 1841; RZ T–1841 (10")

ECHOES (Duffield & Ayer)
    1904–1905: acc unknown: Nicole 4427 (7")

EILEEN ALANNAH (Marble & Thomas)
    (1) 1904–1905: acc orch. Nicole 5815; Sovereign 1; Pelican P–36 (10")
    (2) 1907, October: acc orch. EB 10454 (cyl)
    (3) 1911, September: acc orch. Edison Amb 12365 (cyl)

EL ABANICO (Javaloyes)
    1932, August 30: acc orch & chorus. HMV B–4267; Victor (Canada) 120863 (10")

EMPIRE'S CALLING, THE (Byng)
    1924, June 3: acc orch. HMV B–1858 (10")

EMPTY SADDLES (Hill)
    1936, July 21: acc orch & chorus. HMV B–8475 (10")

ENCORE TO 'PARTED ON THE SHORE'
    1907, January (as Hector Grant): acc orch. EB 10141 (cyl)

ENGLAND (Besly)
    1934, January 11: acc orch. HMV B–8105 (10")

ENGLAND IN THE MORNING (Lumsdaine)
    1942, January 22: acc piano. R–Z G–24524 (10"), Sydney

ENGLAND, LAND OF THE FREE (Harriss)
    1924, June 3: acc orch. HMV B–1858 (10")

ENGLISHMAN, THE (Cook & Blockley)
    1904–1905: acc unknown. Nicole 5714 (10")

ERL KING, THE (Goethe & Schubert)
    (1) 1914, January 26: acc piano. Zono A–146 (12")
    (2) 1926, April 12: acc piano. HMV C–1327 (12")   *Gerald Moore Co 8242*

ETERNAL FATHER, STRONG TO SAVE (Dykes)
    (1) 1904–1905: acc orch. Nicole 4435 (7")
    (2) 1911, June: acc organ. Edison Amb 12334 (cyl)
    (3) 1939, April 13: acc organ. HMV B–8944 (10")

ETON BOATING SONG (A.D.E.W.) (Kaps)
    1917, January 5: duet with Ernest Pike (as Sydney Reeves & Bernard Moss): acc orch.
    HMV 2–4386; HMV E–110 (10")

EVEN BRAVEST HEARTS (Gounod *Faust*)
    1925, December 29: acc orch. HMV C–1267 (12")   *Cc7591 c Geo Byng*

EVER OF THEE (Linley & Hall)
    (1) 1906, July: duet with Walter Hyde: acc orch. Edison 13502 (cyl)
    (2) 1909, April: duet with Ernest Pike: acc orch. Edison Amb 12037; Edison (USA)
    Amb 258 (cyl)

EVERGREEN EVE (Parkes)
    1922, July 19: anonymous solo with Queens Dance Orchestra, dir. Jack Hylton: HMV
    B–1386 (10")

EVERY MAN A SOLDIER (Stanley)
    1913, March 3; acc orch. Zono 1065 (10")
EVERY TIME I SEE YOU (Emmett Adams)
    1920, April, 29 (as Will Strong): acc orch. HMV B–1109 (10")
EXCELSIOR (Longfellow & Balfe)
    (1) 1905, October: duet with Wilfred Virgo: acc orch. EB 6750 (cyl)
    (2) 1907, March: duet with Walter Hyde: acc orch. White 199 (cyl)
    (3) 1909, June: duet with Ernest Pike: acc orch. Edison Amb 12074; Edison BA 23091
        (cyl)
    (4) 1911, November 16: duet with Ernest Pike: acc orch. Zono A–49 (12")
EYE BENEATH THE BUSBY, THE (Kemble)
    1914, March 20: acc piano. Zono 1306 (10")
FAR ACROSS THE DESERT SANDS (Towne & Woodforde-Finden *A Lover In Damascus*)
    1930, September 22: acc orch. HMV C–2096 (12")
FAREWELL (Newbolt & Stanford *Songs of the Fleet*)
    1934, March 1: acc orch & chorus. HMV C–2694 (12")
FAREWELL IN THE DESERT (Adams)
    1917, March 20: acc orch. Zono 1927 (10")
FAREWELL, MY GOLDEN LOVE DREAM (Straus *The Last Waltz*)
    1922, November 24: duet with Bessie Jones: acc orch. HMV C–1100 (12")
FARMER'S PRIDE, THE (Russell)
    1912, January 16: acc orch. Zono 804; HMV (Canada) 120088 (10")
FATHER O'FLYNN (old Irish Melody arr. Stanford)
    (1) 1922, October 13: acc orch. HMV B–1485 (10")
    (2) 1931, March 10: acc orch. HMV B–3838; HMV (Eire) IP–158 (10")
FESTAL SONG (THE CHANT OF BACCHUS) (McCall)
    1920, May 20: acc orch. HMV B–1137 (10")   *c. Geo. Byng Ho. 5665 AE*
FICKLE FORTUNE (Monckton *The Arcadians*)
    1909, June: acc orch. Edison 13881 (cyl)
FIDDLER OF DOONEY (Dunhill)
    (1) 1925, August 19: acc piano. HMV B–2139 (10")
    (2) 1929, September 4: acc piano. HMV B–3874 (10")
FISHERMAN AND HIS CHILD, THE (White)
    1909, January 20: anonymous English bass solo: acc orch & chorus. Zono X–44117;
        Zono 521; Ariel 9473 (10")
FISHERMEN OF ENGLAND (Phillips *The Rebel Maid*)
    1929, August 15: acc orch. HMV B–3301 (10")   *B6 17248 –1*
FISHERMEN, THE (Cabussi)
    1922, December 28: duet with Sydney Coltham: acc orch. HMV B–1497 (10")
FISHIN' IN THE NORTH SEA (Sterndale Bennett)
    1935, July 11: acc orch. HMV B–8695 (10")
FLEET'S NOT IN PORT VERY LONG, THE (Gay)
    (1) 1937, March 4: acc orch & chorus. HMV B–8554; HMV EA–1986 (10")
    (2) 1937: acc orch & chorus. Soundtrack from GFD/Gainsborough motion picture
        Okay for Sound.
FLORAL DANCE, THE (Moss)
    (1) 1912, September: acc piano. HMV 02426; HMV C–441 (12")
    (2) 1912, December: acc orch. Zono 1005 (10")
    (3) 1927, January 14: acc piano. HMV C–1313 (12")

(4) 1934, May 1: acc orch. HMV C–2698 (12")

(5) 1942, July, Auckland, NZ: radio broadcast, acc piano. HMV PD–1 (12" LP set)

(6) 1945? possibly Sydney: radio broadcast, acc piano. Kingfisher STAR–16 (cassette)

FLOW GENTLY, DEVA (Parry)

1922, December 28: duet with Sydney Coltham: acc orch. HMV B–1497 (10")

FLOWERS O' THE FOREST, THE (Mrs Cockburn, old Scottish air)

1908, December 15: acc orch. Zono X–42874 (10")

FOL DOL TOORALLAY

1907, March (as Hector Grant): acc orch. EB 10159 (cyl)

FOLLOW ME 'OME (Ward & Higgs)

(1) 1920, April 12: acc orch. HMV C–958 (12")

(2) 1927, October 12: acc piano. HMV C–1427 (12")

FOLLOWING THE LADIES

1907, July (as Will Danby): acc orch. White 232 (cyl)

FOO THE NOO – see 'Fou the Noo'

FOR ALL ETERNITY (Mascheroni)

1904–1905: acc orch. Nicole 5813; Nicole D–544; Sovereign 29 (10")

FORESAKE ME NEVER (Mason & Saunders)

1944, October: acc organ. HMV EB–209 (12"), Sydney

FOREVER AND A DAY (Kern & Hammerstein)

1942, January 22; acc piano. RZ G–24524 (10"), Sydney

FORTY YEARS ON (Farmer *The Harrow School Song*)

1916, November 23: duet with Ernest Pike (as Sydney Reeves & Bernard Moss): HMV 2–4475; HMV E–110 (10")

FOU THE NOO (Lauder)

(1) 1905, November (as Hector Grant): acc orch. Edison 13396 (cyl)

(2) 1906, March 2 (as Hector Grant): Zono X–42402; (as Victor Graham): G&T 3–2844 (10")

(3) 1906, April (as Hector Grant): acc orch. EB 6876 (cyl)

FRANCESCO DEL FUEGO (Fraser–Simpson *A Southern Maid*)

1920, May 26: acc orch & chorus. HMV B1110 (10")   + Bessie Jones (sop.)

FRET-FOOT (Barron & McCall)

(1) 1937, July 2: acc orch. HMV B–8610 (10")

(2) 1947, October 24: acc orch. HMV B–9592; HMV EA–3694; HMV JO–166 (10"). All matrix OEA 12450–2 & test exists of OEA 12450–1.

FRIEND (Davies)

1914, January: acc orch. Zono 1294 (10")

FRIEND FOR ME, THE (McCall)

1920, c. September 24: acc orch. HMV B–1220 (10")

FRIEND O'MINE (Sanderson)

(1) 1913, December: acc orch. Zono 1248 (10")

(2) 1931, March 10: acc orch. HMV B–3839 (10")

FRIENDS (Alleyn)

1921, September (as Robert Woodville): acc orch. Zono 2172 (10")

FRIENDSHIP (Harvey)

1917, January: acc piano. Zono 2008 (10")

FROM THE OUTBACK TO THE OCEAN (Dodd)

1951, February 21: acc orch. HMV PD–1 (LP set) (12"), Sydney

FULL SAIL (Graves & Buck)
    1937, July 13: acc orch. HMV B–8627 (10")   OEA 5300-1 Sept 37

FUZZY WUZZY (Kipling & Cobb)
    1935, July 5: acc orch & chorus. HMV C–2797; Victor (Canada) 130827 (12" medley)

FUZZY–WUZZY–WOO (Carlton & Whidden)
    1920, February 17 (as Will Strong): acc orch. HMV B–1091 (10")

GALLANTS OF ENGLAND, THE (Scott–Gatty)
    (1) 1905, July 27: acc orch. G&T 3–2311 (10")
    (2) 1907: acc orch. Zono X–42889 (10")

GALLOPING MAJOR, THE (Bastow & Leigh)
    1907, January (as Will Danby): acc orch. White 173 (cyl)

GARDEN OF ALLAH, THE (Marshall)
    (1) 1909, July 1: acc orch. Zono X–42925 (10")
    (2) 1929, April 26: acc orch. HMV C–1689 (12")

GATEWAY TO HEAVEN, THE (Launton)
    1916, October 13: acc piano. Zono 1748 (10")

GAY HIGHWAY, THE (Drummond)
    (1) 1923, May 7: acc piano. HMV B–1698 (10")
    (2) 1925, December 18: acc piano. HMV B–2297 (10"); matrix Bb7566–2
    (3) 1927, February 7: acc piano. HMV B–2297 (10"); matrix Bb9894–1
    (4) 1949, NZ radio broadcast, acc piano (unissued)

GENDARMES' DUET (Offenbach *Geneviève de Brabant*)
    1935, November 9: acc piano & chorus. HMV C–2805 (12" medley)

GENEVIEVE (Cooper & Tucker)
    (1) 1906, March: duet with Walter Hyde: acc orch. Edison 13455 (cyl)
    (2) 1908, July: duet with Ernest Pike: acc orch. Zono X–44093 (10")
    (3) 1912, January 16: duet with Ernest Pike: acc orch. Zono 525 (10")
    (4) 1922, December 28: duet with Sydney Coltham: acc orch. HMV B–1492 (10")

GENTLE LADY (Mozart *Don Giovanni*)
    1920, November 30: acc orch. HMV B–1202 (10", two sides)

GENTLEMAN JIM (Parr & Oliver)
    (1) 1947, December 1: acc piano. European broadcast (BBC Radio Archive)
    (2) 1948, January 7: acc orch. HMV B–9618; HMV EA–3810 (10")

GESU BAMBINO (THE INFANT JESUS) (Yon)
    (1) 1922, January 18: acc orch. HMV C–1089 (12")
    (2) 1928, October 15: acc organ & chorus. HMV C–1582 (12")

GILDED POPINJAY, THE (Greene)
    1909, July 8: acc orch. HMV 4–2039 (10")

GINCHY ROAD (Edwards)
    1932, January 22: acc orch. HMV B–4089 (10")

GIVE ME THE ROLLING SEA (May)
    1932, January 22: acc orch. HMV B–4194 (10")

GIVE ME THE SPICE OF LIFE (North)
    1937, April 10: acc orch. HMV B–8600; Victor (Canada) 120899 (10")

GIVE ME THY HAND, O FAIREST (Mozart *Don Giovanni*)
    (1) 1909, May 19: duet with Eleanor Jones-Hudson (as Alvena Yarrow): Zono X–44130; Zono GO–13 (10"); matrix 10142e
    (2) 1920, c. March: duet with Bessie Jones (as Alvena Yarrow): Zono GO–13 (10"); matrix y21921–2

GLORIOUS DEVON (Boulton & German)

    (1) 1906, December: acc orch. EB 10120 (cyl)

    (2) 1910, March 23: acc orch. Zono 588; Ariel 794 (as Maurice Evans); HMV (Canada) 120058 (10")

    (3) 1922, October 17: acc orch. HMV B–1484 (10")

    (4) 1929, July 9: acc orch. HMV B–3280 (10")

GLORY OF THE MOTHERLAND (McCall)

    1934, Janury 11: acc orch. HMV B–8105 (10")

GLORY OF THE SEA, THE (Sanderson)

    (1) 1917, May 22: acc piano. Zono 1901 (10")

    (2) 1925, December 15: acc orch. HMV B–2275 (10")

    (3) 1933, January 31: acc orch. HMV B–4467 (10")

    (4) 1954, March 29, Sydney: radio broadcast, acc orch.

GLORY SONG, THE (Gabriel)

    1904–1905: acc unknown. Nicole 4423 (7")

GOD BE WITH YOU TILL WE MEET AGAIN (Tomer)

    1906, September 13: duet with Ernest Pike: acc organ. Zono X–44057 (10")

GOD DEFEND NEW ZEALAND (Wood)

    1924, February 4: acc orch & chorus. HMV D–841 (12")

GOD SAVE THE KING

    (1) 1908, September 30: acc orch. Zono X–40303; Zono 425 (10")

    (2) 1911, June: acc orch. Edison Amb 12340; Edison BA 23318; Edison (USA) BA 2438 (cyl)

    (3) 1922, early July: anonymous bass solo, acc orch. Zono 425 (10"); matrix yy1615–2

GOD SEND YOU BACK TO ME (Furber & Emmett Adams)

    (1) 1917, June 20: duet with Ernest Pike: acc orch. Zono 1794 (10")

    (2) 1934, November: anonymous soloist with orch & chorus. HMV C–2716 (12" medley)

GOD'S WITH YOU EV'RY DAY (Cobbett)

    1946, December 13: acc orch. HMV EA–3461 (10"), Sydney

GOG AND MAGOG (Oliver)

    1922, June 21: duet with Sydney Coltham: acc orch. HMV B–1737 (10")

GOIN' HOME (Fisher & Dvorak)

    1937, July 13: acc orch. HMV B–8620 (10")

GOLDEN DREAM BOAT (Nicholls)

    1922, August (as Robert Woodville): acc orch. Zono 2252 (10")

GOOD COMPANY (Adams)

    1907: acc orch. Zono X–42884 (10")

GOOD GREEN ACRES OF HOME (Kahal & Fain)

    1935, July 5: acc orch & chorus. HMV B–8353 (10")

GOOD NIGHT (Scott–Gatty)

    1905, September 4: in chorus acc soloist Nellie Melba: acc orch. G&T 3618; Victor (USA) 94006 (10")

GOOD RHEIN WINE, THE (Gray)

    1905, September–October: acc orch. EB 6693 (cyl); Little Champion Disc (9")

GOODBYE LITTLE SISTER (O'Hara)

    1906, August 21: acc orch. Zono X–42467; G&T 3–2841 (as David Peters) (10")

GRANDFATHER'S CLOCK (Work)

    1908: quartet with Ernest Pike, Stanley Kirkby & Harold Wilde: acc orch. Zono X–44081 (10")

GREATEST LAD WE'VE EVER HAD, THE (O'Hara) *God Bless the Prince of Wales*
Tribute
 1923, March 23: acc orch. HMV B–1632 (10")

GREEN HILLS O' SOMERSET, THE (Coates)
 (1) 1916, November 23: acc orch. HMV B–874 (10") *3308 ae*
 (2) 1950, December 18, Sydney: radio broadcast, acc piano. Kingfisher STAR–16
  (cassette)

GUID NEW YEAR, A
 1906, October (as Hector Grant): acc orch & chorus. EB 10080; EB 20200 (cyl)

GYPSY JOHN (Clay)
 1931, February 16: acc orch. HMV B–3809 (10")

HAIL KING GEORGE (Quentin)
 (1) 1911, March: anonymous solo: acc orch. Edison 14053 (cyl)
 (2) 1911, March: acc orch. Edison Amb 12300 (cyl)

HAME (Davies)
 1907, January (as Hector Grant): acc orch. Edison 13563 (cyl)

HAND IN HAND AGAIN (Whiting)
 1920, c. March (as Will Strong): duet with Ernest Pike: acc orch. HMV B–1108 (10")

HARK! WHAT WAS THAT, SIR? (Gilbert & Sullivan *Yeomen of the Guard*)
 (1) 1920, May: duet with Derek Oldham: acc orch & chorus. HMV D–485 (12")
 (2) 1928, November 2: quintet with Derek Oldham, Arthur Hosking, Leo Sheffield &
  George Baker: acc orch & chorus. HMV D–1557; Victor (USA) 11228 (12")

HARLEQUIN (Sanderson)
 (1) 1922, March: acc orch. HMV B–1348 (10")
 (2) 1930, October 14: acc orch. HMV B–3679 (10")

HARP THAT ONCE THROUGH TARA'S HALLS, THE (Moore)
 1909, July 30: acc orch & chorus. Zono X–42919 (10")

HARVEST HOME (Tate)
 1932, January 5: acc orch. HMV B–4166 (10")

HEAR DEM BELLS
 1908, March: quartet with Ernest Pike, Stanley Kirkby & Harold Wilde: acc orch &
  chimes. Zono X–44080 (10")

HEAR THE BUGLES CALLING (Kahn)
 1913, c. April: acc orch. Zono 1093 (10")

HEARD IN COURT
 1908, October 16: member of sketch. Zono X–49287 (10")

HEART O' THE HILLS (Ruby)
 1920, December 1 (as Will Strong): acc orch. HMV B–1172 (10")

HEART O' THE ROMANY RYE (McCall)
 1920, c. September 24: acc orch. HMV B–1220 (10")

HEARTS OF OAK (Garrick & Boyce *Harlequin's Invasion*)
 (1) 1911, April: anonymous solo: acc orch & chorus. Zono Coronation Record 598;
  Zono Patriotic Record 598; Zono 2261 (10")
 (2) 1911, December: acc orch. Edison Amb 12406; Edison BA 23333 (cyl)
 (3) 1936, October 13: acc orch & chorus. HMV C–2866; Victor (Canada) 36200 (12"
  medley) *Oct 14 '1936 2EA 4079/4080 —)*

HE HEARD THE GREAT SEA CALLING (Andrews)
 1928, March 28: acc piano. HMV B–2747 (10")

HELLO DEAR OLD VIRGINIA (Whidden)
 1920, c. October (as Robert Woodville): acc orch. Zono 2108 (10")

HELLO LITTLE GIRL

    1906, September (as Will Danby): acc orch. White 142 (cyl)

HELLO! HAWAII!, HOW ARE YOU? (Schwartz)

    1916, November 6 (as Will Strong): duet with Ernest Pike: acc orch. Zono 1740 (10")

HEN CONVENTION, THE

    1910, April 30, quartet with Ernest Pike, Harold Wilde & Stanley Kirby, with crowing
        by Gilbert Girard: acc orch. Zono X–44164 (10") possibly unissued.

HERE IS MY SONG (Longstaffe)

    1933, December 5: acc orch. HMV B–8120 (10")

HERE'S TO THE GOOD OLD DAYS (Hulls)

    1934, December 7: acc orch. HMV B–8334 (10")

HERE'S TO THE GOOD OLD DAYS (Neighbour)

    1924, December 2: acc piano. HMV B–1946 (10")

HERE'S TO THOSE WE LOVE (Fraser–Simpson *A Southern Maid*)

    1920, May 26: acc orch & chorus. HMV B–1110 (10")

HEREUPON WE'RE BOTH AGREED (Gilbert & Sullivan *Yeomen Of The Guard*)

    1907, January 29: duet with Stanley Kirkby: acc orch. G&T 4421; HMV B–408 (10")

HEVA, HIVA, HO (Slater)

    1911, November 3: acc orch. Zono 758; HMV (Canada) 120076 (10")

HIGHLAND BIRTHDAY PARTY (Grant)

    1906, March (as Hector Grant): acc orch. Edison 13466 (cyl)

HILLS OF DEVON (Sievier & Jalowicz)

    1932, April 27: acc orch. HMV B–4219 (10")

HINTON, DINTON AND MERE (Holliday)

    1928, September 26: acc piano. HMV B–2936 (10")

HO! JOLLY JENKIN (Sullivan *Ivanhoe*)

    1909, May: acc orch. Edison 13858 (cyl)

HOLY CITY, THE (Weatherly & Adams)

    1938, September 27: acc organ. HMV C–3038 (12")

HOME BOYS, HOME (Jude)

    1910, July 18: acc orch. Zono X–2–42033; Zono 599 (10")

HOME! CANADA! HOME! (Hennessy)

    1917, June 12: acc orch. HMV B–910; HMV (India) GM–1028 (10")

HOMEWARD

    1904–1905: acc unknown. Nicole 4431 (7")

HOMEWARD BOUND (Stanford *Songs Of The Sea*)

    (1) 1928, January 30: acc orch & chorus. HMV C–1479 (12")

    (2) 1933, January 25: acc orch & chorus. HMV C–2580 (12")   2B 6410—2

HONEY BOY (Norworth & Von Tilzer)

    1907, October: acc orch. EB 10451 (cyl)

HONOUR & ARMS (Handel *Samson*)

    (1) 1909, June 23 (as James Osborne): acc orch. Zono 184 (10")

    (2) 1927, November 1: acc orch. HMV C–1500 (12") *acc George Byng* Cc 11744

HOPE, THE HORNBLOWER (Newbolt & Ireland)

    1920, May 31: acc orch. HMV B–1337 (10")

HOTEL PIMLICO (Redstone *A Night Out*)

    1920, November 3: acc orch & chorus. HMV B–1158 (10")

HOUSE OF MINE (Stewart)

    1925, August 19: acc piano. HMV B–2154 (10")

HOW MANY A LONELY CARAVAN (Towne & Woodforde-Finden *A Lover In Damascus*)
 1930, September 22: acc orch. HMV C–2097 (12")
HOW SAY YOU, MAIDEN, WILL YOU WED? (Gilbert & Sullivan *The Yeomen Of The Guard*)
 1907, January 29: trio with Eleanor Jones-Hudson & Stanley Kirkby: acc orch. G&T
  4422; HMV B–406 (10")
HOW'S EVERY LITTLE THING IN DIXIE? (Gumble)
 1917, June 8 (as Will Strong): duet with Ernest Pike: Zono 1813 (10")
HUNDRED FATHOMS DEEP, A (Shattuck)
 (1) 1910, March 23: acc orch. Zono X–2–42036; Zono 866 (10")
 (2) 1924, March: acc orch. Zono 866 (10")
HURRICANE AM I!, A (Garidini)
 1921, February 3: acc orch. HMV B–1242 (10")
HYBRIAS, THE CRETAN (Campbell & Elliott)
 (1) 1905, August 24: acc orch. G&T 3–2319 (10")
 (2) 1912, February 14: acc orch. Zono 818; HMV (Canada) 120187 (10")
 (3) 1912, November: acc orch. Edison Amb 12523 (cyl)
 (4) 1913, April 4: acc piano. HMV 02506; HMV C–438 (12")
 (5) 1936, November 13: acc orch. HMV B–8513 (10")
I AIN'T NOBODY'S DARLING (King)
 1922, December 20: anonymous solo, with Jack Hylton & His Orch: HMV B–1524
  (10")
I AM A FRIAR OF ORDERS GREY (Reeve)
 (1) 1909, July 1: acc orch. Zono X–42918; Zono 512; Ariel 9475 (10")
 (2) 1922, October 17: acc orch. HMV B–1473 (10")
 (3) 1924, June: acc orch. Zono 512 (10") Matrix Yy4686–2
 (4) 1930, July 10: acc orch. HMV B–3593 (10")
I AM A ROAMER (Mendelssohn *Son & Stranger*)
 (1) 1904–1905: acc unknown. Nicole 5736 (10")
 (2) 1908, January 28 (as George Welsh): acc unknown. Zono 42360 (7")
 (3) 1911, October: acc orch. Edison Amb 12402; Edison BA 23164 (cyl)
 (4) 1916, November 23: acc orch. HMV 02727; HMV C–790 (12")
I AM FATE! (Hamblen)
 1923, March 23; acc orch. HMV C–1103 (12")
I AM PRAYING FOR YOU (Sankey)
 1906, September 13: duet with Ernest Pike: acc organ. Zono X–44052 (10")
I ARISE FROM DREAMS OF THEE (Yates)
 1914, April 30: duet with Ernest Pike: acc piano. Zono 1358 (10")
I FEAR NO FOE (Pinsuti)
 (1) 1907, January 24: acc orch. G&T 3–2791 (10"); matrix 9843b
 (2) 1907, January 24: acc orch. G&T 3–2791 (10"); matrix 9844b
 (3) 1912, January 9: acc orch. Zono 789; HMV (Canada) 120069 (10")
 (4) 1913, January 28: acc piano. HMV 02453; HMV C–438 (12")
 (5) 1936, November 13: acc orch. HMV B–8513 (10")
I GOT PLENTY O' NUTTIN' (Heywood & Gershwin *Porgy & Bess*)
 1938, January 27: acc orch. HMV B–8715 (10")
I HAVE TWELVE OXEN (Ireland)
 1920, March 5: acc orch. HMV B–1137 (10") c. Geo. Byng Ho.5577AE

I HEARD A FOREST PRAYING (Lewis & de Rose)
>   (1) 1939, April 12: acc organ. HMV B–8904 (10")
>   (2) 1942, July: radio broadcast, Auckland, NZ: acc organ. HMV PD–1 (LP set) (12")

I LOST MY HEART TO A MELODY (Strachey)
>   1932, January 22: acc orch. HMV B–4174 (10")

I LOVE A LASSIE (Grafton & Lauder)
>   (1) 1905, November (as Hector Grant): Edison 13402 (cyl)
>   (2) 1905, December (as Hector Grant): EB 6800 (cyl)
>   (3) 1905–1907, anonymous vocal: acc orch. London Popular (cyl) most likely pirated from Edison or Edison Bell cylinder issues.
>   (4) 1906, January 9 (as Hector Grant): acc orch. Zono 42289 (7"); matrix 2941d
>   (5) 1906, January 9 (as Hector Grant): acc orch. Zono X–42380; G&T 3–2842 (as Victor Graham) (10"); matrix 3293e
>   (6) 1907, January (as Hector Grant): White 165 (cyl)

I LOVE TO TELL THE STORY (Fischer)
>   1906, September 13: duet with Ernest Pike: acc organ. Zono X–44059 (10")

I LUB A LUBLY GAL I DO
>   1909, June 30: acc orch & chorus. Zono X–42982 (10")

I NEED THEE EVERY HOUR (Lowry)
>   1906, September 13: duet with Ernest Pike: acc organ. Zono X–44053 (10")

I RAGE, I MELT, I BURN recitative – see 'O ruddier than the cherry' (Handel)

I SEE A TREE (Hodges)
>   1936, March 27: acc orch. HMV B–8436 (10")

I SURRENDER ALL (van de Venter & Weeden)
>   1908, quintet with Eleanor Jones-Hudson, Amy Augarde, Ernest Pike & Thorpe Bates: acc orch Zono X–44085; Zono 535 (10")

I TOOK THE PRIZE
>   1906, June 15 (as Hector Grant) acc orch. Zono X–42510 (10")

I TRAVEL THE ROAD (Thayer)
>   (1) 1931, February 16: acc orch. HMV B–3812; matrix OB352–1
>   (2) 1932, February 24: acc orch. HMV B–3812; matrix OB2821–1
>   (3) mid–1930s?, unpublished private recording: acc piano. Permarec label (10")
>   (4) 1945? possibly Sydney: radio broadcast, acc piano. Kingfisher STAR–16 (cassette)

I WANT THE SUN AND MOON (Fraser–Simpson *A Southern Maid*)
>   1920, May 26: duet with Violet Essex: acc orch. HMV B–1114 (10")

I WANT TO HEAR THAT DIXIE MELODY AGAIN (Gorton)
>   1920, September 7 (as Will Strong): acc orch & chorus. HMV B–1138 (10")

I WANT YOU TO SEE MY GIRL (Castling & Godfrey)
>   1908, November: acc orch. Edison 13811 (cyl)

I WISH I HAD SOMEONE TO LOVE ME (Lauder)
>   (1) 1906, December (as Hector Grant): acc orch. EB 10110 (cyl)
>   (2) 1907, January 15 (as Hector Grant): acc orch. Zono X–42559 (10")
>   (3) 1907, February (as Hector Grant): acc orch. White 176 (cyl)
>   (4) 1907, March (as Hector Grant): acc orch. Edison 13577 (cyl)
>   (5) 1911, February 8 (as Hector Grant): acc orch. Zono 842; HMV (Canada) 120153 (10")

I'D JUST LIKE TO MENTION (St. Helier *Ring Up*)
>   1921, September 28 (as Will Strong): duet with Bessie Jones: acc orch. HMV B–1292 (10")

I'LL SING YOU A SONG (ABOUT DEAR DIXIELAND) (Creamer & Layton)
    1920, January 4 (as Will Strong): acc orch & chorus. HMV B–1081 (10")
I'LL WALK BESIDE YOU (Lockton & Murray)
    (1) 1939, April 18: acc piano. HMV B–8904 (10")
    (2) 1945? possibly Sydney: radio broadcast, acc piano. Kingfisher STAR–16 (cassette)
I'M FOREVER BLOWING BUBBLES (Kenbrovin & Kellette)
    1920, February 17 (as Will Strong): acc orch & chorus. HMV B–1092 (10")
I'M ON MY WAY TO DIXIELAND (Ayer)
    1917, June 8 (as Will Strong): duet with Ernest Pike: acc orch. Zono 1813 (10")
I'M VERY MUCH PAINED (Gilbert & Sullivan *Iolanthe*)
    1921, December 13: trio with Derek Oldham & Violet Essex: acc orch. HMV D–635
        (12")
I'VE GOT A LOVER UP IN SCOTLAND
    1907, October (as Will Danby): acc orch. EB 10468 (cyl)
I'VE GOT THE BLUES FOR MY KENTUCKY HOME (Gaskill)
    1922, January 10 (as Will Strong): acc orch & chorus. HMV B–1313 (10")
IF I COULD TURN THE CLOCK BACK A YEAR (Mills & Scott)
    1916, October 26 (as Will Strong): acc orch. Zono 1723 (10")
IF I WERE KING
    1904, July–August: acc orch. Lambert 5092 (cyl)
IF IN THE GREAT BAZAARS (Towne & Woodforde-Finden *A Lover In Damascus*)
    1930, September 22: acc orch. HMV C–2096 (12")
IF MUSIC BE THE FOOD OF LOVE (Travers)
    1937, July 9: acc orch. HMV B–8620 (10")
IF THOSE LIPS COULD ONLY SPEAK (Ridgewell & Godwin)
    (1) 1908 (as Hector Grant): acc piano. Zono 50; HMV (Canada) 120122 (10"). Some
        Canadian issues give the name as Henry Grant.
    (2) 1922, October: acc orch. HMV B–1477 (10")
    (3) 1930, June 24: acc orch & chorus. HMV B–3541 (10")
IF THOU WER'T BLIND
    1904, July–August: acc orch. Lambert 5089 (cyl)
IN A MONASTERY GARDEN (Ketelbey)
    1933, March 3: acc orch, organ & chorus. HMV C–2595 (12")
IN A PERSIAN MARKET (Ketelbey)
    1932, October 6: acc orch, organ & chorus. HMV C–2491 (12")
IN AN OLD–FASHIONED TOWN (Squire)
    1914, April: acc piano. Zono 1318 (10")
IN CELLAR DEEP (Fischer) (An Old German Drinking Song)
    1906, January 25: acc piano. G&T 3–2407 (10")
IN DEAR OLD GEORGIA (Williams & Van Alstyne)
    1907, January: acc orch. White 166 (cyl)
IN GOD'S OWN KEEPING (Geehl)
    1917, January 25: acc orch. Zono 1810 (10")
IN MEMORY OF YOU (Bowden & Dawson)
    1941, August 14: acc orch. RZ G–24398 (10"), Sydney
IN OLD JAPAN (Clare & Tomlin)
    1920, November (as Robert Woodville): acc orch. Zono 2123 (10")
IN THE SHADE OF THE OLD APPLE TREE (Williams & Van Alstyne)
    1906, August–September: acc orch. EB 10012 (cyl)

IL BALEN (AH, COULD I BEHOLD)

IN THE VALLEY WHERE THE BLUEBIRDS SING (Solman)

   (1) 1906, June 7, duet with Ernest Pike: acc orch. Zono X–44046; Zono 525 (10")

   (2) 1922, December 28, duet with Sydney Coltham: acc orch. HMV B–1492 (10")

IN ZANZIBAR – MY LITTLE CHIMPANZEE (Cobb & Edwards *The Medal And The Maid*)

   1904, December: acc orch. EB 6509 (cyl)

INTERRUPTED STORY, AN

   1907, late (as Percy Clifton): sketch with Stanley Kirkby. Zono 154 (10")

INVICTUS (Henly & Huhn)

   (1) 1917, January 20: acc piano. Zono 2008 (10")

   (2) 1937, April 10: acc orch. HMV B–8600; Victor (Canada) 120899 (10")

IT MUST BE YOU (Conrad)

   1920, April 29 (as Will Strong): acc orch. HMV B–1109 (10")

IT'LL BE ALL THE SAME (Gideon *A Night Out*)

   1920, September (as Robert Woodville): acc orch. Zono 2080 (10")

IT'S A DIFFERENT GIRL AGAIN (Scott)

   1906, July (as Will Danby) acc orch. White 111 (cyl)

IT'S CLEAR THAT MEDIAEVAL ART ALONE RETAINS ITS ZEST (Gilbert & Sullivan *Patience*)

   1921, January 31: trio with Ernest Pike & George Baker: acc orch & chorus. HMV D–570 (12")

IT'S MY THISTLE

   1908, October 9 (as Hector Grant): acc orch. Zono X–42858 (10")

IVY GREEN, THE (Mortimer)

   1911, August 22: acc orch. Zono 647 (10")

JACK TAR

   1907, March: acc orch. EB 10171 (cyl)

JANE (Mohr)

   1917, February 15 (as Will Strong): duet with Ernest Pike: acc orch. Zono 1842 (10")

JAPANESE SANDMAN, THE (Egan & Whiting)

   1920, November (as Robert Woodville): acc orch. Zono 2123 (10")

JEALOUS ANNIE

   1907, January 15 (as Hector Grant): duet with Carrie Tubb: acc orch. Zono 59 (10")

JEAN FRAE ABERDEEN (Murphy & Lipton)

   1907, December (as Hector Grant): acc orch. Zono X–42725 (10")

JEAN McNIELL (Lauder & Melville)

   (1) 1906, June 5 (as Hector Grant): acc orch. Zono 42323 (7"); matrix 7428a

   (2) 1906, June 5 (as Hector Grant): acc orch. Zono X–42526 (10"); matrix 8229b

JEANNIE LEE (Russell)

   1906, March (as Hector Grant): acc orch. Edison 13459 (cyl)

JERUSALEM (Blake & Parry)

   (1) 1926, January 12: acc orch. HMV B–2271 (10")

   (2) 1934, March 12: acc orch. HMV B–8196 (10")

JHELUM BOAT SONG (Fraser & Woodforde-Finden *On Jhelum River*)

   1931, February 3: acc orch. HMV C–2177 (12")

JINGLES, JOKES AND RHYMES

   1906, September (as Hector Grant) duet with Arthur Gilbert: acc orch. White 144 (cyl)

JOCK McGRAW (Linn)

   1911, August 25 (as Hector Grant): acc orch. Zono 707; HMV (Canada) 120140 (10")

JOGGIN' ALONG THE HIGHWAY (Samuel)

    1933, December 5: acc orch. HMV B–8120 (10")

JOHN, JOHN, GO AND PUT YOUR TROUSERS ON (Godfrey & Williams)

    (1) 1906, December (as Hector Grant): acc orch. EB 10112 (cyl)

    (2) 1907, January 10 (as Hector Grant): acc orch. Zono X–42535 (10"); matrix 9696b

    (3) 1907, January 10 (as Hector Grant): acc orch. Zono X–42535 (10"); matrix 9697b

    (4) 1907, February (as Will Danby): acc orch. White 162 (cyl)

JOHN MACKEY (Lauder)

    1906, June 5 (as Hector Grant): acc orch. Zono X–42487 (10")

JOKANAAN IS SUMMONED BEFORE SALOME (Strauss *Salome*)

    1924, June, sung in German: acc orch. HMV D–908; HMV (France) W–584 (12")

JOLLY CHRISTMAS, A

    1907, quartet with Ernest Pike, Stanley Kirkby & Arthur Gilbert: sketch with singing.
      Zono X–49279; Zono 694 (10")

JOLLY GOOD LUCK TO THE GIRL WHO LOVES A SOLDIER (Hargreaves)

    1907, June: acc orch. White 218

JOLLY ROGER , THE (Dewar & McCall)

    1936, September 10: acc orch. HMV B–8489 (10")

JONATHAN JONES (Teschemacher & Slater)

    1914, April 30: acc piano. Zono 1345; Ariel 2193 (10")

JOURNEY'S END (Kern *The Cabaret Girl*)

    1922, October 17: duet with Ennis Parkes: acc orch & chorus. HMV B–1412 (10")

JOURNEY'S END, THE (De Rance)

    1929, November 27: acc orch. HMV C–1805 (12")

JOVIAL MONK AM I, A (Audran *La Poupée*)

    (1) 1907, January 24: acc orch. Zono X–42901; Zono 512 (10")

    (2) 1922, October 17: acc orch. HMV B–1473; Ariel 9465 (10")

    (3) 1924, June: acc orch. Zono 512; Ariel 794 (as Maurice Evans) (10")

    (4) 1929, July 9: acc orch. HMV B–3186 (10")

JUG OF PUNCH, THE (Irish Folk Song, arr Charles Wood)

    1920, May 31: acc orch. HMV B–1265 (10")

JUST A CORNER OF HEAVEN TO ME (Stark & Hanley)

    1932, January 22: acc orch. HMV B–4174 (10")

JUST FOR TODAY (Partridge & Seaver)

    1939, March–April: acc piano. HMV B–8919 (10")

JUST KEEPIN' ON (Phillips)

    1936, March 16: acc orch. HMV B–8422 (10")

KANGAROO AND DINGO (German)

    1912, June 4: acc piano. Zono 3013 (10")

KASHMIRI LOVE SONG (Woodforde–Finden *Four Indian Love Lyrics*)

    (1) 1923, March 16: acc orch. HMV B–1686; HMV (Canada) 120805 (10")

    (2) 1925, December 31: acc orch. HMV B–2256 (10")

    (3) 1932, November 8: acc orch. HMV B–4320; HMV (Eire) IP–184 (10")

KEEP IN THE MIDDLE OF THE ROAD

    1909, June 30 (as Charles Handy): acc orch & chorus. Zono 189 (10")

KEEP THOU MY HEART (Lockton & Brahe)

    1946, January 14: acc organ. HMV EA–3303 (10"), Sydney

KERRY DANCE, THE (Molloy)

    (1) 1925, June 3: acc piano. HMV C–1212 (12")

(2) 1927, January 25: acc piano. HMV C–1442 (12")   *acc Gerald Moore*

KILLARNEY (Balfe)

1906, June: acc orch. EB 6931 (cyl)

KILLIECRANKIE (Lauder) – see 'The Lass o' Killiecrankie'

KIND CAPTAIN (Gilbert & Sullivan *H.M.S. Pinafore*)

(1) 1906, June 16: duet with Stanley Kirkby: acc orch & chorus. G&T 4404 (10")

(2) 1908, September: duet with Thorpe Bates: acc orch. G&T 4478; HMV B–440 (10")

KING CHARLES (White)

1921, January 28: acc piano. HMV B–1242 (10")

KING OF THE CLOUDS (Lewis)

1920, April 12: acc orch. HMV C–958 (12")

KINGFISHER BLUE (Fraser & Woodforde-Finden *On Jhelum River*)

1931, February 3: acc orch. HMV C–2177 (12")

LACKADAY (Crampton *Gavotte Songs*)

1914, January 26: acc piano. Zono 1282 (10")   *Ak 17421 e*

LADS IN NAVY BLUE, THE

1936, October 13: acc orch. HMV C–2866; Victor (Canada) 36200 (12" medley)

LADS O' DEVON (Loughborough & O'Reilly)

1913, November 18: acc orch. Zono 1224 (10")

LAMENT OF SHAH JEHAN, THE (Ronald)

1922, June 15: acc orch. HMV B–1723 (Parts 1 & 2) (10")   *Bb 1476-2, 1477-2*

LANAGAN'S LOG (Lohr)

(1) 1905, July 27: acc orch. G&T 3–2295 (10")

(2) 1912, September 24: acc orch. Zono 958 (10")

LANCASHIRE LAD'S TRIP ROUND LONDON, A

1908, early (as Percy Clifton), trio with Arthur Gilbert & Stanley Kirkby: descriptive. acc orch & bells. Zono X–41029 (10")

LAND O' MINE (Farrell & Dawson)

1941, August 14: acc orch. RZ G–24397 (10"), Sydney

LAND OF DELIGHT (Sims, Bovill & Sanderson)

1913, October 15: acc orch. Zono A–128 (12")

LAND OF MINE (Wheeler & Krips)

1951, September 12: acc orch & chorus. HMV EA–4008 (10"), Sydney

LAND OF THE HARLEQUINADE (Oliver)

1913, October 15: acc orch. Zono 936 (10")

LAND OF "WHO KNOWS WHERE" (James *Six Australian Bush Songs*)

(1) 1923, January 25: acc piano. HMV C–1125 (12")

(2) 1927, October 12: acc piano. HMV C–1428 (12")

LARBOARD WATCH (Williams)

(1) 1906, January–February: duet with Wilfred Virgo: acc orch. EB 6829 (cyl)

(2) 1922, October 26: duet with Sydney Coltham: acc orch. HMV B–1453 (10")

(3) 1923, June 15: duet with Browning Mummery: acc orch. Zono 527 (10")

LARGO AL FACTOTUM – see 'Room for the Factotum'

LASS O' KILLIECRANKIE , THE (Lauder)

1906, June 5 (as Hector Grant) acc orch. Zono X–42423 (10")

LASSETER'S LAST RIDE (Harrington & Dawson)

(1) 1942, January 22: acc piano. RZ G–24525 (10") Sydney

(2) 1950, December 18, Sydney: radio broadcast, acc piano. Premium Masters PCD–10123 (5" CD)

1953 Soundtrack "Phantom Gold"   acc. Chas. Cammaleri
(Age T)   *(p.t.o)*

(3) 1951, Sydney: radio broadcast, acc piano. Premium Masters PCD–10123 (5" CD)
(4) 1953, late: acc inst quartet. Prestophone unissued (10" acetate exists)
(5) 1954, May 10, Sydney: radio broadcast, acc orch. Kingfisher STAR–16 (cassette)

LASSIE, DINNA SIGH FOR ME (Grant)
(1) 1906, April–May (as Hector Grant): acc orch. EB 6895 (cyl)
(2) 1906, July 26 (as Hector Grant): acc orch. Zono X–42478 (10")
(3) 1906, August (as Hector Grant): acc orch. White 118 (cyl)
(4) late 1906 (as Hector Grant): acc orch. Pathé 60088, 1136, 226 (cyl & disc)

LAST MAN, THE (Calcott)
1917, May 22: acc piano. Zono 1874 (10")

LAST PATROL, THE (Riesenfeld)
1936, March 16: acc orch. HMV unpublished; test exists (10")

LAUGHING VAMP
1920, September 23 (as Will Strong): acc orch & chorus. HMV B–1145 (10")

LAZILY, DROWSILY (Caryll *Little Christopher Columbus*)
1934, November: anonymous soloist with orch & chorus. HMV C–2716 (12" medley)

LEAD, KINDLY LIGHT (Newman & Dykes)
(1) 1906, September 13: duet with Ernest Pike: acc organ. Zono X–44068 (10")
(2) 1908, July: acc orch. Zono X–42806; Zono 511 (10")
(3) 1939, April 12: acc organ. HMV B–8961 (10")

LEGION OF THE LOST, THE (Western)
1932, October 6: acc orch & chorus. HMV C–2507 (12")

LESS THAN THE DUST (Woodforde–Finden *Four Indian Love Lyrics*)
(1) 1923, May 16: acc orch. HMV B–1685 (10")
(2) 1925, December 29: acc orch. HMV B–2255; HMV (Canada) 120805 (10")
(3) 1932, November 8: acc orch. HMV B–4319 (10")

LET ME LOVE THEE (Arditi)
1906, February 14: acc orch. G&T 3–2483 (10")

LET ME SING
1906, August (as Hector Grant) duet with Arthur Gilbert: acc orch. White 126 (cyl)

LET THE LOWER LIGHTS BE BURNING (Bliss)
1906, September 13: duet with Ernest Pike: acc organ. Zono X–44056 (10")

LET THE MERRY CYMBALS SOUND (Gilbert & Sullivan *Patience*)
1921, January 26: trio with Ernest Pike & George Baker: acc orch & chorus. HMV D–567 (12")

LET THE REST OF THE WORLD GO BY (Brennan & Ball)
1920, March 17 (as Will Strong) duet with Ernest Pike: acc orch. HMV B–1098 (10")

LET'S ALL BE GOOD PALS TOGETHER (Erdman)
1921, September 30 (as Robert Woodville) duet with Ernest Pike: acc orch. Zono 2170 (10")

LIFE AND DEATH (Coleridge–Taylor)
1935, January 23: acc orch. HMV B–8325 (10")

LIFE IS A SONG (Let's sing it together) (Young & Ahlert)
1935, November 9: acc piano & chorus. HMV C–2805 (12" medley)

LIFE ON THE OCEAN WAVE, A (Sargent & Russell) – see 'Trafalgar'

LIGHTERMAN TOM (Squire)
1916, October 23: acc piano. Zono 1901 (10")

LILY AND THE SUN, THE (Arkell & Tchaikovsky *Catherine*)
1923, October, duet with Bessie Jones: acc orch. HMV B–1711 (10")

LINDY'S WEDDING (Gordon)

    1920, September 7 (as Will Strong): acc orch. HMV B–1139 (10")

LINGER A LITTLE LONGER (Ayer)

    1922, January 10 (as Will Strong): acc orch & chorus. HMV B–1312 (10")

LITTLE ADMIRAL, THE (Stanford *Songs of the Fleet*)

    (1) 1920, May 31: acc orch. HMV C–972 (12")

    (2) 1933, January 25: acc orch & chorus. HMV C–2580 (12")   2B 6411–1

LITTLE BROWN JUG (Winner)

    1906, October 31: acc orch & chorus. Zono X–42514 (10")   THE LITTLE WHITE House

LITTLE GREY HOME IN THE WEST, THE (Lohr)

    (1) 1912, December 17: acc orch. Zono 1023; Ariel 247 (as Maurice Evans) (10")

    (2) 1954, March 29, Sydney: radio broadcast, acc orch. Unissued

LITTLE HERO, THE (Adams)

    1907 (as George Welsh): acc orch. Zono X–42658; Zono 520 (10")

LITTLE OLD LOG CABIN DOWN THE LANE (Hays)

    1908, quartet with Eleanor Jones-Hudson, Ernest Pike & Harold Wilde: unaccompanied. Zono X–44115; Zono 533 (10")

LITTLE PRAYER I LOVE (Rizzi)

    1934, October 25: acc organ. HMV B–8244; Victor (Canada) 120882 (10")

LOAD THE COVERED WAGON (Kane & Hunt)

    1936, May 18: acc orch. HMV B–8443 (10")

LOCH LOMOND (Scottish traditional)

    (1) 1904–1905: acc unknown. Nicole (untraced); Pelican P–33 (10")

    (2) 1933, February 28: acc orch & chorus. HMV C–2597 (12" medley)

LOCHNAGAR (Gibson)

    1908, November 12: acc orch. Zono X–42855; Zono 759,

    HMV (Canada) 120077 (10"). Zono 759 & HMV both as Hector Grant

LONDON GIRL (Snodgrass)

    1932, July 19: acc orch. HMV B–4278 (10")

LONDONDERRY AIR (Irish traditional)

    1933, February 28: acc orch & chorus. HMV C–2597 (12" medley)

LONG AGO IN ALCALA (Messager)

    1904, September 5: acc unknown. G&T 2–2495 (7")

LONG LIVE THE KING (Andrews)

    (1) 1910, July 18: acc orch. Zono X–2–42026; Zono 599 (10")

    (2) 1910, August: acc orch. Edison 14010 (cyl)

LOOKING ALL OVER FOR YOU (Kern *The Cabaret Girl*)

    1922, October 17, duet with Ennis Parkes: acc orch & chorus. HMV B–1412 (10")

LORD IS A MAN OF WAR, THE (Handel *Israel in Egypt*)

    1924, January 5, duet with Robert Radford: acc orch. HMV D–967 (12")

LORD IS KING, THE (Dawson)

    1938, September 27: acc organ. HMV B–8832 (10")

LORD IS MY SHEPHERD, THE (Bantock)

    1947, September 18: acc organ. HMV EA–3769 (10")

LORRAINE, LORRAINE, LORRÉE (Capel)

    1928, March 28: acc piano. HMV B–2759 (10")

LOST CHORD, THE (Proctor & Sullivan)

    (1) 1907, duet with Ernest Pike: acc organ, bells, piano, & chorus. Zono X–44073; Zono 526 (10")

(2) 1923, May, duet with Browning Mummery: acc organ, orch, & chorus. Zono 526; Ariel Grand 1000 (as Maurice Evans & George Saunders) (10")

(3) 1938, September 27: acc organ. HMV C–3038 (12")

LOUDLY LET THE TRUMPETS BRAY (Gilbert & Sullivan *Iolanthe*)
1921, December 13, septet with George Baker, Edward Halland, Walter Glynne, Derek Oldham, Harold Wilde & Ernest Pike: acc orch. HMV D–634 (12")

LOUISIANA (West)
1920, June 18 (as Will Strong): acc orch & chorus. HMV B–1119 (10")

LOVE AND WAR (Cook)
1922, June 30, duet with Sydney Coltham: acc orch. HMV B–1495 (10")

LOVE AND WINE (Goatley)
1922, November 8: acc orch. HMV B–1735 (10")   ✓ 15728e

LOVE AND WINE (Ross & Lehar *Gypsy Love*)
1912, September 25: acc orch. HMV 4–2238; HMV B–319 (10")

LOVE ME ALL THE TIME (Brookhouse)
1909, July 8 (as Charles Handy): acc orch. Zono X–42914 (10")

LOVE TRIUMPHANT (Wheeler)
1944, November: acc organ. HMV EB–224 (12"), Sydney

LOVE'S MELODIE (Ford–Barrington)
1922, June 21, duet with Sydney Coltham: acc orch. HMV B–1415 (10")

LOVE'S REQUIEM (Sanderson)
1914, March 11: acc piano. Zono 1479 (10")

LOVE, COULD I ONLY TELL THEE (Capel)
(1) 1925, December 8: acc piano. HMV B–2238 (10")
(2) 1933, January 5: acc orch. HMV B–4411 (10")

LOVELY KIND AND KINDLY LOVING (Breton & Holst)
1923, May 7: acc piano. HMV B–1750 (10")   Bb 2948–2

LOVERS, THE (Lane Wilson)
(1) 1914, March 11, duet with Ernest Pike: acc piano. Zono A–148 (12")
(2) 1924, January 4, duet with Sydney Coltham: acc orch. HMV B–1768 (10")

LOW–BACKED CAR, THE (Lover)
1913, September 26: acc orch. Zono 1179 (10")

LOWLAND SEA, THE (Branscombe *The Golden Vanity*)
1912, July 9: acc orch. Zono 892 (10")

LUTE PLAYER, THE (Allitsen)
(1) 1917, January 29: acc piano. Zono A–238 (12")
(2) 1927, January 14: acc piano. HMV C–1313 (12")
(3) 1934, May 1: acc orch. HMV C–2698 (12")

MAD WILLIE (Scott)
1905, October: acc orch. Edison 13369 (cyl)

MAI PAHI AIPO (Maori song)
1935, November 9: acc ukelele. HMV C–2805 (12" medley)

MAKE BELIEVE (Davies & Shilkret)
1921, September 28 (as Will Strong): acc orch & chorus. HMV B–1282 (10")

MAN IN THE STREET, THE (Longstaffe)
1934, December 7: acc orch. HMV B–8262 (10")

MAN IS MASTER OF HIS FATE (Straus *The Last Waltz*)
1922, November 24: acc orch. HMV B–1512 (10")

MAN WHO BRINGS THE SUNSHINE, THE (Cooper)
    1929, April 20: acc piano. HMV B–3078 (10")

MAN'S A MAN FOR A' THAT, A (Burns)
    1908, December 15 (as Hector Grant): acc orch. The Twin T–2110; The Twin 112; HMV (Canada) 120182 (10")

✓ **MANDALAY** (Kipling & Cobb)
    1935, July 5: acc orch & chorus. HMV C–2797; Victor (Canada) 130827 (12" medley)

MANDALAY (Kipling & Willeby)
    (1) 1910, April 30: acc orch. Zono X–44163; Zono 914 (10"), matrix 11684e
    (2) 1912, August 13: acc orch. Zono 914 (10"); matrix y15468e

MANDALAY POTPOURRI (Kipling, Speaks, Willeby, Hedgcock & Cobb)
    1945, September 12, Sydney: acc organ. HMV EA–3295 (10", two sides)

MANDALAY SCENA (Kipling, Speaks, Willeby, Hedgcock, & Cobb)
    (1) 1954, May 10, Sydney: radio broadcast: acc orch. Kingfisher STAR–16 (cassette)
    (2) 1955, May 4: acc orch. HMV 7EG–8157 (7" EP mono); HMV PD–1 (12" LP set stereo)

MANY HAPPY RETURNS OF THE DAY (Blockley)
    1911, August 22: acc orch. Zono 722; RZ T–722; HMV (Canada) 120195 (10")

MARCH OF LIBERTY – see 'Song of Liberty'

MARCH OF THE CAMERON MEN (Campbell)
    1923, February 1: acc orch. HMV B–1545 (10")

MARLIN CHAPEL (Grant)
    1923, February 1: acc orch. HMV B–1582 (10")

MARNA (Oliver)
    (1) 1911, November 29: acc piano. HMV 02372; HMV C–440 (12"); matrix Ac5795f
    (2) 1911, November 29: acc piano (?) HMV 02372; HMV C–440 (12"); matrix Ac5796f

McPHERSON'S FAREWELL (McCall)   *SOLDIER'S FAREWELL ?*
    1934, October 8: acc orch. HMV B–8343 (10")

MEANDERIN' (Gideon *The Co–optimists*)
    1922, June 26: acc orch. HMV B–1394 (10")

MEET ME IN ROSE TIME, ROSIE (Jerome & Schwartz)
    1909, July 8 (as Mr. C. Handy): acc orch. Zono X–42933; Zono 504; Ariel 9508 (10")

MEET ME, JENNY, WHEN THE SUN GOES DOWN (Castling & Murphy)
    1908 (as Hector Grant): acc piano. Zono 50; HMV (Canada) 120122 (10")

MEMORY OF A SONG (Nicholls)
    1921, September 9 (as Robert Woodville): acc orch. Zono 2185 (10")

MEMORY OF THE DEAD (Johnson)
    1906, June 6: acc orch. Zono X–42424; Zono 515 (10")

MEN OF THE A.I.F (Myers)
    late 1943: acc piano. HMV EA–3042 (10"), Sydney

MENIN GATE, THE (Bowen)
    1930, November 4: acc organ: HMV B–3691 (10")

MERRY–GO–ROUND (Tate)
    1932, January 5: acc orch. HMV B–4166 (10")

✓ **MIDNIGHT REVIEW** (Newmarch & Glinka)
    1929, March 5: acc orch. HMV C–1988 (12")   *c Geo Byng Ce 15967*

MIDSHIPMITE, THE (Adams)
    1909, June: acc orch. Edison Amb 12084; Edison (USA) Amb 418 (cyl)

MIGHTY DEEP, THE (Jude)

    1910, October 21: acc orch. Zono X–2–42042; Zono 866 (10")

MILL WHEEL, THE

    1909, June 30: acc orch, harp & chorus. Zono X–42939; Zono 525 (10")

MINER'S DREAM OF HOME, THE (Godwin & Dryden)

    (1) 1909, June: duet with Ernest Pike: acc orch & chorus. Edison Amb 12103; Edison
        BA 23044 (cyl)

    (2) 1922, October 13: acc orch. HMV B–1477 (10")

    (3) 1930, June 24: acc orch & chorus. HMV B–3543; HMV (Canada) 120838 (10")

MIYA SAMA (Gilbert & Sullivan *The Mikado*)

    1906, August 21, duet with Amy Augarde: acc orch & chorus. G&T 4412; HMV B–427
        (10")

MOLLY OF DONEGAL (Austin)

    (1) 1925, August 19: acc piano. HMV B–2139 (10"); matrix Bb6548–1

    (2) 1927, February 7: acc piano. HMV B–2139 (10"); matrix Bb9895–2

MOLLY, MY OWN (Purssord)

    1917, February 5: acc piano. Zono 1874 (10")

MONARCH OF THE WOODS (Cherry)

    1910, December 8: acc orch. Zono 601: Ariel 9744; HMV (Canada) 120086 (10")

MOON HATH RAISED HER LAMP ABOVE, THE (Benedict *The Lily of Killarney*)

    (1) 1905, December, duet with Wilfred Virgo: acc orch. EB 6763 (cyl)

    (2) 1906, June,:duet with Edward Davies: acc orch. Edison 13494 (cyl)

    (3) 1906, July, duet with Tom Child: acc orch. White 107 (cyl)

    (4) 1906, October, duet with Mr. Stanley: acc orch. White 161 (cyl)

    (5) 1908, duet with Ernest Pike: acc orch. Zono X–44111 (10")

    (6) 1909, June, duet with Ernest Pike: acc orch. Edison Amb 12063; Edison BA 23072
        (cyl)

    (7) 1911, November 16, duet with Ernest Pike: acc orch. Zono A–49 (12")

    (8) 1922, May 18, duet with Sydney Coltham: acc orch. HMV B–1380 (10")

    (9) 1924, September 2 duet with Browning Mummery: acc piano. Zono A–49 (12")

    (10) 1935, November 9: acc piano & chorus. HMV C–2805 (12" medley)

MOPSA

    1904–1905: acc unknown. Nicole 4487 (7")

MORE HUMANE MIKADO, A (Gilbert & Sullivan *The Mikado*)

    1906, August 21: acc orch & chorus. G&T 3–2476; HMV B–434 (10")

MOTHER CAREY (Keel *Salt Water Ballads*)

    1924, January 29: acc orch. HMV B–1785 (10")

MOTHER O' MINE (Kipling & Tours)

    1936, September 10: acc orch. HMV B–8487 (10")

MOTHER'S RUSTIC ROCKING CHAIR

    1909, June 3: acc orch & chorus. Zono X–42954 (10")

MOTORING UP TO DATE

    1906, January, comedy sketch with Alfred Groves: EB 6825 (cyl)

MOUNTAINS O' MOURNE, THE (Collisson & French)

    (1) 1921, January 28: acc piano. HMV B–1265 (10")

    (2) 1931, January 29: acc orch. HMV B–3772; HMV B–9114; Victor (Canada) 120840;
        HMV (Eire) P–158(10")

MOUNTIES, THE (Harbach, Hammerstein, & Friml *Rose Marie*)

    1925, April 14: acc orch & chorus. HMV B–2004 (10")

MRS JEAN MACFARLANE
1907, December (as Hector Grant), acc orch. Zono X–42737 (10")

MY BELOVED QUEEN (Rose)
1916, November 3: acc piano. Zono 2313 (10")

MY CAPTAIN (Scott)
1922, July 13: acc piano. HMV B–1582 (10")

MY DEARIE (Farrells)
1909, June: acc orch. Edison 13895 (cyl)

MY DREAM OF LOVE IS O'ER
1908, quartet with Ernest Pike, Stanley Kirkby & Harold Wilde: acc orch. Zono X–44110; Zono 530 (10")

MY HAWAIIAN SUNSHINE (Gilbert & Morgan)
1917, June 8 (as Will Strong): acc orch. Zono 1798 (10")

MY HEART'S BEST LOVE
1908, quartet with Ernest Pike, Stanley Kirkby & Harold Wilde: acc orch. Zono X–44112 (10")

MY HENLEY GIRL (Chauncey)
1906, July: acc orch. Edison 13506 (cyl)

MY HOME IN U.S.A. (Flynn)
1917, June 8 (as Will Strong): acc orch. Zono 1826 (10")

MY LITTLE EVA
1908, November 12 (as Henry Tucker): acc orch. Zono 80 (10")

MY LOVE SONG TO A TREE (Saunders & Walters)
late 1950: acc probably piano. Vitavox (private) (10" acetate) Sydney

MY MINE OF MEMORIES (Davis & McCall)
1958, April 30, Adelaide: radio broadcast, acc piano. HMV PD–1 (12" LP set).

MY OLD SHAKO (Barron & Trotère)
(1) 1908, May: acc orch. EB 20084 (cyl)
(2) 1909, June: acc orch. Edison Amb 12058; Edison (USA) BA 3590 (cyl)

MY PALE FACE QUEEN (le Brun)
1905, October: acc orch. Edison 13378 (cyl)

MY SONG GOES ROUND THE WORLD (May, Neubach & Kennedy)
1935, November 9: acc piano. HMV C–2805 (12" medley)

MY SUNNY TENNESSEE (Kalmar, Ruby & Ruby)
1922, January 10 (as Will Strong): acc orch & chorus. HMV B–1313 (10")

MY SWORD AND I (Byng)
(1) 1920, April 12: acc orch. HMV B–1141 (10")
(2) 1931, February 16: acc orch. HMV B–3812 (10")

MYSTERY (Cirina)
1920, April 29 (as Will Strong): acc orch & chorus. HMV B–1106 (10")

MYSTIC NILE (Pierce)
1920, April 29 (as Will Strong): acc orch. HMV B–1106 (10")

NANCY LEE (Weatherly & Adams)
(1) 1906, June: acc orch. White 104 (cyl)
(2) 1906, June: acc orch. Edison 13498 (cyl)
(3) 1906: acc orch. Pathé 60084 (cyl & disc)
(4) 1909, June: acc orch. Edison Amb 12071 (cyl)

NATION ONCE AGAIN, A (Davis & Johnson)
(1) 1906, June 6: acc orch. Zono X–42448; Zono 516 (10")

(2) 1922, June 26: acc piano. Zono 516 (10")

NAVAJO (Williams & Van Alstyne)

T Part ✓ (1) 1904, July–August (as Leonard Dawson): acc orch. Lambert 5100 (cyl)

(2) 1904, July–August (some as Leonard Dawson): acc orch. EB 6398 (cyl)

(3) 1904, August 15: acc piano. G&T 2–2479 (7")

(4) latter half 1904 (as Mr. C. Adams): acc orch. Nicole 4457 (7")

NAZARETH (Chorley & Gounod)

(1) 1909, June: acc orch. Edison Amb 12099; Edison BA 23147 (cyl)

(2) 1928, October 15: acc organ & chorus. HMV C–1582 (12")

(3) 1948, October 1: acc organ. HMV C–3808 (12")

✓ **NEARER, MY GOD, TO THEE** (Dykes)

1939, April 13: acc organ. HMV B–8944 (10")

NEW HOOSE, THE (Gillespie)

1911, August 25 (as Hector Grant), acc orch. Zono 707; HMV (Canada) 120140 (10")

NIGHT WATCH, THE (Pinsuti)

1922, May 23: acc orch. HMV C–1103 (12")

NIGHT WATCHMAN, THE (Leo)

1912, August (as Fred Davies), duet with Harry Fay: acc orch. Zono 945 (10")

NO NEWS! OR WHAT KILLED THE DOG (Wills)

1910, September 7 (as Robert Baxter), humorous monologue with Ernest Pike: unaccompanied: Zono X–49328 (10")

NOBODY KNOWS (AND NOBODY SEEMS TO CARE) (Berlin)

1920, June 18 (as Will Strong): acc orch. HMV B–1119 (10")

NONE BUT THE LONELY HEART (Meyer, Goethe & Tchaikovsky)

1947, December 1: European broadcast, acc orch. BBC Radio Archive.

NONE SHALL PART US (Gilbert & Sullivan *Iolanthe*)

1912, December 17, duet with Eleanor Jones-Hudson: acc orch. Zono 1025 (10")

NORTH SEA SKIPPER, A (George)

1924, March: acc orch. Zono 2453 (10")

NOW FOR THE PIRATES' LAIR (Gilbert & Sullivan *The Pirates of Penzance*)

1929, February 19, trio with Derek Oldham & Dorothy Gill: acc orch. HMV D–1685; Victor (USA) 9614 (12")

✓ **NOW YOUR DAYS OF PHILANDERING ARE OVER** (Mozart *The Marriage of Figaro*)

(1) 1920, November 30: acc orch. HMV C–1041 (12")

✓ (2) 1927, September 1: acc orch. HMV C–1401 (12")   CR1496 c. Sea Byng

NURSERY RHYMES – see under 'Uncle Peter'.

NUT BROWN ALE (Booth & Murray)

1951, February 21: acc orch. HMV PD–1 (LP set) (12"), Sydney

O COME, EVERYONE THAT THIRSTETH (Mendelssohn *Elijah*)

1907, January 29 quartet with Ernest Pike, Florence Venning & Eleanor Jones-Hudson: acc orch. G&T 04002; HMV C–486 (12")

O FALMOUTH IS A FINE TOWN (Henley & Ronald)

1922, June 12: acc piano. HMV B–1375 (10")

O GOD OUR HELP IN AGES PAST

1907, October: acc orch. EB 10461 (cyl)

O LORD THOU HAST OVERTHROWN (Mendelssohn *Elijah*)

1907, January 29, duet with Carrie Tubb: acc orch. G&T 04003; HMV C–484 (12")

O MISTRESS MINE (Sullivan)

1917, June 12: acc orch. HMV B–851 (10")

O MISTRESS MINE (Tarpey)
    1912, August 14: duet with Ernest Pike: acc orch. Zono 916 (10")
O RUDDIER THAN THE CHERRY (recit: I Rage, I Melt) (Handel *Acis & Galatea*)
    1927, November 1: acc orch. HMV C–1500 (12")   *cc 11743   c. George Byng*
O SING TO ME AN IRISH SONG (Geehl), see 'Come Back to Erin' and 'Londonderry Air'
O STAR OF EVE (Wagner *Tannhäuser*)
    (1) 1906, January 4: acc piano. G&T 3–2396; HMV B–4504 (10")   *3274e*
    (2) 1907, late: acc piano. Zono X–42811 (10")
    (3) 1925, December 29: acc orch. HMV C–1267 (12")
O! SYDNEY I LOVE YOU (McLeod)
    1930s? or 1940s?: acc unknown. Reported as issued by Vitavox in 1930s (late 1940s seems more likely). No known copies exist.
O'BRIEN IS TRYIN' TO LEARN TO TALK HAWAIIAN (Dubin & Cormack)
    1917, June 20 (as Will Strong): acc orch. Zono 1698 (10")
O, CANADA, MARCH ON! (Wakefield)
    1917, June 12: acc orch. HMV B–841 (10")
ODDFELLOW'S SONG, THE
    1910, October 11: acc orch. HMV 4–2107 (10")
OFF TO PHILADELPHIA (Haynes)
    (1) 1911, May: acc orch. Edison Amb 12325 (cyl)
    (2) 1922, December 20: acc orch. HMV B–1485 (10")
OH, BETTER FAR TO LIVE AND DIE (Gilbert & Sullivan *Pirates of Penzance*)
    1929, March 25: acc orch & chorus. HMV D–1679; Victor (USA) 9608 (12")
OH, COULD I BUT EXPRESS IN SONG (Malashkin)
    1927, January 14: acc piano. HMV B–2425 (10")   *acc Gerald Moore B68241*
OH FOR A SAIL IN THE PIPING BREEZE
    1905, February 21: acc orch. G&T 3–2581 (7")
OH! MOTHER ASTHORE (MacCarthy)
    1917, February 8: acc piano. Zono 1760 (10")
OH! MY WARRIORS (Acworth & Elgar *Caractacus*)
    1928, September 24: acc orch. HMV C–1579 (12")   *c. Sir John Barbirolli Cc 14390*
OH! OH! HEAR THE WILD WINDS BLOW (Mattei)
    1911, September 19: acc orch. Zono 683, HMV (Canada) 120199 (10")
OH! SERGEANT MERYLL, IS IT TRUE? (Gilbert & Sullivan *Yeomen of the Guard*)
    1928, October 5: acc orch & chorus. HMV D–1553; Victor (USA) 11224 (12")
OH! WHAT A DIFFERENCE THE NAVY'S MADE TO ME (Alleyne)
    1920, November (as Robert Woodville): acc orch. Zono 2094 (10")
OH WHAT A NASTY FEELING
    1908, December 15 (as Henry Tucker): acc orch. HMV GC 4–2011 (10")
OH! WHAT A PAL WAS MARY (Leslie, Kalmar, & Wendling)
    1920, March 17 (as Will Strong): duet with Ernest Pike: acc orch. HMV B–1108 (10")
OH, WHO WILL O'ER THE DOWNS WITH ME? (Pearsall)
    1910, July 1 quartet with Eleanor Jones-Hudson, Ernest Pike & Harold Wilde: acc unknown. Zono X–44162 (10") possibly unissued
OL' MAN RIVER (Hammerstein & Kern *Show Boat*)
    1928, September 11: acc orch & chorus. HMV B–2858 (10")
OLD BRIGADE, THE – see 'Boys of the Old Brigade'

OLD BULL AND BUSH, THE – see 'Down At The Old Bull and Bush'

OLD COMRADES (Teike)

> 1930, June 16: acc orch & chorus. HMV C–2045 (12")

OLD DOG SPORT

> 1908, February (as Peter Clifton): descriptive with Gilbert Girard. Zono X–41030 (10")

OLD FATHER THAMES (Wallace & O'Hogan)

> 1933, January 25: acc orch & chorus. HMV B–4374 (10")

OLD FLAGGED PATH, THE (Kelly & Arundale *The Little White House*)

> 1914, January 20: acc orch. Zono 1282 (10") *Ak 17392 e*

OLD FOLKS AT HOME (Foster)

> (1) 1905, September 4, in chorus (Nellie Melba soloist): acc piano. G&T 3617; HMV DA–337; Victor (USA) 94005 (10")
>
> (2) 1908, quartet with Eleanor Jones-Hudson, Thorpe Bates & Harold Wilde: acc orch. Zono X–44092; Zono 532 (10")

OLD JIM'S CHRISTMAS HYMN (Gray)

> (1) 1906, October, duet with Wilfred Virgo: acc orch. White 148 (cyl)
>
> (2) 1908, September, duet with Wilfred Virgo: acc orch. EB 20198 (cyl)
>
> (3) 1923, March 7: acc orch & chorus. HMV B–1596 (10")
>
> (4) 1931, March 24: acc orch & chorus. HMV B–3860 (10")

OLD KETTLE DRUM **OLD MAN NOAH** (Sanderson)

> 1935, January 23: acc orch. HMV B–8334 (10")

OLD PLANTATION (Redmond & David *Cotton Club Parade*)

> 1937, May 10: acc orch & chorus. HMV B–8583; HMV EA–1986 (10")

OLD RUSTIC BRIDGE BY THE MILL, THE (Skelly)

> (1) 1909, February, duet with Ernest Pike: acc orch. Edison Amb 12006; Edison BA 23052; Edison (USA) Amb 243 (cyl)
>
> (2) 1923, March 7: acc orch & chorus. HMV B–1630 (10")

OLD SEXTON, THE (Russell)

> 1916, December 1: acc orch. HMV B–785 (10")

OLD SUPERB, THE (Stanford *Songs of the Sea*)

> (1) 1928, February 24: acc orch & chorus. HMV C–1479 (12")
>
> (2) 1933, January 10: acc orch & chorus. HMV B–4483 (10") *o B 4388–2*

OLD TENNESSEE AND ME (Whiting)

> 1920, January 15 (as Will Strong): acc orch & chorus. HMV B–1087 (10")

ON A SYDNEY HARBOUR FERRY

> 1930s? or 1940s?: acc unknown. Reported as recorded in Sydney by Vitavox in 1930s (late 1940s seems more likely). No known copies exist.

ON THE ROAD TO MANDALAY (Kipling & Hedgcock)

> 1929, September 11: acc orch. HMV C–1770 (12")

ON THE ROAD TO MANDALAY (Kipling & Speaks)

> (1) 1939, March–April: acc piano. HMV B–8886; HMV JO–388 (10")
>
> (2) 1951, August 26, Sydney: 2GB radio broadcast: acc piano. (16" disc)

ON TO THE FIELD OF GLORY (Donizetti *Belisario*)

> 1922, December 29, duet with Sydney Coltham: acc orch. HMV B–1380 (10")

ONAWAY, AWAKE, BELOVED! (Cowen)

> (1) 1914, April 30: acc piano. Zono 1376; Ariel 281 (10")
>
> (2) 1927, January 25: acc piano. HMV B–2561 (10") *acc. Gerald Moore B b 9854*

ONCE ABOARD THE LUGGER (Slater)

> 1911, November 30: acc orch. Zono 758; HMV (Canada) 120076 (10")

ONLY A PANSY BLOSSOM (Rexford & Howard)
　　1908, quintet with Eleanor Jones-Hudson, Stanley Kirkby, Ernest Pike & Harold Wilde: acc orch. Zono X–44084 (10")

ONLY TO SEE HER FACE AGAIN (Chambers)
　　1908, quartet with Ernest Pike, Stanley Kirkby, & Harold Wilde: acc orch. Zono X–44092 as Quartet; G&T 4465 as Minster Singers (10")

OPEN YOUR HEART AND LET THE SUNSHINE IN (Godfey & Scott)
　　1920, October 29 (as Will Strong): acc orch & chorus. HMV B–1166 (10")

ORA PRO NOBIS (Pray for us) (Piccolomini)
　　(1) 1907, trio with Florence Venning & Ernest Pike, soloist Eleanor Jones-Hudson: acc orch. Zono X–43138; Zono 472 (10")
　　(2) 1909, March: acc orch. Edison Amb 12023 (cyl)

ORDER, PLEASE! (Weston & Lee)
　　1916, November 6 (as Will Strong), duet with Ernest Pike: acc orch. Zono 1752 (10")

OTHER SIDE O' JORDAN (Hawley)
　　1913, March 3: acc orch. Zono 1065 (10")

OUR FARM (Caryll & Monckton *Our Miss Gibbs*)
　　1909, June 9 (as Charles Handy), duet with Eleanor Jones-Hudson: acc orch. HMV 2–4005 (10")

OUR HERITAGE (Wheatley & Lewis)
　　1953, December: acc orch & choir. Prestophone A–54–1 (10") Sydney

OUR JACK'S COME HOME (Devers)
　　1910, July 18: acc orch. Zono X–2–42054 (10")

OUR RIVER THAMES (Hennessy)
　　1929, July 10: acc piano. HMV B–3143 (10")

OUR STAR (Baxter & Dawson)
　　1941, August 14: acc orch. RZ G–24397 (10"), Sydney

OUT ON THE DEEP (Cowan & Lohr)
　　(1) 1909, April 27: acc orch. Zono Z–042005 (12")
　　(2) 1909, June 23 (as James Osborne): acc orch. Zono 173 (10")
　　(3) 1910, August: acc orch. Edison Amb 12225; Edison (USA) Amb 591 (cyl)
　　(4) 1911, July 31: acc orch. Zono A–25; HMV (Canada) 130023 (12"); matrix Ac5229f
　　(5) 1924 , January: acc orch. Zono A–25; (12") matrix Zz4039–1

OUTPOST'S VIGIL, THE (Rivers)
　　(1) 1914, April 30, duet with Ernest Pike: acc piano. Zono A–148 (12")
　　(2) 1920, November, duet with Ernest Pike: acc orch. Zono 2313; Ariel 3504 (10")
　　(3) 1922, December 29, duet with Sydney Coltham: acc orch. HMV B–1498 (10")

OUTWARD BOUND (Stanford *Songs of the Sea*)
　　(1) 1928, February 24: acc orch. HMV B–2743 (10")
　　(2) 1933, January 10: acc orch & chorus. HMV B–4482 (10")　　O B 4 3 8 9 –2

OVER THE DARK STILL SILENCE (Rizzi)
　　1933, January 10: acc orch. HMV B–4405 (10")

PADDY'S PERPLEXITY (Kenward)
　　1916, November 3: acc piano. Zono 2214 (10")

PADDY'S WEDDING (Grant)
　　1924, May 21: acc orch. HMV B–1840 (10")

PAGAN, THE (Lohr)
　　1922, December 21: acc orch. HMV B–1735 (10")

PALM TREE ISLAND (Law)

    1920, January 4 (as Will Strong): acc orch. HMV B–1080 (10")

PALMS, THE (Fauré)

    (1) 1907: acc piano. G&T 3–2939 (10")

    (2) 1926, January 12: acc orch. HMV B–2271 (10")

PARADISE FOR TWO, A (Tate *The Maid of the Mountains*)

    1917, March 30, duet with Bessie Jones (on some copies as Louise Leigh): acc orch. HMV B–805 (10")

PARODY ON "I'VE BUILT A BAMBOO BUNGALOW FOR YOU"

    1907, March (as Will Danby): acc orch. Sterling 868 (cyl)

PARODY ON "THE OLD APPLE TREE"

    1906, October (as Will Danby): acc orch. White 149 (cyl)

PARTED (Tosti)

    (1) 1913, December 23: acc orch. Zono A–134 (12")

    (2) 1917, June 8, duet with Ernest Pike: acc orch. Zono 1811 (10")

    (3) 1939, April 12: acc organ. HMV B–8978 (10") *acc. Herbert Dawson*

PAUPER'S DRIVE, THE (Homer)

    1921, January 28: acc piano. HMV B–1311 (10")

PEGGY O'NEILL (Pease, Nelson, & Dodge)

    1922, August 29 (as Robert Woodville): acc orch. Zono 2252; Ariel 904 (as Percy Dalton) (10")

PERFECT DAY, A (Jacobs-Bond)

    1917, February: duet with Ernest Pike: acc orch. Zono 1794 (10")

PETER DAWSON TELLING YOU ABOUT HIS 'HMV' MODEL 570 GRAMO-PHONE

    1934, October: sales talk with musical examples: HMV C–86 (10")

PETER DAWSON'S CHRISTMAS PARTY

    1935, November 9: with Leonard Henry: acc orch & chorus. HMV C–2805 (12", two sides)

PHIL THE FLUTER'S BALL (French)

    1936, December 8: acc orch. HMV B–8515; HMV B–9114; HMV (Eire) IP–928 (10")

PHYSICAL CULTURE EXERCISES

    1922, December 20–29: instructional talk: acc orch. HMV B–1669; HMV B–1670; HMV B–1671 (10", six sides)

PIPES OF PAN, THE (Ross & Elgar)

    1904–1905: acc orch. Nicole 5660; Pelican P–35 (10")

PIRATE GOES WEST, THE – see 'Westward Ho!'

PIRATE SONG, THE (Gilbert)

    (1) 1924, January: acc orch. Zono 2453 (10")

    (2) 1924, February 4: acc orch. HMV B–1815 (10")

PLACE WHERE THE OLD HORSE DIED, THE (Melville)

    1906, November 12: acc orch. Zono X–42546; Zono 517; RZ T–517 (10")

PLUMBER, THE

    (1) 1907, November: sketch with Winifred Harbor. Pathé 727 (8½" disc)

    (2) 1907, November: sketch with Winifred Harbor. Edison 13712 (cyl)

POOR MAN'S GARDEN (Barrie & Russell)

    1938, September 27: acc organ. HMV B–8815 (10")

PORT OF MANY SHIPS (Keel *Salt Water Ballads*)

    1924, January 29: acc orch. HMV B–1799 (10")

PORTO RICO (Royce)

1914, April 15: acc piano. Zono 1330 (10")

POTTED POETRY (Osborne)

(1) 1907, June (as Will Danby): acc orch. White 217 (cyl)

(2) 1907, (as George Welsh): acc orch. Zono X–42657 (10')

POWDER MONKEY, THE (Watson)

1907: acc piano. Zono X–42719; Zono 518 (10")

PRAYER FOR THE SAFETY OF ROAD USERS (Trinsh & Mack)

1951, September 12: acc orch & chorus. HMV EA–4009 (10"), Sydney

'PRENTICE LADS O' CHEAP, THE (Barron & McCall)

1938, January 27: acc orch. HMV B–8723 (10")

PRIDE OF THE EARTH

1904–1905: acc orch. Nicole 5718; Pelican P–33; Sovereign No. 15 (10")

PRIDE OF TIPPERARY, THE (Lockhead)

1926, March 15: acc piano. HMV B–2324 (10")

PRIS'NER COMES TO MEET HIS DOOM, THE (Gilbert & Sullivan *Yeomen of the Guard*)

1920, May 27, duet with Robert Radford: acc orch & chorus. HMV D–483 (12")

PRISON SCENE (Gounod *Faust*)

(1) 1905, September 19, trio with Alice Esty & John Harrison: acc orch. G&T 4381 (10") 7284½ b

(2) 1909, May 19, trio with Eleanor Jones-Hudson & Ernest Pike: acc orch. Zono Grand Opera X–44144; Zono Celebrity GO–7; matrix 10136e

(3) 1909, May 19, trio with Eleanor Jones-Hudson & Ernest Pike: acc orch. Zono Grand Opera X–44144; matrix 10137e

PRIVATE TOMMY ATKINS (Potter)

1936, October 13: acc orch. HMV C–2866; Victor (Canada) 36200 (12" medley)

PROLOGUE, THE (Leoncavallo *Pagliacci*)

(1) 1920, March 5: acc orch. HMV C–968 (12", two sides)

(2) 1925, December 31: acc orch. HMV C–1259 (12", two sides)   Jan 1927 ?

PULL TOGETHER (Blackham)

1920, November (as Robert Woodville): acc orch. Zono 2094 (10")

PUNCH AND JUDY SHOW, THE (Baxter)

(1) 1906, August, comedy sketch with imitator Alf Holt: EB 10005 (cyl)

(2) 1906, August, comedy sketch with imitator Alf Holt: White 130 (cyl)

PUNCHINELLO (Molloy)

1924, May 21: acc orch. HMV B–1840 (10")

PUNJAUB MARCH (Payne)

1933, March 7: acc orch & chorus. HMV B–8015 (10")

QUACK DOCTOR, THE

1907, late (as Percy Clifton): monologue. Zono 154 (10")

QUEEN OF MY HEART (Cellier *Dorothy*)

(1) 1910, June 27: acc orch. Zono X–2–42027 (10") Unissued (?)

(2) 1911, December: acc orch. Edison Amb 12423; Edison BA 23194 (cyl)

(3) 1912, August 14: acc orch. Zono 878 (10")

QUEEN OF THE EARTH (Jaxone & Pinsuti)

(1) 1907, April: acc orch. EB 10167 (cyl)

(2) 1908, July: acc orch. Zono X–42785 (10")

(3) 1908, September: acc orch. EB 20178 (cyl)

(4) 1909, September: acc orch. Edison Amb 12093; Edison BA 23127 (cyl)

(5) 1923, June 22: acc orch. HMV C–1117 (12")

QUI VIVE (Ganz *The Old Guard*)

1909, July 1, duet with Ernest Pike: acc orch. Zono X–44146 (10")

RANN OF EXILE (Colum & Bax)

1938, September 7: acc piano. HMV B–8866 (10")

RAPTURE, RAPTURE (Gilbert & Sullivan *Yeomen of the Guard*)

(1) 1907, February 8, duet with Florence Venning: acc orch. HMV GC–4420; HMV B–403 (10")

(2 1920, May, duet with Edna Thornton: acc orch & chorus. HMV D–500 (12")

(3) 1928, November 2, duet with Dorothy Gill: acc orch. HMV D–1558; Victor (USA) 11229 (12")

READY EVERY TIME (Andrews)

1911, January: acc orch. Edison 14047 (cyl)

RED STAR OF THE ROMANY, THE (Sanderson)

1923, January 16: acc orch. HMV B–1549 (10")

RED, WHITE AND BLUE (Gay *Swing is in the Air*)

1937, April 1: acc orch & chorus. HMV B–8558 (10")

✓ **RED, WHITE AND BLUE** (Russell)

1936, October 13: acc orch & chorus. HMV C–2866; Victor (Canada) 36200 (12" medley)   *14 Oct 1936*

REDEMPTION, THE (Behrend)

1905, December: acc orch. Edison 13411 (cyl)

REFEREE, THE (Lauder)

1906, June 15 (as Hector Grant): acc orch. Zono X–42527 (10")

REGIMENTAL PET, THE

1907, August: acc orch. White 245 (cyl)

REMEMBER (Phipson)

1914, March 20: acc piano. Zono 1330 (10")

REMEMBER (McCall)

1953, late: acc orch quartet. Prestophone unissued (10" acetate survives) Sydney

REQUITAL, THE (Blumenthal)

1917, January 29: acc piano. Zono A–238 (12")

REST, SOLDIER, REST (Morley)

1916, October 13: acc piano. Zono 1748 (10")

RÊVE PASSÉ, LE (A Vision of Victory, 1914–1918) (Helmer & Krier)

1930, June 16: acc orch & chorus. HMV C–2045 (12")

RINGERS, THE (Lohr)

1910, October 21: acc orch. Zono 647 (10")

RIP VAN WINKLE (Carroll)

1910, October 11: acc orch. HMV 4–2100; HMV B–4504 (10")

RISING EARLY IN THE MORNING (Lauder)

(1) 1906, June 5 (as Hector Grant): acc orch. Zono 42336 (7"); matrix 7427d

(2) 1906, June 5 (as Hector Grant): acc orch. Zono X–42422 (10"); matrix 8228b

RIVETTER, THE (Sievier & Arlen)

1937, March 4: acc orch & chorus. HMV B–8554 (10")

ROAD ACROSS THE SEA, THE (Bowen)

1924, August 29: acc orch. HMV B–1901 (10")

ROADSIDE FIRE, THE (Stevenson & Vaughan Williams *Songs of Travel*)
    1922, June 12: acc piano. HMV B–1375 (10")

ROADWAYS (Lohr)
    1921, September 28: acc orch. HMV B–1280 (10")

ROAST BEEF OF OLD ENGLAND, THE (Trad) – see 'A Jolly Christmas'

ROB ROY MACINTOSH
    (1) 1907, July (as Hector Grant): acc orch. White 226 (cyl)
    (2) 1907, October (as Hector Grant): acc orch. EB 10442 (cyl)

ROCK OF AGES (Redhead)
    1939, April 12: acc organ. HMV B–8961 (10")

ROCK–A–BYE, BABY
    1908, quartet with Ernest Pike, Stanley Kirkby & Harold Wilde: acc orch. Zono X–44078 (10")

ROCKED IN THE CRADLE OF THE DEEP (Willard & Knight)
    (1) 1904–1905: acc orch. Nicole 5726; Nicole D–550; Sovereign No. 13 (10")
    (2) 1908, July: acc orch. Zono X–42805 (10")
    (3) 1922, October 13: acc orch. HMV B–1479 (10")
    (4) 1930, July 10: acc orch. HMV B–3593 (10")

ROLLICKING BAND OF PIRATES, WE, A (Gilbert & Sullivan *Pirates of Penzance*)
    1920, July 13: acc orch & chorus. HMV D–513 (12")

ROLLICKING ROLLING STONE, A (Fisher)
    1916, October 23: acc piano. Zono 1927 (10")

ROLLING ALONG (Akst & Richman)
    1936, May 18: acc orch. HMV B–8443 (10")

ROLLING DOWN TO RIO (Kipling & German)
    (1) 1911, June 8: acc orch. Zono 614; HMV (Canada) 120065 (10")
    (2) 1922, October 27: acc orch. Zono 614; HMV B–1475; Ariel 573 (as Maurice Evans) (10")
    (3) 1929, April 3: acc orch. HMV B–3023 (10")
    (4) 1931, March 24: acc orch. HMV B–3860 (10")   *April 1931   OB 687 – 1*

ROLLING IN FOAMING BILLOWS (Haydn *The Creation*)
    1930, November 5: acc orch. HMV C–2099 (12") *Cc2o359*

ROLLING STONE, A (Bevan & Gleeson)
    1946, December 13: acc orch. HMV EA–3462 (10"), Sydney

ROOM FOR THE FACTOTUM (Rossini *The Barber of Seville*)
    (1) 1920, October, 26: acc orch. HMV C–1007 (12")
    (2) 1927, March 30: acc orch. HMV C–1400 (12") *Cc10503 c Lawrence Collingwood*

ROSE OF BLOOMSBURY SQUARE (Hanley)
    1920, September (as Robert Woodville): acc orch. Zono 2081 (10")

ROSE OF VIRGINIA (Caddigan & Storey)
    1920, November (as Robert Woodville): acc orch. Zono 2116 (10")

ROSES OF PICARDY (Wood)
    (1) 1939, April 12: acc organ. HMV B–8932 (10") *acc. Herbert Dawson*
    (2) 1954, March 29, acc orch. Radio broadcast, Sydney

ROUTE MARCHIN' (Kipling & McCall)
    (1) 1930, September 19: acc orch. HMV B–3629 (10")
    (2) 1935, July 5: acc orch & chorus. HMV C–2797; Victor (Canada) 130827 (12" medley)

RUDYARD KIPLING'S BARRACK ROOM BALLADS (Kipling, McCall, Cobb)
1935, July 5: acc orch & chorus. HMV C2797 (Parts 1 & 2) (12" medley)

RULE BRITANNIA (Arne)
(1) 1909, April 20: acc orch. HMV GC 4–2040 (10")
(2) 1911, April: anonymous with orch & chorus. Zono Coronation Record 598; Zono Patriotic record 598 (10")
(3) 1936, October 13: acc orch & chorus. HMV C–2866; Victor (Canada) 36200 (12" medley)

SACRED HOUR, THE (Ketelbey)
1933, March 3: acc orch, organ & chorus. HMV C–2595 (12")

SADDLE YOUR BLUES TO A WILD MUSTANG (Whiting, Bernier & Haid)
1936, March 20: acc orch. HMV B–8425 (10")

SAFTEST O' THE FAMILY, THE (Lauder)
1906, March 5 (as Hector Grant): acc orch. Zono X–42412 (10")

SAILING (Marks)
1910, July 18: acc orch. Zono X–2–42020; Zono 513; Ariel 9473 (10")

SAILOR'S CONSOLATION, A (George)
(1) 1917, June 8, duet with Ernest Pike: acc orch. Zono 1859 (10")
(2) 1923, May 31, duet with Sydney Coltham: acc orch. HMV C–1111 (12")

SAILOR'S PARADISE, A (Richards)
1914, March 20: acc piano. Zono 1318 (10")

SALLY (Kern *Sally*)
1921, September 29: acc orch & chorus. HMV B–1274 (10") Bb 515-1

SALUTE TO AUSTRALIA (Wheeler & Baer)
1951, September 12: acc orch & chorus. HMV EA–4008 (10"), Sydney

SAME GIRL, THE
1905, December: acc orch. EB 6782 (cyl)

SANCTUARY OF THE HEART (Ketelbey)
1932, October 6: acc orch, organ & chorus. HMV C–2491 (12")

SANDY BOY
1907, December, (as Hector Grant): acc orch. Zono X–42724 (10")

SANDY, YOU'RE A DANDY (Grant)
(1) 1906, October (as Hector Grant): acc orch. Edison 13535 (cyl)
(2) 1907, July (as Hector Grant): acc orch. Zono X–42627 (10")

SAVED BY GRACE (Stebbins)
1908, duet with Ernest Pike: acc organ & bells. Zono X–44082; Zono 536 (10")

SCOTS WHA HAE WI' WALLACE BLED (Burns & Old Scottish Air)
1907: acc orch. Zono X–42890 (10")

SCREW GUNS (Kipling & Cobb)
1935, July 5: acc orch & chorus. HMV C–2797; Victor (Canada) 130827 (12" medley)

SEA CALL, A (Ramon)
1934, December 7: acc orch. HMV B–8325 (10") o EA 929 - 2

SEA ROAD, THE (Wood *Three Sea Songs*)
1921, February 3: acc orch. HMV B–1211 (10")

SEA WINDS (Askew & Harrison)
1936, March 27: acc orch. HMV B–8627 (10")

SENTINEL, THE (Oliver & Teschemacher)
1913, October 1: acc piano. Zono 1203 (10")

SERGEANT OF THE LINE (Squire)
1954, March 29: acc orch. ABC radio broadcast, Sydney
SERGEANT RELEASES HUGH, THE (Child & Vaughan Williams *Hugh The Drover*)
1924, sextet with Mary Lewis, Constance Willis, Tudor Davies, William Anderson,
William Waite & chorus: acc orch. HMV D–926 (12")
SERMON ON OLD MOTHER HUBBARD, A
1908, January (as Percy Clifton): monologue. G&T 1391 (10")
SEXTETTE (Donizetti *The Bride of Lammermoor*)
1908, October 13 sextette with Eleanor Jones-Hudson, Amy Augarde, Ernest Pike,
Thorpe Bates & Leonard Stanley: acc orch. Zono X–44113; Zono GO–10 (10")
SHADOWLAND (Johnson)
1910, July: acc orch. Edison 13999 (cyl)
SHALL WE MEET BEYOND?
1906, September 13, duet with Ernest Pike: acc organ. Zono X–44055 (10")
SHE ALONE CHARMETH MY SADNESS (Gounod *The Queen of Sheba*)
1907, (as James Osborne): acc orch. Zono 184 (10")
SHE IS FAR FROM THE LAND (Moore & Lambert)
(1) 1925, December 8: acc piano. HMV B–2238 (10")
(2) 1933, January 5: acc orch. HMV B–4411 (10")
SHE IS MA DAISY (Harper & Lauder)
1906, March 2 (as Hector Grant): acc orch. Zono X–42401; Zono 546; G&T 3–2843
(as Victor Graham) (10")
SHE SELLS SEA SHELLS
1909, January 14 (as Henry Tucker), trio with Stanley Kirkby & Ernest Pike: acc orch.
HMV 04038 (12")
SHE WAS WONDERFUL (Ayer)
1920, September (as Robert Woodville): acc orch. Zono 2081 (10")
SHEIK OF ARABY, THE (Smith, Wheeler & Snyder)
1922, September 4 (as Robert Woodville): acc orch. Zono 2253 (10")
SHEIK, THE – see 'Sheik of Araby, The'
SHEPHERD BOY'S SONG, THE (Pepper)
1936, May 18: acc orch. HMV B–8456 (10")
SHIMMY WITH ME (Kern *The Cabaret Girl*)
1922, October 17, duet with Ennis Parkes: acc orch & chorus. HMV C–1087 (12")
SHIPMATES O' MINE (Teschemacher & Sanderson)
(1) 1913, November 18: acc orch. Zono 1224; Ariel 550 (as Maurice Evans) (10")
(2) 1931, March 10: acc orch. HMV B–3839 (10")
SHIPWRIGHT, THE
1907, January 24: acc orch. G&T 3–2797 (10")   *SIEGE of LA ROCHELLE (Balfe)*
SILENT NOON (Rossetti & Vaughan Williams)
1922, April 25: acc piano. HMV B–1355 (10")   *acc. Mme Adami B6 1235*
SILENT WATCHER, THE (Grant *Eastern Love Songs*)
1922, April 25: acc piano. HMV B–1435 (10")
SILENT WORSHIP (Handel)
1948, December 10: acc organ. HMV (unissued)
SILVER PATROL, THE (Sievier & Thayer *Silver Patrol*)
1937, May 10: acc orch & chorus. HMV B–8583 (10")
SILVER STAR (Nicholls)
1921, September 9 (as Robert Woodville): acc orch. Zono 2160 (10")

SIMON THE CELLARER (Bellamy & Hatton)
- (1) 1905, October: acc orch. EB 6668 (cyl)
- (2) 1909, June 24 (as James Osborne): acc orch. Zono 159 (10")
- (3) 1910, April 14: acc orch. Zono X–2–42013 (10")
- (4) 1910, June: acc orch. Edison Amb 12207 (cyl)
- (5) 1925, December 8: acc piano. HMV B–2324 (10")

SINCERITY (Clarke)
- (1) 1906, January 4: acc piano. G&T 3–2443 (10")
- (2) 1912, February 21: acc piano. HMV 02385; HMV C–439 (12")
- (3) 1927, January 25: acc piano. HMV B–2425 (10")

SING A SONG OF LONDON (Strachey)
1932, July 19: acc orch. HMV B–4278 (10")

SING ME TO SLEEP (Greene)
1905, May: acc orch. EB 6635 (cyl)

SINGER WAS IRISH, THE (Castling & Murphy)
- (1) 1905, December: acc orch. Edison 13424 (cyl)
- (2) 1906, May, with Wilfred Virgo, tenor: acc orch. EB 6898 (cyl)
- (3) 1906, June 7, with unidentified soprano: acc orch. Zono X–42427; Zono 516 (10")
- (4) 1906, with unidentified tenor: acc orch. Colonial (UK) 152 (cyl)
- (5) 1910, September, with Ernest Pike, tenor: acc orch. Edison Amb 12245; Edison BA 23014 (cyl)

SIR DARE (Dale)
1912, December 17: acc orch. Zono 1023 (10")

SIRS! A TOAST – see 'Toreador's Song'

SISTER (Vaughan)
- (1) 1906, July: acc orch. White 112 (cyl)
- (2) 1906, August 7 (as Hector Grant): acc orch. Zono X–42643 (10")

SIX AUSTRALIAN BUSH SONGS (James) – see 'Bush Silence', 'Bush Night Song', 'Land of "Who Knows Where"', 'Comrades of Mine', 'The Stockrider's Song'.

SKIPPER'S YARN, THE (Marks)
1916, November 3: acc piano. HMV B–1057 (10")

SKIPPER, THE (Jude)
- (1) 1911, November 16: acc orch. Zono 742; HMV (Canada) 120192 (10"); matrix Ab14496e
- (2) 1922, April: acc orch. Zono 742 (10"); matrix Yy1277–1

SLEEP, COMRADE, SLEEP (Andrews)
1910, October 11: acc unknown. Zono X–2–42059 (10")

SLEEPY HOLLOW TUNE (Kountz)
1925, July: acc orch. Zono 2623 (10")

SMILE, SMILE, SMILE
1908, May (as Will Danby), duet with Miss Mortimer: EB 20076 (cyl). This is reported to have been announced as Ann Mortimer. If this was so, it is probably Annie Mortimer Noble, Dawson's first wife.

SMUGGLER'S SONG, THE (Kernochan)
1920, October 22: acc piano. HMV B–1311 (10")

SMUGGLER'S SONG, THE (Kipling & Mortimer)
- (1) 1929, June 6: acc orch. HMV B–3072 (10")
- (2) 1948, May 6: acc orch. HMV B–9657; HMV EA–3834 (10")

SMUGGLERS, THE (Popple)
1929, April 29: acc orch. HMV B–3078 (10") *Bb 16886–2 June 1929*

SNOWBIRD (Sievier & Thayer)
    (1) 1938, January 27: acc orch & chorus. HMV B–8715 (10")
    (2) 1948, January 7: acc orch & chorus. HMV B–9634; HMV EA–3737 (10")

SO I LEFT (Grover & Butcher)
    1929, December 12: acc piano. HMV B–3378 (10")

SO IT GOES ON (Gay *Swing Is In The Air*)
    1937, April 1: acc orch & chorus. HMV B–8558 (10")

SOLDIER AND A MAN, A
    1908, October 9 (as Hector Grant): acc orch. Zono 118 (10")

SOLDIER! WHAT OF THE NIGHT? (Dix)
    1914, February 11: acc piano. Zono 1294 (10")   *SOLDIER'S FAREWELL (McPherson's " ?)*

SOLDIER'S SONG, A (Mascheroni)
    1912, June: acc orch. Zono 878; Ariel 550 (as Maurice Evans) (10")

SOLDIERS OF FORTUNE (Hemery)
    1912, August 14, duet with Ernest Pike: acc orch. Zono 916 (10")

SOLDIERS OF THE KING (Stuart)
    1936, October 13: acc orch & chorus. HMV C–2866; Victor (Canada) 36200 (12"
    medley)

SOLDIERS OF THE QUEEN, THE (Gilbert & Sullivan *Patience*)
    1921, January 26: acc orch & chorus. HMV D–564 (12")

SOLENNE IN QUEST'ORA (Verdi *The Force of Destiny*)
    1909, January 14, duet with Ernest Pike: acc orch. Zono X–44118; Zono GO–12

SOME CRIMSON ROSE (Neighbour)
    1922, December 2: acc piano. HMV B–1946 (10")

SOMEBODY WOULD SHOUT 'SHOP'! (Weston & Lee)
    1916, November 6 (as Will Strong), duet with Ernest Pike: acc orch. Zono 1752 (10")

SOMEBODY'S SAILOR BOY
    1904–1905: acc unknown Nicole ? (untraced); Pelican P–36 (10")

SOMETIMES (English)
    1921, February 2 (as Will Strong): acc orch. HMV B–1205 (10")

SOMEWHERE A VOICE IS CALLING (Tate)
    (1) 1914, April 30, duet with Ernest Pike: acc piano. Zono 1358 (10")
    (2) 1939, April 13: acc organ. HMV B–8919 (10")   *Herbert Dawson*

SON O' MINE (Wallace)
    1936, September 10: acc orch. HMV B–8489 (10")

SON OF THE DESERT AM I , A (Phillips)
    1911, May 11: acc orch. Zono 601; Ariel 9744; HMV (Canada) 120086 (10")

SONG FOR YOU AND ME, A (Rizzi)
    1936, May 18: acc orch. HMV B–8456 (10")

SONG OF AUSTRALIA (Carleton & Linger)
    1932, February 24: acc orch & chorus. HMV EA–1093 (10"); matrix 0B 2819–2. A test
    copy of matrix OB 2819–1 exists.

SONG OF AUSTRALIA (Jackson)
    1940, July 11: acc orch. R–Z G–24077 (10"), Sydney

SONG OF LIBERTY (MacAuley & Walters)
    (1) late 1950: acc probably piano: Vitavox (private) (10" acetate) (Diary entry as 'March
    of Liberty') Sydney
    (2) 1951, January 24: acc orch. HMV EA–3957 (10") Sydney

SONG OF TENDER MEM'RIES, A – see 'Prologue, The'

SONG OF THE DRUM (Andrews & McCall)
1933, December 5: acc orch. HMV B–8089 (10")
✓ **SONG OF THE FLEA** (Goethe & Moussorgsky)
1928, September 24: acc orch. HMV C–1579 (12") *Sv J. Barbirolli C. 14397*
SONG OF THE GRATEFUL HEART (Hamilton)
1936, November 13: acc orch. HMV B–8508 (10")
SONG OF THE HIGHWAY (May)
1931, January 29: acc orch. HMV B–3874 (10")
SONG OF THE HOMEWARD–BOUND (Clarke)
1925, July: acc orch. Zono 2623 (10")
⌐ **SONG OF THE KETTLE, THE** (Anthony)
1929, April 29: acc piano. HMV B–3521 (10")
⌐ **SONG OF THE THAMES** (Murray & Mortimer)
1935, July 11: acc orch. HMV B–8373 (10")
SONG OF THE TINKER, THE (Elliott)
1931, February 16: acc orch. HMV B–3809 (10")
✓ **SONG OF THE VOLGA BOATMAN** (Koenemann)
1927, March 30: acc orch. HMV C–1342 (12")
SONG OF THE WHEATLANDS – see 'Wheatlands'
SONG OF TRIUMPH (Anderson)
1914, January 12: acc orch. Zono A–156 (12")
SONG THAT REACHED MY HEART, THE (Jordan)
1907, trio with Ernest Pike & Denise Orme: acc orch & chorus. Zono X–44076 (10")
SONG TO MIRIAM (Grant *Eastern Love Songs*)
1922, July 13: acc piano. HMV B–1435 (10")
⌐ **SONS OF THE BRAVE** (Bidgood)
1932, August 30: acc orch & chorus. HMV B–4267; HMV (Canada) 120863 (10")
SONS OF THE SEA (Coleridge–Taylor)
(1) 1922, May 23: acc orch. HMV B–1815 (10")
(2) 1935, January 23: acc orch. HMV C–2728 (12")
SOUL OF ENGLAND, THE (Barnes)
1917, June 12: acc orch. HMV B–874; HMV (Italy) R–7323 (10")
SOUND ADVICE (Melville & Lauder)
(1) 1906. June 5 (as Hector Grant): acc orch. Zono 42346 (7")
(2) 1906, July (as Hector Grant): acc orch. White 105 (cyl)
⌐ **SOUND, SOUND THE TRUMPET** (Bellini *Puritani*)
1924, January 5, duet with Robert Radford: acc orch. HMV D–967 (12")
⌐ **SPEAK, MUSIC!** (Benson & Elgar)
1938, September 7: acc piano. HMV B–8866 (10")
SPIRIT FLOWER, A (Tipton)
1925, February 19: acc piano. HMV B–1988 (10")
SPIRIT OF ENGLAND (McCall)
1942, July, Auckland, NZ: radio broadcast, acc piano. HMV PD–1 (12" LP set)
✓ **SPIRIT OF THE WOOD** (Parker *Fairyland*)
1912, February 14, duet with Eleanor Jones-Hudson: acc orch. Zono 805; HMV (Canada)
120089 (10") *Ab 14927e*
STAR O' ROBBIE BURNS (Booth)
✓ (1) 1923, February 1: acc orch. HMV B–1545 (10")
(2) 1932, July 19: acc orch. HMV B–4338 (10")

STAR OF GOD (Weatherly & Coates)
    1944, November: acc organ. HMV EB–224 (12"), Sydney
STAR OF THE EAST (Lohr)
    (1) 1923, January 16: acc orch. HMV B–1632 (10")
    (2) 1929, April 26: acc orch. HMV C–1689 (12")
STARLIGHT (Madden & Morse)
    1906: acc orch. Pathé 60086 (disc)
STILL AS THE NIGHT (Gotze)
    1912, August 29: acc unknown. Zono A–89 (12")
STILL THEY KEPT ON LOVING ALL THE TIME (Lee)
    1917, February 15 (as Will Strong), duet with Ernest Pike: acc orch. Zono 1765 (10")
STOCKRIDER'S SONG, THE (James *Six Australian Bush Songs*)
    (1) 1923, January 25: acc piano. HMV C–1125 (12")
    (2) 1927, October 12: acc piano. HMV C–1428 (12")
STOP YOUR TICKLIN', JOCK (Grafton & Lauder)
    1905, October 1: acc unknown. Neophone 15581 (12")
STORM FIEND, THE (Roeckel)
    1911, September 19: acc orch. Zono 683; HMV (Canada) 120199 (10")
STOUTHEARTED MEN (Hammerstein & Romberg *The New Moon*)
    1941, mid–September, Sydney: radio broadcast, acc orch & chorus. HMV PD–1 (12"LP set)
STRANGE ADVENTURE (Gilbert & Sullivan *Yeomen of the Guard*)
    (1) 1920, May: quartet with Derek Oldham, Edna Thornton & Bessie Jones: acc orch & chorus. HMV D–485 (12")
    (2) 1928, November 2: quartet with Elsie Griffin, Dorothy Gill & Derek Oldham: acc orch. HMV D–1557; Victor (USA) 11228 (12")
STRONG GO ON, THE (Thayer)
    1935, July, 11: acc orch. HMV B–8353 (10")
SUE, SUE, SUE (Elliott)
    1908, November 12 (as Henry Tucker): acc orch. Zono Twin 80 (10")
SUMMER LOVE TALE, A (Tchaikovsky)
    1925, February 19: acc piano. HMV B–1988 (10")
SUMMER NIGHT, A (Thomas)
    1912, February 14: duet with Eleanor Jones-Hudson: acc orch. Zono 805; HMV (Canada) 120089 (10") Ab 14924e
SUN GOD, THE (James)
    1921, September 28: acc orch. HMV B–1280 (10")
SUNRISE AT THE ZOO
    1909, July 8, quartet with Ernest Pike, Harold Wilde, Stewart Gardner; sketch assisted by Gilbert Girard, animal imitator: acc orch. Zono X–44136; Zono 3022 (10")
SWEET ALEEN (Greene)
    1909, June 3, quartet with Ernest Pike, Harold Wilde, Stewart Gardner: acc orch. Zono X–44135; Zono 1516 (10")
SWEET AND LOW (Johnson)
    1921, September 9 (as Robert Woodville): acc orch. Zono 2160 (10")
SWEET CHIMING BELLS (Shattuck)
    1907, October 17: acc orch. G&T 3–2905 (10")
SWEET CHRISTMAS BELLS (Shattuck)
    (1) 1906, October, duet with Walter Hyde: acc orch. Edison 13530 (cyl)

(2) 1909, June, duet with Ernest Pike: acc orch. Edison Amb 12100; Edison BA 23143 (cyl)

SWEET GENEVIEVE – see 'Genevieve'

SWEET SIMPLICITAS (Monckton & Talbot, *The Arcadians*)
1909, July 3 (as Charles Handy): acc orch & chorus. HMV GC 4–2036 (10")

SWING ME HIGHER
1907, August (as Will Danby): acc orch. White 248 (cyl)

SWING SONG (Eldee, Greenbank & Messager *Veronique*)
1912, December 17, duet with Eleanor Jones-Hudson: acc orch. Zono A–97 (12")

SWINGING ALONG THE ROAD TO VICTORY (Cohan)
1940, July, 11: acc orch. RZ G–24078 (10"), Sydney

SWORD SONG, THE (Acworth & Elgar *Caractacus*) *Sir John Barbirolli*
1928, September 24: acc orch. HMV C–1988 (12") *Ce 14392*

SYLVIA (Scollard & Speaks)
1939, April 13: acc organ: HMV B–8886 (10")

TAFFY'S GOT HIS JENNY IN GLAMORGAN (Lloyd & Lee)
1916, November 22 (as Llewellyn Morgan): acc orch. HMV B–781 (10")

TAHINI, TARAKINO
1954, May 10, possibly Sydney: radio broadcast, acc orch. Kingfisher STAR–16 (cassette):

TAKE THIS LETTER TO MY MOTHER
1908, quartet with Ernest Pike, Stanley Kirkby, & Harold Wilde: acc orch. Zono X–44079 (10")

TAKE YOUR GIRLIE TO THE MOVIES (If You Can't Make Love At Home) (Leslie, Kalmar & Wendling)
1920, March 17 (as Will Strong), duet with Ernest Pike: acc orch. HMV B–1098 (10")

TANKS THAT BROKE THE RANKS, THE (Castling & Carlton)
1916, October 26 (as Will Strong): acc orch. Zono 1726 (10")

TAR'S FAREWELL, THE (Adams)
1910, March 23: acc orch. Zono X–42003; Zono 518 (10")

TAXI DRIVER, THE
1908, January (as Percy Clifton): Monologue. Zono X–42743 (10")

TEARS OF AN IRISH MOTHER, THE (Nicholls)
1921, November 8 (as Will Strong): acc orch & chorus. HMV B–1305 (10")

TELL ME (Callahan & Kortlander)
1920, February 17 (as Will Strong): acc orch & chorus. HMV B–1092 (10")

TEMPEST OF THE HEART, THE (Verdi *Il Trovatore*)
(1) 1909, June 24 (as James Osborne): acc orch. Zono 173 (10")
(2) 1922, July 19: acc orch. HMV B–1393 (10")
(3) 1930, November 5: acc orch. HMV B–3698 (10")

TEMPLE BELLS, THE (Woodforde–Finden *Four Indian Love Lyrics*)
(1) 1923, May 16: acc orch. HMV B–1685 (10")
(2) 1925, December 29: acc orch. HMV B–2255 (10")
(3) 1932, November 8: acc orch. HMV B–4319 (10")

TENOR AND BARITONE (Lane–Wilson)
(1) 1912, June 14, duet with Ernest Pike: acc orch. Zono A–75 (12")
(2) 1923, May 31, duet with Sydney Coltham: acc orch. HMV C–1111 (12")

TENTS OF ARABS (David)
1920, September 23 (as Will Strong): acc orch. HMV B–1145 (10")

THAT DEAR OLD HOME OF MINE (Ayer *The Bing Girls Are There*)
    1917, March 19, duet with Ernest Pike: acc orch. Zono 1761 (10")
THAT DIVINE MELODY (Ewart & English)
    1920, December 3 (as Will Strong): acc orch. HMV B–1186 (10")
THAT LUCKY OLD SUN (Gillespie & Smith)
    1950, April 6: acc orch. HMV B–9913 (10")
THAT OLD SUNNY WINDOW (Shelley)
    1906: acc orch. Pathé 60143 (cyl & disc); Pathé 8025 (10", 11" & 20" discs)
THAT'S WHY I'M SANTA CLAUS (Philpot)
    1906, October: acc orch. Edison 13532 (cyl)
THEIR FIRST QUARREL
    (1) 1907, February (as Will Danby): sketch with Yolande Noble (sister-in-law, Fan Noble): White 175 (cyl)
    (2) 1908, January (as Will Danby): sketch with Yolande Noble (as Dora Whittaker): EB 10497 (cyl)
    (3) 1908, February (as Will Danby): sketch with Miss Mortimer (probably sister-in-law or possibly his wife, Annie Mortimer Noble): Zono Twin 177; (as Miss Noble & Mr. Clifton in *Their First Parting*): HMV (Canada) 120128) (10")
THERE GOES MY SOLDIER BOY
    1904–1905: acc orch. Nicole 4428 (7")
THERE IS A FLOWER THAT BLOOMETH (Wallace *Maritana*)
    1911, July: acc orch. Edison Amb 12343 (cyl)
THERE IS A GREEN HILL FAR AWAY (Alexander & Gounod)
    (1) 1911, July 1: acc organ. Zono 630; RZ T–630 (10")
    (2) 1948, October 1: acc organ. HMV C–3808 (12")
THERE IS BEAUTY IN THE BELLOW OF THE BLAST (Gilbert & Sullivan *The Mikado*)
    1906, August 21, duet with Amy Augarde: acc orch. G&T 4413; HMV B–430 (10")
THERE IS NO DEATH (O'Hara)
    1938, September 27: acc organ. HMV B–8832 (10")
THERE YOU ARE THEN (Silberman)
    1921, September 30 (as Robert Woodville): acc orch. Zono 2172 (10")
THERE'LL ALWAYS BE AN ENGLAND (Charles & Parker)
    1947–1948, Sydney: radio broadcast, acc orch & chorus. (16" 2GB radio disc)
THERE'LL BE NO SOUTH (Schertzinger)
    1936, March 20: acc orch. HMV B–8436 (10")
THERE'LL COME A DAY (Keyes)
    1946, January 14: acc piano. HMV EA–3317 (10"), Sydney
THERE'S A BIG LOT OF SUNSHINE COMING SOON (Hay)
    1917, January 25: acc piano. Zono 1760 (10")
THERE'S A BRIDLE HANGING ON THE WALL (Robison)
    1936, November 13: acc orch. HMV B–8508 (10")
THERE'S A GIRL IN KILDARE (Norton)
    (1) 1917, January 29: acc piano. Zono 1791 (10")
    (2) 1922, December 20: acc orch. HMV B–1491 (10")
THERE'S A GOOD TIME A-COMING (Gideon)
    1922, May 22 (as Will Strong), duet with Pamela Baselow: acc orch & chorus. HMV B–1358 (10")

THERE'S A MAN IN MANITOBA (Murphy)
> (1) 1906: acc orch. Pathé 60144 (cyl & disc); Pathé 1134 (8½", 11", 20" discs)
> (2) 1906, August: acc orch. White 122 (cyl)

THERE'S A TAVERN IN THE TOWN (Traditional)
> 1917, January 17: acc orch & chorus. Zono 1777; RZ T–1777 (10")

THERE'S A WEE BIT LAND
> 1911, November 30 (as Hector Grant): acc orch. Zono 759; HMV (Canada) 120077 (10")

THERE'S SOMETHING AT THE YARDARM (Gleeson)
> 1932, February 24: acc orch. HMV B–4194 (10"); matrix OB 2820–2. A test copy exists of OB 2820–1

THEY ALL LOVE JACK (Weatherly & Adams)
> (1) 1910, April 14: acc orch. Zono X–2–42014; Zono 513 (10")
> (2) 1910, (possibly April 14) (as Maurice Evans): acc orch. Ariel 573 (10")
> (3) 1910, October: acc orch. Edison Amb 12256 (cyl)

THEY'RE FAR, FAR AWA' (Booth)
> 1923, March 7: acc orch. HMV B–1630 (10")

THIS IS MY LAND (Jones & Jones)
> 1946, January 14: acc piano. HMV EA–3317 (10"), Sydney

THO' P'RAPS I MAY INCUR YOUR BLAME (Gilbert & Sullivan *Iolanthe*)
> 1922, January 13, quartet with Violet Essex, Derek Oldham & Robert Radford: acc orch. HMV D–639 (12")

THORA (Weatherly & Adams)
> 1910, June: acc orch. Edison Amb 12219; Edison BA 23002 (cyl)

THOU'RT PASSING HENCE (Hemans & Sullivan)
> (1) 1909, July 1: acc orch. Zono X–42980; Zono 511 (10")
> (2) 1913, April 2: acc piano, organ & bells. HMV 02553; HMV C–439 (12")
> (3) 1927, October 12: acc piano. HMV C–1427 (12")

THOU, O LORD, ART MY SHEPHERD (Mason, Saunders & Tchaikovsky)
> (1) 1944, October: acc organ. HMV EB–209 (12"), Sydney
> (2) 1947, September 15: acc organ. HMV EA–3769 (10")

THOUGH THE VIEWS OF THE HOUSE HAVE DIVERGED (Gilbert & Sullivan *Iolanthe*)
> 1921, December 13: acc orch. HMV D–635 (12")

THREE BACHELORS (Russell)
> 1916, October 23: acc piano. Zono 1736 (10")

THREE FOR JACK (Weatherly & Squire)
> 1905, August 24: acc orch. G&T 3–2338 (10")

THROUGH THE DARKNESS (Rossini *Stabat Mater*) *c. Lawrence Collingwood*
> 1930, November 5: acc orch. HMV C–2099 (12") *CL 20368*

THROUGH THE SUNRISE (Nutting)
> 1913, December 18: acc orch. Zono 1248 (10")

THY BEAMING EYES (Gardner & MacDowell)
> (1) 1904, July–August: acc orch. EB 6383 (cyl)
> (2) 1904–1905: acc unknown. Nicole 5628 (10")

THY CONQUEROR (Grant *Eastern Love Songs*)
> 1922, April 25: acc piano. HMV B–1435 (10")

TICKLE ME TIMOTHY (Barnes & Weston)
> 1908, January (as Will Danby): acc orch. EB 10516 (cyl)

TICKLIE GEORDIE (Lauder)

(1) 1905, December (as Hector Grant): acc orch. Edison 13415 (cyl)

(2) 1906, January (as Hector Grant): acc orch. EB 6872 (cyl)

(3) 1906, March 2 (as Hector Grant): acc orch. Zono X–42410; Zono 842; Zono 3006; HMV (Canada) 120153 (10")

TILL I WAKE (Woodforde–Finden *Four Indian Love Lyrics*)

(1) 1923, March 16: acc orch. HMV B–1686 (10")

(2) 1925, December 31: acc orch. HMV B–2256 (10")

(3) 1932, November 8: acc orch. HMV B–4320; HMV (Eire) IP–184 (10")

TILL THE SANDS OF THE DESERT GROW COLD (Ball)

(1) 1922, October 27: acc orch. HMV B–1479 (10")

(2) 1929, April 3: acc orch. HMV B–3023 (10")

'TIS A LOVE SONG

late 1905: acc unknown. EB 6694 (cyl)

'TIS I (Pinsuti)

(1) 1904–1905: acc unknown. Nicole 5659 (10")

(2) 1904, December: acc orch. EB 6594 (cyl)

(3) 1905, February 21: acc orch. G&T 3–2586 (7"); matrix 879d

(4) 1905, February 21: acc orch. G&T 3–2223 (10"); matrix 1820e

(5) 1929, November 27: acc orch. HMV B–3410 (10")

TO GAIN A BRIEF ADVANTAGE (Gilbert & Sullivan *Pirates of Penzance*)

(1) 1920, July 9, quintet with George Baker, Robert Radford, Violet Essex, Edna Thornton: acc orch & chorus. HMV D–514 (12")

(2) 1929, March 25, quintet with Leo Sheffield, George Baker, Elsie Griffin, Dorothy Gill: acc orch & chorus. HMV D–1688; Victor (USA) 9617 (12")

TO MY FIRST LOVE (Lohr)

(1) 1904, July–August (as Leonard Dawson): acc unknown. EB 6384 (cyl)

(2) 1904, July–August: acc unknown. Lambert 5091 (cyl)

TO THE FOREST (Tolstoy & Tchaikovsky)

(1) 1922, July 19: acc orch. HMV C–1169 (12")

(2) 1930, October 14: acc orch. HMV C–2097 (12")   *c. Geo. Byng Cc 20295*

TOBACCONIST'S DUMMY, THE (Murphy & Lipton)

1906, December (as Hector Grant): acc orch. Edison 13556 (cyl)

TOBERMORY (Lauder)

(1) 1906, June 5 (as Hector Grant): acc orch. Zono 42348 (7"); matrix 7439a

(2) 1906, June 15 (as Hector Grant): acc orch. Zono X–42539 (10"); matrix 8331b

TOILERS, THE (Piccolomini)

(1) 1910, July 18: acc orch. Zono X–2–42019 (10")

(2) 1911, April: acc orch. Edison Amb 12312 (cyl)

TOMMY LAD (Teschemacher & Margetson)

(1) 1907: acc orch. Zono X–42625 (10")

(2) 1936, December 8: acc orch. HMV B–8540 (10")

TOMORROW IS ANOTHER DAY (Kahn, Kaper & Jurmann)

1937, May 10: acc orch. HMV B–8576 (10")

TOMORROW WILL BE FRIDAY (Molloy)

1905, November: acc orch & chorus. Edison 13383 (cyl)

TOREADOR'S SONG (Sirs! A Toast) (Bizet *Carmen*)

(1) 1909, May 19: acc orch & chorus. Zono Grand Opera X–42917; Zono GO–12 (10")

(2) 1911, October: acc orch. Edison Amb 12388; Edison BA 23065 (cyl)

(3) 1920, October 26: acc orch & chorus. HMV C–1007 (12")

(4) 1927, September 1: acc orch. HMV C–1400 (12") *CR 1495 e, Geo. Byng*

TOWER WARDERS, UNDER ORDERS (Gilbert & Sullivan *Yeomen of the Guard*)

1920, March 18: acc orch & chorus. HMV D–496 (12")

TRADE WINDS (Keel *Salt Water Ballads*)

1921, February 3: acc orch. HMV B–1211 (10")

TRAFALGAR (*Descriptive Sea Songs*)

1907; dramatic sketch with singing: acc orch & effects. Zono X–49278; Cinch 5300 (10")

TRAMP'S SONG, THE (Gleeson)

1934, March 16: acc orch. HMV B–8191 (10")

TRAMP, THE (Sawyer)

1924, August 29: acc orch. HMV B–1914 (10")

TRAMP, TRAMP, TRAMP (Root)

(1) 1905, December: acc orch. EB 6788 (cyl)

(2) 1907, January 10 (as Hector Grant): acc orch. Zono X–42555 (10")

TRAMPING THROUGH THE COUNTRYSIDE (Allison)

1934, October 8: acc orch. HMV B–8267 (10")

TRAVELLER, THE (Godard)

1925, February 19: acc piano. HMV C–1212 (12")

TRAVELLERS ALL, OF EVERY STATION (Balfe *The Siege of Rochelle*)

(1) 1923, May 16: acc orch. HMV C–1169 (12")

(2) 1927, October 12: acc piano. HMV C–1442 (12")

TRAWLERS, AHOY! (Elliott)

1920, September 24: acc orch. HMV B–1164 (10")

TREES (Kilmer & Rasbach)

(1) 1934, October 25: acc organ. HMV B–8244; Victor (Canada) 120882 (10")

(2) 1945? possibly Sydney: radio broadcast, acc piano. Kingfisher STAR–16 (cassette)

TRIO FINALE *FAUST* – see 'Prison Scene'

TRIP TO INVERARY, A (Lauder)

1906, June 15 (as Hector Grant): acc orch. Zono X–42488 (10")

TROOPER JOHNNY LUDLOW (Temple)

1926, June 16: acc piano. HMV C–1275 (12")

TROT HERE AND THERE (Messager *Veronique*)

1912, December 17, duet with Eleanor Jones-Hudson: acc orch. Zono A–97 (12")

TRUE TILL DEATH (Scott-Gatty)

(1) 1905, July 25: acc orch. G&T 3–2617 (7")

(2) 1905, July 27: acc orch. G&T 3–2314 (10")

(3) 1909, April: acc orch. Edison Amb 12041 (cyl)

TRUMPETER, THE (Barron & Dix)

(1) 1905, October: acc orch. EB 6669 (cyl)

(2) 1909, February: acc orch. Edison Amb 12002; Edison BA 23335 (cyl)

(3) 1929, April 26: acc orch. HMV C–1770 (12")

TUNE THE BO'SUN PLAYED, THE (Loughborough)

1930, October 14: acc orch. HMV B–3679 (10")

TURN YE TO ME (old Scottish Air arr. Lawson)

(1) 1927, January 14: acc piano. HMV B–2561 (10") *acc Gerald Moore Bb 9822*

(2) 1948, December 10: acc organ. HMV (unissued)

TWENTY LARGE DOMAINS (Balfe)

1920, November (as Robert Woodville), duet with Ernest Pike: acc orch. Zono 2093 (10")

TWO BEGGARS, THE (Lane–Wilson)

    (1) 1913, March 3, duet with Ernest Pike: acc orch. Zono A–117 (12")

    (2) 1923, May 24, duet with Sydney Coltham: acc orch. HMV B–1768 (10")

TWO GRENADIERS, THE (Schumann)

    (1) 1914, April 15: acc piano. Zono A–146 (12")

    (2) 1937, July 9: acc orch. HMV B–8695 (10")

TWO LITTLE SOLDIER BOYS

    1904–1905: acc piano. Nicole 5720; Nicole D–561 (10")

TWO OLD TRAMPS (Holloway)

    1927, September 14: acc piano. HMV B–2651 (10")

UNCLE PETER'S CHILDREN'S PARTY

    1936, November 7, set of seven nursery rhymes, of which Dawson sings three: acc orch & children's chorus. HMV B–8509 (10", two sides)

UNCLE PETER'S NURSERY SINGSONG

    1932, November 7: acc inst trio. HMV C–2502 (12", two sides)

UNCLE PETER'S PARTY (*Children's Nursery Series*)

    1932, October, a set of nine nursery rhymes, of which Dawson sings three. The set was originally recorded acoustically on 14 September 1923 with George Baker as 'Uncle Peter': acc unknown. HMV AS–1 (7", two sides)

UNDER THE DESERT STAR (Temple)

    (1) 1920, November (as Robert Woodville): duet with Ernest Pike: acc orch. Zono 2093 (10")

    (2) 1922, June 21, duet with Sydney Coltham: acc orch. HMV B–1415 (10")

UNLESS (Caracciolo)

    (1) 1904–1905: acc orch. Nicole 5737; Pelican P–35; Sovereign No. 69 (10")

    (2) 1906, January 4: acc piano. G&T 3–2433 (10")

    (3) 1912, February 21: acc orch. HMV 02422; HMV C–440 (12")

UP FROM SOMERSET (Weatherly & Sanderson)

    1913, October 15: acc orch. Zono A–128 (12")

V FOR VICTORY (Dawson)

    1941, August 14: acc orch. RZ G–24398 (10"), Sydney

VACANT CHAIR, THE (Washburn & Root)

    (1) 1909, June: duet with Ernest Pike: acc organ. Edison Amb 12081 (cyl)

    (2) 1911, October 20: acc orch. Zono 722; RZ T–722; HMV (Canada) 120195; Ariel 840 (as Maurice Evans) (10")

VAGABOND, THE (Stevenson & Vaughan Williams *Songs of Travel*)

    (1) 1923, May 7: acc piano. HMV B–1698 (10") *acc J Bratch Bb1253*

    (2) 1925, December 18: acc piano. HMV B–2297 (10")

    (3) 1954, March 29 Sydney: acc orch. Radio broadcast.

VANITY FAIR (Carolan)

    1909, June: acc orch. Edison Amb 12158 (cyl)

VEAU D'OR, LE (Gounod *Faust*)

    1923, July 2: in chorus (soloist Feodor Chaliapin): acc orch. HMV 7–32080; HMV DA–554; Victor (USA) 960 (10") (in French)

VETERAN'S SONG, THE (Adams)

    (1) 1911, March: acc orch. Zono 573; HMV (Canada) 120061 (10")

    (2) 1932, August 30: acc orch & chorus. HMV C–2507 (12")

VICAR OF BRAY, THE (Old English melody)

    1904–1905: acc piano. Nicole (untraced); Pelican P–34 (10")

VILLAGE BAND, THE (Lohr)

    1917, January 17: acc orch. Zono 1858 (10")

VILLAGE BLACKSMITH, THE (Longfellow & Weiss)

    (1) 1908, April: acc orch. EB 20000 & EB 20001 (2 cyl set)

    (2) 1909, June: acc orch & chorus. Edison Amb 12106 (cyl)

    (3) 1909, June 23: acc orch. Zono X–42912 (10")

    (4) 1913, January 21: acc orch. Zono A–107 (12")

    (5) 1923, May 31: acc orch. HMV C–1116 (12")

    (6) 1929, August 15: acc orch. HMV C–1816 (12")

VOLUNTEER ORGANIST, THE (Glenroy & Lamb)

    (1) 1909, February: acc orch & organ. Edison Amb 12015; Edison BA 23026 (cyl)

    (2) 1922, October 13: acc orch. HMV B–1493 (10")

    (3) 1930, July 10: acc orch & organ. HMV B–3630 (10")

VOUS QUI FAITES, L'ENDORMIE (Gounod *Faust*)

    1923, July 2: in chorus, where sings duet at beginning of aria with soloist Feodor Chaliapin: acc orch. HMV 7–32081; HMV DA–554; Victor (USA) 960 (10") (in French)

VULCAN'S SONG (Gounod *Philemon et Baucis*)

    (1) 1904, July–August: acc orch. Lambert 5094 (cyl)

    (2) 1904–1905: acc orch. Nicole 5653; Sovereign 65 (10")

    (3) 1930, May 1: acc orch. HMV B–3464 (10") *c. Geo. Byng Bb 19282*

WAIATA POI (Hill)

    (1) 1938, March 3: acc orch & chorus. HMV B–8771; Victor (USA) 10–1025; Victor (Canada) 120970; HMV (Eire) IP–995 (10")

    (2) 1954, May 10, Sydney: radio broadcast, acc orch & chorus. Kingfisher STAR–16 (cassette)

WAIT (d'Hardelot)

    1917, February 5: acc piano. Zono 1810 (10")

WALK DOWN THE ROAD (Sievier & Thayer)

    1947, October 24: acc orch. HMV B–9592; HMV EA–3694 (10")

WALTZ ME, BILL

    (1) 1908, January (as Will Danby): duet with his sister-in-law, Yolande Noble (as Dora Whittaker): acc orch. EB 10508 (cyl)

    (2) 1908, February (as Will Danby): duet with Miss Mortimer (probably sister-in-law, Yolande Noble, or possibly his wife, Annie Mortimer Noble): acc orch. Twin 177; HMV (Canada) 120114 (as Mortimer & Derby) (10")

WALTZ ME ROUND AGAIN, WILLIE (Shields & Cobb)

    1906, September (as Will Danby): acc orch. White 140 (cyl)

WALTZING MATILDA (Paterson & Cowan)

    (1) 1938, March 3: acc orch & chorus. HMV B–8771; HMV B–9191; HMV (Eire) IP–995; Victor (USA) 10–1025; Victor (Canada) 120970 (10")

    (2) 1942, c. July: acc piano. HMV PD–1 (LP set 12") broadcast Auckland, NZ.

    (3) 1949, August 22: acc piano. unpublished newsreel or film short soundtrack probably from Wellington NZ.

WANDER THIRST (Ronald *Song Fancies*: No.4)

    1924, December 2: acc piano. HMV B–1930 (10")

WANDERER'S SONG, THE (Keel *Salt Water Ballads*)

    1922, May: acc orch. HMV B–1785 (10")

WANDERING THE KING'S HIGHWAY (Leslie Coward)

(1) 1938, January 27: acc orch & chorus. HMV B–8723 (10")

(2) 1948, May 6: acc orch. HMV B–9739 (10")

WANDERTHIRST (Gould & Fordell)

1949, November 3: acc piano. HMV PD–1 (LP set) (12") concert broadcast, Rotorua, NZ.

WARATAH AND WATTLE (Lawson & McCall)

(1) late 1950, acc probably piano: Vitavox (private) (10" acetate), Sydney

(2) 1958, April 30, radio broadcast Adelaide: acc piano. HMV PD–1 (LP set 12")

WATCHMAN, THE (Squire)

(1) 1916, October 23: acc piano. Zono A–230 (12")

(2) 1916, December 1: acc orch. HMV 02699; HMV C–756; HMV (India) M–874 (12")

(3) 1921, September 28: acc orch. HMV C–756 (12")

WATCHMAN, WHAT OF THE NIGHT (Sarjeant)

(1) 1909, May, duet with Ernest Pike: acc orch. Edison Amb 12052 (cyl)

(2) 1909, June 17, duet with Ernest Pike: acc orch. Zono X–44131; Zono 526 (10")

(3) 1922, December 29, duet with Sydney Coltham: acc orch. HMV B–1496 (10")

(4) 1923, May, duet with Browning Mummery: acc orch. Zono 526; Ariel Grand 230 (as George Saunders & Maurice Evans) (10")

(5) 1935, January 29, duet with himself (trick record): acc orch. HMV C–2728 (12")

WAVE YOUR HAND AS THE BAND GOES BY (Murray & Everard)

1907, May: acc orch. Edison 13580 (cyl)

WE PARTED ON THE SHORE (Lauder)

(1) 1906, August (as Hector Grant): acc orch. EB 10000 (cyl)

(2) 1906, September (as Hector Grant): acc orch. White 135 (cyl)

(3) 1906, October (as Hector Grant): acc orch. Edison 13525 (cyl)

WE SAW THE SEA (Berlin)

1936, March 20: acc orch. HMV B–8425 (10")   *o EA 2723 – 1   May 1936*

WE SHALL PREVAIL (Bowden & Gerity)

1940, July 11: acc orch. RZ G–24077 (10"), Sydney

WEDDING OF LAUCHIE McGRAW, THE

1906, June 5 (as Hector Grant): acc orch. Zono X–42538 (10")

WEST'S ASLEEP, THE

1906, June 6: acc orch. Zono X–42425; Zono 515 (10")

WESTWARD HO! or THE PIRATE GOES WEST (Moore & McCall)

(1) 1933, December 5: acc orch. HMV B–8089 (10")

(2) 1935, November 9: acc piano. HMV C–2805 (12" medley)

WHALIN' UP THE LACHLAN (Esson & McCall)

(1) 1942, January 22: acc piano. RZ G–24525 (10"), Sydney

(2) 1947, October 24: acc orch. HMV B–9618; HMV EA–3810 (10")

WHAT DO YOU MEAN BY LOVING SOMEBODY ELSE (Gottler)

1920, February 17 (as Will Strong): acc orch & chorus. HMV B–1091 (10")

WHAT SHALL WE DO WITH THE DRUNKEN SAILOR? (Sea shanty)

1935, 9 November: acc piano & chorus. HMV C–2805 (12" medley)

WHAT HAVE I TO DO WITH THEE? (Mendelssohn *Elijah*)

1907, January 29, duet with Eleanor Jones-Hudson: acc orch. G&T 04004; HMV C–484 (12")

WHAT'S THE USE OF BEING WISE?

1904, July–September: acc unknown. Lambert 5088 (cyl)

WHEATLANDS (Shave & Mason)
    1947–1948, acc orch & chorus. Radio broadcast, Sydney (16" 2GB radio disc)
WHEN A FELON'S NOT ENGAGED … (Gilbert & Sullivan *Pirates of Penzance*)
    1920, October 1: acc orch & chorus. HMV D–512 (12")
WHEN ALL THE WORLD IS YOUNG, LAD (Parry)
    1917, June 19: acc piano. Zono 2387; Ariel 831 (as Maurice Evans) (10")
WHEN BRIGHT EYES GLANCE (Hedgcock)
    1923, June 22: acc orch. HMV C–1117 (12")
WHEN BRITAIN REALLY RULED THE WAVES (Gilbert & Sullivan *Iolanthe*)
    1922, January 13: acc orch & chorus. HMV D–638 (12")
WHEN HIELAND MARY DANCED THE HIELAND FLING (Von Tilzer)
    1908, October 9 (as Hector Grant): acc orch. Zono X–42826) (10")
WHEN I COME BACK HOME (Rizzi)
    1939, March–April: acc piano. HMV B–8978 (10")
WHEN I FIRST PUT THIS UNIFORM ON (Gilbert & Sullivan *Patience*)
    1921, January 26: acc orch & chorus. HMV D–565 (12")
WHEN I GET HOME (Wenrich)
    1920, November (as Robert Woodville): acc orch. Zono 2108 (10")
WHEN JOHNNY COMES MARCHING HOME (Gilmore)
    1917, January 17: acc orch & chorus. Zono 1777; RZ T–1777 (10")
WHEN MY SHIPS COME SAILING HOME (Darel)
    1913, December 23: acc orch. Zono A–134 (12")
WHEN THAT HARVEST MOON IS SHINING (Stevens)
    1920, September 7 (as Will Strong): acc orch & chorus. HMV B–1138 (10")
WHEN THE BOYS GO MARCHING BY (Dix)
    1906, February: acc unknown. Edison 13444 (cyl)
WHEN THE CHRISTMAS BELLS ARE RINGING (Cleve, Stroud & Watson)
    1921, September 30 (as Robert Woodville), duet with Ernest Pike: acc orch. Zono
        2170 (10")
WHEN THE EBBTIDE FLOWS (Gordon)
    (1) 1906, November: acc orch. Edison 13549 (cyl)
    (2) 1907, August: acc orch. White 249 (cyl)
    (3) 1912, July 9: acc orch. Zono 892 (10")
WHEN THE FOEMAN BEARS HIS STEEL (Gilbert & Sullivan *Pirates of Penzance*)
    1920, July 9: trio with Violet Essex & George Baker: acc orch & chorus. HMV D–510
        (12")
WHEN THE GUARDS GO MARCHING BY (Barker)
    1931, March 10: acc orch. HMV B–3838; HMV B–8983 (10")
WHEN THE LIGHTS GO ROLLING ROUND (Blake & Ireland)
    1922, January 9: acc piano. HMV B–1337 (10")
WHEN THE LITTLE SINGING BIRDS FORGET THEIR SWEETEST TUNE
    (Francis)
    1909, April: acc unknown. Edison 13855 (cyl)
WHEN THE SERGEANT-MAJOR'S ON PARADE (Longstaffe)
    (1) 1926, January 12: acc orch. HMV C–1245 (12")
    (2) 1934, January 11: acc orch & chorus. HMV B–8158; HMV B–8983; Victor (Canada)
        120873 (10")
WHEN THE STARS WERE YOUNG (Rubens)
    (1) 1904, September 5 (as Arthur Walpole): acc unknown. Zono X–42118 (10"); matrix
        5740b

(2) 1904, September 5: acc unknown. G&T 3–2126 (10"); matrix 5741b

(3) 1904, c. September: acc orch. EB 6417 (cyl)

WHEN THE SUN GOES DOWN IN SPLENDOUR (Smith)

1910, September: acc orch. Edison 14025 (cyl)

WHEN THEY GET DIXIE ON THE WIRELESS TELEPHONE (Law)

1920, July 20 (as Will Strong): acc orch & chorus. HMV B–1129 (10")

WHEN YOU COME HOME (Weatherly & Squire)

(1) 1913, October 15: acc orch. Zono 1203; Ariel Grand 800 (as Maurice Evans) (10");
matrix Ak17037e

(2) 1925, July: acc orch. Zono 1203 (10"); matrix Yy6291–2

WHEN YOU HAD LEFT OUR PIRATE FOLD (Gilbert & Sullivan *Pirates of Penzance*)

1929, February 19, trio with Derek Oldham & Dorothy Gill: acc orch. HMV D–1685;
Victor (USA) 9614 (12")

WHEN YOU'RE A LONG, LONG WAY FROM HOME (Mayer)

1916, October 20 (as Will Strong): acc orch. Zono 1723 (10")

WHEN YOU'RE TIRED OF ROAMING (McGlennon)

1907: acc orch. Clarion 773 (cyl)

WHERE THE ABANA FLOWS (Towne & Woodforde-Finden *A Lover In Damascus*)

1930, September 22: acc orch. HMV C–2096 (12")

WHERE THE BLACK-EYED SUSANS GROW (Radford & Whiting)

1917, June 8 (as Will Strong): acc orch. Zono 1797 (10")

WHERE THE HILLS OF BEN LOMOND LOOK DOWN ON THE DELL (Ray)

1920, July 20 (as Will Strong): acc orch. HMV B–1129 (10")

WHERE THE NORTH ROAD LEAVES THE MINSTER CITY

(1) 1907, March: acc orch. White 198 (cyl)

(2) 1907, (as George Welsh): acc orch. Zono X–42656 (10")

WHERE'S THE SERGEANT? (Longstaffe)

1936, December 8: acc orch. HMV B–8540 (10")

WHERE, OH WHERE

(1) 1907, January (as Will Danby): acc orch. White 172 (cyl)

(2) 1907, February (as Will Danby): acc orch. Sterling 869 (cyl)

WHIP-POOR-WILL (Kern *Sally*) Bb 517-1

1921, September 29, duet with Bessie Jones: acc orch. HMV B–1274 (10")

WHIST! THE BOGIE MAN

1909, June 9 (as Walter Wentworth): acc orch. Zono X–42990 (10")

WHITE SQUALL, THE (Baker)

1909, June: acc orch. Edison Amb 12125 (cyl)

WHITE WINGS (Winter)

1907: acc orch. Zono X–42671 (10")

WHOSE BABY ARE YOU? (Caldwell & Kern *The Night Boat*)

1921, November 8 (as Will Strong), duet with Bessie Jones: HMV B–1305 (10")

WHY DO THE NATIONS? (Handel *Messiah*)

1934, March 12: acc orch. HMV C–2694 (12") 2B5939 c. Lawrence Collingwood

WHY SHOULDN'T I? (Russell)

1923: January 16: acc orch. HMV B–1549 (10")

WIDOW OF PENZANCE (Coates)

1917, May 22: acc piano. Zono 1919 (10")

WILD COLONIAL BOY, THE (Traditional)

1951, February 21: acc orch. HMV PD–1 (LP set) (12"), Sydney

WILL O' THE WISP (Cherry)
    1932, April 27: acc orch. HMV B–4350 (10")
WINDING ROAD, THE (Arale & Andrews)
    1934, December 7: acc orch. HMV B–8262; HMV B–9191 (10")
WINDMILL, THE (Nelson)
    1912, February 15: acc orch. Zono 804; HMV (Canada) 120088; Ariel 552; (as Maurice
        Evans) (10")
WITH A SONG (May)
    1933, January 5: acc orch. HMV B–4374 (10")
WITH MY SHILLELAGH UNDER MY ARM (O'Brien & Wallace)
    1936, December 8: acc orch. HMV B–8515 (10")
WITH SWORD AND LANCE (Starke)
    1933, March 7: acc orch & chorus. HMV B–8015 (10")
WITH YOUR HAIR OF SILVER
    1908, February (as George Welsh): acc orch. Zono X–42760 (10")
WOLF, THE (Shield *The Castle of Andalusia*)
    (1) 1908, January 28: acc piano. Zono X–42773; Zono 514; Ariel 9475 (10")
    (2) 1912, August: acc orch. Edison Amb 12495 (cyl)
WOMBA
    1909, July 2, in chorus providing Indian war whoops: acc Black Diamonds Band. Zono
        X–40345 (10"). Possibly unissued.
WOO THOU THY SNOWFLAKE (Sullivan *Ivanhoe*)
    1922, June 15: acc orch. HMV C–1079 (12")
WOOD MAGIC (Shaw)
    1925, August 19: acc piano. HMV B–2154 (10")
WORD ALLOW ME, A – see 'Prologue, The'
WOULD-BE DRAMATISTS, THE
    1908, sketch with Winifed Harbor: Pathé 727 (8½" disc)
WRAP ME UP IN MY OLD STABLE JACKET (Major & White)
    1906, November 12: acc orch. Zono X–42545; Zono 517; RZ T–517 (10")
WRECK OF A TROOPSHIP, THE
    1907: member of descriptive sketch with effects & singing. Zono X–41027; Zono 564
        (10")
WRECK, THE (Little)
    1909, July 1: acc orch. Zono X–42945; Zono 3040 (10")
YEOMEN OF ENGLAND (German *Merrie England*)
    (1) 1911, March 7: acc orch. Zono 573; Ariel 798 (as Maurice Evans); HMV (Canada)
        120061 (10")
    (2) 1929, April 26: acc orch. HMV B–3111 (10")
YES! I AM BRAVE! OH, FAMILY DESCENT (Gilbert & Sullivan *Pirates of Penzance*)
    1920, October 1, duet with Violet Essex: acc orch & chorus. HMV D–512 (12")
YON ASSASSIN IS MY EQUAL (Verdi *Rigoletto*)
    (1) 1922, June 26: acc orch. HMV B–1393 (10")
    (2) 1930, May 1: acc orch. HMV B–3698 (10")
YOU (Hamblen)
    1922, November 8: acc orch. HMV B–1449 (10")
YOU ARE MY IRISH LILY (Darewski)
    1906, May: acc orch. Edison 13482 (cyl)

YOU ARE STILL MY HIGHLAND LASSIE
　　1908, January (as Hector Grant), acc orch. EB 10505 (cyl)
YOU CAN'T DO WITHOUT A GIRL
　　1907, October (as Will Danby): acc orch. EB 10452 (cyl)
YOU'D BETTER ASK ME (Lohr)
　　1904, July–August: acc unknown. Lambert 5090 (cyl)
YOU'LL BE SOME WONDERFUL GIRL (McCarthy)
　　1920, January 4 (as Will Strong): acc orch & chorus. HMV B–1081 (10")
YOU'LL WANT ME BEFORE I WANT YOU (Scott)
　　1922, January 10 (as Will Strong): acc orch & chorus. HMV B–1312 (10")
YOU, JUST YOU (Thompson)
　　1914, February 9: duet with Ernest Pike: acc piano. Zono 1377 (10")
YOUNG BRITISH SOLDIER, THE (Kipling & Cobb)
　　1935, July 5: acc orch & chorus. HMV C–2797; Victor (Canada) 130827 (12" medley)
YOUNG BRITON'S HERITAGE (Hennessy)
　　1929, July 10: acc piano. HMV B–3143 (10")
YOUNG TOM O' DEVON (Russell)
　　(1) 1909, July 1: acc orch. Zono X–42946; Zono 588; HMV (Canada) 120058 (10");
　　　　matrix 10408e
　　(2) 1909, July 1: acc orch. HMV GC 4–2034 (10"); matrix 10409e
　　(3) 1922, December 20: acc orch. HMV B–1484 (10")
　　(4) 1929, July 9: acc orch. HMV B–3301 (10")
YOUR ENGLAND AND MINE (Simpson)
　　1917, June 12: acc orch. HMV B–910 (10")
YOUR SMILE (Forster)
　　1909, July 1: acc orch. Zono X–42915 (10"). Possibly unissued.
YOUR WONDERFUL HEART OF GOLD (Long & Scott)
　　1920, December 1 (as Will Strong): acc orch. HMV B–1172 (10")
YOUTH (Allitsen)
　　1914, January 20: acc orch. Zono 1265 (10")

Abbreviations

ABC Australian Broadcasting Commission, later Corporation.

ABC/AA (1936–1969) Australian Broadcasting Commission's Peter Dawson files are now held by Australian Archives: SP 368/1, 7/18/2, Box 4, ABC 1938–1962 (+69); press files, SP1011/2, Box 27, Job 10946/96, 303/6/3/33.

ADB *Australian Dictionary of Biography*. Melbourne University Press.

AMN *Australian Musical News*.

APRA Australasian Performing Right Association.

BBC British Broadcasting Company, later Corporation.

BBC/AC (1922–1971) Written Archives Centre, Caversham.

EMI (1905–1992) Electric and Musical Industries Ltd Archive, Hayes, Middlesex. File 2818, *Peter Dawson*, plus selected extracts from the *Voice*.

New Grove *New Grove Dictionary of Music and Musicians*, ed. Sadie.

PDAS Peter Dawson Appreciation Society, (1982–1991). Formed in Wales by Ron Hughes to collect any available information about Peter Dawson. The society only proved viable for a limited period. A body of documentary evidence collected was sent to archivist, Peter Burgis, who lodged the documents with other Peter Dawson documents at National Film and Sound Archive (see SSA). Some of these documents are in MS5030; the bulk in MS6829.

RSL Returned Services League, originally Returned Sailors and Soldiers Imperial League of Australia.

SSA ScreenSound Australia, formerly National Film and Sound Archive, Canberra. There are two groups of pertinent documents:

    (1) MS5030: Peter Dawson personal documents, sheet music and mss (1903–1962);

    (2) MS6829: ephemera – Peter Dawson Appreciation Society.

Notes

CHAPTER 1: 1882–1902

1. P. Moss, *Modern World History*. St Albans: Collins 1978, pp.9–10.
2. Marjorie Barnard, *A History of Australia*. Sydney: Angus & Robertson 1963, p.436.
3. Family tree by Jessie's daughter, Alison Mullin, 21 January 1996, Peter Dawson's diary, and birth certificate.
4. EMI, April 1931.
5. Ancillary information from E. Richards (ed.), *The Flinders History of South Australia*. Adelaide: Wakefield Press 1986.
6. Family tree 21 January 1996: James (1868–1912), Violet (1870–1954), Agnes (1872–1912), Thomas (1873–1937), Alison (1876–1900), David (1878–1936), William (1880–1955), Peter (1882–1961), Jessie (1883–1968). Family names from Dawson's diary: Dad, Mum, Jim, Val, Aggie, Tom, Else, Dave, Will, Pete, Jess. Diary entry 11 July 1953, 'Violet dies age 84.'
7. Population of Australia 1891: 3,177,823. SA census 30 April 1881: 275,344; Census 31 March 1901: 358,346. Adelaide City Council Medical Officer Report 12 November 1902: 1898–99 38,913; 1901–02 39,345.
8. Information about Adelaide based on B. Dickey (ed.) *William Shakespeare's Adelaide 1860–1930*. Adelaide: Association of Professional Historians, 1992. Painter, 'Hotels and Drinking'; Riddle, 'Adelaide's Parklands'; Hillard, 'The City of Churches', with support from Richards 1986 and M. McKernan, *Australian Churches at War: Attitudes and Activities of the Major Churches 1914–1918*. Canberra: Australian War Memorial, 1980.
9. Melba, born 1861 in Melbourne as Helen Porter Mitchell, was 20 years older than Dawson.
10. The 'birth certificate produced' held by Dawson was issued in 1934. The amendment to 1882 was typed on the back so it is probable the issuing passport officer did not see it.
11. *Advertiser*, Adelaide, 19 September 1931.
12. Jessie, 30 October 1960: 'you were born in the South East of the City of Adelaide, Peter. I suppose 80 years ago Castle [sic] St was out in the <u>never never</u>'. J. Hopkins, *Phonograph Society of S.A. Newsletter*, September 1993, supports the genealogical correction to 1882 and, using the City of Adelaide citizen rolls establishes that Cassel Street is since defunct. Initially the houses were not numbered; when they were the Dawson house acquired the number 7 but the numbering was altered in 1920/21 'and the Dawson property became numbers 17 and 19 Castle Street'.
13. G.H. Manning, *Place Names of South Australia*: Grange, SA: East Adelaide 'Healthy locality, no deep drainage, no unpleasant smells'. 'Saint Peters: 1884 … took its name from the adjacent college.' *East Adelaide School 1886–1986*, East Adelaide School 1986: It was only after a drain had been constructed along the length of St Peters Street to channel and tame Second Creek, which meandered through the area creating awkward little hills and hollows and causing frequent flooding, that subdivision of the area could proceed.

14. Information on education generally from Richards 1986. Unless otherwise noted Dawson's primary schooling source is East Adelaide Primary School Record, handwritten.

15. General information about music in Adelaide is based on: Szuster: 'Concert Life in Adelaide'; Swale: 'Liturgical & Choral traditions'; Silsbury: 'Secular Choral Music'; Clark: 'Music in the Home' in McCredie, A. (ed.), *From Colonel Light into the Footlights*. Adelaide: Pagel 1988.

16. P. Gammond, 'Drawing-room ballad' in *New Oxford Companion to Music*. Oxford University Press, 1984.

17. L. Marsh, *The Price of a Song*, 2 November 1959. London: *Punch Almanack*, pp.23–26, 'Smallwood's Piano Tutor sold over three million copies.' 30 guineas may sound cheap but today its equivalent would be c.$A3,500.

18. *People*, Sydney, 25 April 1951.

19. *People*, Sydney, 25 April 1951.

20. W.J. Reynolds, *A Survey of Christian Hymnology*. New York: Holt, Rinehart, Winston, 1963. *Hymns Ancient and Modern* first edition, Novello, 1860, consisted of 273 hymns, 131 of English origin, 132 Latin translations, 10 German translations. Only 12 of the English hymns were new.

21. *People*, Sydney, 25 April 1951.

22. Quotations about Sankey's and Alexander's are from Joan Mansfield, 'The Music of Australian Revivalism' in *Reviving Australia*. Sydney: Centre for the Study of Australian Christianity, 1994. When Moody toured Australia in 1877 he used Sankey's *Sacred Songs and Solos*. By 1900 Sankey's had sold 80 million copies worldwide. Alexander was the Scottish evangelist/composer Alexander Somerville, who had been associated with Moody in his Glasgow mission in 1874. 'Their words have almost always the same nostalgia and yearning for heaven which is heard in negro spirituals; it is only one step from "Swing low, sweet chariot" to "Safe in the arms of Jesus".'

23. Hillard in Dickey 1992.

24. Given to Dawson by Mr Foale and reported by the *Advertiser*, 22 May 1933. We do not know what young Peter sang.

25. G. Moore, *Am I too loud? Memoirs of an Accompanist*. London: Hamish Hamilton 1962, p.38. John McCormack, one of the finest Irish tenors of the Peter Dawson era, was created a count by the Pope.

26. *People*, 25 April 1951, and nephews, 25 March 1993.

27. J. Mansfield 1994.

28. Correspondence with Boosey & Hawkes, London, 1 January 1996: Collection by Bayley & Ferguson in 'the latter part of the last century' under the editorship of Sir Arthur Sullivan & Josiah Pittman'; precursor to Boosey Imperial Edition c.1890.

29. Secondary education: correspondence with Pulteney Grammar School 9 May 1996, and 20 August 1996. The name was changed from the Pulteney School to Pulteney Grammar School when the school moved to its present site on South Terrace in 1921.

30. Biography, *Daily Telegraph Mirror*, Sydney, 23 August 1991.

31. *Advertiser*, Adelaide, 26 September 1931.

32. *Advertiser*, 26 September 1931. 'The drill Sergeant at Peter Dawson's school, Pulteney St School in 1898'. The caption suggests that the S-M was a Boer War veteran when he was Peter Dawson's drill sergeant, but Dawson had left school before the Boer War began.

33. According to Dawson's nephews, 26 January 1996; and family tree, 21 January 1996.

34. *People*, 25 April 1951.

35. C. Fenner, 'Apprenticeship Training', in *S.A. Education Department Bulletin No.1*. Adelaide, Government Printer, 1924, p.5: '[until] 1917, when the [technical education of apprentices] Act was passed, apprenticeship was a wholly haphazard matter in the city of Adelaide; no one in authority knew whether any new worker was an apprentice or not, what school or workshop training he was receiving (if any), and no information was available as to the number of apprentices in any particular trade or calling.'

36. EMI, 20 March 1931.
37. Family tree, 21 January 1996.
38. Interview, *Advertiser*, Adelaide, 19 September 1931; *Daily Telegraph Mirror*, Sydney, 23 August 1931.
39. See Silsbury, p.213. If Stevens had been contemporaneous with Sullivan he must have been with him in the Chapel Royal from about 1854. As Mendelssohn died in 1847 the presumed collaboration must be fictitious. As *Redemption* dates from 1882 he could have worked with Gounod only on other compositions. Some performances cited can also be found in G.H. Manning, *50 Years of Singing: A History of the Adelaide Harmony Choir Inc.*. Eastwood, SA. The Choir, 1996, p.87.
40. A. Harman & W. Mellors, *Man and his Music*. London: Barrie 1962. R. Longyear, *Nineteenth Century Romanticism in Music*. Eaglehawk Cliffs, N.J.: Prentice Hall 1973. D.J. Grout, *A History of Western Music*. London: Dent, 1980. J. Machlis, *The Enjoyment of Music*. New York: Norton, 1984. G.B. Shaw, *GBS on Music*. Harmondsworth: Penguin, 1962.

    R. Covell, *Themes of a New Society*. Melbourne: Sun Books, 1967, p.17. 'In nineteenth-century Britain the choral society and its repertory were the true nucleus of formal music-making – the history of concert-going in the various cities and towns of Australia is largely reducible to the founding of one society of this kind after another.'
41. J.J. Virgo, *Fifty Years Fishing For Men*. London: Pilgrim 1939, p.35. Don Virgo provided the extract in 1994 with a note about John James Virgo, CBE: 'my great grandfather was general secretary of the Y.M.C.A. who travelled the world extensively preaching and singing'.
42. *Advertiser*, Adelaide 19 September 1931, 5 December 1950.
43. R. Rene, *Mo's Memoirs*. Melbourne: Reed & Harris, 1945, p.18. Born Harry van der Sluys (changed later to Sluice) in Hindley Street, Adelaide, 15 February 1892.
44. Manning 1996, p.89. EMI, February 1926, *Reuters*, 24 October 1938, unidentified newspapers, 26 August 1955, 12 October 1933.
45. Quotes Dawson in *People*, 25 April 1951; Glennon, 1968, pp.47–48.
46. Programme, 28 July 1900.
47. *Advertiser*, 19 September 1931, and 22 September 1931: Dawson on tour at an Adelaide Town Hall luncheon. Appears also in J. Glennon, 'Peter Dawson' in *Australian Music and Musicians*. Adelaide, Rigby, 1968, p.47 as 'red tie'. Championship not confirmed.
48. 18 January 1901, the two Ballarat newspapers.
49. Information on Kent Town Choir based on Silsbury in McCredie, 1988 and Hillard in Dickey, 1992.
50. S. Brooke, *The Railways of Australia*. Melbourne: Dreamweaver 1984. South Australia completed its section to Servicetown in 1886 and the Victorian component was completed on 19 January 1887.
51. Moss, 1978, pp.294–95. Certain British colonies were granted a form of independence: Canada, 1867, Australia, 1901, New Zealand, 1907, and South Africa, 1910. The term 'Dominion' was not used until 1907: 'After 1907, to distinguish them from other colonies, these independent colonies were called dominions.'
52. J. Glennon, 'Peter Dawson' in *ADB* 1981, p.246; *People,* 25 April 1951.
53. *People*, 25 April 1951.
54. Interview with nephews, 25 March 1993.
55. EMI January 1949 (typed article by F.W. Gaisberg, 1 September 1948 appeared in *Voice*, January 1949).
56. *Register*, Adelaide, 26 December 1901.
57. EMI, *Voice,* April 1931.
58. Unidentified newspaper clipping among Peter Dawson papers held privately.
59. Dawson papers held privately.
60. P. Dawson, *Fifty Years of Song,* London: Hutchinson, 1951, p.17. Others have written 'S.S. Medic,' another White Star liner.

61. Dalgety & Co Ltd, agents, in the *Register,* Adelaide, Monday 24 March 1902.
62. 29 March 1902, ship's manifest, Victorian State Archives: All passengers are listed as 'Third Class' but in the Summary as 'Steerage', the Dawson brothers being two of '338 Persons', who equalled '315 Statute Persons'. Confusingly, the figure 25 has been entered against P. Dawson in the age column.
63. 26 May 1951.
64. A Portugese island off the coast of Morocco.
65. *People*, 25 April 1951.

CHAPTER 2: 1902–1904

1. Dawson 1951 and *Morning-Tea Chat with Edith Pearn* at Radio 7LA, 1951.
2. Shipping details Lloyd's Register, 1902 and *Lloyd's Weekly Shipping Index*, 1902.
3. *Daily Express*, London, 20 March 1931; EMI, April 1931; *Daily Mail* and *Evening News*, London, 31 October; Dawson, 1951, p.17; and many more.
4. Dawson, 1951, p.18; *Advertiser*, Adelaide, 27 May 1954, family tree, 21 January 1996.
5. Photos held by Dawson's niece on the Noble side, Ann Jacquet. Others titled by Dawson include 'Quay builders on Holy Isle', another 'Key Builders on Holy Isle'; another of Peter, James, cousin Daniel and Captain Riddell sailing the '*Aglaia* off Holy Isle 1902'.
6. MS5030: 'Wardlow Hill Parish Church, Rev Jack, 1902, Peter Dawson, Rutherglen', in Dawson's handwriting. Three anthems are marked for use. 'Holy Isle' painting SSA MS5030/6/8; photo of same, MS5030/12/342.
7. Dawson, 1951, p.18.
8. *Advertiser*, Adelaide, 27 May 1954; *AMN*, May 1954.
9. EMI, April 1931; Dawson, 1951, p.17; photo held by Ann Jacquet: 'Dick Martin & Peter, 25 Finchley Road Kennington, 1903'. Kennington is south of the Thames near Lambeth. The S.S. *Afric* arrived in London on 18 May 1902, then proceeded to Liverpool, arriving 30 May, which leads to the supposition that the boys travelled from Liverpool to Glasgow, that Peter first studied with Bamford in Glasgow (1902) and that James returned home when Peter went to London to audition for Santley in May 1903. Lessons began in September following the summer holiday break. We have respected Peter's story to a certain extent, but as he was obviously such an outstanding young singer it is likely he was accepted without delay.
10. Thumbnail sketch of Sir Charles Santley mainly from H. Rosenthal, *New Grove*, 1980; also 'Messiah', 7 January 1891 in *G.B.S. on Music*, 1962; D. Blaikley, 'Ballad Concerts', *New Grove*. 1980; EMI, January 1949.
11. J.N. Moore, *A Matter of Records*, New York: Taplinger 1977, p.86. Santley not only recorded 'Non piu andrai' on 10 June 1903 but also 'Thou'rt passing hence, my brother'. Two days earlier he had also recorded 'Simon the Cellarer', 'The Vicar of Bray' and 'To Anthea' – all with Landon Ronald, piano.
12. EMI, February 1926.
13. Albani: *New Grove*, 1980 and Dawson, 1951, p.19. MS5030/9/226: photograph of Madame Albani dated London 1903. Dawson retained this as a keepsake of the tour.
14. J.D. Vose, *Once a Jolly Swagman*. Blackpool: Vose 1987, p.16, quotes the *Western Daily Mercury* of 7 December 1903, also quoted in the *Gentlemen's Journal*, 1905.
15. Vose, 1987, p.13, taken from Dawson, 1951, p.26. J. Walsh, 'Peter Dawson' in *Hobbies*, Vol 66, January–June 1962, taken from Dawson, 1951, p.24. Dawson sang 'Long Ago in Alcala' as his Gramophone Company audition, 1904, and recorded 'Blow, Blow Thou Winter Wind' (1905), 'Rocked in the Cradle of the Deep' (1908), 'Hybrias the Cretan' (1905), 'I Fear No Foe' (1907), 'The Bandolero' (1907).
16. Constance, aged 75, interview with Peter Burgis, February 1975.

17.   J & J. McMenamin, 'Peter Dawson, a Great Australian Singer' in *Phonographic News,* Vol 1/4, Adelaide 1975, pp.42–53; p.44 taken directly from Dawson, 1951, p.24. 13 February 1905 programme, Royal Alhambra, National Theatre of Varieties: item No.4, Mr Peter Dawson Bass.

18.   Walsh, April 1962.

19.   *Pictorial Show,* Sydney, 25 November 1957.

20.   MS5030/8/134: photograph dated 1902 of 'Daniel Dawson, Lieut. Highland Light Infantry'. The subject of the memorial was one of the Rutherglen Dawsons but whether it was this cousin in the 1902 photograph could not be established. The manuscript paper was from a supplier in Ealing, which confirms that Dawson was living there in December.

21.   Due to the change at puberty, the male vocal ranges are generally an octave lower than the female range. In the preparation of this manuscript we used the technically correct range description: C for the note below the bass stave, then at the octave c, c', c", c".The baritone voice does not exceed a'. However, we have reverted to colloquial parlance for the general reader: in this case a low G to a top E.

22.   William Mann, in *The Operas of Mozart.* London: Cassell 1977, p.293, writes that this song, 'In tiefem Keller' was written by Karl Ludwig Fischer (1745-1825), Mozart's Osmin, the greatest German bass of his day. He had a florid technique that was unexcelled and a vocal compass from bottom C to the baritone high A. Originally the song had a top F and a final low F to show off the two extremes of Fischer's voice. The editing to G in most English versions meant a low G but the top was altered to a top D, which made the song very popular with amateurs. Dawson sang this version.

        In B. Dean & V. Carell, *Gentle Genius: A Life of John Antill.* Sydney: Akron, 1987. Antill, one of Australia's leading post-World War II composers, recalls a recording session with Dawson after the war: 'Dawson's grand bass-baritone went slowly down the scale in the 'Drinking Song' enunciating D.R.I.N.K.I.N.G, hitting a low 'G' firmly in the middle. I was staggered to hear Dawson say, "That's a low note, John".'

CHAPTER 3: 1904–1908

1.   Belloc, H, 'Epigramophones', December 1929, in *The Gramophone Jubilee Book, 1923-1973.* London: The Gramophone, 1973, p.52.

2.   Dawson in unidentified English newspaper, 21 December 1925, *Making Records* (3 million to date).

3.   *Gramophone Jubilee Book 1923-1973,* p.78 appeared originally in *Gramophone,* December 1929 as 'Forty Years of the Gramophone' by Alfred Clark, managing director of the Gramophone Co. of London.

4.   Phonograph: from Greek *phōné* (sound) + *gráph-ma* (write). gramophone (German: grammophon): *grámma* (writing), which derives from *gráph-ma* + *phōné.* Historical information about the industry may be found in several publications produced for the centenary: J.N. Moore, *A Matter of Records.* New York: Taplinger 1977; O. Read & W. Welch, *From Tin Foil To Stereo.* Indianapolis: Sams 1976; *100 Years of Recorded Sound.* City of London Phonograph & Gramophone Society 1977; R. Gelatt, *The Fabulous Phonograph,* London: Cassell 1977; W.R. Isom, 'Centenary of recorded sound' in *Phonographs & Gramophones.* Royal Scottish Museum Edinburgh, 1977; V.K. Chew, *Talking Machines.* London: National Science Museum, 1981.

5.   The first demonstration of disc recording and reproduction was on 16 May 1888. First marketed as a child's toy by Kammerer & Reinhardt in Berlin circa 1890.

6.   EMI, 26 November 1996. The Manager of EMI Archives advised the authors that although the literature indicates that the company was established in 1898 'the company actually started trading in August 1897'. 1898 would be the year the company was registered.

7.   Later became the independent *Deutsche Grammophon.*

8.   R. Gelatt, *The Fabulous Phonograph: The Story of the Gramophone from Tin-foil to High Fidelity*. London: Cassell 1977, p.86.

9.   Gelatt, 1977, p.27. By 1891 Columbia had already issued a catalogue, 'thin in format and only three pages long', which included thirty-six selections of 'John AtLee, the famous whistler' with piano accompaniments by Professor Gaisberg'.

10.   '2 August' is etched on Lamonte's first Berliner disc. Some discographers suggest the recording engineer got the date wrong and believe that her first recording was made some weeks later. However, we favour 2 August. Later, in 1905, she made eight titles for English Columbia. Information from Brian Rust, who received it from Fred Gaisberg in 1949.

11.   J.N. Moore, 1977, p.86.

12.   Remark from *Gramophone Jubilee Book*, 1973, p.38 in J.N. Moore, 1977, pp.76–77.

13.   Gelatt, 1977, p.43

14.   Glennon, *ADB,* 1981, p.245; unidentified London newspaper, 26 April 1955; McMenamin, 1975, pp.44–45.

15.   Walsh, May 1962.

16.   EMI, 16 Jan 1978; Glennon, *ADB*, 1981.

17.   Walsh, 1962. Similarly, Winifred Ponder, *Clara Butt*, London: Harrap 1928. Harrap complained that Ponder's biography of Dame Clara was too bland, too clean, because the singer had taken great pains to put herself in a perfect light and had been very careful not to offend any other artist.

18.   In G. Meadmore, 'Interview with Peter Dawson', *Gramophone*, September 1935, Hough knocked on Dawson's front door and invited him to audition. In Dawson, 1951, p.30, Hough approached Dawson after a concert. Hough was active on the music-hall circuit as the 'Lancashire Laddie' and may have known of Dawson through his father-in-law.

19.   EMI, *Voice*, January 1949; but also EMI, *Voice*, April 1931, Dawson, 1951 and elsewhere.

20.   Fred Gaisberg in EMI; *Voice*, January 1948.

21.   Dawson, 1951, p.33

22.   *People*, Sydney, 25 April 1951, Dawson, 1951, p.30ff; Walsh, 1962: Leonard Dawson also appeared on an Edison Bell poster in December when dealers displayed a 'musical menu' with 'Item 1: Soup: L. Dawson with Morse's great hit "Blue Bell".'

23.   Walsh, April, May 1962.

24.   J.N. Moore, 1977, p.86.

25.   Fred Gaisberg, EMI, *Voice*, January 1948.

26.   J.N. Moore, 1977.

27.   J.N. Moore, 1977.

28.   Walsh, 1962; Gaisberg, *Voice*, 1949, Moore quoting Gaisberg's memoirs.

29.   The version of 'Asleep in the Deep' which stayed in the catalogue until 1930 was the one recorded for *Zonophone* in December 1907 – as George Welsh, bass.

30.   EMI, *Voice*, January 1949.

31.   J.N. Moore, 1977, p.89.

32.   'Sun and Song', Music: Peter Dawson, Words: C. Bingham. London: Elkin, 1904.

33.   Meadmore, 1935.

34.   *Observer*, Adelaide, 13 May 1915: in an interview Dawson lists Glasgow City Hall, October 1904 among others.

35.   MS5030/5/4/folder 7: 4 November 1904.

36.   Dawson, 1951, p.24; unidentified London newspaper. 'Pirate baritone…', 26 April 1955. £100 in 2000 terms is about £4,600, nearly $A11,500.

37.   This date accords with the certificate of marriage; but in *Who's Who in Australia* 1933 and 1959 the date is given as 5 May 1905.

38.   Adelaide, Dawson's nephews, 25 March 1993.

39.   *Sunday Despatch*, London, 26 March 1950.

40.   EMI, 11 October 1905: board meeting minutes No. 94.

41. Sir Alfred Clark (1873–1950): started his career on 12 September 1889 with the North American Phonograph Company, which had acquired Edison's patents. When Edison regained his patents Clark went to work for him and divided his time between the phonograph and another invention, the kinetoscope, the forerunner of the cinema. Clark created the first film scenario.

    Sir Louis Sterling (1879–1958) initially lived in the Gaisberg household in London. He became manager of British Zonophone, which was soon acquired by the Gramophone Co. He went into partnership with Russell Hunting, who had left Edison Bell to start his own Russell Hunting Record Co (cylinders) which made Sterling records. It later became Sterling & Hunting. But the cylinder business failed so Sterling brought out Rena discs which were pressed from Columbia masters, before consolidating with Columbia. Sterling ran Columbia until it merged with the Gramophone Co. in 1931 to become EMI.

    Russell Hunting (1854–1943), 'unquestionably the most popular pre-1900 recording artist', was a monologist and 'originator of the famous Casey series'. (Gelatt, 1977, p.30). When cylinders lost their commercial viability in England around 1914, Hunting returned to the USA.

42. J.N. Moore, 1977, p.90, referring to typewritten article on John McCormack.

43. Walsh, February 1962: 'The Gaisbergs persuaded Peter Dawson to sign an exclusive contract minimum £25, though he earned £72 that year. It seems incredible that the young singer would accept a contract with such a paltry guarantee … after all he made £75 in five days with "John John".'

44. Programme, 13 April 1906: Woolwich Nonconformist Choir Union, soloists Miss Perceval Allen, Mr Alfred Heather, Miss Lucie Johnstone, Mr Peter Dawson.

45. Dawson, 1951, p.24.

46. *Gramophone Jubilee Book*, 1973, p.187, 'Pseudonyms and Anonyms'.

47. K. Brisbane (ed.) *Entertaining Australia,* Sydney: Currency 1991. Confirmed by Ernie Bayly, English *Zonophone* historian.

48. All recording pseudonyms are listed against the appropriate recording in our Complete Song Title Discography.

49. Dawson may not have chosen them; it is likely that the record companies had the final say.

50. Nephews, 21 January 1996.

51. J.N. Moore, 1977, p.89, referring to EMI, *Voice,* Winter 1948; Dawson, 1951, pp.42–43.

52. Gordon Irving, *The Great Scot.* 'I Love a Lassie' was composed by Lauder and Gerald Grafton.

53. Piracy is referred to at length in Marsh, 1959, also Dawson, 1951. The practice forced publisher William Boosey to put pressure on Parliament to push through the Copyright Act 1911. See Boosey, *Fifty Years of Music,* London: Benn, 1931 p.145.

54. SSA, MS5030/music folio O. Recorded July 1907 *Zonophone* X–42627.

55. MS5030/1/73: Dawson, 10 March 1961, to Tierney referring to first meeting with Bransby Williams, by then 91 years old.

56. Advertising poster about 3ft. x 9in. Glasgow Coliseum, 25 June 1906. Advertising poster, Ardwick Green Empire, Manchester, 2 July 1906, printed as No.8 but note by Dawson that he appeared as No.6. A Glasgow newspaper advertisement from 27 June 1906 misprints him as Hector Macdonald.

57. Unidentified newspaper, 26 April 1955: his allowance was cut after 'three £100 credits' because his father was angry that he should think of marrying at 22 and to a girl 'who danced and sang in theatres'.

58. Dawson, 1951, p.42: he was not earning enough to survive 'the dead-summer season for vocalists in those early days'.

59. Dawson, September 1909, letter to Nan from Amy Castles' tour.

60. ABC, 4 April 1945, Commonwealth Club interview; *Stage*, London, 10 June 1948.

61. Dawson recorded 'John, John' as Hector Grant for Edison Bell in December 1906 and for *Zonophone* in January 1907, but as Will Danby for *White* in February .

62. Billy Williams co-composed the song with Fred Godfrey. He not only recorded this number for Edison in late 1906; between 1908 and 1911 he made four studio recordings for disc companies, which have been traced to 23 different labels around the world.

63. Dawson, in unidentified London newspaper, 26 April 1955.

64. J.N. Moore, 1977.

65. Dawson, 1933, 'Thirty Years of Record Making' in *Gramophone*, repeated in *Gramophone Jubilee Book*. London: 1973, repeated by Chislett for EMI record sleeve *Peter Dawson Sings Opera* c.1985.

66. 26 May 1951: Radio 7LA Launceston, *Morning-tea Chat with Edith Pearn,* during the Red Cross tour of Tasmania.

67. Dawson, 1951, p.33; *Evening News,* London, 26 August 1947, '2500 Songs in Wax... he often sang the same song six hours a day for three weeks, he tells me, in order to make sufficient matrices.' The figure of five shillings in Walsh, February 1962, derived from Peter Dawson interview, Meadmore 1935.

68. In a last spasm two popular tunes, 'Meet me Jennie when the sun goes down' and 'If those lips could only speak,' appeared in 1908 on 'twins', double-sided discs which were still a rarity. Walsh, April 1962, cites Edison Bell but these two songs were actually marketed by *Zonophone* in October as Catalogue No. 50. According to Brian Rust the first Edison Bell discs – 10¾ in. diameter appeared in September 1909. *Zonophone* released three more Hector Grant discs, the last, Cat. No. 118, 'A Soldier and a Man', about March 1909. Yet another, No.707, 'The New Hoose', was recorded on 25 August 1911. By 1915 the *Zonophone* catalogue carried 106 solos by Peter Dawson, 32 by Harry Lauder – and one lone disc by Hector Grant.

69. J.N. Moore, 1977, p.86: 'then as now the bulk of record sales were confined to ephemeral, popular music'; also referred to above.

70. Fred Gaisberg , EMI, *Voice,* January 1948.

71. 'The Moon Hath Raised Her Lamp Above' – from *The Lily of Killarney* – is one of Dawson's most recorded titles: with Tom Child, Edward Davies, Mr Stanley, Wilfred Virgo, Browning Mummery, Sydney Coltham and three times with Ernest Pike. 'In the Shade of the Old Apple Tree' (1904) is by the young Americans, Egbert van Alstyne, aged 22, and Harry Williams, 24, also the composers of the earlier 'Navajo'.

72. In his autobiography Dawson recalled the name as Frank Danby.

73. This collaboration for about half a century innocently disadvantaged many other fine British baritones, who were forced to align themselves with less influential recording companies. There was not much room at the top of the HMV baritone pyramid.

74. This was the first extended contract: 24 April 1907 to 23 April 1910, the forerunner of all later exclusive contracts.

75. In relative 2000 terms £200 = £7,000, $A18,000.

76. Walsh, February 1962, quoting Meadmore, 1935.

77. G. Moore, 1962, pp.59–60.

78. English newspaper, n.d. The text suggests a Peter Dawson interview c.1931; *People,* Sydney, 25 April 1951; Roger Pilgrim, (n.d.) *Frozen Music in The Making,* 'Secrets of Gramophone Recording'. G. Moore, 1962: c.1921 'session then as now three hours but often two or more [used] solving tonal and balance problems'.

79. J.N. Moore, 1977, pp.173–75.

80. The *Sovereign* issues also turned up on other discs such as *Pelican* and *Britannic,* but were in fact material published on *Nicole* back in 1904/05.

81. Dawson recorded 'Calvary' eight times between 1904-1911 on both cylinder and disc.

82. EMI, *Voice,* August 1937.

83. Dawson, 1933, in *Gramophone,* republished 1973 in *Gramophone Jubilee Book, 1923-73*. It had also appeared in EMI, *Voice,* February 1926.

84. EMI, *Sound Waves and Talking Machine Record,* November 1907.

85. Walsh, March 1962: 'James H. White was a monologist who made records for Edison in the U.S.A.' He went to London as Edison's manager, but later set up his own company.
86. The label of the Premier Manufacturing Company. Walsh, 1962: from January 1908 review, therefore probably recorded late 1907. Premier stayed in business until electrically recorded discs were introduced. It was probably one of the last companies to make wax cylinders after Edison discontinued them in 1912. It made both cylinders and discs until its plant was destroyed by fire in the 1920s.
87. It had a total playing time of 4 (2 x 2) minutes.
88. EMI, 20 May 1908, believed the other company had made 'disc-records direct without the knowledge of Dawson ... it looks very much like fraud.'
89. EMI, 26 January 1909.
90. EMI, c.1909, *Talking Machine News* and J.N. Moore, 1977, p.76, among others. The programme for *Die Meistersinger* 2 February 1909 carries an *HMV* advert for 'The New Melba Gramophone'. Dawson claims that he met the artist, Barraud, whose only job was painting replicas for display by agents. The vague shadow of the phonograph can be seen on the original HMV painting, which was sighted in EMI Archives at Hayes in 1992.
91. Fred Gaisberg, EMI, *Voice*, January 1949.

CHAPTER 4: 1909

1. Mrs Lin Fraser-Smith from Lincolnshire to authors as recently as 16 May 1999.
2. Mrs B.V. Bennet, of Hackney Rd, St Peters, 1 May 1991.
3. For example *Advertiser*, Adelaide, 28 April 1933, 'opera at Covent Garden ... did not appeal to him, and he decided to confine himself to concerts and gramophone recording.' *Reuters*, 24 October 1938: 'The Singing Plumber: An operatic career did not appeal to him and he decided to confine himself to concerts and gramophone recording.'
4. Dawson, 1951, p.19 ff.
5. *Music in Australia*, 20 June 1931.
6. Kenneth Neate, 14 June 1984, p.14 to PDAS. Neate was one of Australia's first post-war international tenors; he sang at Covent Garden then moved to Paris and finally Munich, where he remained until he died in 1997.
7. Correspondence Covent Garden, 12 January 1996: Monday 25 January, Tuesday 2 February, Tuesday 9 February and Saturday 13 February 1909. The conductor was Hans Richter. Programme held by Dawson: first performance of 3rd series, Tuesday 2 February at 6.30pm. The programme lists Dawson as Schwarz and Robert Radford, his recording colleague in the 1920 G&S series, in the more substantial role of Pognor the goldsmith.
8. Dawson, 1951, p.19ff; H. Rosenthal, *Opera*, 1983, p.1375: '"Too much work for too little pay," he is said to have remarked, a pity, as his performances of operatic excerpts clearly show.'
9. It has been suggested to us that Dawson could have performed lighter roles at Sadlers Wells, like Figaro in *The Marriage of Figaro*. In 1909 Mozart was not yet part of the standard repertoire, nor did the Sadlers Wells Theatre exist as a home for the British National Opera Company. Many noted Australians sang with the BNOC, formed in 1922. Dawson did not. (Most BNOC singers were aligned with English Columbia, the chief rival to HMV. By this time Dawson may have lost interest in opera; on the other hand he may not have been asked.) Managements appear to have pigeon-holed him as 'recordings and concerts only'.
10. Walsh, February 1962.
11. J.N. Moore, 1977, p.89.
12. *Observer*, Adelaide; 13 May 1915, *Daily Chronicle*, London, 24 November 1926, '20 years ago' [c.1906]; Dawson, 1951, pp.39–40. *Talking Machine News* was an advertising magazine promoting Dawson, so its accuracy cannot be relied on.
13. 1998, Charles A. Hooey, biographer of Caroline Hatchard, correspondence with the authors.

At the Prom Dawson sang 'Vulcan's Song' and 'My Old Shako'. He sang many of Madame Lehmann's compositions, including 'Myself When Young' from *In a Persian Garden*, which has remained a classic to this day.

14.   MS5030/1/70–72: Dawson, handwritten, to Nan, September 1909, pp.6–8 only: 'and everything they touch is successful, as they have such smart business tact'.

15.   MS5030: programme, 1909. Dawson, 1951, p.47 and photos.

16.   EMI 2 June 1909: 'I have also fixed up with Miss Amy Castles for several of my songs; she is going to sing them at every concert'. EMI, 1 June 1909, to agent Hoffnung: 'local representatives in each town which these artists visit [should] arrange to exhibit in their windows and by means of sandwich men' that records of the artistes could be heard at their shops.

17.   Information from Boosey, 1931; Blaikley, 1980; Gammond, 1984; R. Cowan, *The London Ballad Concerts*, London: Boosey n.d.; D.M. Randel (ed), 'Ballad', *New Harvard Dictionary of Music*, Cambridge, Mass: Belknap, 1986; B. Bronson, 'Ballad' in *New Grove*, 1980.

18.   Dawson 1951, pp.39–40.

19.   Biography in Glennon, 1968 (has incorrect date of birth); information booklet to Amy Castles CD, Armidale, Vic: Distronics, 1988.

20.   Thorald Waters, *Bulletin*, review of 1902 Williamson concert; Cargher in *Bulletin*, 1988. James Farrell of Castlemaine, Victoria, to the editor of *Opera Australia*, June 1989.

21.   Dr Jeff Brownrigg, 'Amy Castles', unpublished manuscript, Canberra, 1996; chapter '1909–1910: Touring Australia with Peter Dawson'.

22.   Dawson, 1951, p.49.

23.   SSA, MS5030, 1/70; 1/71; 1/72: Peter to Nan, handwritten, September 1909.

24.   Brisbane, 1991, p.157; Walsh, 1962; McMenamin, 1975; *People*, 25 April 1951; *Daily Telegraph*, Sydney, 23 August 1991; 'John Tait in the "Sydney Morning Herald" Sept 29, 1909' quoted in notes to Amy Castles CD, 1988.

25.   Dawson, 1951, p.50 – an anecdote, true in principle but as Dawson was in Melbourne 23 August, Adelaide 7 September it is doubtful that Newcastle was 'a week or so after the Melbourne concert'.

26.   MS5030: photographs, 1909: the company in 'the turnout that took us the rounds of the town in grand style' and 'the brake that drove us round the Town at a gallop'.

27.   Dr Brownrigg visited many of the towns for his research.

28.   These 'bare essential' concert reviews are extrapolated from Brownrigg: Dubbo, 27 October; Goulburn, 1 November.

29.   Programme, 1909; Dawson, handwritten, September 1909. In his book (p.52) he writes 7 August.

30.   Dawson, 1951, pp.62–63. 'Little Grey Home in the West' published 1913; 'Phil the Fluter's Ball', 1912.

31.   Dawson, 1951, p.60.

32.   Walsh, April 1962, from *Talking Machine News*, February 1911. Dawson, 1951, p.49: in 1909 his concert and gramophone successes had already 'been hailed throughout Australia'. 'Shade of the Old Apple Tree' was in fact an Edison Bell cylinder.

33.   *Advertiser*, Adelaide, 18 May 1912.

CHAPTER 5: 1910–1913

1.   Moss, 1978, pp.10–11.

2.   J.N. Moore, 1977, p.131.

3.   Walsh, 1962, paraphrased from Dawson 1951, pp.64–65.

4.   Dawson, 1951, p.29. Despite his 'rejection' of opera in 1909 the December 1910 *Talking Machine News* reported that 'Peter Dawson is now studying to sing grand opera under Professor Kantorez.'

5. M. Scott, *The Record of Singing*. New York: Holmes & Meer, 1979, pp.180–82.
6. The pair star together in later recordings. Radford (1874–1933) became director of the British National Opera Company in 1921.
7. EMI, 20 January 1911; EMI, 23 February 1911; EMI, 25 April 1911. Total £300 = year 2000 c. $A23,000.
8. EMI, 16 November 1912: contract 16 November 1912–15 May 1914 (year 2000 = $A41,500 per annum).
9. EMI, 25 April 1912 – mostly at the old rates.
10. H. McQueen, *Tom Roberts*. Sydney: Macmillan 1996, p.549. Music in MS5030: 'Kangaroo & Dingo', Folio Gi; 'Rolling Down to Rio', Folio J.
11. Walsh, 1962. 1912 review. Smacks of Gramophone Co. blurb.
12. These reviews infer that Dawson had sung in such concerts before his 1909 tour.
13. *Argus*, Melbourne, 4 August 1913, review of final concert in Melbourne 1 August 1913.
14. *AMN*, April 1915, p.286.
15. *Daily News,* Perth, 1 October 1931.
16. Scott, 1979, pp.180–82.
17. *AMN*, July 1913 p.13
18. Dawson, 1951, pp.51–52. The same story appears in the *Daily Telegraph Mirror,* 'The enduring Peter Dawson', Sydney, 23 August 1991. Like journalists before him this writer has relied on secondary sources.
19. *AMN*, August 1913.
20. MS5030/music folio A. Published London: Chappell, 1912.
21. Programme, Warrnambool Town Hall, 17 July 1913.
22. *Corowa Free Press*, 25 July 1913.
23. William James was in his eighties when he told the story to Peter Burgis. According to James the town was Geelong. He added that after observing the shock his remark had caused, Peter's stern countenance broke into a broad grin, he patted James on the shoulder and said: 'Yer doin' well, lad.'
24. *AMN*, November 1913, p.151. Henry Wood had played the organ at the inaugural Queen's Hall concert in 1893. He conducted the Proms for 46 years, from their inception in 1895 until 1941.

CHAPTER 6: 1914–1919

1. Photos G. Moore, 1962, pp.104–105. Today Hayes is a 20-minute bus ride along a crowded suburban thoroughfare from Ealing Common; but in those days Hayes was well out in the country. Boris Semeonoff, *Record Collector,* August 1972: Chaliapin was making recordings at City Road. He did not record at Hayes until 9 October 1921.
2. EMI, 26 March 1929.
3. Poster and programme.
4. *AMN*, January 1914.
5. *AMN*, August 1914, p.48.
6. Dawson, 1951, p.82.
7. Following detail from Moss, 1978; Barnard, 1963; and McKernan, 1980.
8. Dawson, 1951, pp.82–83.
9. *Argus*, Melbourne, 19, 21, 25, 26, 28 September 1914.
10. Collation from *Theatre*, July 1915; programmes; *AMN*, March 1915. All these reports derive ultimately from Dawson himself. Newspaper reviews tell us he was in Melbourne in September and again in October.
11. Based on Barnard, 1963 and McKernan, 1980: 'Forty-two place names were changed in South Australia alone because they had a German flavour.' This anti-German feeling lasted

well into the post-war period. (The English Royal House of Saxe-Coburg-Gotha resisted the change to Windsor till 1917.)

12. Often written MacIntosh but birth certificate (1876) gives McIntosh.

13. John West in *Theatre in Australia*. Sydney: Cassell, 1978, states that he took over the theatre in late 1913. Frank Van Straten in 'The Tivoli: A Chronology of the Melbourne Home of Vaudeville'. Melbourne: Victorian Arts Centre, May 1981, wrote that McIntosh established 'the Tiv' as the enduring home of Australian vaudeville in 1914.

14. Programme 12 November 1915: Dawson contributed 'at least one Sandbag for every ticket sold'.

15. *Argus*, Melbourne, 3 April 1916. Dawson may have sung in 1915 as Van Straten states; on the other hand, this could have been his first appearance at the Tivoli in Melbourne.

16. Quote from *Hawklet*, December 1915, per Frank Van Straten.

17. State Library of Victoria holds a royalty statement for Aileen Neighbour from 1919 which shows that two songs, 'Just for Today' and 'Because of You', had been published by John Church of London. Dawson recorded 'Because of You' (Zonophone 2387) at Hayes on 19 October 1916 but it was not issued until December 1923. He did not record 'Just for Today' but he did record two other Neighbour songs, 'Some Crimson Rose' (2 December 1922) and 'Here's to the good old days' (2 December 1924) issued on HMV B-1946. Another, 'Australia's Starlit Flag', was published by McCarron, Melbourne c.World War I.

18. Moss, 1978, p.33. One of these ships was the veteran S.S. *Afric*, on which Dawson had sailed to England in 1902: it was being used as a troopship when it was torpedoed off Eddystone on 12 February 1917.

19. EMI, 25 September 1916. 2000 equivalent would be c. $A28,000.

20. Quoted in Walsh, 1962; but Dawson, 1951, p.14.

21. *Chu Chin Chow*, a musical play by Australian-born author-actor, Oscar Asche, with music by Frederick Norton, had opened at His Majesty's Theatre, London on 31 August 1916. Peter recorded the song on 11 November.

22. *Gramophone*, January 1933; Dawson, 1951, pp.37–38: 'Fred Gaisberg handed me a song and said, "You might have a look at that, Peter." After glancing through it I said I thought it was a good number and asked, "Do you want me to make it?" "Yes", replied Fred, "right away." I was recording the song in ten minutes.'

23. These statistics from Jose, Carter, Tucker, *Australian Encyclopaedia*, Sydney: Angus & Robertson 1927. The average cost per man had risen from £280 to £800.

24. Australian Archives, CSN: CP78/23, item 1917/89/411, 1 March 1917.

25. Dawson, 1951, pp.83, 87.

26. Interview, *Daily News,* Perth, 1 October 1931.

27. Dawson, 1951, p.87 quoting *Adelaide Herald.*

28. Barnard, 1963, p.485.

29. Statistics from *Australian Encyclopaedia*, 1927. Barnard, 1963, writes 'nearly 300,000'.

30. Moss, 1978, p.25.

31. (i) *Smiths Weekly*, Sydney, 25 November 1933; (ii) *Who's Who In Australia,* 1933 through to 1959; (iii) *Courier Mail*, Brisbane, 25 August 1939; (iv) Dawson, 1951, p.87; (v) *People*, Sydney, 24 May 1951; (vi) *Mercury*, Hobart, 24 April 1951; (vi) already in *Reuters*, 24 October 1938, 'in the world war served as a Company Sergeant-Major with the Australian Forces in Europe.' The information came ultimately from Peter Dawson himself, through newspaper interviews or the chapter, 'The First World War', in Dawson, 1951.

32. Following service detail from Service Record, War Memorial, Canberra: Australian Archives CRS: B2455.

33. Ruddle to Dawson, Brisbane, 24 May 1918.

34. *Daily News*, Perth, 1 October 1931.

35. Programme, 11 June 1918.

36. War Memorial, 1933: a report to an adjutant-general refers to him only as private. The 1918 ship's manifest at the NSW State Archives has 'Acting Sergeant' typed in the right-hand margin. The Soldier Career Management Agency (23 November 1994) advised that he would have returned to the rank of private when he joined the troops on the ship. This sequence is confirmed by his pay allocation, which shows that he was originally paid as 'Private', later as 'Provisional Sergeant', then from 1 November as 'Private' again.

37. NSW State Archives: S.S.*Carpentaria* left Sydney for London via New Zealand on 7 November 1918. AWM embarkation records lists '65041 Private Peter Dawson, Vocalist and Plumber' among the embarking troops. Army Service Record, Australian Archives, 1918 has '28th November' but NSW State Archives ships' manifests: *Riverina* berthed in Sydney on 20 November 1918 'with 14 Officers, 23 Sergeants, 440 Troops ex Carpentaria from Auckland'.

38. MS5030/11/273, photograph.

39. Dawson 1951, p.91; and *People*, 25 April 1951.

40. *Argus*, Melbourne, 27 January 1919.

41. 'Licence to Drive a Motor Vehicle' was issued on 8 April to 'Peter Dawson of 6 South Terrace Adelaide for One Year'.

42. Dawson, 1951, p.92; EMI, *Voice*, March 1920.

43. South African Library, 2 June 1998.

44. *AMN*, August 1919.

CHAPTER 7: 1920–1925

1. Moss, 1978, pp.294–95 partly paraphrased. Australia did not actually send ambassadors abroad until 1940.

2. C. Cook & J. Stevenson, *Modern British History 1714-1987*. London: Longman 1988 p.386.

3. The Gramophone Company now dominated the market throughout the British Empire. Its only serious rival was Columbia Records. Back in May 1900 the Columbia Phonograph Company of New York had opened a branch in London. It started pressing discs about June 1906 at its factory in Surrey. Disc recordings of British artists – who included Yolande Noble – started in 1907. In the 1920s Columbia groomed the Sydney baritone Harold Williams as a rival to Peter Dawson.

4. EMI, 1 December 1919. Today's equivalent of £1,200 = c $A70,000.

5. 'News from the Recording Theatre' in *Voice*, Vol.4, No.3, March 1920. The Gramophone Co. monthly magazine *The Voice* was established in January 1917. Though a popular source of information about the company today, it was a promotional trade publication and therefore is only relatively reliable.

6. Dawson, 1951, p.92; EMI, *Voice*, November 1920: 'Tetrazzini concert last season'.

7. Dawson, 1951, p.134. '[The Barbers Song] is the easiest to sing, as it comes tripping off the tongue, and I revel in it.'

8. EMI, *Voice*, October 1920. Photograph held courtesy of PDAS.

9. EMI, 26 May 1985, recorded 26 May 1920. One title is a duet with Violet Essex.

10. Dawson, 'Thirty Years of Record Making' in the *Gramophone,* 1933, p.315.

11. Among others: Gelatt, 1977, p.163; Dawson, 1951, p.96; Burgis, 1981. The original and blow-up of a section sighted at EMI archives 1992.

12. J.N. Moore, 1977, pp.173–74.

13. Boult, 'Making the Records', in the *Gramophone Jubilee Book*, 1973, p.15 paraphrased. The young Boult was assigned to the first ballet recordings in 1919.

14. *Daily Chronicle*, 'Recording Room Secrets', London, 11 September 1928.

15. W. Booth & A. Ziegler, *Duet*. London: Stanley Paul 1951, pp.52–53, 86–87. This is supported by EMI Librarian, 16 July 1992.

16. First Violin part signed 'Peter Dawson London 1914'.

17. For example: 'Chant of Bacchus' (1920); 'Heart of the Romany Rye' (1923); 'Boots' (1928); 'Westward Ho!' (1933); 'Deep-Sea Mariner' (1934); 'Old Kettledrum' (1937); 'Lasseter's Last Ride' (1950).

18. MS5030/3/25: M & J. Robarts, 2 May 1957.

19. *Daily News*, Perth, 1 October 1931.

20. Correspondence from Stuart Booty, naturopath, friend of the Dawsons, to a distant cousin, when Dawson was in NZ late 1949: 'Mrs Dawson has been left in my care (she is a diabetic) whilst he's away.'

21. Letter from Dawson, 1 February 1921, held EMI.

22. MS5030/8/186: India album, 1921, Dawson handwritten.

23. Dawson, 1951, p.99ff. EMI, *Voice*, March 1920, 'constant globe-trotter' – 'India, Ceylon, Straits Settlements and Burma'; *AMN*, September 1921, p.45, Notes from Ceylon: 'full season of music April to July', 'has given eight recitals in Ceylon'. The Straits Settlements – Singapore, Malacca, and Penang – were a British Crown Colony, as distinct from the Federated Malay States, which were under British protection.

24. *Talking Machine Review* No.70, UK 1985.

25. An undated programme printed in Madras. Although this programme was for Madras, it would have been repeated elsewhere. Dawson does not mention Selwyn Driver in correspondence, nor is he identified in any of the photographs. He was born in Leamington in 1879, was a member of the Savage Club and composed 'Songs at the Piano'. He toured India, China, Malaya, Australia and New Zealand; and appears to have been working in India when Dawson was there.

26. *Daily Chronicle*, London, 24 November 1926. English newspaper, n.d., MS5030/15/box 6/folder 24, sent by Ron Hughes, PDAS; Walsh, January 1962 quoting Meadmore, 1935: 'I've toured Australia and New Zealand seven times, South Africa three and I've also sung in India, Burmah, the Straits Settlements, and China and Japan.' Hughes comments: 'Would it mean Hong Kong or Shanghai for China? Or visited as a tourist?' There is no evidence he ever got to Singapore.

27. 9 September 1921.

28. The two files of Gramophone Company recording sheets from 1922–25 indicate that as well as a variety of solo numbers he continued to sing duets and ensembles. For example, on 2 July 1923 he sang in the chorus backing Chaliapin in Moussorgsky's 'Death of Boris', from *Boris Godounov*.

29. J.N. Moore, 1977, p.77.

30. Dawson, 1951, p.94.

31. As programme, 23 January 1922. We may assume there were many encores too, not necessarily from opera. As was quite common at the time, German opera, in this case *Martha*, was sung in Italian.

32. Obituary, *Woman's Day*, Sydney, 16 October 1961.

33. BBC/AC, 14 November 1922. Information on BBC from Written Archives Centre, Caversham. S. Goslich, 'Broadcasting', in *New Grove*, 1980, gives Thursday 16 November.

34. MS5030/8/146i, ii: photograph; 'A Mighty Man of Song', *Radio Times*, London, 26 August 1955.

35. BBC/AC, 26 January 1923. Malcolm McEachern, (1883-1945) in Brisbane, 1991, p.156: 'Two young Australians who had yet to leave the country made strong impressions in Sydney in August 1908 … W.M. McEachern revealed an excellent bass voice and made a successful debut. This was Malcolm McEachern who many years later, as half of the Flotsam & Jetsam duo, made a famous recording "Is 'E an Aussie, Lizzie?"' (p.179. 'Is 'E an Aussie' was recorded in London on 20 October 1939). The bass M.M. sang in Tivoli theatres in 1917; p.201: 'By 1930 many local and expatriate performers could be heard on discs, not all

recorded here. They included: ... Malcolm McEachern.'

36.   *Radio Times*, London, 26 August 1955. BBC, 26 January 1923, confirms he sang Bedford's 'Ships That Pass In The Night' unaccompanied, followed by Lohr's 'Star Of The East' (accompanied!), which Dawson had recorded for HMV ten days earlier. Herbert Bedford, the husband of Liza Lehmann, had conducted the 1908 concert tour.

37.   Dawson, 1951 and elsewhere; confirmed in Dawson's obituary, *Woman's Day*, Sydney, 16 October 1961.

38.   SSA, MS5030/music folio K.

39.   S. Goslich, 'Broadcasting' in *New Grove*, 1980.

40.   His name only appeared 'among others' in a carol concert from the Royal Albert Hall on 20 December 1924; and on 25 April 1925 as soloist with the Barclays Bank Male Voice Choir, for whom he sang 'Phyllis' (Anthony Young), 'I'll sail upon the Dog-star' (Purcell) and 'Recognition of the Land' (Grieg).

41.   See *Who's Who in Australia* and obituary in *Sydney Morning Herald* 1967 which refers to her as 'Contralto Madame Lily Payling'. She was the same age as Amy Castles, i.e. two years older than Peter Dawson.

42.   Dawson, 1951, p.110 ff.

43.   D. Hickey & J. Doherty, *Irish History since 1800*. Totowa, N.J.: Barnes 1980; J. Doherty & D. Hickey, *A Chronology of Irish History*. Dublin: Gill & Hamilton Malcolm 1989; R.F. Foster, *Modern Ireland 1600-1972*. London: Allen Lane 1988.

44.   G. Moore, 1962, p.38.

45.   G. Moore, handwritten, to PDAS, 1961.

46.   Walsh, January 1962, from Meadmore, 1935.

47.   Dawson, 1951, p.191.

48.   For example, programmes of *Peter Dawson's Concert Tour*, managed by Harold C. Lloyd, 1924; concert in aid of St Anthony's Orphanage, Grimsby, 1 January 1924; also Nan's diary. Their relationship was much longer and more complex than either of their memoirs would suggest.

49.   Nan always writes 'Rider'. Sometimes these meetings are called lessons, sometimes practice.

50.   SSA, MS5030/15/box 6/folder 24/envelope 3. Only this programme is detailed in his book: 'Sei mir gegrüsst' (My Greetings), 'Erstarrung' (Frozen), 'Wasserfluth' (Flood), 'Die Krähe' (The Crow), 'Ungeduld' (Impatience), 'Die Mainacht' (May Night) 'Botschaft' (Message). 'Ständchen' (Serenade), 'Der Tod, das ist die kühle Nacht' (Death is like a cool night), 'Blinde Kuh' (Blind Cow [a children's game]), 'Nun wandre Maria' ([Joseph says to Mary] Keep walking Mary [we'll soon be there]), 'Verschwiegene Liebe' (Secret Love), 'Frühlingsnacht' (A Night in Spring), 'Du bist so jung' (You are so young) 'Traum durch die Dämmerung' (Dreaming at twilight).

51.   From Dawson, but here from *Daily Telegraph*, 'Last Song of Peter Dawson', Sydney, 7 July 1956; and *Daily Telegraph Mirror*, 'The Enduring Peter Dawson', Sydney, 23 August 1991.

52.   *Daily Chronicle*, 'British Songs for Britain', London, 17 June 1927; repeated verbatim in *AMN*, May 1933, pp.10–11; surprisingly similar in Dawson, 1951, p.187.

53.   EMI, August 1937, *Voice*, 'Peter the Practical Joker'; and Dawson, 1951, p.129 combined.

54.   For example *Mercury*, Hobart, January 1962: 'in 1923 earned £23000' taken from earlier standard *Reuters* biography; also *Daily Telegraph Mirror*, Sydney, 23 August 1991.

55.   G. Moore, 1962, pp.59–60. *Sunday Times*, 'Gerald Moore', London, 18 October 1953: 'The first gramophone records (the singer was Peter Dawson) appeared in the early twenties'; Moore, handwritten, c.1961 to PDAS: 'It was Peter Dawson with whom I made my first records'. Renée Chemet, see also Tetrazzini concert 20 September 1919.

56.   Recorded 5 January 1925.

57.   J.N. Moore, 1977, p.174.

CHAPTER 8: 1925–1931

1.   J.N. Moore, 1977, Gelatt, 1977, and *Gramophone Jubilee Book*, 1973, pp.28, 53. The recording,
      American Columbia No. 50013–D, featured 850 voices from 15 glee clubs and an audience
      of 4,000. Some sources say that the Gramophone Co. promoted the demonstration, but, as
      the product was from Columbia, it seems more likely that Columbia would have taken the
      initiative.

2.   Vose, 1987, pp.124–25.

3.   Dawson, 1951, pp.96–97; Dawson also in *People*, Sydney, 25 April 1951; reported in *M(anchester)
      Post*, 26 January 1926. Walsh, 1962, taken from Dawson, 1951.

4.   Hospital report from Ward 16 Register No. 9218, handwritten in Dawson address book. The
      entry for 4 October 1925 refers to 'Morphia'; entry 5 October 1925 specifies 'Gangrene';
      entry 6 October 1925 prescribes 'Gangrene serum 100cc'; and later 'Gangrene serum 50cc';
      'Morphia 1/6 gr' until 15 October; entry 16 October:

> Ether – Incisions round leg 3" or 4" above and below the heel of the
> wound on [?] aspect of thigh down to the mussell – Intervening skin
> and superficial structure removed in muss – all blood clots, torn and
> bruised pieces of mussell removed $-^{HC}/_2$ injected freely into the
> mussels and surrounding tissues, dressings; Four fractured ribs, fractured
> left [?] – Scapular [?] 4547–25; Head wounds.

5.   EMI board minute 11 November 1925: 'We shall be extremely glad if you will make a
      special effort to rush this contract through.' The accountants put the payment through on
      25 December.

6.   Dawson, 1951, pp.128–129.

7.   *Daily Express,* London, 11 May 1932.

8.   EMI, 9 September 1925.

9.   Gale Pedrick, 'A Mighty Man of Song', in *Radio Times*, London, 26 August 1955. Pedrick was
      using some licence as Dawson's only *Elijah* recordings were in 1905 and 1907.

10.   Walsh, 1962.

11.   Dawson, 1951, p.33, photograph.

12.   G. Moore, correspondence with PDAS c.1961.

13.   Booth & Ziegler, 1951, pp.52–53, 86–87. The tenor, Webster Booth and soprano, Anne
      Ziegler were married. They were the most famous 'romantic couple' of their era.

14.   Photos, Vose, 1987, p. 62, p. 127.

15.   SSA, MS5030/15/box 6/folder 24: unidentified newspaper 8 April 1926. Ada Crossley
      (1871-1929) 'One of the greatest oratorio contraltos of her time', was renowned for her
      encouragement of fellow-Australian artists. She made her London debut in 1895, toured
      USA 1902-03 where she was the first musician to have a record issued in the *Victor* 'red seal'
      series. Toured Australia with Percy Grainger 1903-04 and 1908-09. See Glennon, 1978, W.
      Bebbington, (ed.) *Oxford Companion to Australian Music*. Melbourne, OUP 1997. Gertrude
      Johnson OBE (1894–1973) was a protegée of Melba. She became principal soprano at
      Covent Garden, BNOC; was first to broadcast opera for BBC; recorded for Columbia and
      Regal in England. In 1935 she returned to Melbourne. Founded the National Theatre
      Movement of Australia from 1936; and was influential in the beginnings of the Australian
      Opera. See *Who's Who in Australia*, 1959 and Bebbington, 1997. May Brahe (1884–1956) had
      a prolific and successful career in Britain as a songwriter; most famous for 'Bless This
      House'.

16.   Gladys Moncrieff, 'The Peter Dawson I Knew', obituary in *Woman's Day*, Sydney 16 October
      1961.

17.   Sir Henry continued to conduct at the Queen's Hall until it was destroyed by a German
      incendiary bomb on the evening of 23 May 1941. Information here from J.R. Wrigley,

'Queen's Hall London: An affectionate Tribute', in *Historic Record*, No.46, January 1998.

18. The Tuesday after Dawson's concert a 26-year old from Geelong, John Brownlee, was there, putting his foot on the bottom rung of the ladder of fame.

19. Dawson, 1951, pp.67–68; Blaikley, 'Ballad Concerts', *New Grove,* 1980: 'The new Queen's Hall was leased by [Chappell], which ran the Promenade Concerts there from 1915 until 1926 when the BBC took over their management.' The commercial British Broadcasting Company was nationalised to become British Broadcasting Corporation in 1927. Retained the same acronym. The Proms were taken over by the Corporation in 1927.

20. Any altercation is more likely to have occurred at rehearsal.

21. Dawson, 1951, pp.153–156. MS5030/music folio B: 'Boots', J.P. McCall, London: Chappell, 1928. Dawson writes 'duly published by Swan …'.

22. This recording of 'Boots' has remained in the EMI catalogue somewhere in the world continuously, either as 78rpm, LP or CD, for more than 70 years. Although it was normal practice to try to emulate the success of a 'hit song' only two – unsuccessful – attempts were made: English Columbia made a version with Raymond Newell in 1929, American Columbia produced a version with Nelson Eddy in 1942. Dawson became identified with the song. On the BBC television programme, *Music Makers,* 4 September 1947, he was introduced by 'Boots, McCall, play-in 25".' The manuscript (M55030, music folio K) is marked 'entrance & Bowing Music for Boots. To be repeated at Conductor's discretion'.

23. Rudyard Kipling (1865–1936) received the Nobel Prize for literature in 1907. Many settings of Kipling texts appear in Peter Dawson's repertoire: 'Danny Deever', 'Kangaroo & Dingo', 'Rolling Down to Rio', 'A Smuggler's Song', several settings of 'Mandalay', and among Dawson's own compositions 'Cells', 1930; 'Route Marchin'', 1930; 'The Ladies', Dawson mss, n.d.

24. Latent ideas of independence and republicanism may have been fuelled by American soldiers during World War II, but not for Dawson: on 10 March 1961 he wrote to James Tierney: 'Attacks on royalty – Margaret & her husband – the Aussie Press is the worlds worst, sons of blasted convicts & champion American boot-lickers.'

25. *Daily Express,* 'Topicality in Records' London, 23 March 1929: mentions Gracie Fields and carries a contemporary photo of Peter Dawson: 'in the more modern and light-hearted sections of the new lists I notice we have Peter Dawson singing "Hinton, Dinton, and Mere" (HMV) a cheery ballad of the "rollicking baritone" type, with "Curtain Falls", a rather sombre affair, on the other side.'

26. Fred Gaisberg, 1946, p.176. Also referred to by William James, Peter Dawson obituary, *Woman's Day,* Sydney, 16 October 1961: 'using the great Russian's gestures and mannerisms, even singing like him'.

27. Chaliapin anecdotes, Dawson, 1951, pp.124–26, 131.

28. Concerts on Tuesday 30 October, the afternoon of Saturday 10 November, Thursday 13 December. Extant text MS5030/music folio C. Original song dedicated to H. Plunket Greene. Arthur Somervell (1863-1937) was knighted in 1929.

29. 'Come into the garden Maud' had been set by Balfe in 1858. The recording of this 'Come into the garden Maud', sung by John McCormack for Victor in New York in 1915, stayed in the catalogue for over 30 years.

30. Also in Dawson, 1951, p.113 as 'that happy home at Templeogue'.

31. MS5030/4/12, n.d: Dawson, 1929, programme stuck together. Dawson, 1951, pp.111–112.

32. EMI, 11 November 1925, board minute: 'Sullivan & Carte, <u>Gilbert & Sullivan Opera</u>, payment of £5.5.0 each to Sullivan & Carte for supervising each rehearsal and recording performance, plus reasonable out-of-pocket expenses'. This was the meeting that approved Dawson's bonus.

33. These recordings were outside Dawson's normal contract. He was paid an extra £100 each for the 1929 recordings (=2000, c. $A4,000.)

34. *Gramophone Jubilee Book,* 1973, p.79.

35.   Dawson, 1951, p. 131 ff.
36.   Dawson, correspondence with 'Javal', EMI, 5 June 1929, 8 July 1929, 27 July 1929.
37.   *Encyclopedia Britannica*, 'Motion Pictures'; *dtv Encyklopedea*, 'Cinema': from 1930 silent films were a thing of the past. The first English talkies, *Kitty* (half-sound) and Hitchcock's *Blackmail* (all sound), were produced by British International Pictures (BIP) about 1929 with musical scores by Hubert Bath of the Carl Rosa Opera Company, who had conducted Gramophone Company studio orchestras for Peter Dawson in 1919. As early as 1905 the Gramophone Company had been associated with Gaumont Chronophone Films, which produced 'Sound' shorts, an attempt to synchronise gramophone discs with moving images. Dennis Gifford's *British Film Catalogue (1895–1985)*, Newton Abbot: David & Charles, 1986, lists G&T recordings used in Gaumont Films:

01700	The Fireman	Hamilton Hill	16.9.1905
01705	The Bedouin's Love Song	Peter Dawson	21.2.1905
01712	Wait Till the Work Comes Round	Gus Ellen	4.9.1906
01713	Cupid	Ernie Mayne	19.9.1905

    Hamilton Hill (1873-1910), baritone, born in Bendigo, Victoria. From 1903–1910 he recorded more than 350 titles for a variety of cylinder and disc companies. Dawson's November 1929 recording of 'Journey's End' was used as background to the mounting tension of men dying in French trenches in the 1930 Gainsborough film of the same name.
38.   EMI correspondence 18 May 1998 – referring to Javal 1929, concludes: 'The letters of recommendation were perhaps when Dawson was seeking alternative work as his career failed in the U.K. He did, I believe, return to Australia on more than one occasion to "launch" his career.'
39.   MS5030/8/3-6. EMI hold negative H104/2 [Harrods] stamped 100742. Smoking photo can be seen, for example, in advertisement, Melbourne Programmes 1&2, 1931; Scott, 1979, pp.180–182.
40.   EMI, 26 November 1929: Dawson to Mr Dines of Gramophone Co. There was a new machine photo for the 1931 Australasia tour, for the 1933 tour, and in 1934 he even made a spoken recording backed by a snippet of 'The Floral Dance'.
41.   Ann is now Ann Jacquet living in Sydney. She has helped us document much of the Noble family history. Her father, Montgomery (Mont) Gilbert appears in many family photos with Dawson, often larking about together.
42.   Sir Donald Bradman to Colin Slater, Canberra, 8 July 1988.
43.   Don Bradman had been talked into recording this 'friendly chat' by his baritone friend and Columbia artist, Harold Williams. It took place on 18 September, 1930 when Bradman recorded 'Old-Fashioned Locket' and 'Our Bungalow of Dreams'. When Bradman returned to Australia Davis & Co. of Sydney published his composition 'Every Day is a Rainbow Day' to words by Jack Lumsdaine.
44.   As mentioned in Note 19, initially BBC meant the private British Broadcasting Company; it changed to the British Broadcasting Corporation when nationalised in 1927. Dawson had a long association with the British Broadcasting Corporation but he had been singularly absent from British Broadcasting Company programming; possibly because one pivotal administrator favoured Columbia artists.
45.   Programme: 'London's High-Speed Variety Theatre: Sets the Vaudeville Pace for the World'.
46.   Dawson, 1951, p.175 among others. £250 in 2000 terms = c. £3,500 pw. We believe that Dawson actually appeared at the Palladium *before* 1930. *Voice*, April 1926, listed Dawson for the Palladium on 2 April, two days before the Dublin concert – a bit of rush by boat and train! According to Ian Bevan's *The Story of the Palladium*, 1952, at that time the Palladium producer, Harry Day, did fill in the gaps between major productions with weekly variety bills. Although Dawson was listed for one performance, not a week, 2 April would fit neatly between a four-month run of *Folies Bergère* and 102 performances of *Cinderella*. So

other performances before 1930 cannot be excluded.

47. Programmes: 29 September, 1 December 1930. Artists appeared from Monday to Sunday, twice nightly (6.30 pm & 9 pm) plus matinees on Tuesday and Thursday at 2.30pm: a total of 16 performances a week.

48. MS5030/15/box 6/folder 24; *Daily Sketch*, London, 4 October 1930.

49. Mozart's aria became so popular during the composer's lifetime that he parodied it himself in *Don Giovanni*. BBC, 2 December 1930: Peter Dawson: Song Recital from the Palladium with a Mr Johnson as accompanist. Gerald Moore was officially programmed.

50. Programme, 6 June 1931; tour advertisement for Melbourne season c. May/June 1931; newspaper, 22 September 1931.

51. EMI, April 1931, *Voice*; ref also EMI, *Voice*, January 1948.

52. EMI, 9 March 1931.

53. *Daily Express*, London, 18 November 1931. George Baker (1885-1976) made his recording debut with Pathé in 1909, recorded for *Zonophone* and *Columbia* in 1913 then *HMV* in 1916. His last recording was for a stereo G&S LP in 1961. His recorded repertoire was as varied as Dawson's and he worked for as many disc companies, often under pseudonyms. Claims for his record output appear exaggerated; more likely about half the publicity estimates. Despite his long and successful career, neither his record sales nor his notoriety matched Dawson's.

54. MS5030/4/23.

55. Moss, 1978, pp.294-5; Barnard, 1963, p.543 'gave legal form to the Balfour Declaration of 1926'.

56. EMI, 16 April 1931.

57. EMI, 25 February 1931: agreed, provided that the break-even sales of 'Four thousand five hundred ten inch Plum records' could be guaranteed. See also EMI, 6 March 1931; 16 April 1931. The numbers, backed by a male quartet, were recorded on 24 March, a week before Peter Dawson sailed.

58. Programmes; *AMN*, March 1931; Perth, *Daily News*, 1 October 1931; *People*, Sydney, 25 April 1951.

59. *AMN*, April 1931, p.7; *AMN*, May 1931, pp.10–11; advertisement, Perth, 26 September 1931.

60. Mark Hambourg, 51, 'Russian born child prodigy', married to 'Dorothea Mackenzie, daughter of Lord Muir Mackenzie'. Mark Hambourg was already an established artist when Dawson first arrived from Australia in 1902. He had toured Australia as a teenager in 1895 and again in 1903. He had also been associated with Dawson on other occasions, e.g., advertisement Town Hall Oxford, Friday 23 November 23 at 8pm. Peter Dawson (photo), Albert Sammons and Mark Hambourg (as silhouettes), accompanist Gerald Moore.

61. MS5030/7/161, photograph from *Courier Mail*, 16 May 1931: with Kingsford-Smith; autographs of each person; MS5030/5/3, photograph, 7 July 1931: with Lord & Lady Bledisloe; MS5030/5/1, postcard, 8 July 1931: Bledisloe to Dawson at Hotel George, Wellington.

62. *Advertiser*, Adelaide, 19 September 1931.

63. *Advertiser*, Adelaide, 22 September 1931; *Listener In* Vol 7 No. 25, 29 August 1931; EMI, *Voice*, April 1931.

64. Menu, 1931: the framed menu with 29 signatures – not the total number of persons named as present – could be seen on the 1st Floor, ABC building, Collinswood, Adelaide, 1991. Many of the personalities were also caricatured in the Maegraith booklet *Who's Who in Adelaide: Well-known people caricatured by Kerwin Maegraith*, 'Published by Advertiser Newspapers Limited, in aid of The Lord Mayor's Unemployment Fund, sales, no deductions, straight to fund, cost 1/–.' This booklet (c.1930) predates the dinner. Although the menu thanks '*The Bulletin* for permission to use caricatures of our guests', a similar booklet published by Maegraith in 1933 carries the note: 'Peter Dawson sketched during his recent tour of his native Australia for the *Sketch*', that is, the 1931 tour. This cartoon held MS5030/6/21c.

65. From the Cantata *Wachet, betet* (1716) – as he was wont to write on each programme. This

became one of his most enduring standard opening numbers.

66. *People*, Sydney, 25 April 1951: Peter Dawson said he had sung it all over the place since 1912. The story of 'Edward' from the *Manchester Guardian* of 8 September 1922 was pasted on the inside front cover of his copy, which had been torn out of a Loewe Album No.1, Braunschweig, edition Litolff, No. 2241A. Although Peter Dawson sang 'Edward' at many concerts, it seems he never recorded it.

67. Peter Dawson had announced his encores with the names of the poets. 'Boots' was composed by J.P. McCall – as we are well aware; the often-featured 'A Banjo Song' is by Sidney Homer.

68. Taken from *Music in Australia*, 20 June 1931; *AMN*, July 1931; *West Australian*, Perth, 4 October 1931.

69. *Music in Australia*, 31 July 1931.

70. These are Dawson's figures. Ticket prices were 7/6, 5/– and 3/–. Taking an 'average price' as 5/– the team would have needed to draw average houses of 1600 per concert; for 60 concerts 96,000, say 100,000 paying customers.

CHAPTER 9: 1932–1939

1. MS5030/8/162: Dawson, handwritten.

2. *AMN*, February 1932. Dawson may have written to *AMN* at Christmas but BBC programmes prove that he was in London at the time.

3. *People*, Sydney, 24 April 1951; *Daily Telegraph Mirror*, Sydney, 23 August 1991. Story turned into direct speech. This was their only international trip together. South African sources could not trace any concerts at this time.

4. J.N. Moore, 1977, photo XII, opp. p.169.

5. 'Bells & Hobbles', 5 January, Studio 1; 'Song of Australia', 24 February, Studio 2. Songs recorded on *HMV EA* series were for Australia only.

6. In Dawson, 1951, p.133, the year is incorrect. Dawson attributed the words of these songs to 'a young assistant at Chappell's', who 'set them to some of the fine old tunes played by military bands'; but the labels credit Javaloyes, Bidgood, Starke and Payne.

7. Stanford's *Songs of the Sea* published Boosey, 1904. Dawson first recorded the cycle in early 1928 but he would have performed it much earlier.

8. Byng used an orchestra of 19 on 16 February 1931. Something must have happened to the master because Collingwood used the same arrangement but with 27 players. Both recordings were issued as HMV B–3812. It is difficult to tell the two apart, especially as neither conductor received label credit.

9. F. Gaisberg, *Music on Record*. London: Hale 1946. (Ref also p. 34: Byng named on *Alhambra* programme.)

10. Dawson was supported by Charlie Higgins (Lancashire Comedian), the Six Henriette Fuller Dancers, The Cycling Astons, Gordon Freeman (the world's worst inventor), and Anna Roth and Lew Grade (Specialty Dancers). Lew Grade and his brother Bernard Delfont – later Lord Grade and Lord Delfont – moved from vaudeville hoofing to become the most powerful agents in London with an empire of show business interests and associated activities. In 1964 they took over two great theatrical chains, Stoll and Moss Empire Theatres.

11. MS5030/music folio N: 'Westward Ho! or The Pirate Goes West', music: J.P. McCall, words: Lockwood Moore. London: Swan, 1933. Dawson used either title in his programmes.

12. Dawson documents held privately. The letter is typed, the signature illegible, but it could be Bowker Andrews. Dawson mentioned him in connection with the publication of 'Boots' and he organised the 1935 tour to South Africa.

13. Dawson, 10 March 1961, to Tierney: (see also extended quote in final chapter).

14. J. Cooper, 'Gerald Moore' in *Dictionary of National Biography, 1986-1990*, Oxford: OUP, 1996.

15. February 1975.

16. J.&N. Tait, previously solely concert promoters, set up in opposition to J.C. Williamson's following the founder's death in 1913. The companies amalgamated in 1920.

17. Concerts usually Tuesday, Thursday, Friday, Saturday.

18. £66/13/4 = 2000 equivalent £880, c. $A2,200 per concert (on which he had to 'pay his own Income-Tax'). The claim that the Hambourg/Dawson 1931 tour averaged £400 per concert, i.e. £200 each now sounds excessive.

19. Correspondence E. Juan Dzazopulos, 8 April 1993: (paraphrased) Arnaldo Tapia Caballero (1907–) Chilean pianist, specialist in Debussy. Tapia: father's family name; Caballero: mother's family name. At 14 he received degree of Professor of Piano; 1930 to London; 1931 first Wigmore Hall recital; 1933 Australian tour. He lived in Vienna until WWII; USA debut 1949, Carnegie Hall; 1956, 1960–85.

20. MS5030/music folio I: 'Old Father Thames', music: Betsy O'Hogan, words: Raymond Wallace, London: Wright, 1933. O'Hogan was a pseudonym used, this once only, by composer-publisher Lawrence Wright, who had an enormous output of popular songs.

21. Bradman had recaptured the Ashes the month the article was published. 'Victorian monarch' is a bit unsettling as Bradman played for NSW (1927–34), SA (1935–49), Australia (1928–48). Amy Johnson was, in fact, a Yorkshire lass.

22. Practical because it was the first port of call in Australia, but the contract had said Melbourne or Sydney.

23. MS5030/8/196, *Advertiser*, Adelaide, 28 April 1933, and photographs.

24. Official War History, Canberra, AWM43: *Reveille*, Sydney, June 1931 and August 1933.

25. *AMN*, August 1933.

26. Tapia Caballero had not yet earned the reputation of Mark Hambourg. He had made no gramophone records. The programmes tell us little about him and a lot about Dawson: in Perth he was even introduced as 'the Celebrated Spanish Pianist'.

27. Claude Kingston, letter to Dawson, 17 August 1933. Kingston wrote a book of memoirs of great artists who toured for the Taits. He makes a deferential reference to the Scottish tenor, Joseph Hislop, who made the next tour, but omitted any reference to Dawson.

28. Also on Hotel Windsor notepaper. 'The "Mallee Root" went splendidly. The audience were quite interested.' 'The Mallee Root', Sydney: Palings, 1932. Photo of Peter Dawson on cover; 'Mr Peter Dawson' above title.

    Sound motion picture making in Australia was in its infancy. The only motion picture being made in Sydney at that time was the J.C. Williamson Picture Production, *The Hayseeds*, which started shooting at Cinesound's studio, Rushcutter's Bay in August – (opened Civic Theatre, Sydney 12 August 1933). It contained musical scenes to music of well-known English composer, Alf Lawrence, who was no doubt known to Peter Dawson. However, Dawson does not feature in the cast. If the Sydney offer came from another producer it did not eventuate.

29. In effect a summary of his popular repertoire. Keen observers will note some errors, omissions and repetitions.

30. EMI, 18 November 1933.

31. MS5030/4/22: Nan's copy, signed by those present.

32. 22 April 1998: correspondence Charles Gatty, author of *Luisa Tetrazzini, The Florentine Nightingale*, Aldershot: Scolar 1995.

33. 2000 = c. $A23,000.

34. A hot property like Gracie Fields only put down 55 sides in the two years 1933-34; Dawson put down 46 titles.

35. EMI, 7 November 1933, board minute. Dawson was contracted to earn £7,500 but there was a shortfall of £250 on the previous contract. Threat to go to another company an interesting bluff. The other major catalogues with separate stables of singers were *Columbia* and *Parlophone* but they were already under the EMI umbrella. The most likely was the fledgling

Decca Gramophone Co. formed in 1929, which absorbed Edison Bell in 1933.

36. EMI, 14 December 1933.

37. For the duet itself one voice was recorded with orchestra on 23 January; on 29 January the voice alone. Using a trick pioneered by Richard Tauber for Parlophone in 1933, the technicians then married the two versions. 'Floral Dance' review picked up by Walsh, 1961. 'Trees' and 'Little Prayer' EMI, 28 January 1935: publicity when records were sent to South African agents for Dawson's 1935 tour. Report on Alba Rizzi's funeral, *Daily Express*, London, 9 April 1950.

38. Dawson, 1951, pp.144–45. No programme was exclusive to German lieder. Lieder included in BBC broadcasts were: Beethoven: 'Adelaide' (28 July 1932); Brahms: 'Botschaft': (11 May 1932, 7 October 1934), 'Die Mainacht': (11 May 1932, 7 October 1934); 'O liebliche Wangen' (28 July 1932); Schubert: 'Du bist die Ruh' (29 January 1933); 'Sei mir gegrüsst': (29 January 1933, 7 October 1934); 'The Erl King' (16 November 1933); 'Erstarrung' (29 January 1933).

39. Vose, 1987, may have had access to BBC sources.

40. Herbert William Dawson, born London 1890, died 1976, organist and choirmaster, member of the Savage Club, first recorded with Dawson in October 1928 playing the Kingsway Hall organ. Played piano for the 1923 Payling concert. Made many records with Peter Dawson.

41. Correspondence to PDAS 14 January 1983; 18 October 1983.

42. Actually Löhr – usually anglicised as Lohr – to Dawson, 1 December 1934.

43. 27 January 1935.

44. Bowker Andrews: see note 11 about 'Westward Ho!' above.

45. His recording contract guarantee was £1,250. £1,115 in the year 2000 would be worth c£14,000, $A35,000.

46. MS5030/1/65-69, Dawson, handwritten, c.1952?

47. Dawson's membership, 10 February 1932. Nan joined the Ladies' Chapter.

48. May 1935, Primrose League: Lord Ebbisham, Chancellor; Sir Reginald Bennett, Vice Chancellor.

49. MS5030/4/17; MS5030/1/2; MS5030/1/3.

50. MS5030/7/42.

51. *Daily Sketch*, London, 6 August 1935.

52. *Daily Sketch*, London, 9 January 1934.

53. Dawson recording 5 January 1933: HMV B4405 in 1934 catalogue.

54. EMI, 8 June 1934.

55. EMI, 23 November 1935, 4 December 1935, 5 December 1935, 9 January 1936. For the first time a document, EMI, 4 December 1935, reveals that Tom Noble was Peter's manager. Dawson would write letters but Tom did the negotiating.

56. *Gramophone Jubilee Book*, 1973, p.192: 'Broadcasting Records'.

57. EMI, 18 December 1935, £1,500 + £500 pa, total £2,500, av. £1,250 = 2000 $A39,000 pa.

58. 'We Saw The Sea', 'There'll Be No South', and 'Saddle Your Blues To A Wild Mustang' were all recorded on one day, 26 March 1936. 'With A Shillelagh Under My Arm', manuscript, MS5030/music folio N. Reviews picked up by Walsh, June 1962.

59. Dawson, 1951, p.133.

60. Dawson's version of 'Empty Saddles' was recorded on 21 July 1936, one week after Bing Crosby had recorded the same number for Decca in Los Angeles.

61. W.A. McNair, *Radio Advertising in Australia*. Sydney: Angus & Robertson 1936. Richard Crooks' 'big lead in this particular survey is undoubtably due to the fact that he was in Sydney giving concerts at the time of the survey.'

62. MS5030/4/7: log book.

63. MS5030/13/348.

64. BBC/AC: 'Fri Sept 4 1936 TV 4.31–6.34 repeat programme of Aug 28 omitting film "First a Give" and incl: Peter Dawson (Bar.)'.

65. EMI, 13 July 1937. Only a few Australians who actually lived and worked in the United

States, like Marjorie Lawrence or John Brownlee, were successful there. Most Australians were drawn to London.

66. Permission EMI, 14 January 1937. *The Crazy Gang* comprised Nervo & Knox, Naughton & Gold, Flanagan & Allen. 'The Fleet's Not In Port Very Long' was sung with the Sherman Fisher Girls.

67. The drafts 'Written & Composed by Rover Peter Dawson' are dated November 1937. In the fourth draft the song was called 'The Sea is the Life for Me', the title under which it was published in 1938. The film was cut dramatically and re-issued in mid-1939.

68. EMI, 13 July 1937; from Peter Dawson EMI, 5 October 1937; EMI, 27 January 1938; 12 March 1938.

69. EMI, 3 February 1938.

70. EMI, 21 March 1938, Dawson to Sir Louis Sterling.

71. 10 November 1938. To get some relative idea of the the tax bill: £1,500 in 2000 would be about £17,000 or $A41,500. At '4/- in the £' Dawson today would have paid the equivalent of more than A$8,300 plus costs.

72. Dawson, 1951, p.159.

73. *Advertiser*, Adelaide, 2 October 1961, 'Wrong bar – the story of Waiata Poi', a posthumous Peter Dawson anecdote.

74. 1927: John Collinson, believed to be a Queenslander. It appeared on a 10in. *Vocalion* disc, No. X-10221, probably for export to Australia. 4 November 1930, Colin Crane, later Mr. Crump of ABC Radio's Village Glee Club, 1937: The Hill Billies' 'Waltzing Matilda' on *Regal-Zonophone* sold 2,312 copies in Australia between 1938-50; their biggest hit, 'Roll Along Covered Wagon', sold 23,000+ copies.

75. 'Matilda's Ghost', *Australian,* Sydney, 25 March 1995: 'Waltz of Words', *Australian Weekend Magazine*, Sydney, 1 April 1995:

76. T. Radic, 'Waltzing Matilda' in *New Oxford Companion to Music*, Oxford University Press 1984, 'wife of Scottish-born manager, William Cowan'.

77. Dawson, 1951, p.159. The extract prefaces the Oxford University Press publication: OUP noted as publisher in the recording ledgers.

78. BBC/AC, 14 January 1938.

79. *Advertiser*, Adelaide, 24 May 1939, 4 June 1939.

80. 'Old Kettledrum', London, Boosey, 1937; 'Fret Foot', London, Prowse, 1938; 'The 'Prentice Lads o' Cheap', London, Ashdown, 1938.

81.

Old Kettledrum	C major	G–E	$^4/_4$	tempo di marcia;
Fret-Foot	A minor	A–F	$^4/_4$	marziale;
'Prentice Lads	B^b	B^b–F	$^2/_4$	allegretto.

82. C.W.S. Male Voice Choir, Newcastle Branch, 17th Annual Concert, with Hubert Greenslade at the Piano.

83. While these names appear on manuscripts and concert programmes, several – Evelyn Bird, Gilbert Munday, Denton Toms and Charles Weber, for example – do not appear on discs, nor on APRA membership or Kenneth Snell's *Australian Popular Music Composer Index*, East Malvern: Quick Trick Press, 1991. We believe Dawson may have used other unacknowledged and unproven composer pseudonyms.

84. K.S. Inglis, *This is the ABC*. Melbourne University Press, 1983, p.45.

85. Inglis, 1983, p.68: 'He always enjoyed demonstrating his strength. In 1938 he was challenging other strong men to competition in tearing up telephone books.'

86. ABC/AA, 9 August 1951. In the case of 'Variety' the recommendation came from the federal director of variety. Information was also passed to other departments such as publicity and finance.

87. In his memoirs Dawson makes little reference to the ABC and none to Moses; in Inglis' highly regarded *This is the ABC* Dawson is mentioned only once – as one of many who spoke about Melba.

88. J. Davidson, *A Showman's Story: the Memoirs of Jim Davidson*, Adelaide: Rigby, 1983: 'In New Guinea I visited Moses in hospital and he urged me to rejoin the ABC as soon as the war was over as he would need a head of Variety – but by 1946 his affection seemed to have turned to disenchantment.'

89. The cautious publisher modified 'forced me out' to 'worked with me'.

90. William James was commonly known as 'Bill' but the memos from which our information is taken used the official 'William'.

91. To put the sum into a modern perspective: £300 sterling per week in 1938 = 2000 £3,800 pw or $A9,500; so 12 weeks would be c. $A114,000. To reiterate a former point, it is not possible to simply translate a sum from one period to the other: even after the war an income of £20 per week was above average; in 1938 terms that would only be c.$22,500 today. It indicates how high Peter Dawson's demands were.

92. ABC/AA, 23 November 1938.

93. ABC/AA, 26 November 1938.

94.

Contract Period	Royalty Advance	Earned	Unearned Balance	
1930–33	7500	4907	2592	(w/off Dec '33!)
1933–35	2500	861	1639	
1935–37	2500	659	1841	
current	350	45	305	
			6377	
[+] Loan Feb 1938			500	
Balance		(in red)	(£6877)	

95. EMI, 23 January 1939.

96. 2000 equivalent = c. $A7,800.

97. EMI, 21 January 1939.

98. J.N. Moore, 1977:

Sir Hugh Allen
Wilhelm Backhaus
John Barbirolli
Sir Thomas Beecham
Sir Adrian Boult
Adolf Busch
Fritz Busch
Pablo Casals
John Christie
Albert Coates
Alfred Cortot
Richard Crooks
Ben Davies
Peter Dawson
Ania Dorfmann
Edwin Fischer
Kirsten Flagstad
Sir George Franckenstein
Elena Gerhardt
Walter Gieseking
Beniamino Gigli
Eugene Goossens
James Gray

Sacha Guitry
Richard Haigh
Mark Hambourg
Jascha Heifetz
Myra Hess
Harold Holt
Edward Johnson
Serge Koussevitzky
Fritz Kreisler
A.T. Lack
Wanda Landowska
Sir Harry Lauder
Lotte Lehmann
Frida Leider
Compton Mackenzie
Sir Robert Mayer
Giovanni Martinelli
Jan Masaryk
Lauritz Melchior
Count John McCormack
Yehudi Menuhin
Ivor Novello

Ignaz Paderewski
Egon Petri
Yvonne Printemps
Sergei Rachmaninoff
Elisabeth Rethberg
Artur Rubinstein
Tito Schipa
Elisabeth Schumann
Rudolf Serkin
L.G. Sharpe
Artur Schnabel
Malcolm Sargent
Herbert Sinclair
Christopher Stone
Leopold Stokowski
Georg Szell
Luisa Tetrazzini
Lawrence Tibbett
John Tillett
Bruno Walter
Felix Weingartner
Vaughan Williams
Sir Henry J. Wood

99. MS5030/8/190–195: photographs.

CHAPTER 10: 1939-1947

1. ABC/AA, 6 January 1939. Dawson is referring to Moses' letter of 10 December 1938, (see also previous chapter p. 160).

2. These 'celebrity' singers were profiled in *ABC Annual 1939*; five Australian women singers lumped together in one paragraph.

3. ABC/AA, 26 January 1939, 11 February 1939.

4. ABC/AA, 2 March 1939.

5. *Advertiser*, Adelaide, 31 May 1939.

6. ABC/AA, *Mail*, 10 June 1939.

7. Inglis, 1983, p.66. ABC/AA, 28 September 1939.

8. ABC/AA, 2 May, 28 September, 11 October, 1939.

9. SSA series note: 'Launched Nov 7 1931 and running to Oct 1970 Cinesound Review was part of Cinesound Productions famous for its kangaroo logo and voice of commentator Charles Lawrence.' Cover No 28238; Series ID 138005; episode No.0396; segment 79448: 'Peter Dawson Arrival Perth 2 June 1939'. Note is incorrect: Dawson arrived in May; tour began in Sydney 2 June.

10. *Advertiser*, Adelaide, 31 March, 24 May, 29 May, 4 June 1939; programme, June 1939.

11. For *Voice of the Voyager* on GUT affiliate, Melbourne's 3KZ.

12. ABC/AA, 17 June 1939, *Radio Times*, Letter to the Editor.

13. *Wireless Weekly*, 31 May 1939; *Radio Times*, 3 June; *Broadcasting Business*, 8 June, 15 June.

14. The Christmas letter, 'written from South Africa' 1931, (discussed in text Chapter 9, p. 137), appeared in *AMN* February 1932.

15. Brisbane, 1991, p.244. Kenneth Neate, 14 June 1984, wrote: 'Peter … was over 60: he sang without michrophone "Largo al factotem", "The Lute Player", "Old Man River", "Old Father Thames", "There'll always be an England" etc.'

16. Inglis, 1983, p.78.

17. Based on Barnard, 1963, p.565.

18. Family tree, 21 January 1996, 'the name is still decipherable today'; interview with nephews, 25 March 1993.

19. Dawson to Ted Hopgood, 4 October 1939, newspaper interview, 25 April 1951; B.V. Bennet, 1 May 1991: 'When Uncle Peter settled in Sydney his brother Will Dawson put him on his payroll as publicity officer to help finances'. 'Princely' is Dawson's phrase, implying 'not much', but £624 p.a. was an adequate executive salary at the time.

20. Brisbane, 1991, p.251.

21. *Allan's Music Edition* 22, Melbourne, c.1950 p.68. Full text of the three songs in Dawson, 1951, pp.163–165.

22. *AMN*, August 1940, p.18. Brisbane, 1991, p.251, quoting *Bulletin*.

23. MS5030/3/71a; MS5030/3/71b: 2 June 1940; in *Women's Weekly*. Vol.8, No.4, p.5, 29 June 1940.

24. *Evening News*, London, 30 October 1939.

25. Confirmed EMI, 29 July 1941. Local content was chosen by producer, Arch Kerr, to comply with government orders and broadcasting needs. Dawson was accompanied by Brian Lawrance and his Orchestra. Lawrance, an Australian, successful in London 1932-40 as a 'hot fiddler' and vocalist, was also forced to return to Australia by the outbreak of war. Later ABC music producer.

26. The 1940 ABC Orchestral Season booklet began: 'The ABC is proud to announce its decision to follow the Prime Minister's "Business as usual" slogan during the war'. There were ten conductors, 15 instrumentalists and six singers: the other singers were Maria Markan, Lord Lurgan, Lawrence Power and his wife, Annunciata Garrotto, who were returning home.

27. Today's equivalent = c.$A20,000; or c. $1,667 per broadcast. ABC counter offer was $16,000+, $1,333+ per week.
28. ABC/AA, 24 August 1940.
29. ABC/AA, 30 July 1940, 8 August 1940.
30. Inglis, 1983, p.45.
31. ABC/AA, 1940, pp.11, 22.
32. 'V for Victory', published by Chappell's towards the end of 1941. Dawson copy: MS5030/ music folio L. Dawson later revealed (Dawson, 1951, p.62) that the words had been cobbled together by himself and the Lord Mayor. Words and announcement from MS5030.
33. Barnard, 1963, p.558.
34. The substitution of 'Advance Australia Fair' for 'The British Grenadiers' caused a flurry of letters to the CEO, Bearup, complaining that 'Advance Australia Fair' belonged only to NSW. Dawson (Dawson, 1951, p.166) had hoped that the South Australian composition, 'Song of Australia' (Carl Linger, 1858) would be retained as the National Anthem; but due to 'strange inter-State jealousy … the basic reason why we had to create the capital at Canberra', a NSW composition, 'Advance Australia Fair', was receiving precedence. Etta Clark, 'Music in the Home' in McCredie, 1988, p.444ff: the popularity of Carl Linger's 'Song of Australia' can be seen from the numerous editions in which it appeared, several locally produced. 'Advance Australia Fair', 1878, was composed by Peter Dodds McCormick (1834-1916).
35. MS5030/7/53: newspaper, c.1943, 'Waltz by Wizards of Aus'. A clipping among Dawson's papers has no date or source. Article suggests an Australian newspaper of the time when American servicemen were stationed in Australia during WW2.
36. *People*, Sydney, 25 April 1951.
37. For example *Humphrey Bishop Presents*, which was heard throughout Australia. 16in. diameter 33rpm discs, giving half an hour's entertainment per record, would be shuttled from one radio station to the other by train. Humphrey Bishop, producer and compere, London-born (1884) bass, knew Dawson from earlier days.
38. ABC/AA, July 1941.
39. ABC/AA, 26 August 1941.
40. ABC/AA, 2 March 1942.
41. ABC/AA, 5, 6 March 1942.
42. Harold Williams (1893-1976): 'A baritone, teacher and broadcaster who brought credit to Australia'. At 26 he went to England and for 15 years was one of the leading soloists in opera, oratorio and recitals. He made regular appearances with British National Opera and Covent Garden and was famous as Mendelssohn's Elijah. Returned 1952 to become professor of singing at NSW Conservatorium of Music. (See Glennon, 1978; *AMN*, September 1949) Obituary *Sydney Morning Herald* 6 November 1976: 'At the height of his career [he] was as well-respected and well-known as Peter Dawson.'
43. Inglis, 1983, p.91: *Argonauts* launched 1941.
44. ABC/AA, 6 March 1942; 2 April 1942; 22 April 1942.
45. ABC/AA, 6 May 1942; 8 May 1942.
46. J.D.Vose, 1987, pp.80-86: recollecting in 1961, the conductor referred to the New Zealand Air Force Band. Peter Burgis, information booklet to *Peter Dawson, Ambassador of Song*, EMI/ National Library 1981, EMI OXLP7661–70; and correspondence sighted at ScreenSound Australia, dated recordings in Wellington on 1 June, in Auckland on 14 June and in Wellington again on 7 July; but Dawson was only in NZ for three weeks so these must be broadcast dates.
47. MS5030/8/171.
48. MS5030/1/65–69, Dawson, c.1946, handwritten. *British Australian*, 22 October 1948: '2 weeks'.
49. ABC/AA, 11 July 1942; Dawson to Senator Ashley, Postmaster General.
50. ABC/AA, 3 August 1942, from the acting general manager.
51. ABC/AA, 6, 7, 9, 21 April 1943.

52. Music folio A; music folio F; melody blocked out in ink, piano accompaniment not composed; words altered, melody altered in pencil; key signature on first stave of each of three pages only.

53. 'The Anzac House Song', published (sponsored) by Chappell's, had a photograph of Peter Dawson and Marjorie Lawrence on the front. Peter Truman is listed as a composer in Snell's 1971 APRA directory. No compositions are listed against his name but there is no indication that the name is a pseudonym.

54. MS5030/4/1.

55. Unfortunately, sales of these mainly Australian compositions on 12in. discs at 6/8d each were not inspirational:

The Lord is my Shepherd/ God Make Me Kind	HMV EB 208	303
Forsake Me Never/Thou, O Lord, Art My Shepherd	HMV EB 209	302
Star of Eve/Love Triumphant	HMV EB 224	354
The Cry of the Fighting Forces/Bring Back the Simple Faith HMV EB 225		311

56. On a 10in. disc, leading to greatly improved sales: 1,200 in ten years.

57. *Woman's Day*, Sydney, 16 October 1961.

58. ABC/AA, 16 April 1945, *Radio Pictorial*, publicity, 9 June 1945: 'Peter Dawson sings *Drakes Drum* Wed 6 June 415, Sat 315 Nat.'

59. MS5030/1/65–69: Dawson, handwritten; n.d.; c.1946.

60. 11 December 1946; entrepreneur, Begg's Celebrity Artists, an offshoot of Charles Begg & Co., Dunedin distributor of musical and electrical goods.

61. *Advertiser*, Adelaide, 4 July 1946; New Zealand *Listener,* 12 July 1946.

62. EMI, 10 September, 3 November, 9 November, 12 November 1945; 28 November 1946; 21 March 1947.

63. ABC/AA, 24 November and 25 November 1946.

64. ABC/AA, 30 January 1947.

CHAPTER 11: 1947—1955

1. With apologies to Hilaire Belloc, *Epigramophones* December 1929, in *Gramophone Jubilee Book,* 1973, p.52 – in original 'Prima Donna'.

2. *Daily Telegraph*, Sydney, 7 July 1956: Charles Buttrose, 'Last Song of Peter Dawson'. Melba was so renowned for making 'final' appearances that 'more (final) appearances than Nellie Melba' or 'more farewells than Melba' became colloquialisms.

3. *Times of Colombo*, Colombo, 5 August 1947; *Evening Standard*, London, 26 August 1947: 'to sing 140 concerts in a year here, which means … singing on average once every 56 hours'.

4. Poster.

5. Mrs Doris Walker of Swanage, Dorset, to PDAS, 1983.

6. *Sunday Despatch*, London, 26 March 1950: 'Peter Dawson Is "Broke",' also reported in *Sydney Morning Herald*, 27 March 1950: 'Peter Dawson says he is "broke".' Amount upon which tax was due: EMI, 28 November 1946, plus 5 December 1947 (£1,977/2/2 + £300/3/8; today would equal $A42,000+).

7. J.N. Moore, 1977; EMI, 4 July 1947, 8 July 1947; EMI 15 September 1947: original offer six titles per annum became six record sides in the contract.

8. 19 May 1948.

9. 'Wandering the King's Highway', published 1935, first recorded by Dawson in 1938, was one of the numbers advertised by Chappell's in 1939. Other songs of this type that Dawson recorded included: 'Comrades Of Mine' (James) recorded 1923; 'The Tramp' (Sawyer) 1924; 'I Travel The Road' (Thayer) 1931; 'Tramping Through The Countryside' (Allison) 1934; 'The Tramp's Song' (Gleeson) 1934; 'A Rolling Stone' (Gleeson) 1946.

10. As told to Peter Burgis by Harry Pringle. Noel Harry Lempriere Pringle (1903-1985), son of international Tasmanian bass, Harry Lempriere Pringle (1870–1914), had a long association with Dawson. Harry (jnr) was one of the original BBC TV producers. When it shut down for the war he returned to Australia to produce programmes for commercial radio. He rejoined BBC TV in 1946 but came back to Australia in 1956 to produce for TCN9 (now Channel 9).

11. BBC/AC 4 September 1947: Television (Music): *Music Makers*. Dawson was accompanied by Ernest Lush.

12. Mrs Thelma Smith wrote to PDAS in 1983 that she had sung in the choir on this occasion; and that Dawson replaced Richard Tauber who had fallen ill. (Tauber died in London soon after; on 8 January 1948.)

13. Extrapolated from Dawson diaries.

14. EMI, *Voice*, December 1948, EMI, 9 January 1949, EMI, 17 March 1949: Dawson left the modern instrument with Tom Noble, but the Trade Mark Model Gramophone was despatched to Australia on S.S. *Port Hobart*; 31 December 1948. Late in life Dawson was photographed beside it.

15. *British Australasian*, London, 22 October 1948.

16. *ABC Weekly*, Sydney, 5 February 1949; *AMN*, February 1949, p.16.

17. ABC/AA, several memoranda 1 November – 17 January 1948.

18. *AMN*, April 1949, p.8; *Advertiser*, Adelaide, 30 March 1949: 'Geoffrey Parson [sic], a self-effacing accompanist, played arrangements of Bach, and a group of side-slipping moderns, the flippant dryness of which suited him better.'

19. ABC/AA, 8 February 1949.

20. *Advertiser*, Adelaide, 11 May 1949.

21. ABC/AA, 16 June 1949, 11 June 1949, p.18: Peter Dawson with Queensland Symphony Orchestra; *AMN*, August 1949, p.24.

22. *AMN*, January 1950. In his diary he has carefully listed and calculated the mileage at 9,971 miles. ABC/AA, 18 June 1949, gross income was £2,720/11/0; about one third spent on personal expenses, such as taxis, entertaining, cost of music.

23. *Advertiser*, Adelaide, 22 March 1949, 30 March 1949, *AMN*, May 1949 p.20.

24. ABC/AA 11, 16, 18 June 1949; *AMN* August 1949.

25. Photograph, July 1949. Dates of tour were estimated from NZ radio recordings and the fact that he was back in London by December. No evidence of entrepreneur. Could have been ABC/NZ radio agreement or independent. *AMN*, January 1950.

26. Dawson, 1 December 1949.

27. Letter signed B.R. Edwards, 4 January 1950.

28. *Sunday Despatch*, London, 26 March 1950.

29. Peter Dawson diary.

30. See M.J. White, 'Geoffrey Parsons' in 'Music Lover's Guide to the Bicentennial Concert Season' in *Symphony Australia*. Sydney: Australian Consolidated Press, 1988. Interview language personalised.

31. BBC/AC, 24 January 1950, 26 January 1950, on *Australia Calls*. Fee for this broadast 75 guineas, all others 50 guineas. (today = c.$A1,200, $800)

32. *Rainbow Room*, 'Radio's Musical Rendezvous' with host Alan Skempton and Majestic Orchestra conducted by Lou Whiteson, played to an invited audience.

33. EMI, 30 March 1959; 5 April 1950. Burgis found no programme evidence for this song, so it must have been either a substitute number or, more likely, an off-air encore.

34. Dawson, 1951, p.149: Peter Dawson lists the 12 consecutive programmes as an Appendix.

35. EMI, 8 January 1935: 'four samples of test made at 123 threads to the inch which gives six minutes on a 12 inch and 4¼ minutes on a 10in. ... compared with the standard recording ... Peter Dawson Test 5450–1, Band 1 against "Sea Call" (OEA 929–1) fine thread down 2db.'

(Teddy Joyce equal; Stuart Robertson equal; London Philharmonic down 3db) ... it is doubtful therefore whether the market is yet ripe for a finer thread record ... leave matter for the present.'

36.   *Gramophone Jubilee Book*, 1973, p.193; Gelatt, 1977; J.N. Moore, 1977: 'February 1949 RCA Victor introduced 7in. 45rpm. 331/3rpm 'long playing' records were first introduced to London by Decca on 17 September 1950.' According to *Guinness Book of Records* professional tape decks were introduced into America in 1950, into the UK in 1951: the first pre-recorded tapes appearing 1954.

37.   EMI, 15 February 1950; 4 April 1950. Recorded Abbey Road 6 April. Dawson may have suggested the titles himself because his professional copy of 'Wild Goose' was published in Sydney in 1949.

38.   BBC/AC, 8 June 1950; in BBC, 3 March 1953. Tom Noble claimed that it was his idea. BBC/AC, 6 June 1950: 'not right as it stands', 13 June, 16 June: BBC/AC, 6 June 1950. It was agreed that the programmes would be kept 'under lock and key so that other Services may not pre-empt & therefore invalidate'.

39.   BBC/AC, 30 April 1953, 4 May 1953. As there was no named fee for Louis Voss it was presumably included in the orchestra's and would have been at least as much as Freddy Grisewood's. On these terms each orchestral player would have earned about half as much for the whole series as Dawson for one programme.

40.   Dawson wanted to pre-record the programmes. BBC response 13 June 1950: 'possible problem of pre-recording with Musicians Union but OK if Peter Dawson out of country'.

41.   *Radio Times*, London, 26 August 1955, 'A Mighty Man of Song'.

42.   ABC/AA, 22 May 1950. He actually arrived in Australia in November.

43.   Programme, 19 November 1950; ABC/AA, 20 November 1950; SSA, cover no. 264690; segment 264691.

44.   *People*, Sydney, 25 April 1951.

45.   *Mildura Daily*, Mildura, 26 October 1951: review of ABC concert.

46.   Programme, 7 December 1950; *Advertiser*, Adelaide, 5 December 1950.

47.   *Daily Telegraph*, Sydney, 7 July 1956, 'Last Song of Peter Dawson'.

48.   26 April 1951: Dawson in 'Morning Tea Chat with Edith Pearn': 'the older ones, I can remember them in a flash but later ones are a bit hard to learn up, to get them in the subconscious mind.'

49.   ABC/AA, 30 April, 1 May, 12 May 1951, and diary.

50.   Kenneth Harrison, *Dark Man, White World*. Melbourne: Novalit Press, 1975, p.165.

51.   ABC/AA, *ABC Weekly*, 4 March 1951.

52.   *People*, Sydney, 25 April 1951. The song, titled 'Song of Liberty', was recorded with the Eastern Command Band.

53.   *People*, Sydney, 25 April 1951. He had thought differently in 1939.

54.   *Mercury*, Hobart, 25 April 1951.

55.   'Gentleman Jim', recorded 1948, 'Potpourri', 1945; Dawson told the *ABC Weekly* that he had picked up 'Snowbird' on his last trip to England; in fact, he had first recorded it in 1938.

56.   *Daily Telegraph*, London, 17 May 1951.

57.   John Amis interviews Geoffrey Parsons, BBC *Talking About Music*, undated.

58.   SSA. MS5030/1/39, letter from J. Kowin to Dawson, 21 August 1958.

59.   *Daily Telegraph*, London, 4 October 1951. Tierney, October 1957: 'LAG Strong is giving a half-hour programme about you next Friday afternoon at 4'.

60.   *People*, Sydney, 25 April 1951.

61.   *Orcades* arrived Fremantle 13 October, Adelaide 16, Melbourne 18, left Melbourne 20, Sydney 22. When the boat docked in Sydney Peter was singing in Castlemaine. Stan and Ruby Staton were friends through the RSL. 1951 diary entry Christmas Day: 'Stan and Ruby to dinner.'

62.   Conversation with Ann Jacquet, 5 July 1997.

63.   Dame Mary Gilmore quoted in the *Bulletin*, 30 March 1982, 'A Tribute to Peter Dawson' for his centenary.

64.   Australian Archives, CRS: A463/61, item 58/2094.

65.   Ruby Staton's husband. See note 61.

66.   Interview with grandson, September 17 1997. MS5030/6/18: print. In 1947 William Dargie painted a portrait of Jim Beveridge to honour his 25 years with the printing firm. He had prints made, which he signed and distributed to many friends, including Peter Dawson.

67.   MS5030/4/13; 4/18; series 12/box 6/folder 19: Melbourne Scots programmes 1949, 53, 60.

68.   Bradman was Australian Captain 1936–48 for 52 test matches; both his batting average, 99.94 and his 29 Test centuries were Test records. He was knighted in 1949.

69.   For a nett profit of £300 (2000 = c.$A4,000).

70.   Dawson's diary. Bill and Matie were his brother William and his wife.

71.   *Daily Express*, London, 26 April 1955.

72.   *Prestophone*: 'Our Heritage', 'China Sea', 'Child of Mine'; *Vitavox*: 'Waratah & Wattle', 'My Love Song to a Tree', 'March of Liberty'.

73.   26 July 1935; 24 May 1951.

74.   Gerald Moore, handwritten, c.1961 to Ron Hughes, PDAS. Peter and Con were not married at that time. Ref also G. Moore, 1962: 'Australia'.

75.   ABC/AA, 8 March 1954, and others: Peter Dawson, Jim Gussey and orchestra, script John McLeod, producer John Wiltshire. Scheduled 10-week series: 8 March, 1900-05; 15 March 1905–10; 22 March 1910–15; 29 March, 1915–20; 5 April, 1920–25; 12 April, 1925–30; 19 April, 1930–35; 26 April 1935–40; 3 May, 1940–45; 10 May, 1945–50.

76.   Jack McNamara (father of Ian of ABC Radio's *Australia All Over*) in Jacqueline Kent, *Out of the Bakelite Box*. Sydney: Angus & Robertson, 1983, reprint ABC Books, 1990. At that time it was Moses' policy to insist on BBC-type public voices.

77.   BBC/AC, 26 January 1955.

78.   Peter Dawson diary.

79.   BBC/AC, 27 February 1955.

80.   *Advertiser*, Adelaide, 8 June 1955.

81.   Walter Eastman, of publishers Asherwood, Hopwood & Crew, 5 October 1955.

82.   EMI, 19 January 1955; EMI, 27 January 1955, who was 'in wonderful voice (possibly because he has married a new wife!)'.

83.   Dawson is not mentioned in Nancy Phelan's biography of Sir Charles Mackerras, *A Musician's Musician*, Oxford University Press, 1987. This engagement kick-started the career of the 29-year-old Sydneysider. The talented Mackerras (b. 1925) had made an auspicious recording debut with *Pineapple Poll* for Columbia in 1951 but little had followed until this recording. After that there was such a steady stream of EMI work that he became one of the most prolific conductors on record.

84.   EMI, 7 April 1955.

85.   Constance's interview with Peter Burgis, February 1975.

86.   'On the Road to Mandalay' (Speaks) published 1935. Dawson recorded Willeby's 1909 'Mandalay' in 1910 and 1912; Hedgcock's 'Mandalay', featured in programmes from 1914 to 1933, was recorded in 1929; Cobb's 'Mandalay' can be found in a 1937 BBC programme.

87.   *Gramophone*, March 1956. EP 45 rpm: these extra-play 7in. vinyl discs provided up to six minutes of sound on both sides. Bi-aurally or binaural = double mono, potentially stereo. Dawson had bridged the gap from wax cylinders to stereophonic sound.

88.   London newspapers, 26 April 1955.

89.   Dawson, 1951, pp.138, 190.

90.   Collage of London newspapers 26, 28 April 1955, converted to direct speech; and Dawson's diary.

CHAPTER 12: 1955–1961

1. ABC/AA, 16 June 1955. Announcement *AMN*, December; ABC/AA, 3 December 1955, accompanied by a photo of Peter Dawson listening to the 1898 model Gramophone presented to him at the Savoy reception in 1950.

2. On some earlier sheets Dawson wrote: 'on behalf of Tommy Tycho & his players I bid you goodnight' but on programme 4, 31 December 1955, he has crossed out 'Tommy' and inserted 'Thomas'. The 27-year old Hungarian pianist had emigrated to Australia in the early 1950s. He worked as a storeman for David Jones for two years until he could obtain a musician's union card. His work with Dawson was a stepping stone to a long and illustrious career as conductor, pianist, and arranger.

3. *ABC Weekly.* 3 December 1955. The opening programme was 'Arrow & the Song', 'Snowbird', 'Floral Dance', and 'Clancy of the Overflow'; other programmes were a mixture of songs from his early days ('The Lute Player', 'The Holy City'), others relatively new ('Waltzing Matilda', 'Mandalay Scena', 'Marri'd'), and a good sprinkling of solid McCall numbers such as 'Fret-Foot' and 'Westward Ho!'. ('Marri'd', music: A. Harrison, words: Dame Mary Gilmore, Peter Dawson mss, MS5030/music folio I).

4. ABC/AA, 27 April 1956.

5. Constance's Diary. It was ABC executive Norman Shepherd who described Dawson's manner of presentation above.

6. 17 April 1956.

7. Charles Osborne, *Last of the Matinee Idols*, London: Michael O'Hara Books, 1988.

8. Enid Conley, *Clem and I*, Sydney: Wentworth Books, 1972. Enid Conley was an ABC accompanist and wife of baritone Clem Williams.

9. *Advertiser*, Adelaide, 30 April 1956.

10. Unidentified newspaper article, winter of 1961, by C.C. Wicks, a former South Australian ABC manager. Glenda Raymond became the wife of Melbourne radio and television producer, Hector Crawford.

11. *Daily Telegraph*, Sydney, 7 July 1956, long article, the substance copied from Dawson's current ABC recital programme.

12. 19 November 1956: 'My nephew Jeffrey Ernest Gilbert 2/4, My brother-in-law William Charles Noble 1/4, My niece Sally Ann McNair 1/4'. William had spent some time in Australia. He managed one of Dawson's New Zealand tours, but Masonic Lodge clearances show that he returned to England.

13. MS5030/2/33–39: household accounts, 1956.

14. Boosey, 1931, p.66.

15. AA/ABC, 26 January 1957: Dawson and Dame Mary advertised on *Picture Page*.

16. Nephews, 29 March 1993.

17. Text by Leslie Davis, lyricist for 'The Aussie Spirit'. Lashmar considered the song 'too difficult to develop successfully' but the score was developed further and signed by Dawson 'Sydney Australia 1958'. A final version was signed 'P. McCall & James Kimlin'. It was broadcast on 30 April 1958.

18. ABC/AA, 16 April 1958; in Burgis, 1982 called 'Anzac Memoriam' with piano and bugle accompaniment.

19. Dawson was a member of the Savage Club in London, which had affiliates throughout the Empire. Savage Club, London to PDAS, 11 May 1985: Peter Dawson joined 21 March 1929; 'proposed by Mark Hambourg, seconded by the Hon. Sec. & G. L. Skampe, the artist'. *London Encyclopedia*, 1983: Savage Club, 9 Fitzmaurice Place, Berkeley Square, W.1, founded in 1857 as a gregarious club to which many actors, writers and lawyers belonged. Dawson had visited the Savage Club in Adelaide on his 1931 and 1933 tours. In this case, (29 April 1958) he was invited again (Savage Club, 24 April 1958). A photo shows Dawson singing at the

piano; others named are Geo. Harris, Rolf Boehm, Bob Cross, with Roy Mellish at the piano.

20. Glennon, 1968.

21. Burgis, 1982 'My Mine of Memories', 30 April 1958, ABC radio, accompanist Ronda Gehling.

22. Photograph MS5030/7/6: *Daily Telegraph*, Sydney, 11 December 1958, Winifred Atwell kissing Peter on his bald pate as the two remembered their tour of the 'English provinces together ten years ago'.

23. Correspondence, 21 January 1996.

24. Con to 'Dear G', early 1961. Refers to the exciting Test series between Australia and the West Indies captained by Richie Benaud and Sir Frank Worrell.

25. *New Grove*, 1980, p.708: Florence Mary Austral (Fawaz, Wilson) 1892–1968 'particularly famous as Wagnerian singer; toured Australia and America with husband John Amadio interspersing recitals with operatic appearances … many admirable HMV recordings in 1920s and 30s, incl early-electric German language series of Wagner's Ring cycle from Covent Garden.' Dawson, 1951, p.191: 'She certainly possessed a grand voice, but I must confess that I was astonished at her success following the *Daily Mail's* remarkable write-up. Nevertheless, she deserved her triumph.'

26. Inglis, 1983, p.165.

27. Vose, 1987, p.134.

28. The programme which is dealt with in John Thompson, *On the Lips of Living Men*. Melbourne: Lansdowne, 1962, also appears under 'As They Remembered Her', in William R. Moran, *Nellie Melba, A Contemporary Review*. Westport, Conn: Greenwood, 1985, pp.341–343.

29. 11 January 1960: In the programme *In the Mood* he sang 'Snowbird'. At the Regent Theatre on 17 January 1960 he sang 'Lute Player', 'Glorious Devon', 'Boots'.

30. 2 February 1961, Sydney *Daily Mirror* column, 'Talk of the Town'.

31. AA/ABC, press cutting, 25 May 1951, Smoky Dawson, *Smoky Dawson: A Life*. Sydney: Allen & Unwin, 1985.

32. 27 March 1998.

33. ABC/AA, press cutting, 29 June 1961.

VALE

1. EMI, 9 October 1962; EMI, 15 January 1963. The only avenue for sales was a few reissues by World Record Club at 2.5%.

2. Bank deposit slips.

3. *Mercury*, Hobart, 4 January 1962: EMI, file 2818, 1 March 1962, Supreme Court of NSW, document No. 534582 'the said estate and effects do not amount in value to the sum of £1724'; stamped 'Not liable to Death Duty K4462'.

4. M. Scott, *The Record of Singing*, New York: Holmes & Meier, 1979, pp.180–82.

5. Obituaries, *Age*, Melbourne, 27 September 1961.

6. BBC/AC, 12 March 1955.

7. We would like to thank Wayne Turner, LRAM, Bass, of Chester, UK, for his contribution supplied 8 October, 1997.

8. *Woman's Day*, 16 October 1961.

9. Barnard, 1962, p.669.

10. G. Moore, 1962.

Bibliography

Barnard, M. *A History of Australia*. Sydney: Angus & Robertson, 1963.

Bebbington, W. *Oxford Companion to Australian Music*. Melbourne: Oxford University Press, 1997.

Boosey, W. *Fifty Years of Music*. London: Benn, 1931.

Booth, W. and Ziegler, A. *Duet*. London: Stanley Paul, 1951.

Brisbane, K. (ed.) *Entertaining Australia: an Illustrated History*. Sydney: Currency Press, 1991.

Brownrigg, J. '1909-1910: Touring Australia with Peter Dawson' in 'Amy Castles': unpublished ms. Canberra: 1996.

Burgis, P. information booklet, *Ambassador of Song*, (EMI OXLP 7661-70), Sydney: EMI/National Library, 1981.

Cook, C. & Stevenson, J. *Modern British History 1714–1987*. London: Longman, 1988.

Dawson, P. *Fifty Years of Song*. London: Hutchinson, 1951.

Dawson, P. 'Thirty Years of Record Making' in *Gramophone Jubilee Book*. London: Gramophone, 1933.

Dickey, B. (ed.) *William Shakespeare's Adelaide 1860–1930*. Adelaide: Association of Professional Historians, 1992.

Doherty, J. & Hickey, D. *A Chronology of Irish History since 1500*. Dublin: Gill & Macmillan 1989.

Edge, R. and Petts, L. *The Collector's Guide to 'His Master's Voice'*. London: Nipper Souvenir, EMI 1997.

Foster, R.F. *Modern Ireland 1600–1972*. London: Allen Lane, 1988.

Gaisberg, F, *Music on Record*. London: Hale, 1946.

Gelatt, R. *The Fabulous Phonograph: The Story of the Gramophone from Tin-Foil to High Fidelity*. London: Cassell, 1977.

Glennon, J. 'Peter Dawson' in *Australian Dictionary of Biography*. Melbourne University Press, 1981.

Glennon, J. "Peter Dawson and other famous Australian singers" in 'The Music Makers': *1000 Famous Australians*. Adelaide: Rigby, 1978.

Gramophone Jubilee Book 1923–1973. London: Gramophone, 1973.

Hickey, D. & Doherty, J. *Irish History Since 1800*. Totowa, NJ: Barnes 1980.

Inglis, K.S. *This is the ABC*. Melbourne University Press, 1983.

Kesting, J. 'Peter Dawson', in *Die Grossen Sänger*. Dusseldorf: Classen, 1983.

Maegraith, K. *Who's Who in Adelaide: Well-known People Caricatured by Kerwin Maegraith*. Adelaide: Advertiser Newspapers, 1930.

Manning, G.H. *50 Years of Singing: Chorales, carols and community service. A history of the Adelaide Harmony Choir inc.* Eastwood, SA: The Choir, n.d.

Manning, G.H. *Place Names of South Australia*. Grange, SA: Manning, n.d.

Mansfield, J. 'The Music of Australian Revivalism' in *Reviving Australia*. Sydney: Centre for the Study of Australian Christianity, 1994.

Marsh, L. 'The Price of a Song' in *Punch Almanack*. London: Punch, 1959.

Marsi, L. *Index to the Australian Musical News 1911–63*. Melbourne: Lima, 1990.

Martland, P. *EMI: The First Hundred Years*. Portland (USA): Amadeus, 1997.

McCredie, A. (ed.) *From Colonel Light into the Footlights*. Adelaide: Pagel, 1988.

McKernan, M. *Australian Churches at War. Attitudes and Activities of the Major Churches 1914–1918*. Canberra: Australian War Memorial, 1980.

McMenamin, J. and J. 'Peter Dawson: a Great Australian Singer' in *Phonographic News*. Adelaide. Vol.1 no.4, pp.42–53.

Meadmore, G. 'Interview with Peter Dawson' in *Gramophone*, London: September 1935.

Moore, G. *Am I Too Loud? Memoirs of an Accompanist*. London: Hamish Hamilton, 1962.

Moore, J. *A Matter of Records*. New York: Taplinger, 1977.

Moss, P. *Modern World History*. St Albans: Collins, 1978.

Reynolds, W.J. *A Survey of Christian Hymnology*. New York: Holt, Rinehart, Winston, 1963.

Richards, E. (ed.) *The Flinders History of South Australia*. Adelaide: Wakefield, 1986.

Rosenthal, H. 'record review: Peter Dawson' in *Opera*. Vol.34, no.12. London: 1983.

Sadie, S. (ed.) *New Grove Dictionary of Music and Musicians*. London: Macmillan, 1980.

Seidner, G. *Peter Dawson Centenary Stamp Cover*. Melbourne: Australian Stamp Monthly, 1982.

Snell, K. *Australian Popular Music Index*. East Malvern: Quick Trick Press, 1987.

Van Straten, F. 'The Tivoli: a Chronology of the Melbourne Home of Vaudeville'. Melbourne: Victorian Arts Centre, 1981.

Vose, J.D. *Once a Jolly Swagman*. Blackpool: Vose, 1987.

Walsh, J. 'Peter Dawson' in *Hobbies,* Vol.6, January–June 1962. Chicago: Lightner.

West, J. *Theatre in Australia*. Sydney: Cassell, 1978.

Who's Who in Australia, 'Peter Dawson', in Vols. 1933–59. Melbourne: Herald.

Australia Post Centenary logo for Dawson first day stamp cover.

Index

PERCY GRAINGER
By John Bird

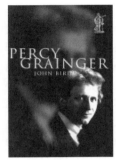

In few creative figures can such artistic brilliance, demonic drive, idiosyncrasy and uncompromising ideology be so inextricably mixed as in the extraordinary life of Percy Grainger. John Bird's acclaimed biography of this Australian composer and pianist gives the first account of the life and works of one of the strangest figures in twentieth-century music. Behind Grainger's highly original compositional achievements, folksong collecting and glittering career as a virtuoso concert pianist lay a tragic and chaotic personal life — long domination by his mother, unorthodox sexual predilections, an eccentric athleticism, a demonic spiritual drive and widely inconsistent personal philosophy with Anglo-Saxon obsessions such as his famous 'Blue-Eyed English.' A list of published compositions, a current discography of performances by Grainger and a selection of his seminal writings, complete what has already proved to be a standard work. Now fully revised and containing new material from Bird's continuing research, this compelling biography is published at a time when Grainger's reputation and popularity as a uniquely individual composer have never been higher.

ANNA BISHOP: The adventures of an intrepid prima donna
By Richard Davis

Anna Bishop was a remarkable and unconventional woman, driven by ambition and curiosity. The rebellious soprano, wife of the 'English Mozart', Henry (*Home, Sweet Home*) Bishop, eloped in 1839 with dissolute French harpist, Nicholas Bochsa and began an adventure lasting 40 years. They survived snow and jungle, shipwreck and impassable mountains, bandits, cholera and civil wars. She sang in great opera houses, concert halls and makeshift venues in the outposts of civilisation. She visited Australia 3 times, meeting and performing with many of our musical pioneers; while in Europe she crossed 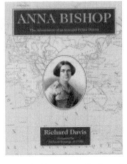 swords with, or delighted , such luminaries as Verdi and Donizetti. Extensively researched and generously illustrated, this is a fascinating combination of travelogue, cultural and social history and adventure story. Richard Bonynge writes in the introduction, '*reads like a modern thriller... Richard Davis... has produced a book I could not put down.*'

SOUND BEGINNINGS
By Ross Laird

Sound Beginnings is the first publication to document in detail the early history of the Australian record industry. It focuses on a single decade from the period of more than 100 years since Edison invented the phonograph. The tumultuous decade between 1924 and 1934 has been selected because it is without question the most significant decade in the history of the industry; seventy years later the events of those years are still being felt by our musical culture. Laird briefly documents the initial reception in Australia of Edison's phonograph during the late 1870s and the eventual commercialisation of his invention, together with the pioneering of small-scale efforts to begin a cylinder record industry — fledgling attempts quickly undercut by the importation of superior products at cheaper prices. Post First World War all records sold in Australia were imported. Within a few years, however, several disc record factories had been established and the first locally recorded discs had been made and marketed.

FLORENCE AUSTRAL
A biography by James Moffat

Described by Nellie Melba as 'one of the wonder voices of the world', Austral was one of the world's greatest Wagnerian sopranos, making her debut at Covent Garden in 1922, in her most famous role, Brunnhilde in *Die Walkure.* Her overwhelming voice was captured on many HMV recordings, some now re-issued on CD. Struck by multiple sclerosis at the height of her career, she abandoned the operatic stage for the concert hall, touring widely throughout Australia and America in recital programs with her husband, flautist John Amadio. Theirs was a marriage fraught with fire and controversy and this biography  reveals a woman passionate, yet capable of great self control. Co-published with the National Library of Australia. *"...painfully honest and revealing, as biographies should be."* (Fred Blanks)

For a full list of our titles, visit our website:

www.currency.com.au

Currency Press
The performing arts publisher
PO Box 2287
Strawberry Hills NSW 2012
Australia
Tel: (02) 9319 5877
Fax: (02) 9319 3649
E-mail: enquiries @currency.com.au